James Proude

History of England

from the Fall of Wolsey to the Defeat of the Spanish Armada, Vol. II

James Proude

History of England
from the Fall of Wolsey to the Defeat of the Spanish Armada, Vol. II

ISBN/EAN: 9783741130700

Manufactured in Europe, USA, Canada, Australia, Japa

Cover: Foto ©ninafisch / pixelio.de

Manufactured and distributed by brebook publishing software (www.brebook.com)

James Proude

History of England

HISTORY OF ENGLAND

FROM THE FALL OF WOLSEY TO THE DEATH OF ELIZABETH.

REIGN OF ELIZABETH.

VOLUME I.

LONDON
PRINTED BY SPOTTISWOODE AND CO.
NEW-STREET SQUARE

HISTORY OF ENGLAND

FROM

THE FALL OF WOLSEY

TO

THE DEFEAT OF THE SPANISH ARMADA.

BY

JAMES ANTHONY FROUDE, M.A.

LATE FELLOW OF EXETER COLLEGE, OXFORD.

 VOLUME VII.

LONDON:
LONGMANS, GREEN, AND CO.
1870.

PREFACE.

LARGE extracts being made in these volumes from the despatches of the Spanish ambassadors residing at the court of Elizabeth, it is necessary for me to say briefly to what extent I consider those despatches worthy of credit. Foreign ministers in England or elsewhere are not usually admitted to domestic secrets of state. Their private information is generally imperfect; they are often purposely deceived; and their reports at all times if unsupported by other evidence must be received with hesitation and distrust. To a large extent these considerations will qualify the belief which we can give to the letters of the Count de Feria, the Bishop of Aquila, and their successors; but there were circumstances in the position of the representatives of Philip the Second which gave them unusual opportunities of knowing the truth, while at the same time exact information was of especial importance to their master. At the accession of Elizabeth three-fourths of the population of England, a third of the Privy Council, and a large minority of the lay Peers, were opposed to the alteration of religion. When the Queen had declared for the Reformation, it was to Philip that the Catholics looked for advice and support; and it was the chief duty of his ambassadors to keep the party together, and to communicate to them the wishes of the court of Spain. The more moderate of Mary's ministers who were retained upon the Council, were Philip's personal friends, and were in receipt of pensions from the Spanish Crown; while Philip again at the outset of his reign was Elizabeth's single foreign ally, and the necessity of keeping on good terms with her brother-in-law, which no one felt more acutely than Elizabeth herself, obliged her to treat his ministers with exceptional confidence.

For these reasons I think it likely that the Spanish ambassadors possessed sources of information which the representatives of foreign states are usually without. I think that no deception could have been long practised upon them by either party in the Council which would not have been betrayed by the other. They write at all times with a certain mastery of the situation; and in no instance, where their statements can be tested by other criteria, have I found them to have been seriously mistaken.

The Spanish archives are preserved in admirable order in the Castle of Simancas, a state fortress eight miles from the city of Valladolid. The courtesy of the Madrid Government gave me unrestricted access to every document in the collection; and I take the opportunity of acknowledging gratefully the attention and assistance which I received from the Archivero, Don Manuel Gonzalez. I desire also to express my obligations to the accomplished Count de Laborde, who has the care of the Imperial Archives at Paris; to the keepers of the MSS. in the Imperial Library; and to Mr. Hardy, Mr. Brewer, and Mr. Gairdner, in the English Record Office. Nor can I omit to mention the late Mr. Turnbull, who, before the intolerance of a part of the religious world deprived the country of his services, was also employed in the Record Office, on the Calendar of the Elizabethan State Papers. Mr. Turnbull could have felt no sympathy with the work in which I was engaged, but he spared no pains to be of use to me: and in admitting me to a share of his private room, enabled me to witness the ability and integrity with which he discharged his own duties.

A further and most important assistance I have received from the Marquis of Salisbury, who has permitted me to examine the private papers of Lord Burleigh, which are preserved at Hatfield. It is impossible to overrate the value of these documents. To know at any given conjuncture the opinion of Sir William Cecil upon it, is to know all which any modern inquirer is likely to arrive at. A large portion of the earlier Cecil papers are in the Record Office, or in the British Museum; and so far as the history has been at present carried, the information which I have derived from the Hatfield collection, though most important in itself, is in extent comparatively small. If I live to continue my work, and the same permission is kindly continued to me, it will be of inestimable moment.

The frontispiece is from a miniature in the collection of the Duke of Buccleuch, who has been good enough to allow it to be engraved.

I have made an alteration in the form of the book, for which I must request the indulgence of the public. The accession of Elizabeth is the commencement of a new epoch in the history of the Reformation. There may be persons who having gone so far with me, may not care to accompany me further; others may be interested in the later and brighter period, who may not care to encumber themselves with the earlier volumes: while the story therefore is continued without interruption, I have made the present publication the commencement as it were of a second work; and the portion already before the world will be made complete as soon as possible by the addition of an Index.

J. A. F.

CONTENTS OF VOLUME I.

CHAPTER I.

	PAGE
Accession of Queen Elizabeth	1
Popular unanimity	3
Death of Cardinal Pole	4
Condition of the finances	5
Social changes	7
State of parties	8
Effect on the nation of the Marian persecution	10
Creed of Elizabeth	12
Mission of the Count de Feria	13
Sir William Cecil	14
The Privy Council at Hatfield	15
Address of the Queen	16
The Court removes to London	17
Changes in the Council	18
Proposals for Ecclesiastical Reform submitted to Cecil	20
Opinion of Goodrich	21
Final resolution	25
Revision of Edward's Prayer-book	26
Anxiety of the Spanish Ambassador	27
The Queen's marriage	28
The Conference at Cercamp	29
Proposal for a secret peace with France	32
Philip offers his hand to Elizabeth	35
The Coronation	40
Opening of Parliament	42
Elizabeth's Statesmen	43
Speech from the Throne	46

Contents.

	PAGE
The Subsidy	49
The Commons request the Queen to marry	50
Answer of Elizabeth	51
The Supremacy Bill	53
Protest of Convocation against the alteration of religion	55
Speech of the Archbishop of York	56
Elizabeth declines to marry Philip	57
National Defences and state of the Navy	58
Calais	59
Peace concluded with France	65
Speeches in Parliament on the Supremacy Bill	66
Reports of de Feria	68
Lady Catherine Grey	70
Theological controversy at Westminster	73
The Supremacy is reannexed to the Crown	76
De Feria and Philip	78
The Church of England	79
Restoration of the English Prayer-book	80
Embarrassment of Philip	83
De Feria leaves England	85
Lord Robert Dudley	86

CHAPTER II.

The Clergy and the Reformation	88
The Bishops refuse the Oath of Supremacy	91
Alvarez de Quadra, Bishop of Aquila, comes to England in the place of de Feria	92
Letter of de Quadra to Philip	93
The Queen's Suitors	97
Remonstrances of Philip	99
Relations with Scotland	101
The Scotch Reformation	103
John Knox	104
Burning of Walter Milne	106
Mary Stuart assumes the English arms and style	107
Outbreak at Perth	111
Knox preaches at St. Andrew's	115

	PAGE
Destruction of the Abbeys	116
The Scots apply to England for help	117
Proposed marriage of the Earl of Arran and Elizabeth	118
Cecil encourages the Scots	121
Death of the King of France	123
Designs of France upon the English Crown	124
Dilemma of Elizabeth	125
Letter of Knox	126
The Scotch Protestants are dispersed	128
Advice of Cecil to them	130
Arguments for and against interference in Scotland	132
Sir Ralph Sadler is sent to the Border with money	135
The Earl of Arran in England	136
Temper of the Scots	138
Elizabeth, to humour the Spaniards, gives hopes that she will marry the Archduke Charles of Austria	142
Elizabeth and de Quadra	143
The Crucifix is replaced in the Royal Chapel	144
De Quadra's opinion of the Queen	146
The English Nobility in favour of the Austrian marriage	149
Arran returns to Scotland	150
Elizabeth threatens France	153
Preparations for war	154
Weakness of the Scotch Protestants	156
Debate in the English Council	158
Plan for a union of the Crowns of England and Scotland	159
Opinions of the Spanish Ministers as to Elizabeth's prospects	161
Uncertainty in England	163
Sir Nicholas Bacon declares against interference	164
Elizabeth determines to persevere, and the English fleet sails for the Forth	169
Letters of de Quadra	172
Consecration of Archbishop Parker	175

CHAPTER III.

Difficulties of the Court of Spain	177
Elizabeth again hesitates	179

	PAGE
D'Oysel with the French army invades Fife	181
Influence of Cecil	183
A French fleet going with reinforcements to Leith is lost in a storm	184
Admiral Winter arrives in the Forth	186
The French transports on the coast of Fife are destroyed	187
Escape of D'Oysel	188
Philip proposes to send a Spanish force into Scotland	194
Conference at Berwick	197
Fresh Alliance between Elizabeth and the Scotch Protestants	199
Naval preparations of England	201
Despair of the Catholics	202
De Quadra urges Philip to interfere in England	204
The Conspiracy of Amboise	205
Uncertain humour of the northern English counties	208
Mission of the Bishop of Valence	211
The English army enters Scotland	212
Their cold reception	213
Skirmish at Leith	214
An armistice and fresh efforts of diplomacy	216
Menaces of Philip	219
Elizabeth refuses to recall her troops	221
Distrust of the Scots	224
Situation of the French	225
Siege of Leith	229
Frauds in the English army	231
Unsuccessful assault of Leith	232
Despondency of Elizabeth	235
Religious disturbances in France	239
Distress of the garrison in Leith	240
Cecil goes to Scotland	241
Elizabeth and a Papal Nuncio	245
Death of Mary of Lorraine	249
Conference at Edinburgh	251
The Treaty of Leith and the departure of the French	258
General results of the War	262
Position of the King of Spain	264

CHAPTER IV.

	PAGE
Return of Cecil to the Court	266
Ecclesiastical character of the Reformation in Scotland	269
The Confession of Faith	270
Dissatisfaction in England	272
The Scotch Estates request Elizabeth in form to marry the Earl of Arran	273
Cecil is out of favour with Elizabeth	274
He proposes to retire from the public service	276
Relations between the Queen and Lord Robert Dudley	278
Communication of Cecil to de Quadra	279
Death of Lady Dudley	281
Inquest at Cumnor	284
Suspicion of foul play	287
Subsequent declaration of Lady Dudley's half-brother	288
General expectation that the Queen will marry Lord Robert Dudley	290
Opinion of Lord Sussex	293
Fresh dangers from France	295
Sir N. Throgmorton protests against the Dudley marriage	297
Death of Francis the Second	300
Elizabeth declines the Earl of Arran	301
Resentment of the Scots	302
State of parties in France	303
Projected Catholic League	306
Secret advances through Sir Henry Sidney are made to the Spanish Ambassador	309
The Queen and the Dudley marriage	312
Advice of Lord Paget	316
The Queen of Scots and her subjects	320
Parties in Scotland	323
Advances of Lord R. Dudley to the Spanish Ambassador	326
Interview between Elizabeth and de Quadra	327
The House of Lennox	329
Elizabeth is invited to admit a Nuncio from the Pope	330
Conditions on which Elizabeth will take part in a General Council	335

Philip and Lord Robert Dudley	337
Refusal to admit the Nuncio	342
The burning of St. Paul's	344
A water party on the Thames	348
Addresses of the Scots to Mary Stuart	352
Lord James Stuart invites Elizabeth to recognise Mary Stuart as her Heir-presumptive	353
Mary Stuart refuses to ratify the Treaty of Edinburgh	354
She prepares to return to Scotland	356
Letters of Elizabeth to the Scotch Estates	357
Mary Stuart sails from Calais	361
Consequences expected from her return	363

CHAPTER V.

Mary Stuart lands at Leith	365
Her welcome to Holyrood	366
Interview with Knox	367
The Scots agree to support her claims on the English Succession	369
Proposed marriage of Mary Stuart with Lord Darnley	370
Lady Catherine Grey is found to have been married secretly to Lord Hertford	371
The Treaty of Edinburgh remains unratified	373
Protestant riots	375
Suggestion of an interview between the two Queens	377
The Conference at Poissy	381
The Huguenots at Paris	382
Apostasy of the King of Navarre	385
Elizabeth and Lord Robert Dudley	385
Uncertain attitude of Philip	386
Lady Margaret Lennox	387
The Duke of Guise	390
The massacre of Vassy	391
Civil War in France	393
Sir N. Throgmorton entreats Elizabeth to support the Huguenots	394
The Bishop of Aquila and his secretary	397

Discovery of Catholic intrigues in England 400
The recognition of the Queen of Scots 405
Conspiracy of Arran and Bothwell 406
Elizabeth desires the interview with the Queen of Scots 410
Opposition of Sir N. Bacon 411
Probable coalition of the Catholic Powers 413
The interview is abandoned 417
The laws against the Catholics are enforced more strictly 418
The civil war in France 420
The Prince of Condé offers Havre to Elizabeth as the price of assistance 421
Alliance between Elizabeth and Condé 422
Want of sincerity on both sides 424
The English occupy Havre 425
Siege of Rouen 426
Conspiracy of the Poles 428
Elizabeth is attacked by smallpox 429
Philip requires Elizabeth to abstain from interference in France 432
Death of the King of Navarre, and the fall of Rouen ... 435
Condé takes the field 437
Unsuccessful negotiation for peace 438
The Battle of Dreux 441
Expedition of Mary Stuart to Inverness 445
Battle of Corrichie Burn 448
Mary Stuart again demands her recognition 451

CHAPTER VI.

Reform of the English currency 454
Condition of England 460
Character of Cecil 461
Social disorganization 462
State of the Clergy 464
Deans and Chapters 465
Ruinous condition of the parish churches 467
Temper of the country Clergy 469

	PAGE
Difficulties of the Bishops	470
The English Catholics apply to the Pope for permission to attend the English Service	472
The request is refused	473
Sir N. Throgmorton is taken prisoner by the Duke of Guise	475
The English Catholics are threatened with persecution	478
Meeting of Parliament	479
Debate on the Succession	482
Penal Laws against the Catholics	484
Petition to the Queen to name a successor	487
Trial of Bonner	491
Story of Châtelar	493
Murder of the Duke of Guise	495
Proposed marriage between Mary Stuart and Don Carlos	498
Elizabeth wishes her to marry Lord Robert Dudley	500
Speech of the Queen in Parliament	502
Proceedings of Convocation	504
The Civil War in France is brought to an end	507
Elizabeth refuses to evacuate Havre	508
War with France	511
Siege of Havre	512
The Plague attacks the garrison	513
Surrender of Havre	516
The Plague in London	519
Philip consents to the marriage between the Queen of Scots and Don Carlos	520
Death of de Quadra	525
The marriage of the Queen of Scots with a safe person is made a condition of her recognition	528
Knox protests against her marriage with a Catholic	530
He sends warning to Cecil	532
Relations between England and Spain	534
The Carlos project cools	537
Elizabeth again attempts to work on the Queen of Scots	539

CHAPTER I.

QUEEN MARY ceased to breathe an hour before daylight on Thursday the 17th of November. Parliament opened as usual at eight for the morning session, when a message from the Peers required the immediate presence of the Commons. As they appeared at the bar of the Upper House, the Chancellor Archbishop Heath rose and said—

'The cause of your calling hither at this time is to signify to you that all the lords here present are certainly certified that God this present morning hath called to His mercy our late Sovereign Lady Queen Mary; which loss, as it is most heavy and grievous to us, so have we no less cause another way to rejoice with praise to Almighty God, for that He hath left unto us a true lawful and right inheritress to the crown of this realm, which is the Lady Elizabeth, second daughter to our late Sovereign Lord of noble memory King Henry the Eighth and sister to our late said queen; of whose most lawful right and title in the succession of the Crown, thanks be to God! we need not to doubt. Wherefore the lords of this House have determined, with your assents and consents, to pass from hence to the palace, and there to proclaim the said Lady Elizabeth Queen of this realm without further tract of time.'

CHAP I.
1558
Nov 17

The Commons answered; 'God save Queen Elizabeth! long may she reign over us!' The vacancy of the throne had dissolved parliament; and at once, while it was still morning, the Duke of Norfolk, the Marquis of Winchester, Lord Shrewsbury, and Lord Bedford rode through London with the heralds, making known from Palace Yard to the Tower the change which had passed over the realm.

The proclamation had been sketched in haste by Sir William Cecil. It declared Elizabeth 'the only right heir by blood and lawful succession,' and charged all persons of every degree, under pain of the new Queen's indignation, to keep themselves quiet, and under no pretence to break the order of the established law.

In the sudden snapping of the chain which had bound them there was a fear that the citizens might be tempted into dangerous excesses.

But for a moment the past was forgotten in the present. The bells which six years before had rung in triumph for Mary's accession now pealed as merrily for her death. The voices which had shouted themselves hoarse in execrations on Northumberland were now as loud in ecstacy that the miserable reign was at an end. Through the November day steeple answered steeple; the streets were spread with tables, and as the twilight closed blazed as before with bonfires. The black dominion of priests and priestcraft had rolled away, like night before the coming of the dawn. Elizabeth, the people's idol, dear to them for her sister's hatred, the morning star of England's hope, was Queen.

So deep had been the indignation at the Smithfield cruelties, so intense the national humiliation at the loss of Calais, that Catholics and Protestants forgot their animosities in the prospect of change. Elizabeth was the favourite daughter of Henry, whose character she was supposed to inherit, and whose reign was the last bright spot on which the nation looked back with pride. The Reformers saw in her their child and pupil, whose life had all but paid the forfeit of her fidelity to their instructions; in her ultimate submission and conformity the orthodox found a guarantee that they need not fear from her a return to revolutionary fanaticism; while, as Philip had declared in her favour, the Conservative peers and statesmen, who inherited the national traditions, supported her as the best security for the maintenance of the Spanish alliance and for the protection of the country against foreign invasion. One rival only possessed claims which would bear inspection. But Mary Stuart was Dauphiness of France. In the possible eventual union of the crowns of Scotland, France, and England, the politicians of Spain and the Low Countries saw their own ruin; and even in religion, however uncertain they might feel as to her real convictions, Elizabeth seemed preferable to the daughter-in-law of the sovereign who had fostered Wyatt's insurrection, and taught every Catholic in the realm to fear and hate him. Philip therefore having failed to secure the entail of the crown for himself, had signified his desire, through the Count de Feria, for the undisputed succession of his sister-in-law. And though Philip had left behind him no single personal friend, his position as England's solitary ally, as the most powerful sovereign in Europe, and as the most faithful servant of the Church, gave him still weight in the council, and an authority almost absolute among the sincere and earnest Catholics.[1]

---

[1] 'No tiene su Majestad en todo el Reyno hombre á su devocion, pero la parte de los Católicos entiende todavia que el bien y conservacion de la religion consiste en la ayuda y asistencia que su Majestad les quisiere hacer, en

CHAP I.
1558
November

Philip expects that she will act as he shall dictate.

Elizabeth herself he trusted that he could bind by gratitude, if not by a closer tie.[1] That a young unmarried woman in a situation so critical should choose a course and policy of her own was the one possibility which neither he nor any one else anticipated. Her conduct, he naturally supposed, would be dictated by the husband to whom she would immediately be allied; and the choice of the person he conceived to rest with himself.

Alone among the Catholic leaders, Reginald Pole shared the ineradicable suspicion with which Elizabeth had been regarded by her sister. But Pole was on his death-bed when Mary died. Among the last sounds which fell upon his ears must have been the bells of Westminster ringing the knell of the cause to which he had sacrificed his life; and before the evening he too had passed away—a blighted, brokenhearted man, detested by those whom he had laboured most anxiously to serve.[2] Singled out, in connexion with Bonner, for

---

la qual parece que van colocando todas sus esperanças y remedio. Porque entienden si el Rey de Francia metiese aqui el pie, se perderia lo espiritual y temporal del Reyno, porque saben que no curarian sino de desfrutarlos y traerlos en su sugecion, sin atender á lo de la religion.'—*Memorial del Conde de Feria. MS. Simancas.*

'Los Católicos que hay en este Reyno, que son muchos tienen puesta toda su esperansa en V. M^d., y es cosa estraña la cuenta que tienen con saber que hago yo; y quando el negocio hubiese de venir á los manos V. M^d. tendra esta parte por suya, porque piensan que seran perdidos si el Rey de Francia mete aqui el pié.'—*De Feria to Philip, Jan. 31, 1559. MS. Ibid.*

[1] The recent connexion between the English Protestants and the Court of France was so considerable, and so notorious, that Philip attempted to make Elizabeth suspicious of them by dwelling upon it. 'Mirad si convendria decir tan bein á la Reyna que tenga sospechosa á la parte de los ereges, porque con aquellos tienen mas platica los Franceses, y confian mas dellos; y que los Católicos nunca se fiéran de Franceses.'—*Philip to de Feria, Feb. MS. Ibid.*

[2] 'Murió á noche. El dia que falleció su Maj^d. sus criados pusieron mala guarda para encubrille la muerte de la Reyna, y la pena que recibió creo que abrevió la suya. Dios le hizo misericordia en llevarle, y V. M^d. perdió muy poco en el.'—*De Feria to*

the especial aversion of the new Queen, he was taken away in mercy to escape a second exile, or the living death of the Tower.[1]

Thus it was that Elizabeth was welcomed to the throne without a dissentient voice, and perhaps without a dissentient heart, save only among the fanatic ecclesiastics, whose bloody work was at an end. And yet her position was beyond example difficult; difficult at the best—more difficult tenfold, if she cared to act on any deeper principle than the immediate expediency of the moment.

Statesmen who remembered the resources at the command of Henry the Eighth when, twenty years before, he had built fortresses round the coast out of the spoils of the monasteries, and had replied to the menaced coalition between Charles the Fifth and Francis the First by calling the united nation under arms, must have felt mournfully how keen was the contrast with the ruined inheritance of his daughter.

The war in which Henry's reign had closed had left a legacy of debt behind it, for which the capture of Boulogne had poorly compensated. The minority of Edward had been a time of mere thriftless waste and plunder, while east, west, north, and south the nation had been shaken by civil commotions. The economy with which Mary had commenced had been sacrificed to superstition, and what the hail had left the locusts had eaten. She had brought herself to believe that the confiscation of the abbey lands had forfeited the favour of heaven; and stripping the already embarrassed crown of half its

---

[1] Philip, MS. Ibid. . . 'Este maldito Cardinal,' de Feria calls him elsewhere.—De Feria to Philip. MS. Simancas.

[1] 'Con el Cardinal (la Reyna) esta malisimamente y comenzó mi a contar los enojos que la habia hecho.'—Ibid.

remaining revenues to re-establish the clergy, she had sacrificed, at the same time, the interests of England to her affection for her husband, and forced the nation into a war in which they had neither object to gain nor injury to redress. She had extorted subsidies only to encounter shame and defeat; and in the midst of the general exasperation at the disgrace which had fallen upon England, she had allowed Philip to avail himself of the scanty revenues of the treasury, and had made him a present of unknown thousands of pounds, with valuable jewels of the crown.[1]

Although the country was financially ruined, there was still the land, and there were still the people to fall back upon; but in the last two sad years, famine and plague had been added to other causes of suffering, and the long gaps in the muster rolls told a fearful tale of the ravages which they had made. The revolt of the Commons under Edward had led also to a general disarmament. The art of war was changing; and the English peasantry, so far from having been taught the use of harquebuss and pistol, were no longer familiar even with their own bows and bills. Themselves untrained and undrilled, their natural leaders the young men of family had been entangled one side or other in rebellion or conspiracy, and had been executed or driven into exile. The nobility were scanty and weak. The new owners of the soil, the middle classes who had risen to wealth on the dissolution of the monasteries, were unwarlike

---

[1] 'Se quejó Isabel al Conde de Feria que sabia que el Rey se lo habia dado grandes sumas de dinero. Contradijó lo el conde pero en el hecho era verdad que la Reyna Maria lo habia dado de una vez siete mil libras y algunas joyas de valor para pagar ciertas tropas Alemannas.'—*De Feria to Philip,* November 11. *MS. Simancas.*

It was believed in London, that shortly before her death Mary had sent Philip as much as 100,000 ducats.

men of business, given merely to sheep farming and making money. The peasantry hated them as the chief enclosers of the commons; the crown and the lords despised them as the creation of a new age; while as evading in all ways the laws of military tenure, and regarding their estates as a commercial speculation for the building up of their private fortunes, they were looked on by the Englishmen of the old order of things as poisonous mushrooms, the unwholesome out-come of the diseases of the age.

'The wealth of the meaner sort,' wrote some Tory correspondent of Sir William Cecil, 'is the very fount of rebellion, the occasion of their insolence, of the contempt of the nobility, and of the hatred they have conceived against them. It must be cured by keeping them in awe through the severity of justice, and by providing as it were of some sewers or channels to draw and suck from them their money by subtle and indirect means.'[1]

On all sides the ancient organization of the country was out of joint. The fortresses from Berwick to Falmouth, although in the preceding summer some faint efforts had been made to repair them, were half in ruins, dismantled, and ungarrisoned. The Tower was as empty of arms as the treasury of money. The volunteer fleet which had been called together for the ineffectual demonstration against Brest was scattered; and thus bare of the very necessaries for self-defence, the Queen found herself with a war upon her hands which the experience of Crêpy made her fear that she might be left to endure alone, with Calais lost, the French in full possession of Scotland, where they were

---

[1] 'The distresses of the Commonwealth, with the means to remedy them, addressed to the Lords of the Council, Dec., 1558.'—*Domestic MS., Eliz.*, vol. i.

fast transporting an army, and with a rival claimant to her crown whose right by the letter of the law was better than her own.[1]

Her position and the position of England were summed up in a few pregnant sentences. 'The Queen poor; the realm exhausted; the nobility poor and decayed; good captains and soldiers wanting; the people out of order; justice not executed; all things dear; excesses in meat, diet, and apparel; division among ourselves; war with France; the French king bestriding the realm, having one foot in Calais and the other in Scotland; steadfast enemies, but no steadfast friends.'[2]

Beyond all these political difficulties and at the heart and root of them, lay the differences of religion. The alternate supremacy of the two extreme parties had taught the nation to loathe them equally. Yet men were in that strange state that they still believed in the necessity of some defined conviction. They believed it still to be their duty to profess, as a Christian people, a national creed, while yet there was no third form of opinion visible to them on which they could rest with security. Happily there was one point on which, with but few exceptions, all sides were united—the dread

---

[1] 'The wars have consumed our captains, men, money, victuals, and have lost Calais. The axe and the gallows have taken away some of our captains. It is necessary, that in every shire at the towns' charge, there might be discipline and exercises used to prepare and frame the rude men into captains and soldiers, to serve in case of need. All other plagues that before and since the death of good King Edward have happened unto us, have been in respect tolerable, and as it were but preludes of one great and grievous plague to come. The loss of Calais is the beginning of the same great plague, for it has introduced the French king within the threshold of our house; so as now or else never your honours must bestir you and meet with this mischief. Else, if God start not forth to the helm, we be at the point of greatest misery that can happen to any people, which is to become thrall to a foreign nation.'—Address to the Council. *Domestic MS.*

[2] Ibid.

and hatred of those ecclesiastical tribunals whose yoke had been broken by Henry, and who had so fearfully abused their recovered power.

A bishop's chancellor sitting in court and proceeding *ex-officio*, unrestrained by statute or common law, and enabled at all times to command the services of the secular arm, was the incarnate representative of iniquity. No fireside was safe from the intrusion of his familiars. No act no word was so innocent but that it could be construed into a crime; and the conduct of the priests in the three last years showed that they had learnt from their humiliations only a lesson of revenge. Towards them and their doings there was no doubt at all of the feeling of the English laity. As it had been in the days of Cromwell so it remained—an irrepressible detestation and scorn.

Here however unanimity was at an end. The secular power of the priesthood was no necessary adjunct of the Catholic faith. The accession of Mary had found the new opinions equally dishonoured by tyranny; and if the reaction had not stained itself with crimes beside which the iniquities of the Duke of Northumberland looked pale, the profession of Protestantism as a positive creed would have been confined to a minority, strong in the fire and force of their convictions, but numerically small and politically weak. But the fanaticism of the Catholic clergy had discredited their doctrines and forfeited for them the confidence of moderate and reasonable men. They had clutched so passionately at the privileges to which they pretended that their theories entitled them, they had betrayed so incautiously their unslaked thirst for power, for wealth, for blood, that the world was taking them at their word, and judging the tree by its fruits. Their foreign policy had been as unfortunate as their domestic administration had been cruel. A blight as if from heaven had rested on them and their deeds; and thus the teaching of the Reformers which had passed away like a dream was beginning again to find its way into men's minds. The figures of the murdered Cranmer and his fellow sufferers stood out against the dark background of those wretched times as the victims of an accursed tyranny; and with the halo of martyrdom shining round them, they became silent preachers of righteousness, more effective in death than in life. While again the reformed opinions had this advantage, equivalent at the bottom of it to certain eventual victory. However men might argue and wrangle, however they might persuade themselves that they believed what they did not believe, Catholicism had ceased to be the expression of the true conviction of sensible men on the relation between themselves and heaven. Credible to the student in the cloister, credible to those whose thoughts were but echoes of tradition, it was not credible any more to men of active and original vigour of understanding. Credible to the uneducated, the eccentric, the imaginative, the superstitious; credible to those who reasoned by sentiment, and made syllogisms of their passions, it was incredible then and ever more to the sane and healthy intelligence which in the long run commands the mind of the world.

In the long run—yet the force which eventually maintains the ascendancy is the slowest in rising to it. The strongest nations are the most reluctant to change, and in England especially, opinions, customs, laws, hold their ground because they exist, although their logical defences may have long crumbled to pieces, and their warmest friends may have long ceased to plead for them. Healthy people live and think more by habit than by reason, and it is only at rare intervals that they are content to submit their institutions to theoretic revision. The interval of change under Edward the Sixth had not shaken the traditionary attachment of the English squires and peasantry to the service of their ancestors. The Protestants were confined chiefly to the great towns and seaports; and those who deprecated doctrinal alteration, either from habit, prudence, or the mere instinct of conservatism, still constituted two-thirds, perhaps three-fourths of the entire people.[1] They were willing to resume the tenths and first-fruits which Mary had restored, to revise the relations with the Pope, to suppress the re-established monasteries; a cautious adviser suggested that it might be even possible to expel the bishops from the House of Lords, take from them their palaces, their lands, their titles, and reduce them to stipendiaries of the crown:[2] yet the same writer thought it eminently dangerous to meddle with the established creed.

Such was the condition of England, and such the humour of the English people, when Elizabeth a young untried woman of twenty-five was intrusted with their destiny. Every course open to her was beset with objections. She could not stand still, she could move in

---

[1] 'In perusing the sentences of the Justices of the Peace in all counties of the realm, scantly a third part was found fully assured to be trusted in the matter of religion.'—Note on the State of the Realm, in the hand of Sir William Cecil.—*Cotton MSS.*, Calig. B. 10.

[2] 'Peradventure it was not amiss as the time and things would suffer, to take from all your bishops the titles of lords, with their places in Parliament, remitting them to the House of Convocation, with all their temporal lands and stately houses—to give to the archbishops a thousand pounds per annum in specialties out of the shire where they reside—to the bishops a thousand marks per annum in specialties—and the temporalities to be given to noblemen having need of the same.'—Distress of the Commonwealth, December, 1558. *MS. Domestic*, Eliz., Rolls House.

no direction without offence to some one; and she herself in her own internal uncertainties was a type of the people whom she was set to rule. She had been educated in a confused Protestantism which had evaded doctrinal difficulties, and had confined itself chiefly to anathemas of Rome. Left to herself on her father's death, while the Anglican divines had developed into Calvinism, Elizabeth had inclined to Luther and the Augsburg Confession. For herself she would have been contented to accept the formulas which had been left by her father, with an English ritual, and the communion service of the first prayer-book of Edward the Sixth. But the sacramentarian tendencies of English Protestant theology had destroyed Henry's standing ground as a position which the Reformers could be brought to accept. It was to deny transubstantiation that the martyrs had died. It was in the name and in defence of the mass that Mary and Pole had exercised their savage despotism. Elizabeth had borne her share of persecution; she resented with the whole force of her soul the indignities to which she had been exposed, and she sympathized with those who had suffered at her side. She was the idol of the young, the restless, the enthusiastic; her name had been identified with freedom; and she detested more sincerely than any theologian living, the perversity which treated opinion as a crime. In her speculative theories she was nearer to Rome than to Calvinism. In her vital convictions she represented the free proud spirit of the educated laity, who would endure no dictation from priests of either persuasion, and so far as lay in them, would permit no clergy any more to fetter the thoughts and paralyse the energies of England.

With such views it was impossible for her to sanction

permanently the establishment of a doctrine from which
the noblest of her subjects had revolted, or to alienate
the loyalty of the party who in her hour of danger had
been her most ardent friends.

What she would do those most interested conjectured
by their wishes. The Protestants expected a good time
when they could score out their wrongs on Bonner and
Harpsfeld, and have their crusade against idolatry.
Philip of Spain flattered himself that Elizabeth, whatever her wishes, would recognise her weakness, lean
for support on him and his friends, and by a convenient
marriage be secured to the Catholic confederacy. He
had sent the Count de Feria to be at her side at the
crisis of her accession, and it is clear that he entertained
no sort of misgiving that she would not act as he might
dictate or desire.

De Feria himself thought otherwise. Connected by
marriage with the great English Catholic families (he
had married the daughter of Sir William Dormer, one
of Mary's maids of honour), the Spanish minister had
access to the under-currents of court intrigue, and from
his own personal impressions he anticipated evil. In
her first interview with him before her sister's death,
Elizabeth had spoken with admiration of the government of Henry the Eighth. The ladies of her household
were 'suspect' of heresy, and 'every schismatic and
traitor in the realm seemed to have risen from the grave
to flock about her.'[1] She spoke favourably to him indeed
of Heath the Chancellor, of Paget, Petre, and Mason, all
of whom had been on the council of Mary, and were
either Catholics, or politically disinclined to change;
yet she had no near relation to guide her, and she

---

[1] De Feria to Philip, Nov., 1558, GONZALEZ.

talked as if she intended to act on her own judgment. Her more chosen intimacies were with the younger noblemen: 'gentlemen abandoned all of them,' de Feria admitted, 'to the new religion,'[1]—men like Sir Nicholas Throgmorton, Sir Peter Carew, Sir John Harrington, and Lord Bedford—and the most dangerous of this party for his virtues and his genius, Sir William Cecil, she had chosen for her secretary.[2]

To Cecil indeed it was that Elizabeth had turned with exceptional and solitary confidence. He had received her instructions beforehand how to act; and while she herself remained at Hatfield, without waiting to communicate with her he assumed the instant direction of the government. Within an hour of Mary's death he had sketched the form of the proclamation. The same day he changed the guard at the Tower. The ports were closed. Couriers sped east, west, north, and south, to Brussels, to Vienna, to Venice, to Denmark. The wardens of the marches were charged to watch the Northern Border. Before the evening of the 17th of November, the garrisons on the Kent and Sussex shores had trimmed their beacons and looked to their arms. A safe preacher was selected for the Sunday's sermon at Paul's Cross, 'that no occasion might be given to stir any dispute touching the governance of the realm.'[3]

The next step, characteristic both of Cecil and his mistress, was to staunch the wounds without the delay of a moment, through which the exchequer was bleed-

---

[1] 'En la nobleza todos los mozos estan dañados de eregias.'—*De Feria to Philip. MS. Simancas.*

[2] 'Cecil qui fué secretario del Rey Eduardo me han dicho cierto que sera secretario de Madama Isabel. Este dicen que es hombre entendido y virtuoso pero herege.'—*De Feria to Philip, Nov., 1558,* GONZALEZ.

[3] Memoranda in Cecil's hand, Nov. 17, 1558.—*MS. Domestic,* ELIZ., vol. i. *Rolls House.*

ing to death. More than 200,000*l.* was now owing to the Flanders Jews, bearing interest of 14 and 15 per cent.; and money was wanted for immediate expenses. The accounts were in confusion. The thoughts of Mary and those about her had been absorbed in higher considerations; and two of the last bonds which had been lying in her room for signature had been used by the women in 'cering the corpse.'[1] On the 18th Sir Thomas Gresham accompanied Cecil to Hatfield, received his instructions from Elizabeth herself, and departed for Antwerp on the instant to raise an immediate loan, and to reside there afterwards, till by humouring the merchants by honest payments and by tricks of finance, he could clear the black incubus away.

Meanwhile, peers, courtiers, knights and gentlemen, rode down to do homage and congratulate. By Saturday night the Privy Council with every statesman of any side or party of name or note had collected at Hatfield. On Sunday the 20th Elizabeth gave her first reception in the Hall. The oaths of allegiance were sworn; the promises of faithful service official and private were duly offered and graciously accepted. The Queen then stood forward and said a few words,—

'MY LORDS,

'The laws of nature move me to sorrow for my sister; the burden that has fallen upon me maketh me amazed; and yet considering I am God's creature ordained to obey his appointment I will thereto yield; desiring from the bottom of my heart that I may have assistance of his grace, to be the minister of his heavenly will in the office now committed to me. And as I am but one body naturally considered, though by his

---

[1] *MS. Domestic*, ELIZ., vol. i. *Rolls House.*

permission a body politic to govern, so shall I desire you all my Lords, chiefly you of the nobility, every one in his degree and power to be assistant to me; that I with my ruling and you with your service may make a good account to Almighty God, and leave some comfort to our posterity in earth.

'I mean to direct all my actions by good advice and counsel. And therefore, considering that divers of you be of the ancient nobility, having your beginnings and estates of my progenitors, kings of this realm, and thereby, ought in honour to have the more natural care for maintaining of my estate and this Commonwealth; that some others have been of long experience in governance, and enabled by my father of noble memory, my brother, and my late sister, to bear office; the rest of you being upon special trust lately called to her service; my meaning is to require of you all nothing more but faithful hearts in such service as from time to time shall be in your powers towards the preservation of me and this Commonwealth. And for council and advice, I shall accept you of my nobility, and such others of you the rest as in consultation I shall think meet and shortly appoint; to the which also I will join to their aid and for ease of their burden, others meet for my service. And they which I shall not appoint, let them not think the same for any disability in them, but for that I consider a multitude doth make rather discord and confusion than good counsel. And of my good will you shall not doubt, using yourselves as appertaineth to good and loving subjects.'[1]

Nothing definite had been said; yet the words seemed

---

[1] Words spoken by the Queen to the Lords, Nov. 20, 1558.—*MS. Domestic*, ELIZ, vol. i.

to imply that the Queen did not contemplate immediate or sweeping change. The Lords withdrew: Pembroke, Clinton, Lord William Howard, and Sir Ralph Sadler, remained in the Hall. Sir Thomas Parry was admitted as Controller of the Household. Cecil took the oaths as Secretary, and when he was led up to Elizabeth she said to him,—

'I give you this charge that you shall be of my Privy Council, and content yourself to take pains for me and my realm. This judgment I have of you, that you will not be corrupted with any manner of gifts, and that you will be faithful to the state; and that without respect of my private will you will give me that counsel that you think best: and if you shall know anything necessary to be declared unto me of secrecy, you shall show it to myself only; and assure yourself I will not fail to keep taciturnity therein.'[1]

Two days later the Court removed to London. The last time that Elizabeth had travelled that road she was carried in a litter as a prisoner, could her sister's lawyers so compass it, to die upon the scaffold. Times had changed. Her sister's bishops came to meet her at Highgate. They were admitted to kiss hands—all except one: but from Bonner's lips she shrank as if contaminated by their approach, and in that evidence of her temper they read all their coming fate. No formal alteration could be ventured till the meeting of Parliament; but every hour brought with it some new indication that the moments were numbered of ecclesiastical dominion. Silently and swiftly the Privy Council was transformed: Montague, Englefield, Cornwallis, Boxall, Peckham—bigoted Catholics, and Mary's

[1] Words spoken by Her Majesty to Sir William Cecil, Nov. 20, 1558.— *Domestic MS.*, ELIZ., vol. i.

personal friends—withdrew or were removed. Even Paget the most moderate of the opponents of change was allowed to plead infirmity and retire; while the vacant places were filled by Bedford, Northampton, and the Puritan Sir Francis Knolles. The Archbishop of York in spite of Elizabeth's regard for him ceased to be Chancellor. Sir Nicholas Bacon Cecil's brother-in-law was made Lord Keeper; and within a week or two the alterations were going on so fast that 'fathers did not know their children.'[1]

Notwithstanding some efforts to check their zeal, the London mob tore down the new crucifixes. Priests if they showed in the streets were kicked into the kennels,[2] and the Protestant clergy coming forth out of their hiding-places, began unpermitted to read the English services again. The bishops distracted between fear and fury knew not what to do or where to turn. Maurice Griffin the Bishop of Rochester died, and carried his mute appeal to a higher tribunal. The Queen's almoner Dr. Bill had preached at Paul's Cross on the 20th, bidding the people be quiet and orderly. Christopherson Bishop of Chichester, he who burnt the bones of Bucer and Fagius at Cambridge, got possession of the pulpit the next Sunday, to rave mere treason, to be sent to the Tower for his violence, and to die like Griffin, a week or two later, either by grief or passion. The Catholics clamoured that they were being betrayed by Spain;[3] and de Feria could but write 'that his worst fears were confirmed;' 'that he was himself a cipher;'

---

[1] 'Con la mudanza del Principe y de los officiales anda tal barahunda y confusion que no conocen los padres á los hijos.'—*De Feria to Philip, Nov. MS. Simancas.*

[2] Ibid.

[3] 'Todos los fieles y Catolicos del Reyno ponen la principal culpa á su Magestad por no haberse querido ocupar en ellos y hacer lo que pudiera si quisiera.'—*Memorial Del Conde de Feria. MS. Simancas.*

'that Philip's voice had no more weight with the Council than if he had never married into the realm; and that in all likelihood there would be an insurrection, of which the French would take advantage to invade the realm.' 'His Majesty had but to resolve, and he might be master of the situation; the Catholics would rise to support his interference in arms,[1] and to lose time was useless and dangerous.' 'The truth is,' de Feria said, 'the realm is in such a state that we could best negotiate here sword in hand. They have neither men, money, leaders, nor fortresses, while the country contains in abundance every requisite for the support of an army.'[2]

A large Spanish force was lying idle in the Netherlands. The Scheldt was crowded with vessels which could be converted with ease into transports. Philip himself was on the spot and must have felt how tempting was the opportunity. Happily for England he was incapable of a sudden resolution, and could only act when the critical moment had passed. He believed that the difficulties of her position would work their effect on Elizabeth as soon as she began to feel them, without his interference. He contented himself with charging his ministers to bribe, to promise, to persuade, to force upon the Council the certainty of which he was himself convinced, that without his support the country must become a province of France.

Meanwhile Cecil, with a conviction that let Elizabeth do what she would Philip would be compelled to stand by her, went boldly forward. In preparation for the meeting of Parliament, he circulated questions on the principal points of uncertainty among the leaders

---

[1] 'Quando lo negocio hubiese de venir á las manos V. Magestad tendra esta parte por suya.'—*De Feria to Philip. MS. Simancas.*
[2] Ibid.

of the different parties. The opinion of the Catholic clergy it was needless to ask. The Catholic clergy had nothing to desire beyond the existing order of things, except it was a more complete restoration of their estates and immunities. As easily may be divined the views of the reforming divines. The pupils of Zuingle and Calvin saw in religion an absolute and universal rule for all times and circumstances; and by religion they understood the profession of a special body of doctrinal formularies, with the absolute prohibition of every other creed or system. They implored the Queen to admit no carnal compromise with Satan, and to regard herself as a Deborah or Judith, raised up by Providence for the deliverance of the Church.[1]

The secular politicians had less confidence in truth, or were less certain that the Protestants had exclusive possession of it. The author of the paper on the 'Distresses of the Commonwealth'[2] advised 'wary handling.' 'The Catholics were in the majority in every county in England except Middlesex and Kent.' 'The Pope was a dangerous enemy:' 'theological intolerance was not found by experience to produce healthy convictions;' 'glasses with small necks, if liquor was poured into them suddenly and violently, would not be so filled, but would refuse to receive it.'[3]

Goodrich a lawyer of some eminence, was more explicit and decided. The Premunire Statute might, he thought, be enforced safely. The laws of the realm forbade the introduction of bulls, briefs, or letters of excommunication. The bishops might be forced again to submit to the Crown. They might be forbidden under

---

[1] *Zurich Letters*, 1558, 1559.
[2] Probably Armigil Wade, who had been clerk of the council at the close of Henry the Eighth's reign.
[3] *Domestic MS.*, Eliz., vol. I.

the old penalties 'to deal with suits in their courts for matters determinable in the King's courts.' Before Parliament met, it would be well 'that certain of the principal prelates and their addicted friends, councillors to the dead queen, should be committed to the Tower, and the rest commanded to keep their houses;' while the whole body of the bench might be specially excepted from the pardon which would be proclaimed at the coronation. All these measures, high-handed as they were, might be prudently ventured; but it was more dangerous to meddle with opinion, or even to take a step against the spiritual functions of the Papacy. King John revolted against the Pope, and 'was brought in danger of his state.' The clergy it was true were weaker than they had been; but they were 'more wily and wise;' 'their tempers were more malicious, and the times more dangerous;' and before they could be 'handled effectually' they should be 'dissembled with and bridled.' Even in the approaching Parliament it would be better to attempt nothing beyond the repeal of the Lollard Statutes of Henry the Fourth and Fifth, which Queen Mary had revived. Deprived of these the bishops could no longer institute their processes *ex officio*; 'quiet persons could live safely;' and meantime 'her Majesty and all her subjects might by license of law use the English Litany and suffrages used in King Henry's time;' 'her Majesty in her closet might use the mass, without lifting up the Host, according to the ancient canons; and might also have at every mass some communicants with the minister in both kinds.' The married priests might be 'winked at, so as they used their wives secretly;' and 'the learned and discreet sort' might preach 'the Gospel,' if they would avoid direct controversy, abstain from irritating the Catholics, and reserve their invectives for Anabaptists and Arians.[1]

Seven years later Elizabeth told Guzman de Silva then Philip's ambassador, that at the beginning of her reign she had not been wholly a free agent, and that she had been driven by the pressure of the Protestants beyond the point where she would have preferred to rest. It is possible that she was intentionally deceiving de Silva; but it is likely also that if left to herself she would have accepted the policy which was thus marked out for her by Goodrich. Politically there was much to recommend it. The Council of Trent had proved a failure. The Lutherans had recovered the ascendancy in Germany; and the Ultramontanes had not yet succeeded in dividing the Church of Rome by any sharply-defined line from the communion of the more moderate Reformers. The chances were equal that if a general council should reassemble the Confession of Augsburg might be acknowledged; while the Genevan theology, the articles and the second prayer-book of Edward the Sixth, would be certainly condemned. The Premunire Statute would secure the national independence; and so long as the critical doctrine of the Eucharist was unimpugned, the Church of England might still consider itself in communion with Catholic Christendom; while the Great Powers could have no pretext for interference or complaint. Personally and individually the dogmatism of Calvin was as distasteful to Elizabeth as the despotism of Rome. The practical complexion of her genius gave her a dislike and distrust of speculation; she was herself in her own opinions studiously vague,

---

[1] 'Judgment of Thomas Goodrich,' Dec., 1558.—*Domestic MS.*, ELIZ., vol. i., *Rolls House.*

and she could have been well contented with a tolerant
orthodoxy, which would have left to Catholics their
ritual deprived only of its extravagancies, and to the
more moderate of their opponents, would have allowed
free scope to feel their way towards a larger creed.

Yet revolution cannot be controlled with the logic of
moderation; and toleration of those who are themselves
intolerant is possible only when the common sense of
mankind compels them to an inconsistency with their
theories. The Lutheran might seem nearer to the
Romanist than he was to Beza or Zuingle; but the
vital differences were not the apparent differences; and
the distinctions between the Reformers were after all
but insignificant shades of variety, compared with the
principle which parted all of them from the orthodox
Catholic. The Catholic believed in the authority of the
Church; the Reformers in the authority of reason.
Where the Church had spoken, the Catholic obeyed.
His duty was to accept without question the laws which
councils had decreed, which popes and bishops administered, and so far as in him lay to enforce in others the
same submission to an outward rule which he regarded
as divine. All shades of Protestants on the other hand
agreed that authority might err; that Christ had left
no visible representative, whom individually they were
bound to obey; that religion was the operation of the
Spirit on the mind and conscience; that the Bible was
God's word, which each Christian was to read, and which
with God's help and his natural intelligence he could
not fail to understand. The Catholic left his Bible to
the learned. The Protestant translated the Bible, and
brought it to the door of every Christian family. The
Catholic prayed in Latin, and whether he understood his
words or repeated them as a form the effect was the

same; for it was magical. The Protestant prayed with his mind as an act of faith in a language intelligible to him, or he could not pray at all. The Catholic bowed in awe before his wonder-working image, adored his relics, and gave his life into the guidance of his spiritual director. The Protestant tore open the machinery of the miracles, flung the bones and ragged garments into the fire, and treated priests as men like himself. The Catholic was intolerant upon principle; persecution was the corollary of his creed. The intolerance of the Protestant was in spite of his creed. In denying the right of the Church to define his own belief, he had forfeited the privilege of punishing the errors of those who chose to differ from him.

Liberty as opposed to submission; the natural intelligence of the living man as opposed to the corporate sovereignty of the outward and visible Church: these were the sharp antitheses which were dividing Christian Europe; and between them, and not between any special and detailed conclusions, lay the essential and irreconcilable antagonism. A *via media* might be found for opinion: words could be used which admitted of uncertain interpretation, so long as there was no authority to invest them with a definite meaning. On the question of authority itself, it was as little possible to hesitate as between rival claimants of the same throne. The Pope was a reality or he was nothing; and no government could seem to acknowledge him without consenting sooner or later to enforce his decrees.

Thus when Elizabeth had chosen her place on the moving side, she found it would be necessary to reclaim the spiritual jurisdiction of the Crown; and in taking a step which of itself would make enemies of the Catholics, to restore the Bible, to restore the English

service, and in the question of the mass to leave a latitude
which would conciliate the Calvinists.

The last of the papers addressed to Cecil indicates,
with a rare combination of piety, good sense, and
courage, the course to be pursued, showing at the same
time that the dangers to be anticipated were not too
great to be encountered.

'The sooner religion was restored,' the writer said,
'God was the more glorified, and it might be trusted
would better save and defend her Highness from all
dangers.' The Pope would perhaps excommunicate the
Queen, interdict the kingdom, and invite the Catholic
powers to a crusade. The French king would attempt
an invasion in the name of Mary Stuart; Scotland would
go with France, and Ireland would mutiny. The bishops
and clergy would do their worst to make a rebellion in
England itself; and the ultra-Protestants would be discontented if they were not permitted their turn at persecution.

On the other hand, though all this was possible
enough, it was worse in appearance than in reality. The
Pope had been looked in the face already, and his terrors
had proved chiefly imaginary. 'Evil will, cursing and
practising,' might be expected from him, but little else.
France and Scotland were formidable; but there too as
well as in England were religious differences, which
could be kindled and fanned into a flame; while the disaffection at home might be held in awe by judicious and
prompt severity. The extreme Catholics who had been
placed in office by Queen Mary might be quietly and
gradually removed. The old-fashioned country gentlemen, constitutionally reactionary and conservative, might
be dropped out of the commission of the peace; and
'men of discretion, meaner of substance, and younger in

years,' be put in their place; while the musters or militia should be called under arms, officered 'by young gentlemen which did earnestly favour her Highness;' and 'so far as justice or law might consent, no jurisdiction or authority should be left in any discontented man's hand.'

The laity against the clergy; the middle classes against the higher; the young generation against the old—society was split in two, in the normal line of revolution between the representatives of the future and the past.[1]

Revision of the Prayer-book.

The intended measures were concerted with the strictest secrecy. A body of divines sat in the house of Sir Thomas Smith to revise the Prayer-book, and take from it that sectarian character which in its latest form it had assumed. Northampton, Pembroke, Bedford, and Lord John Grey, formed with Cecil a committee of council to consult privately with the Queen; and innovation and change until sanctioned by Parliament were strictly forbidden by proclamation.[2]

Irritation of the Spanish ambassador.

But however cautious they might be the outline of the intended policy became every day more clear; and the Spanish ambassador wrote with louder emphasis that England was lost and Elizabeth lost unless she was checked in the mad career on which she was entering. He did not anticipate the ultimate success of heresy. He believed only that the Queen blinded by vanity, passion, and ill advice, was bringing on a catastrophe in which she must inevitably lose her throne to the Queen of Scots. Nothing could save her, nothing could prevent

---

[1] The device for the alteration of religion in the first year of Elizabeth, offered to Secretary Cecil.—*Cotton MSS.* Printed in BURNET's *Collectanea.*
[2] STRYPE, *Annals*, vol. I. part ii. Appendix iv.

so disastrous a consequence, except her immediate marriage to some prince or nobleman in the Spanish interest.[1] 'The more I reflect on this business,' he said, 'the more clearly I see that all will turn on the husband which this woman will choose.' That she would marry some one was assumed as a matter of course; and at home as well as abroad the question who was to be her husband was the prominent subject of anxiety.

The opportunity of securing a powerful continental alliance, not a statesman in Elizabeth's cabinet would encourage her to neglect. Her life was the single bulwark between the nation and civil war or incorporation with France. She was the last of her race. All England was impatient for an heir, and was uncertain only whether it desired her to chose a husband from abroad or from among her own subjects. A subject would bring no increase of strength. The antipathy of the English to strangers had been shown remarkably in the opposition to the alliance of Mary with Philip. But the peril of the nation was now so great, the necessity of the case so overwhelming, that minor objections were overlooked; and the first prayer of every loyal man or woman in the country, alike Catholic and Protestant, was to see Elizabeth married somewhere, and to see her a mother.

To this matter therefore de Feria's attention was now turned exclusively. On his first arrival in London the ambassador, regarding the Queen as the creature of his master, had spoken to her in a tone which she resented. High words had passed between them, and de Feria had absented himself from Court. Elizabeth however was

---

[1] 'Quanto mas pienso en este negocio entiendo que todo el consiste en el marido que esta muger tomará, porque si es tal qual conviene, las cosas de la religion irán bien, y el reino quedará amigo á V. Mag⁴.; si no todo va borrado.'—*De Feria to Philip. MS. Simancas.*

afraid to quarrel with him. In a few days she sent for him again, and affected to listen with interest to his proposals for her marriage. Philibert of Savoy, Philip's landless cousin, was the first suggestion. But Philibert had been already proposed and rejected while she was princess. England it was thought would be involved in endless war for the recovery of his lost inheritance. There were the Austrian Archdukes, to either one of whom there was less objection. But the person desirable above all others for her, in the eyes of Spanish statesmen, was Philip himself. 'If she marry out of her own realm,' wrote de Feria to him, 'may she place her eyes on your Majesty.'[1] There would be the true solution of all difficulties. The daughter of Anne Boleyn accepting the hand of her brother-in-law, and submitting to a Papal dispensation in order to obtain it, would make a refined expiation to the Catholic world for the divorce of Queen Catherine and would exquisitely stultify the English revolt. The political combination of England, Spain, and the Low Countries, would be cemented more firmly than ever. There would be no more danger from France and the Queen of Scots; and Philip himself would be rewarded for his late martyrdom by a wife more suited to his years.

A thousand motives recommended Elizabeth to the Spanish Court. To understand their weight we must revert to the conference at Cercamp, and the relations between Spain and France.

In the close of the preceding volume it was seen how the languid but expensive campaign of the last summer had terminated in an armistice, and in an effort to make

---

[1] 'Si determine de casa fuera del Reyno ella ponga los oyos en V. M^t.'— *De Feria to Philip. MS. Simancas.*

peace. Behind the shield of the forty years' war, half Europe had revolted from the Church. The poison of heresy was spreading in France, in the Low Countries, in Italy, and even in Spain—exciting disorder and revolt, and allying itself with dangerous doctrines of popular liberty. The Great Powers were recognizing at last that it was high time to close their secular quarrels, and turn their swords towards holier objects. In the presence of their common enemy the ultramontanes everywhere saw the necessity of drawing together; and for the moment the Catholic party was superior at the court of Henry the Second.

Thus when the conference opened it had seemed that there was nothing to discuss. The French relinquished without a struggle their claims on Naples and Milan. They were willing to retire from Piedmont, to leave Navarre to Spain, to sacrifice every object for which they had wasted their blood and treasure. They insisted only on keeping Metz, which the Duke of Guise had defended against the Emperor, and Calais which he had wrested from the English. Measured by their intrinsic value, these two poor towns were as nothing when compared with the concessions in Italy; and about Metz there was little difficulty. But the English, who had been dragged reluctantly into the war by Mary, who had lost all and gained nothing, required that in the restitution of conquests, their claim should not be disregarded. The loss of Calais had touched the national honour in the point where it was most sensitive, and they insisted and required Philip to insist with them, on its restoration.

The Spaniards were sensible of their obligations, and their own interest assisted in keeping them firm. The possession of Calais by the English was one of the securities of the Low Countries. It had been lost in a war undertaken solely at Philip's entreaty; and the Duke of Alva, perhaps in fear that his master's anxiety for peace might make him hesitate, dwelt with distinctness on the danger of forgetting their duty to their allies.

'We have told the French,' he said to the King of Spain, at the end of October, 'that your Majesty will make no peace without the Queen of England's consent, though all Christendom perish for it. If you give way you will lose utterly the hearts of the English nation, who will turn from you to France; and the French king having Scotland and Calais, will soon be master of England also.'[1]

Both Alva and the Bishop of Arras agreed in advising that the negotiation should be broken off, and the war be resumed. Philip would recover his popularity in London, and England would be roused to fresh exertions. If Spain was exhausted, France was more exhausted. The difficulty had perhaps been raised but as a feint to divide the Anglo-Spanish alliance; and if Philip was firm, the point would probably be given up.

So matters stood a fortnight before Mary's death. The change of sovereigns voided the commission of the English representatives. The armistice was prolonged, the conference prorogued till January, and the interval occupied with intrigue.

Affecting to suppose that the interests of Spain in England must have died with the late Queen, the French commissioners at once, on the arrival of the news, challenged Elizabeth's right.[2] They made an immediate effort to separate Philip from her, and

---

[1] *Papiers d'État du Cardinal Granvelle,* vol. v. pp. 324-5.
[2] Lord Cobham, writing in December to Elizabeth from Brussels, told her, on the authority of Ruy Gomez, the colleague of Alva and Arras, 'that at Cercamp the French did not let to say and talk openly

scarcely cared to conceal their intention of striking an immediate blow, if Spain would look on and hold its hand.[1]

The Spaniards however had no intention of letting England become an appanage of France. Elizabeth was Philip's nominee, and not yet to be set aside for the Queen of Scots. On the 21st of November the King of Spain wrote to assure the English council that he would never desert them, and so he would have all men understand.[2] Doctor Wotton and the Bishop of Ely accompanied Arras from Cercamp to Brussels, and the diplomatic relations of the Spanish and English courts remained as close as ever.

Philip was then confident that he could retain Elizabeth. Elizabeth, while peace was unconcluded, was compelled to keep on terms of cordiality with Philip. Ruy Gomez it was true suggested that it might be better to come to terms without extorting the restoration of Calais; but this was only that the allies might replenish their treasures, and begin the war again at better advantage.[3]

But French intrigues were double-edged. Untroubled by scruples religious or political, Henry cared only to make the most of the situation; and of the two parties and two policies which divided France, he was indifferent which he employed, provided he could gain a march upon an adversary. While the Cardinal of Lorraine, at

---

how your Highness is not lawful Queen of England, and that they have already sent to Rome to disprove your Majesty's right.'—*Spanish MSS. Eliz., Rolls House.*

[1] Arras and Alva to Philip, Nov. 26.—*Granville Papers*, vol. v.

[2] 'Ita enim ab omnibus accipi atque intelligi volumus, nullo tempore Anglos quibus multas ob causas bene volumus desertum sed omnibus in rebus adfuturos.'—*Philip II. to the English Council*, Nov. 21. *Spanish MSS., Eliz., Rolls House.*

[3] Cobham to Elizabeth, Dec. 13.—*Spanish MSS.*

Cercamp, would have persuaded Spain to sacrifice England, the King of Navarre was allowed to tempt England to sacrifice Spain. If Elizabeth would become French, and if he could secure for his daughter-in-law the peaceable reversion of the English crown, Henry might turn the tables upon Philip, keep Piedmont, and possibly extend his frontier to the Rhine.

No sooner was the armistice extended than Lord Grey de Wilton, who had been taken prisoner at Guisnes, was sent over to Elizabeth with proposals for a secret peace. Guido Cavalcanti, who had been employed in Edward's time on a similar errand, followed to 'practice' among the lords; and Henry himself wrote to 'congratulate Elizabeth on her accession, to assure her that he ever had been and ever would be her truest friend, and to express his hope that with her sister's death the only cause had been removed which had made a difference between the two countries. While the conference was suspended, a second set of commissioners might meet in some remote French village where their presence would be unobserved; and Philip could not complain if Elizabeth treated him as Charles the Fifth had treated her father at Crêpy.'[1]

Ignorant whether Henry was sincere, or was trying only to divide her from Philip—ignorant how far she might trust Philip himself when the changes which she was contemplating were daily embroiling her with his ambassador, perhaps knowing that notwithstanding his fair speeches the Count de Feria was already urging his master to an armed interference in England, Elizabeth would not reject these overtures, yet would not so admit them as to give Philip an excuse for complaint. She

---

[1] The King of France to Elizabeth.—Forbes, vol. I.

declined the secret conference yet professed herself ready to make a separate peace; at the same time she directed Wotton to inform the King of Spain of the advances which had been made to her; to tell him that she would agree to nothing which would prejudice the Spanish alliance, without giving him notice; but to say frankly that as England had been entangled in the war against the declared wishes of the people, if advantageous offers were made to her she would not think it right to refuse them.[1]

The habitual ambiguity of Philip had provoked this partial menace. Although his ministers at Cercamp had been true to England, his own language had been less decided. He had declared himself willing to continue friendly towards England, but the treaty remained unrenewed, although Lord Cobham had been sent over to him to exchange the ratifications; and Wotton could only pray 'that it were well done and past,' without expecting to see it done. 'The King,' Wotton wrote, 'doth well consider that if he should agree to the peace without us, we were not able long to resist the French and the Scots and others whom the French would set on our tops. What would ensue thereof a blind man can see; and these reasons persuade that he will make no peace without our satisfaction.'[2] Yet on the other hand Philip was inclined to make demands on England, which he knew could not be complied with; and Spain was impatient of the expenses of the war, and cried out to be at rest. In this uncertainty Henry's advances to England quickened his resolution, and from other quarters probably, as well as from Elizabeth's

---

[1] The Queen to Wotton, Dec. 30, 1558.—*Spanish MSS. Rolls House.*
[2] *MS. Ibid.*

letter, he learnt that no time was to be lost. The King of France had followed up his first step by more decided overtures. Going at once to the central difficulty, he instructed Guido Cavalcanti to say to the Queen that although 'Calais was part of the ancient patrimony of France, and the French nation would give all their substance to keep it,' yet that 'where there was a will on both sides, no difficulties were insuperable.' 'So long as it was uncertain where Elizabeth might marry, he might if he restored it be opening a door to give his enemies an entrance into his kingdom;' 'but if she would marry in a quarter from which France had nothing to fear,' 'an expedient would be found for Calais to the honour of both princes and the satisfaction of their subjects;' while an alliance might be formed between himself, the Dauphin, the Dauphiness, and the Queen of England, for 'a perpetual union' of England, France, and Scotland, 'with a final determination of all quarrels, rights, and pretensions whatever.'[1]

It is uncertain to whom the King of France was alluding as the husband whom he would desire for Elizabeth; but her marrying at all in the French interest was a contingency which Philip dared not risk; and as little could he afford that she should remain—as from her words to de Feria she seemed to desire—neutral in the quarrels of the continent.[2] On the 9th of January Philip was still wavering; on the 10th he declared his final determination.

'Touching the Queen's marriage,' he wrote to de Feria, 'I directed you in one of my last letters to throw all

---

[1] 'Mission of Guido Cavalcanti.—FORBES, vol. I.

[2] Particularmente dió señal de su resolucion de querer estar neutral.'—*De Feria to Philip, Dec.* MS *Simancas.*

possible obstacles in the way of her marriage with a subject. For myself, were the question asked, I bade you say nothing positively to commit me, yet so to answer as not to leave her altogether without hope. In a matter of so great importance I had to consider carefully; and I wished before coming to a resolution to have the advice both of yourself and others. At length, after weighing it on all sides, I have concluded thus:—

'There are many and serious reasons why I should not think of her. I could spend but little time with her: my other dominions require my constant presence. The Queen has not been what she ought to be in religion; and to marry with any but a Catholic will reflect upon my reputation. I shall be committing myself perhaps to an endless war with France, in consequence of the pretensions of the Queen of Scots to the English Crown: my subjects in Spain require my return to them with indescribable anxiety; while so long as I remain in this country, the hospitalities expected of me are, as you well know, a serious expense; and my affairs, as you know also, are in such disorder that I can scarce provide for my current necessities, far less encounter any fresh demands upon me.

'There are other objections besides these, equally considerable, which I need not specify. You can yourself imagine them.

'Nevertheless considering how essential it is in the general interests of Christendom to maintain that realm in the religion which by God's help has been restored in it—considering the inconveniences, the perils, the calamities which may arise, not only there but in these States also, if England relapse into error—I have decided to encounter the difficulty, to sacrifice my private inclination in the service of our Lord, and to marry the Queen of England.

'Provided only and always that these conditions be observed: First, and chiefly, you will exact an assurance from her that she will profess the same religion which I profess, that she will persevere in it and maintain it, and keep her subjects true to it; and that she will do everything which in my opinion shall be necessary for its augmentation and support.

'Secondly, she must apply in secret to the Pope for absolution for her past sins, and for the dispensation which will be required for the marriage; and she must engage to accept both these in such a manner that when I make her my wife she will be a true Catholic, which hitherto she has not been.

'You will understand from this the service which I render to our Lord. Through my means her allegiance will be recovered to the Church. I should mention that the condition that gave the Low Countries to the issue—should any such be born—of my marriage with the late Queen, cannot be again acceded to. It is too injurious to the rights of my son Don Carlos.'[1]

In announcing his resolution to make this cruel sacrifice, Philip nevertheless felt it necessary to add that 'although he was ready to marry Elizabeth, she must not expect him to remain long with her.' 'He was absolutely required in Spain, and to Spain he must go, whether he left her pregnant or not. There was no such pressing haste as there had been when he married her sister; she was young, and he could go and come at convenient intervals.' And here it seemed, as if for the first time it occurred to him, that his offer of himself

---

[1] Philip II. to the Count de Feria, Jan. 10, 1559.—*MS. Simancas.*

might possibly not be welcome; for he told de Feria not to mention the likelihood of his absence, or indeed any of the other conditions, until he had discovered how she was affected towards him. He bade the Count feel his way, 'and not expose him to a refusal which would make his condescension appear ridiculous.' 'For himself he was ready to do anything which his duty to God demanded of him.'[1]

Seen by the light of later history, a proposal of marriage from Philip of Spain to Elizabeth of England can scarcely be thought of without a smile; yet Philip was indisputably serious, and in offering his hand he was offering the most splendid alliance in the world. Had the proposal itself been simply communicated to her, unaccompanied by Philip's thoughts about it, Elizabeth would have felt herself bound to refuse with courtesy. But the fates were unfavourable. The improvident Count de Feria permitted his master's letter to be seen by the ladies of the palace, whom he was endeavouring to interest in the cause. The contents of it, or perhaps the despatch itself, reached Elizabeth's eye;[2] and the value of the offer was not improved when it was represented as a sacrifice to duty.

When the Count opened the subject with her, she was already prepared with her reply. She was conscious, she said, of the honour which had been done her; she was aware of the value to the realm of the King of Spain's alliance; but His Majesty's friendship was as sufficient for her protection as his love. She had

---

[1] *MS. Simancas.*

[2] 'Despues que su M⁴. escribió la resolucion destos negocios, se comenzará á tratar, usando el buen modo que pareció convenir, que fue ganar las voluntades de sus mugeres de camara. Parece que la Reyna ha visto las cartas de su M⁴. lo qual debe advertirse mucho.'—*Memorial del Conde de Feria. MS. Simancas.*

no desire to marry, and she did not believe in the power of the Pope to allow her to have her sister's husband.

De Feria threatened her with the Queen of Scots. She declined to consider the Queen of Scots' chances to be as large as he described them; and finally, her sense of humour getting the better of her, she said, laughing, she feared the King of Spain would prove a bad husband, he would come to England and marry her, and then desert her and go home.[1]

True to her nature however Elizabeth would not give a positive refusal. If she was determined she affected to be irresolute; and the Count could only conjecture that her final answer would be unfavourable.

Thus at home and abroad the new year found all parties watching each other, and 'practising' under the surface. The English Parliament was to meet on the 23rd of January; a fortnight later the Conference was to reassemble at Cambray. On Sunday the 15th, the day after she had received Philip's proposals, the Queen was crowned at the Abbey.

The week preceding was spent according to custom at the Tower. On the Saturday there was the usual pageant, when she was taken in state to Westminster.

Elizabeth had been disciplined into self-control by danger and suffering. Her more serious feelings she habitually concealed; and when she spoke on such subjects, it was either with diplomatic reserve or with an elfish and mocking irony. On occasions however her deeper emotions refused to be stifled; and as she passed out to her carriage under the gates of the Tower, fraught

---

[1] 'Diversas personas le habian dicho que su M⁴. habia de venir aqui á casarse con ella y irse luego á España, lo qual dijó con mucha risa.'—*Memorial del Conde de Feria. MS. Simancas.*

to her with such stern remembrances, she stood still, looked up to heaven, and said:—

'Oh Lord, Almighty and Everlasting God, I give Thee most humble thanks that Thou hast been so merciful unto me as to spare me to behold this joyful day; and I acknowledge that Thou hast dealt wonderfully and mercifully with me. As Thou didst with Thy servant Daniel the prophet, whom Thou deliveredst out of the den, from the cruelty of the raging lions, even so I was overwhelmed, and only by Thee delivered. To Thee, therefore, only be thanks, honour, and praise for ever. Amen.'

She then took her seat, and passed on,—passed on through thronged streets and under crowded balconies, amidst a people to whom her accession was as the rising of the sun. Away in the country the Protestants were few and the Catholics many. But the Londoners were the first-born of the Reformation, whom the lurid fires of Smithfield had worked only into fiercer convictions. The aldermen wept for joy as she went by. Groups of children waited for her with their little songs at the crosses and conduits. Poor women, though it was midwinter, flung nosegays into her lap. In Cheapside the Corporation presented her with an English Bible. She kissed it, 'thanking the City for their goodly gift,' and saying 'she would diligently read therein.' One of the crowd, recollecting who first gave the Bible to England, exclaimed, 'Remember old King Harry the Eighth;' and a gleam of light passed over Elizabeth's face—'a natural child,' says Holinshed, 'who at the very remembrance of her father's name took so great a joy that all men may well think that as she rejoiced at his name whom the realm doth still hold of so worthy memory, so in her doings she will resemble the same.'

CHAP I
1559
January
The coronation.

The ceremony the next day was performed by Oglethorpe, the Bishop of Carlisle. The Archbishop of York, to whom the duty would naturally have fallen, had been alarmed by the English litany and refused to officiate; but his example was not followed. The bishops waited till the quarrel was commenced by the Queen, and were generally present at the Abbey. Mass was sung as usual, and the occasion passed off with no particular remark.

The opening of Parliament was the one subject which absorbed attention. How would the Houses accept the intended policy of the Queen? Four new peers had been created at the coronation. The earldom of Hertford was revived in favour of Edward Seymour, son of the Protector. Lord Thomas Howard, Surrey's younger brother, was made Lord Howard of Binden. Sir Henry Carey, the Queen's cousin, became Lord Hunsdon; and Sir Oliver St. John was created Baron St. John of Bletso. Including these, the lay peerage of England consisted but of sixty-one persons, of whom it is to be observed that eighteen were either unable or unwilling to appear at Elizabeth's first Parliament, while twelve who were present at the opening very soon discontinued their attendance. Their proxies for the most part were held by Bedford and Clinton, and their votes therefore were given to the Government. But the personal absence of half the peers implied but a cold welcome to the new sovereign.

The Bench of Bishops also was proportionately thin. Reginald Pole, for some unknown reason, had left several sees untenanted. The accession of Elizabeth had been followed by a remarkable mortality among those whom it found in possession; and before Parliament met there were a dozen bishoprics vacant for the

Queen to fill, as de Feria expressed it, with as many ministers of Lucifer.[1] Of the surviving prelates, some were incapacitated by age, some by sickness, from attending to their places; and thus, without violence being used to thin their phalanx, ten was the largest number which they were ever able to muster on the most important debate of the session.

For the Commons, the Catholics were loud in their complaints of the unfairness of the elections; and it may be assumed as certain that a government which had contemplated the removal of every Catholic magistrate in the kingdom, exerted itself to the utmost in securing the return of its friends. It is equally certain—inasmuch as five years later two justices of the peace out of three were even then reported to be unfavourable to the Reformation—that when parties approached an equality the Crown was in no condition to use violence. Constitutional opposition however was as yet imperfectly understood; and the disaffected on either side looked rather to rebellion when the government was against them than to the tedious processes of Parliament. The universal horror of the late reign forced the defenders of its principles into the shade, and the moving party though numerically the weakest were the young, the eager, and the energetic. The Catholics left the field to their adversaries; and town and country chose their representatives among those who were most notorious for their hatred of popes and priesthoods.[2]

A slight indisposition obliged Elizabeth to postpone

---

[1] De Feria, in his irritation, credited Pole with the whole deficiency —' Aquel maldito Cardinal dexó doce obispados por proveer en los quales podran ahora doce ministros de Lucifer.'—*De Feria to Philip, Feb.* 20. *MS. Simancas.*

[2] ' Esto Parlamento es de personas escogidas en todo el Reyno los mas enemigos y perversos.'—*Ibid.*

the opening for two days. On the 25th the session began, and for the first time she stood as Queen face to face with her subjects.

Her position was singularly lonely. The mortality in the Tudor race which had raised her to the throne had left her also with scarcely a relation in the world. Her nearest kinswoman was the rival claimant of her crown; and she herself, as she appeared in the House of Lords, a young woman not yet twenty-six, must have felt that in her high estate she had but herself alone, her own resolution, her own prudence, her own energy, to depend upon; the last of the royal blood, the centre of a revolutionary hurricane, which with such skill as she possessed she was set to guide and to curb.

Of those who were round her, the figures of some few, with the help of such scanty light as remains, may be looked at specially and distinctly. First on the bench of bishops sat Heath, and next him Bonner, standing out with unshaken daring to brave the execration which was heaped upon his name. After Bonner came Pates, Bishop of Worcester, attainted by Henry the Eighth for high treason—one of Pole's missionaries of treason, who had sat in the Council of Trent. Next him was White, Bishop of Winchester, who had distinguished himself by a violent sermon at Queen Mary's funeral. Of the three other bishops, Baynes, Scott, and Oglethorpe, the two first were equally notorious fanatics. The Abbot of Westminster, Feckenham, was he who had gone on the vain mission to shake the faith of Lady Jane Grey.

Leaving the churchmen, soon to disappear all of them into their proper darkness, we look next to the Keeper of the Great Seal. Sir Nicholas Bacon, father of the more famous Chancellor, had grown into notice as a lawyer in the time of Henry the Eighth. He had married a daughter of Sir Antony Cooke, being thus Cecil's brother-in-law; and, with Lady Bacon, was an advanced Protestant, inclining over the borders towards Calvinism.[1] His eldest son Antony was a child, Francis was not yet born. He himself was approaching middle age—a large corpulent man, with a square massive face deeply lined, high arched eyebrows, and a high nose, the expression keen, hard, and unsparing, yet upright and noble. Unknown as yet as a statesman, Bacon it is likely owed his advancement to the recommendation of Cecil.

If Bacon represented the incoming era, the Marquis of Winchester represented the era which was passing away. Paulet Marquis of Winchester could remember a Plantagenet king, and Bosworth field. He was advanced in years when Queen Catherine was divorced; and having survived all changes of creed, having been made a peer by Henry, created a marquis by Edward, and having afterwards been the chief instrument in saving Mary's crown—'the Shebna' of Knox, 'the crafty fox with a fair countenance,'—he was to be seen in his office of High Treasurer in Elizabeth's first Parliament, eighty-four years old, still vigorous and serviceable. His letters continued for years to show a mind as clear and a hand as steady as those of the best of the contemporaries of his grandchildren. His principle was loyalty to the family of Henry VIII.; his creed, faith in God and English freedom, and hate of fanatics, Catholic or Protestant.

The Duke of Norfolk, first of the English peers, was young and untried. He for the present was guided, and

---

[1] Sir Antony Cooke, ἀρχαιδγνωσς as he was called, had been spoken of for Chancellor, he too being in close intimacy with the Genevans, yet not disposed to go all lengths with them. —ZURICH *Letters*, pp. 1, 17, and 32.

the Howard family was represented, by his uncle William Lord of Effingham, to whom above all other Englishmen Elizabeth owed her life and throne.

Fitzalan Earl of Arundel, Norfolk's father-in-law, like the Marquis of Winchester, had served under three sovereigns and under three creeds. He had been one of the executors of the will of Henry the Eighth; it was he who arrested Northumberland at Cambridge; he had been steward of Mary's household; he had acted as High Constable at Elizabeth's coronation; and being a widower he was named among those who might aspire to the Queen's hand. But he moved in a cloud, suspected of aims which he would not avow, without a conviction, without a purpose, feared by all men and trusted by none.

The Earl of Pembroke was a soldier, and the ablest which England possessed. Pembroke, with Lord Russell, had suppressed the insurrection under Edward. Pembroke led the English contingent at St. Quentin, and had commanded in London on the memorable morning when Sir Thomas Wyatt came in from Knightsbridge. His wealth was enormous: as President of the Welsh Marches, he was supposed to be able to bring two thousand men into the field. But he had been employed by Mary chiefly because she could not afford to alienate so powerful a subject. He had looked coldly on her proceedings, and in turn had been coldly regarded. He had been among the first to support Elizabeth with his presence at Hatfield; and his growing allegiance to Protestantism placed him on the committee of four which had determined on the change of religion.

Lord Francis Russell Earl of Bedford was the favourite above all English noblemen of the extreme reformers. In the late reign he was one of the few of high rank who had not cared to conceal his opinions;

and although Mary had not dared to proceed to extremities against him, he had been imprisoned and had been released only to go into voluntary exile. He had travelled into Italy, paying a visit by the way to the refugees at Zurich; and the Genevans looked to him afterwards as their surest friend in Elizabeth's cabinet. In appearance he was a heavy ungainly man, distinguished chiefly by the huge dimensions of his head. When Charles of Austria was a suitor for Elizabeth's hand, and questions were asked of his person, the Earl of Bedford's large head was the comparison made use of in his disparagement:[1] but his expression, like that of Bacon, was stern and powerful; the world as he knew it was no place for the softer virtues; and those only could play their parts there to good purpose whose tempers were as hard as the age and whose intellects had an edge of steel.

The Catholic leader among the Peers, in default of Norfolk, was Antony Browne, son of Henry the Eighth's Master of the Horse, created by Mary Lord Montague, in right of descent by the female line from the Nevilles. In the distraction of families, one of his sisters was the wife of the Puritan Lord John Grey, the other was Countess of Kildare. Montague himself, with the estates of the Countess of Salisbury, had inherited her principles and her fearlessness. But his character with that of all others then passing into prominence will unfold itself with the story.

The Queen took her seat upon the throne. The Commons were called to the bar. Sir Nicholas Bacon then rose and spoke.

---

[1] 'Del Carlos dicen que tiene la cabeza mayor que el Conde de Bedford.'—*The Bishop of Aquila to the Count de Feria, May 29, 1559. MS. Simancas.*

Chap I
1559
January

After throwing himself on the courtesy of the Houses, he said that he was directed by her Majesty to explain the causes for which they were assembled.

Her Majesty having God before her eyes, desired to seek 'before all things the advancement of His honour and glory as the sure and infallible foundation on which to erect her policy.' 'This foundation being well laid, good success would follow in all else; without it nothing could be looked for but continual alteration and change; things much to be eschewed in all good governance, and most of all in matters of faith and religion.' 'Her Majesty's desire was to secure and unite the people of the realm in one uniform order to the honour and glory of God and to general tranquillity;' 'she required the Parliament therefore, for the duty they owed to Him whose cause it was, and for their country's sake whose creed it concerned, to use their best diligence for the establishing of that which should be most convenient for so godly a purpose.' They would consider no private interests or personal respects. They would 'forbear, and as a great enemy to good counsel flee from all contentious reasonings and disputations, all sophistical, captious, and frivolous arguments and quiddities meeter for ostentation of wit than a consultation in weightier matters, more beseeming for schools than for the Parliament House '— the Queen required them to 'eschew contumelious and opprobrious words as heretic, schismatic, and Papist, as causes of displeasure and malice, enemies to concord and unity, the very marks which they were now to shoot at;' and as on the one hand they would 'devise nothing which in continuance of time might breed idolatry and superstition,' so 'they would take heed by no licentious or loose handling to give occasion for contempt and irreverent behaviour towards God or godly things.'

Touching then on scriptural illustrations of the dangers of both these extremes, and expressing, in a graceful comparison with Esther, Elizabeth's earnest aim to do only what should be just and acceptable in God's sight, he concluded that part of his subject in these words:—

'Forced by our duties to God, forced thereto by His punishments, provoked by His benefits, drawn by our love to our country, encouraged by so princely a patroness, let us in God's name go about this work, endeavouring ourselves with all diligence to make such laws as may tend to the establishment of God's Church and the tranquillity of this realm.'

Turning next to the condition of the country, he spoke of the change of sovereigns. The Crown, he said, had fallen to a princess who intended to govern with the advice of the estates of her realm ; to put down evil-doers 'without rigour and extremity,' yet without 'indulgence or foolish pity;' a princess that neither was nor ever would be 'so wedded to her own will and fantasy,' that 'for the satisfaction of it' she would bring her people into bondage 'or give occasion for tumults and stirs,' such 'as had risen of late days ;' a princess that never for private affection would advance the quarrel of a foreign prince and impoverish her realm; a princess to whom 'nothing—no worldly thing under the sun—was so dear as the love and goodwill of her subjects.'

All this was of happy augury. On the other hand Calais was lost—Calais the glory of England the fear of England's enemies ; Calais the mart for its merchants; Calais the guardian of the Channel. The particular loss would have been of less consequence if 'what had been lightly lost might lightly be recovered;' but the revenue of the Crown had been wasted; guns, men, ships, stores, squandered and lost; enormous debts were owing abroad, with 'biting interest' so long as they were left unpaid. War was daily growing more expensive; and England surrounded with enemies was unprovided with the commonest means of defence. The Parliament must look to it; when there was danger of fire 'they plucked down part of their houses to save the rest.' 'The wise merchant in adventures of danger' insured himself against loss. The Queen was most unwilling to burden her subjects; but 'the ragged State torn by misgovernment' could no longer be trifled with.

'Her Highness,' the Lord Keeper concluded, 'has commanded me to say, that were it not for the preservation of your ownselves and the surety of the State, she would rather have adventured her own life than troubled you. And albeit you yourselves see that this is no matter of will, no matter of displeasure, no private cause of her own; but for the defence of our country and the preservation of every private man's home and family, her Majesty's pleasure is that nothing shall be demanded of her loving subjects but that which they of their own free liberality be contented frankly and freely to offer; so great is the trust and confidence that she reposeth in them, and the love and affection that she bears towards them.'[1]

Five days passed. On Monday the 30th the business of the Session commenced. In the Commons, the first question was of supply; a committee of twenty-four was appointed to draw up a Money Bill. In the Lords, the same day, an Act was introduced to reannex the first fruits of ecclesiastical benefices to the Crown. In both Houses, the general policy which the Queen intended to pursue was sketched in outline; Cecil, Bed-

---

[1] Speech of Sir N. Bacon, 1558-9. *MS. Harleian*, 398. Printed in Dewes' *Journals*.

ford, and Sussex most distinguishing themselves. 'The Parliament has begun,' de Feria wrote on the 31st. 'It is already proposed to repeal the late laws, and to change religion. The Catholics are in the utmost alarm, and have no hope but in your Majesty.'[1]

The First Fruits Bill—so slight regard was there anywhere for the temporal interests of the clergy—was swept in four days through the Upper House, amidst the clamours of the bishops.[2] The Commons were no less expeditious. On the 1st of February a Tonnage and Poundage Act was introduced.[3] On the 3rd the Committee was prepared with the Subsidy Bill.

It will be remembered that in Mary's last Parliament the Commons, in distrust of Philip's influence on the Queen, had granted half only of the sum which was then demanded of them, undertaking to furnish the remainder at a future time, should it be absolutely required. The preamble of the present bill admitted the necessity, yet in terms which implied a belief that England was weak only by misgovernment, and was capable as ever of maintaining its freedom and greatness. They voted at once, and without reservation, more than all which they had refused to Mary—two-fifteenths and tenths, half-a-crown in the pound on all personal property, and four shillings in the pound on the rents of land. With peculiar significance they took upon themselves on this occasion to legislate for the clergy also, and extended

---

[1] 'Los Catolicos estan muy temorosos de la resolucion que se tomará en este Parlamento. De los del Consejo, Cecil y el Conde de Bedford son los que mas se señalan en destruir esto; de los de fuera el Conde de Sussex hace lo que puede. Los Catolicos tienen puesta toda su esperanza en V. M^d.'—*De Feria to Philip, Jan.* 31. *MS. Simancas.*

[2] LORDS' *Journals,* 1 ELIZ.

[3] In money bills, the reason for the grant was always specially assigned. Tonnage and poundage, or a duty on exports and imports, was supposed to be given for the police duty of the seas.

CHAP I
1559
February

the act to all persons in the realm, spiritual as well as temporal.[1]

But there was a more pressing anxiety than any which could be removed by money. Elizabeth's single life alone lay between England and annexation to France, and no foreign prince could be more anxious about her marriage than her own subjects. To Philip or Henry the question was but of the balance of power in Europe, to the English it was life itself.

The Queen's marriage.

There were many suitors—Philip, his cousin Philibert, the Austrian princes, and the King of Sweden. At home Arundel's name had been mentioned, and Sir William Pickering's. On the whole, the Queen was thought more likely to choose a subject than a foreigner;[2] but the desire to see her married to some one was so great that the person seemed nothing in comparison. On the 6th of February the Speaker Sir T. Gargrave, with the Privy-Council and thirty members of the House of Commons, demanded an audience, and without mentioning person or country they requested her in the name of the nation to be pleased to take to herself a husband.

How Elizabeth received the petitioners is unknown, but she took time to consider her answer. On Thursday the 9th, a bill was introduced into the Lower House to restore the royal supremacy, and was referred to a committee of which Sir Antony Cooke was chairman.[3] It

---

[1] 1 ELIZ. cap. 11.

[2] 'Entiendo que estos consejeros se comienzan desengañar de que ella no se quiere casar en al Reyno, y esto les hace dar mas priesa á lo de la cregia.'—*De Feria to Philip, Jan.* 31. *MS. Simancas.*

[3] De Feria says the heretics made the more haste for fear the Queen might marry a Catholic. Cooke himself complained that he could move no faster. On the 12th of February he wrote to Peter Martyr, 'We are busy in Parliament, casting out the tyranny of the Pope, restoring the authority of the Crown, and re-establishing true religion, but we move far too slowly.'—ZURICH *Letters*, p. 19.

was not till the morning of the 10th that the deputation was desired to return to the Queen's presence.

She then said she most heartily thanked her faithful subjects for the care they showed for her. For herself, from the time when she had first determined to live for God's service, she had preferred to remain unmarried. There had been a time when her life was in danger. She would not blame her sister, nor although she had good grounds for suspicion would she name the person by whose advice her sister was acting; but it had seemed then as if her marriage alone could save her. Yet she had refused, and God, who had defended her before, she was confident would not desert her now. She approved of the form of the petition, which left her choice unfettered, and should it please God to incline her heart to another kind of life they might assure themselves she would do nothing of which the realm should have cause to complain. She intended to spend her own life for the good of her people, and if she married she would choose a husband who would be as careful for them as herself. If, on the contrary, she continued in her present mind she could not doubt but that with the help of Parliament the succession might be secured, and some 'fit governor be provided, peradventure more beneficial to the realm than such offspring as might come of her.' Children were uncertain blessings, and might grow up ungracious. For her it would be enough 'that a marble stone should declare that a Queen having reigned such a time lived and died a virgin.'[1]

A vague answer, yet not intended to mislead; the obligation to marry for political convenience, detestable under all its aspects, painful to a man—to a woman so

---

[1] Speech of the Queen.—*Commons' Journals*, Dewes 1 Eliz.

painful that a crown might be thought too poor a price to pay for it—the proud Elizabeth would not wholly repudiate. Even that sacrifice she might make at last, if the welfare of the country required it of her. But the time had not come as yet, and it was convenient to leave the prize of the English throne open for a while to the competition of the Catholic powers. The Reformation could be carried on with less danger and interference so long as Philip could hope to undo it again constitutionally; nor could he interfere at all, while a suitor in his own behalf or his cousin's for Elizabeth's hand, without blighting his chance of acceptance.

Agitation of Philip.

The King of Spain, on his side, was watching her with tremulous anxiety. On the first intimation of the measure brought forward in Parliament, he feared it would be his duty to withdraw the offer of his hand;[1] but Alva whom he consulted dissuaded him. The Duke was unable to believe that she could reject such a magnificent alliance. Her allegiance to the Church would be a condition of the contract, and the acts of one Parliament could be undone by another.[2] Still impatient, Philip wrote to de Feria, bidding him implore Elizabeth to reconsider what she was doing; if entreaties failed, he left it to the ambassador's discretion to menace her with the chance of losing him.[3] De Feria however agreed with Alva: if Elizabeth would become Philip's wife the Catholics would resume their ground with ease; if not, neither menace nor remonstrance would be of any avail. 'I have ceased,' he wrote on the 20th of February, 'to speak to her about religion, although I see her rushing

---

[1] Philip II. to the Duke of Alva, Feb. 9.—*MS. Simancas.*
[2] Alva to Philip.—*Ibid.*
[3] Philip II. to de Feria, Feb. 12.—*Ibid.*

upon perdition. If the marriage can be brought about, the rest will provide for itself; if she refuse, nothing which I can say will move her. She is so misled by the heretics who fill her court and council that I should but injure our chances in the principal matter by remonstrating.'[1]

Elizabeth understood the situation, and used her advantage. The Parliament, after thanking her for the gracious answer which they construed into a consent,[2] went on with their work. On the 11th of February the English Litany was read in the Lower House, the members all kneeling; on the 13th the Supremacy Bill came on again, and large differences of opinion at once revealed themselves.[3] As first brought before the Commons, the act restored to the Queen the title of Supreme Head of the Church, which was originally assumed by her father.[4] Two days' discussion led to no result; and to judge from the surviving fragment of a single speech, the language of the Catholics was indecently passionate. Dr. Story had been a notorious instrument in the Marian persecution, and serving, as such men ever serve, the cause which they most oppose, he dared to boast of his past atrocities. 'I wish for my part,' he said, 'that I had done more than I did, and that I and others had been more vehement in executing the laws! I threw a faggot in the face of an earwig at the stake at Uxbridge as he was singing a psalm, and set a bushel of thorns

---

[1] De Feria to Philip II., Feb. 20.—MS. Simancas.

[2] Five days later, a committee of the Commons had a conference with the Lords in the Star Chamber, to determine the rank which the Queen's husband should hold.—DEWES' Journals, 1 ELIZ.

[3] 'Sir Antony Cooke defends a scheme of his own, and is very angry with all of us.'—Jewel to Peter Martyr. ZURICH Letters, p. 32.

[4] Speech of Archbishop Heath.—STRYPE'S Annals, vol. i. part ii p. 405

under his feet, and I see nothing to be ashamed of or sorry for. It grieves me that they laboured only about the young and little twigs, whereas they should have struck at the root.'[1]

Story perhaps thought less triumphantly of his Uxbridge exploit when long years after he was entrapped on board a trader at Antwerp, and carried to London to die there. He could boast of his crimes in the English Parliament, but the hate which he had generated against himself dogged his footsteps and overtook him at last.

The Supremacy Bill went back to a Committee: a week later it was re-introduced, slightly, though not materially, altered; and again the opposition was so violent that it would have been lost except for Cecil, who in de Feria's words 'flung the question into a garboyl,' and carried his point in the confusion.[2] In the shape in which it was sent to the Peers the new act scarcely differed from that of Henry the Eighth, either in the title which it gave to the Queen, in the oaths which every subject was required to swear, or in the penalties which were to follow on refusal. The bishops assured the Spanish ambassador that they would sooner die than submit;[3] and, encouraged by the resistance in the Commons, and conscious that they were secretly supported by the majority of the English people, they settled down into resolute opposition. In point of learning

---

[1] Strype's *Annals*, vol. i. part i. p. 115.

[2] 'Los del Parlamento en la camara de abajo determináron que la suprema potestad ecclesiastica se comprehendera en la corona de los Reyes de Inglaterra; aunque hubo algunos que habláron en favor de la razon; de manera que fué necesario para salir con su maldad que el secretario Cecil metiese la cosa en garbullo, y assi pasó. Quieren hacer que todo el Reyno jure de guardar este articulo y que quien no lo hiciese sea tenido por traydor, como lo hizó hacer el Rey Henrico.'—*De Feria to Philip II. MS. Simancas.*

[3] Ibid.

there was no lay peer capable of arguing with them.[1] The vacant sees could not be filled with Protestants till the oaths to the Pope, required at their institution, had been removed by Act of Parliament. Their audience was for the most part neutral or favourable; and, but for Pole's neglect in leaving so many bishoprics unoccupied, de Feria thought the Catholics might have been altogether successful.

Convocation had been sitting by the side of Parliament—the clergy with the bishops at their head had drawn up a protest against the threatened changes, and in five articles had signified their adherence to the Catholic doctrine of the Eucharist, and to the established constitution of the Church.[2]

They asserted their absolute belief in transubstantiation, in the sacrifice of the mass, in the sovereign rights of the successors of St. Peter, in the authority of priests over laymen in 'all matters of faith and discipline;' and the first step of the opposition in the House of Lords was the presentation of the unanimous petition of the entire 'spirituality of England,' embodying their convictions.[3]

---

[1] 'The bishops being, as you know, of the Upper House, and having none there of our side to expose their artifices, they reign as sole monarchs in the midst of ignorant and weak men, and easily overreach our little party by their numbers, or their reputation for learning.'—*Jewel to Peter Martyr.* Zurich *Letters*, p. 22.

[2] The five articles were these:—
1. 'That the natural body and blood of Christ is really present in the sacrament by virtue of the words duly spoken by the priest.

2. 'That after consecration no other substance remains.
3. 'That the mass offered is a propitiatory sacrifice.
4. 'That Peter and Peter's successors are Christ's vicars, and supreme rulers in the Church.
5. 'That the authority in all matters of faith and discipline belongs and ought to belong only to the pastors of the Church, and not to laymen.'—Strype's *Annals*, vol. I.

[3] And yet we are told that the Church of England reformed herself —meaning by the Church, not the

Ch. I
*1559
February*

Speech of the Archbishop of York.

The Archbishop of York followed it up in a careful and elaborate speech. Avoiding as much as possible all irritating topics, he argued for the papal authority on its own merits, on the evidence of history, the decisions of councils, and the judgment of the fathers of the Church. The system which had been established by Henry the Eighth had been condemned, he said, both by Catholic and Protestant; and if the Queen desired to return to it she would be without a friend in either party. There was no intelligible sense in which a temporal sovereign could be head of the Church, and in dealing with the subject at all he considered that Parliament was going beyond its powers.

There was nothing new in these arguments. The supremacy was the well-trodden battle-field of the old campaign between More and Cromwell, Fisher and Cranmer; yet there was no one among the Peers who was capable of answering the archbishop. Heath who had been raised to the bench by Henry had acquiesced once in what he now opposed; and he could represent himself not as new to the subject, but as having gone astray, and as having been brought back to the truth. In its existing shape the Bill could not be carried. English opinion alone would have prevented a measure from again passing into law which might send honest Catholics to the scaffold, and give the longing Protestants their turn at persecution; while even the debate of such a question was compromising English interests at Cambray, and exercising a perilous influence on the humour of Philip, who if pushed too far might make his own terms, and leave England to its fate.

---

laity, who alone did the work, but the bishops and clergy, who never consented, as a body, to any measure of reformation whatever, except under the judicious compulsion of Henry the Eighth.

When pressed to say decisively whether she would marry him, Elizabeth at last refused. On the 20th of February de Feria made his final effort. He spoke to her again of the Queen of Scots. He warned her that if Spain ceased to have an interest in England, the peace of Europe could not be sacrificed because her sister's carelessness had lost Calais. But 'the devil,' he said, 'had taken possession of her;' 'she was more impatient of menace than of entreaty,' she repeated 'that the Pope could not allow her to marry her brother-in-law,' and she refused entirely to be afraid of France; 'her realm,' she said, 'was not too poor, nor her people too faint-hearted, to defend their liberties at home and to protect their rights abroad; she would not marry, and she would agree to no peace without the restoration of Calais—that was her answer.'[1]

As there was no hope that she would change her mind, de Feria recommended Philip not to trouble himself about any other marriage for her, but to instruct his ministers at Cambray to complain to the English representatives of the alteration of religion, and if their remonstrances were unheeded, to make peace at once.

Had nature given Philip a capacity for prompt action, Elizabeth's career might have run out before its time. The shrewdest statesman in England, Lord Paget, though for some reason excluded from her confidence, could not refrain from pressing on Cecil the peril of the crisis. 'If the French invade us by sea or by Scotland,' he said, 'the King of Spain will enter also as our friend or our foe; if we take part with neither of them, they will fasten their feet both of them here and make a Piedmont of us; if we take part with the one, we

---

[1] De Feria to Philip, Feb. 20.—*MS. Simancas*.

ourselves shall afterwards be made a prey by the victor. God save us from the sword! we have been plagued of late with famine and pestilence. For God's sake move that good Queen to put her sword in her hand; she shall make the better bargain with her doubtful friends and enemies.'[1]

It was easy to advise; it was difficult to execute. At this time, England being actually at war with the second power in the world, the whole naval force in commission amounted to seven coast-guard vessels, the largest of which was but 120 tons; and eight small merchant brigs and schooners, altered for fighting. Of ships in harbour fit for service there were twenty-one; one newly built of 800 tons, one of 700, one of 600, one of 500, and one of 400, four from 300 to 200, the rest sloops and boats.

In artillery the destitution was even more pitiable. Of cannon and 'demicannon' in all the dock-yards, there were but thirty which were reputed sound; with two hundred culverins, 'minions,' and 'falconets.' Of bows, arrows, lances, corselets, and harquebusses, there were not enough to arm 3000 men.[2] For the troops, Captain Turner, who was sent to command at Portsmouth, and was in daily expectation of a visit from the French, reported to Cecil on the 6th of March that they were all 'grown to misorder and mischief, and to the greatest ill that man's head could imagine.'[3]

To such a point had England been brought after eleven years of the government of doctrinaires, Protestant and Catholic. If the suspicions and jealousies

---

[1] Paget to Cecil, Feb. 20, 1559.—BURLEIGH *Papers*, vol. i.
[2] Naval Report, March, 1559.—*Domestic MS.*, ELIZ, Rolls House.
[3] Ed. Turner to Cecil, March 6.—*MS. Ibid.*

of France and Spain had not come to the assistance
of Elizabeth's diplomacy, it might have gone hardly
with her. She had continued her private correspondence
with France. Calais, she insisted, must be restored;
her people were determined to have 'that blot to their
nation wiped and taken away.' As to its falling to
Spain, she was descended of English blood, and not
Spanish like her sister; and she and her people might
be trusted to take care of it. She was 'good friends'
with Philip, 'yet not otherwise bound to him than was
for the good of her country and subjects.' The French
king had said 'that a way might be found,' and it was
not for her to close any avenue that promised her an
escape from her difficulties. Her sister had done nothing
without the privity and direction of the minister of
Spain; she herself being a free princess, intended 'to
proceed without participation to the Spaniards of anything, otherwise than for the nature of her matters
should seem expedient.'[1]

The 'way' intended by Henry he indicated by sending over in return a confidential agent, with the portrait
of some unknown prince or nobleman who should take
Calais back with him as Elizabeth's dowry. The Queen
examined it long and earnestly, but as it seemed with an
unfavourable conclusion.[2] The negotiation fell through,
and in a letter still full of friendly expressions, the King
of France intimated his regret that he had changed his

---

[1] Instructions to Guido Cavalcanti, Jan. 29,—FORBES, vol. 1.

[2] 'Hoy he sabido que esta mañana arrivó aquí de vuelta de Francia Guido Cavalcanti, y luego la Reyna le oyú y ha estado con el un gran rato. Trae en su compañía un Frances, hombre pequeño. Hasta ahora no he podido saber mas sino que me dicen que el Guido traye un retrato que estuvó mirando la Reyna un gran rato.' —*De Feria to Alva, Feb. 29. MS. Simancas.*

mind, and that the plan by which he had hoped to end the quarrel was found impracticable.

Thus Elizabeth found herself thrown back upon the solid facts of her position, with her Spanish allies alone to trust to. The congress reopened at Cambray on the 5th of February. The Bishop of Arras, the Duke of Alva, Ruy Gomez, and the Prince of Orange, represented Spain. The Constable Montmorency, the Cardinal of Lorraine, the Bishops of Orleans and Limoges, appeared for France, with the Duchess of Lorraine as a neutral and independent president. Doctor Wotton and the Bishop of Ely returned from Brussels. The third English commissioner, Lord William Howard, was delayed in London, and did not appear till four days after the opening.

On the evening of his arrival Howard had a private interview with Alva and his colleagues. His last instructions from Elizabeth were to surrender anything except Calais; but to remain firm upon that. Philip on the other hand was weary of the war; he was irritated with Elizabeth, and insisted that he was penniless and that peace must be made.[1] Between these contradictory positions the middle term was difficult to find. The Calais question happily was one in which the Low Countries were interested; and Alva, though he spoke bitterly of the carelessness with which it had been lost, promised that he would do his best for its recovery.

The next day the commissioners met in public. Towns taken in war, Lord Howard said, were as a matter of course restored at the making of peace; Calais belonged to England, and the French had no right to persist in

---

[1] 'Porque yo os digo que yo estoy de todo punto imposibilitado á sostener la guerra.'—*Philip II. to the Duke of Alva, Feb. 11.* GRANVELLE *Papers*, vol. v.

keeping it. The French replied promptly that Calais was a French town which at all hazards they meant to keep; their commission in fact did not allow them to consider the surrender of it as possible. A long argument ensued, but absolutely without result; and the day closed apparently without a hope of agreement.

No sooner however had the meeting broken up than the Constable drew Howard apart, and warned him against trusting Philip, who desired only to annex Calais to the Low Countries. From Howard Montmorency went to Alva to express his astonishment that the Spaniards should sacrifice themselves to the selfish interests of England; there was Crêpy for a precedent, and the peace of Europe was more important than a single town. The Dauphiness moreover was the true Queen of England, and if France surrendered Calais, it must be to her.[1]

It was fortunate for Elizabeth that the Dauphiness was the one person whose pretensions in the existing state of Europe the Spaniards could not recognize, and to whom Elizabeth with all her heresies was preferable. For Elizabeth herself they cared nothing; but they dreaded an increase to the power of France; and they cared much for the sympathies of the English Catholics, whom they would alienate for ever by deserting English interests. Notwithstanding Philip's orders, Alva was compelled to assure Montmorency that Spain would be true to her ally. Montmorency with equal firmness insisted that Calais if it belonged to England at all belonged to Mary Stuart, and that to her alone should it be given. Thus much only Henry might be induced to yield. Elizabeth might be left in undisturbed pos-

---

[1] 'Donnant assez à entendre qu'ils ne tiennent la Reyne pour Reyne.'— *Alva and Arras to Philip II., Feb.* 13. GRANVELLE *Papers*, vol. v.

session of the Crown of England, on condition that her children should intermarry with Mary Stuart's children, son to daughter, and daughter to son; France meanwhile should keep Calais for eight years, as England had kept Boulogne, and the question of right could be referred in the interval to arbitration.

Proposals of marriage between children not yet born meant obviously nothing. In communicating to Lord Howard what Montmorency had said, the Duke of Alva expressed no opinion on the course which England should pursue; he desired only that this proposal should be made known to Elizabeth, and he accompanied Howard's despatch with a letter of his own to the Count de Feria. By accepting the French offer Elizabeth would gain breathing time; if the conference broke up ineffectually on her account, he said she must be prepared for exertions of which, in its present exhaustion, he believed England to be incapable—at the same time it was not to be supposed that the French would keep any promise which they might make of restoring Calais at the completion of the term; if the Queen accepted peace on the terms now proposed, it must be by her own act; the King of Spain would neither advise nor dissuade, and if she cared to continue the struggle in a serious spirit, she might rely on his co-operation.[1]

If England had remained orthodox—if Elizabeth had accepted Philip, he would have spent his last ducat to bring France upon her knees; under existing circumstances the Spaniards were justified in adhering to the letter of their engagement. Elizabeth inquired what

---

[1] Alva and Arras to the Count de Feria, Feb. 13.—GRANVELLE Papers. Howard, Wotton, and Ely to Elizabeth, Feb. 14.—FORBES, vol. i. De Feria to Alva, Feb. 19.—MS. Simancas.

Alva meant by larger exertions, and in what time and by what means he thought that Calais could be recovered. If the allied armies, Alva replied, were to invade France in force for two or three consecutive years, there was no doubt that they could force the French king to any condition they pleased; and in that case the King of Spain would sell all that he had to see England righted.[1] But Alva well knew what England must answer; and after a pang of indignation and disappointment, Elizabeth commissioned Howard to accept the best terms which he could obtain.

'It appeared,' the Duke wrote to Philip, 'that all they could do was to attack Scotland, leaving the Continent to us. We told them that to such conditions your Majesty could not agree: if they would do their part, your Majesty would do yours; but they must remember that your Majesty's differences were already arranged, and that your people could not and would not endure the burden of the war only in a quarrel of theirs. They asked us what we would have them do, and we brought them at last to this: we undertook to demand and to urge, by all means short of breaking off the negotiation, the restoration of Calais pure and simple; if this was refused, to demand the town and harbour without the Pale: if we could not obtain this, the English would consent to leave France in possession for eight years; we, on our parts engaging, if the place was not then restored, to go to war, and assist them to recover it.'[2]

So matters stood at Cambray when the Supremacy Bill was first introduced to the Upper House, and it is

---

[1] 'Y que en este caso sabiamos cierto que V. M^d. aunque se hubiese de vender todo se esforçaria para ayudar á la Reyna.'—*Alva and Arras to Philip II., Feb. 26.* GRANVELLE *Papers*, vol. v.

[2] Ibid.

easy to understand why the Government at such a crisis were in no haste to press it.

The two first conditions the French rejected immediately and absolutely. The third would have been rejected also, but to their vexation and no small astonishment, Philip's commissioners united with the English to present it as an ultimatum; and with the certainty that if they refused, the conference would break up, they referred for instructions to Paris.

Since he had resolved at all hazards to keep Calais, the King of France was unwilling to bind himself by a promise which he had predetermined to break. He flinched however before the attitude of Spain, and said that he would restore it after the eight years if the English would take his word for their security; and if in the meantime the fortifications might be dismantled, and the port be made purely mercantile. Again however the English found their allies faithful to them. The Bishop of Arras would have had Philip put his troops in motion, 'the French being a people more affected by force than argument.'[1] 'For myself,' Arras wrote to the Duke of Savoy, 'I hold it certain that if we yield to them in a matter so unreasonable they will presume on our weakness and will withdraw from many things which they have accorded in Piedmont and elsewhere; there is no fair dealing to be had unless we show our teeth.'[2]

It was insisted that the works should be maintained unimpaired; that when the eight years were expired, the town should be given up in the condition in which it had been lost; and the bare word of France not being considered good,[3]

---

[1] Arras to the Comte de Megha, February 28.—GRANVELLE *Papers*, vol. v.

[2] Arras to the Duke of Savoy, March 11.—*Ibid.*

[3] 'Los Franceses les prometerán de volver á Calais dentro de los seis [ocho] años y despues guardarán la verdad que suelen.'—*De Feria to Alva*, Feb. 19. MS. Simancas.

the allies demanded further the ignominious guarantee of hostages.

Seeing that it was useless to persevere further, the French gave way, and on the 12th of March a final arrangement was concluded by which they bound themselves to deliver Calais, Guisnes, and the whole Pale intact in its existing condition at the time stated, or else to forfeit half a million crowns, and leave the English claim unimpaired; to evacuate and raze the fortresses which they had built on the Scotch border; and to give substantial bonds for the money. As a last precaution, the Spanish commissioners required that the Dauphin and Dauphiness should confirm the treaty, and directly recognize Elizabeth's right to the Crown.

Thus had Spain fulfilled its bond, and England was extricated from its difficulties with better conditions than might have been looked for. The King of Navarre wrote indeed to Elizabeth to assure her of the lasting regard of Henry; to tell her that all which she had gained at Cambray would have been conceded more willingly in a private treaty; and that although the immediate opportunity was lost, 'a way' would soon be found again to settle the question more definitively. But Navarre was a feeble rival to the Duke of Guise. The liberal party in France had been permitted to try their hand at making a separate treaty with England, but they had failed, and with their failure they lost their influence at Henry's court. The Guises, ultramontane in creed, and haters of England in politics, were only eager for an occasion to reopen the war, and set themselves free from their embarrassing engagements. The treaty was signed by the King and ratified by the Dauphin and Dauphiness in the terms which had been extorted. But Mary Stuart at the same moment assumed the royal arms of England;

and the Dauphin in the ratification of the separate treaty concluded with Spain, dared to subscribe himself 'Francis by the grace of God King of Scotland, England, and Ireland, Dauphin of France.'[1]

In England the first and immediate effect of the peace was the reappearance of the Supremacy Bill. On the 13th of March it was read a second time. On the 18th, after 'certain provisions and amendments,' it came on again, and Scot, Bishop of Chester, made a last effort to throw it out. At length, and with some power, he exhausted the usual arguments for the unity of the Church; he dwelt upon the distractions of Christendom since the introduction of the new opinions; and asking what security there would be for the preservation of the faith in a Church cut off from the body of Christ, he said that there were already in Europe thirty-four Protestant communions, all differing from one another, yet 'every one of them saying and affirming constantly that their profession was builded upon Christ, alleging Scripture for the same.'[2]

But he spoke to a deaf audience. The bishops had the best of the argument; but they had fallen on evil times, and were outvoted. Montague supported them, and Shrewsbury supported them; but to the great body of the English laity orthodox and unorthodox a foreign jurisdiction was essentially hateful. They did not mean to imitate Henry the Eighth, and make war upon it with the axe and quartering knife; but the thing itself they were determined to end. The bill was read a third time,

---

[1] 'Quand ledict Arras eust entendu que l'Angleterre estoit comprise le dedans il se print a rire.' Intelligence of a commission, wherein the French king used the style of England.—*Scotch MSS., Eliz., Record Office.*

[2] Speech of the Bishop of Chester in Parliament.—Strype's *Annals,* Appendix No. 7.

and in its altered shape went back to the Commons; and Elizabeth could now receive the Spanish ambassador with confidence and smiles.

'I found her resolved,' de Feria wrote to Philip,[1] 'to maintain the proceedings in Parliament; Cecil, Sir Francis Knolles, and their friends, have gained her over.

'After we had talked a short time, she said she could not have married your Majesty because she was a heretic. I said I was astonished to hear her use such words; I asked her why her language was now so different from what it had been. But she would give me no explanation; the heretics, with their friend the devil, are working full speed; they must have told her that your Majesty's object in proposing for her was only to save religion.

'She spoke carelessly, indifferently, altogether unlike herself, and she said positively that she meant to do as her father had done. I told her I would not believe that she was a heretic—I could not think it possible she would sanction the new laws—if she changed her religion she would ruin herself. Your Majesty, I said, would not separate yourself from the Church for all the thrones in the world.

'So much the less, she replied, should your Majesty do it for a woman.

'I did not wish to be too harsh with her, so I said men sometimes did for a woman what they would do for nothing else.

'She told me she did not intend to be called Head of the Church, but she would not let her subjects' money be carried out of the realm to the Pope any more, and she called the bishops a set of lazy scamps.[2]

---

[1] De Feria to Philip II., March 19.—*MS. Simancas.*
[2] 'Y que los obispos eran grandes poltrones.'

'The "scamps," I said, were the preachers to whom she had been listening; and I added that it was small credit to her to allow any vagabond from Germany to get into the pulpit in her presence, and to talk trash to her.

'At this moment Knolles came in to tell her that supper was ready—a story made for the occasion I fancy. They dislike nothing so much as her conversations with me. I took my leave for that time, saying merely that she was no longer the Queen Elizabeth whom I had known hitherto, that I was ill-satisfied with her words to me, and that if she went on thus she was a lost woman.

'Cecil governs the Queen; he is an able man, though an accursed heretic. Parliament came to its resolution on the morning on which the news came from Cambray; it was this which gave them confidence; and it is a bad return for all your Majesty's kindness. That she will confirm their hateful and vile measures there is no sort of doubt. The bishops if necessary are ready to die for the truth; your Majesty would admire the courage which they are showing. With your Majesty's leave I would sooner spend your money upon them than on the false traitors who have sold their God and their country's honour.[1] Religion will triumph at last; of that I am sure, for the Catholics are two-thirds of the realm; but I had rather the work was done by your Majesty than that it should lapse to the French. Your Majesty will pardon me if I pass beyond my office. I am so wretched at what I see that I cannot refrain from speaking.'

A few days later de Feria wrote again—'I know for certain that the news of the peace gave the Parliament

---

[1] 'Estos fomentidos.' The allusion is to the many English noblemen to whom life-pensions were given by Philip at the time of his marriage with Mary.

the courage to act as they have done—they were afraid before, lest your Majesty should leave them in the lurch. I told the Queen I was indeed astonished that she should have permitted such a thing; I could only hope that after all she would refuse her own consent. I reminded her that she had desired me to write nothing to your Majesty so long as that consent had been withheld; I had relied upon her word, and now I feared your Majesty might hear of what had passed from some other source, and be justly displeased.

'She repeated what she said before, that she was not going to be Head of the Church, or to administer the sacraments, with more of the same sort which was both false and foolish. She asked me haughtily if your Majesty intended to be angry with her for having mass in English. I said I could not tell that; but this I could tell, that she was on the high road to lose her throne, and I for my own part should be sorry to see it. She had had opportunities enough of judging what your Majesty's feelings were towards her, and my business was to tell her the truth, and to point out to her the danger in which she stood. I knew what her resources were, I knew what your Majesty's resources were, and what those of France were, and her only chance was to remain on good terms with your Highness.

'She said she did not mean to quarrel with France; she intended only to maintain herself in her own realm as her father had done.

'I told her she was mistaken; she could not do it. She talked of imitating her father; and yet she kept about her a parcel of Lutheran and Zuinglian rogues that King Henry would have sent to the stake. May God and your Majesty provide a remedy for these misdoings! The Pope must be informed of what has taken place in Parliament here. It is not at all as it was in the times of Henry or Edward, when all alike were compromised. If his Holiness proceed against the Queen and the realm, he must exempt the bishops and Convocation, who have been loud in their protests of allegiance to the Church. The majority of the people out of Parliament are innocent also; and it is of high importance that the distinction be observed in the bull, to confirm the faithful in their allegiance, while it blasts and overwhelms the heretics.

'I had forgotten to tell your Majesty that Lady Catherine[1] is a good friend of mine, and talks to me in confidence. The Queen, she says, does not like to think of her as her possible successor. The late queen took her into the privy chamber and was kind to her. She complains that now she is out of favour and finds nothing but discourtesy. I keep on good terms with my Lady Catherine. She promises me for her part not to change her religion, and not to marry without my consent.'[2]

The fear of Philip on receiving this letter was that Elizabeth in despair of retaining his own friendship would accept the hand which France had at first held out to her. In the late reign Henry the Second had been her firmest friend. His religion all Europe was aware depended on the convenience of the moment; and although the opportunity had probably passed and the French court had now determined to play the card of the

---

[1] Lady Catherine Grey, Lady Jane's sister, who had been married (in form only) to the son of Lord Pembroke at the time of the Northumberland conspiracy. The marriage had been declared invalid, but Lady Jane being dead, Lady Catherine, by the will of Henry the Eighth, was next in succession to the Crown.

[2] De Feria to Philip II., March 23.—*MS. Simancas.*

Queen of Scots, the uneasy orthodoxy of the King of Spain was haunted with the dread of an Anglo-Gallican alliance, which would at once turn the scale in the balance of power against himself, and would postpone or prevent for ever his intended crusade against heresy. Or, if this danger were no longer to be anticipated, the English Catholics might declare for Mary Stuart; and the political mischief would be at least equally serious. France would then have earned the chief gratitude of the Papacy. France would be the first power in Europe; and Piedmont, Lombardy, and perhaps the Low Countries themselves, would drop into Henry's hands.

Philip therefore replied with charging de Feria to prevent if it was not too late the passing of the Acts of Parliament; but whether they were passed or not to say nothing to alarm Elizabeth, and to assure her he was as much her friend as ever.[1] He directed him to do everything in his power to prevent an insurrection; to soothe the Catholics privately with promises, and if they broke out into rebellion to avoid committing himself to their support. If he saw them likely to succeed, he might secretly give them money; but even then he must not offend the friends of the Queen, lest they should call in the French.

For himself, Philip said, he had determined to stay for the present in Flanders: he had put off his intended

---

[1] 'Y en caso que no se pudiese remediar esto, procuraseis de entretener con la Reyna en buena gracia y detenerla muy descuydada y asegurada en mi amistad: porque no se le diese ocasion temiendo lo contrario de llegarse á los Franceses y valerse dellos; aunque no parece que sea verisimil que ella se ose fiar de que tiene en ese Reyno tal pretencion, y no desea sino ocasion para procurar de echarla del.'— *Philip II. to the Count de Feria. MS. Simancas.*

return to Spain, and would hold his ships and troops in readiness to take advantage of any opportunity which might offer itself.[1]

At the same moment bidding adieu to his hope of Elizabeth of England the King of Spain transferred his addresses to Elizabeth of France. Among the conditions of peace sketched in the preceding autumn at Cercamp, the daughter of Henry and Catherine de Medici had been proposed as a bride for Don Carlos. The father was now substituted for the son. After a brief private correspondence the exchange was brought forward at Cambray, on the 2nd of April, by Montmorency. It was accepted on the spot by Alva; and so rapidly was everything arranged, that the very next day the marriage treaty complete in all its parts received the signatures of the French and Spanish commissioners.

Meantime the Supremacy Bill with its new provisions went back to the Commons, where it was once more altered, and sent again to the Lords—flying between the two Houses like a shuttlecock, till the 22nd of March, when it appeared to be at last settled, the title of Supreme Head being given by it to the Queen. The more dangerous question of doctrine was yet untouched; and on Good Friday the 24th, Parliament was prorogued to celebrate Easter with a scene of spiritual pageantry. The mass still continued; the Catholic ritual had possession of the churches, and the litany with parts of the communion service alone as yet were read in English. The clergy, with remarkable unanimity, had pronounced against all change; and decency required that for a re-

---

[1] Philip II. to the Count de Feria.—*MS. Simancas*. Thinking it likely that Elizabeth might ask to see his letter, Philip sent a second with the same date, and in the same packet, containing vague expressions of general friendliness, which de Feria, if necessary, could show.—*MS. Simancas*.

ligious reformation there should be some semblance or shadow of spiritual sanction.

On the 31st therefore there was held in Westminster Abbey a theological tournament. Eight champions on either side were chosen for the engagement. Sir Nicholas Bacon and the Archbishop of York kept the lists; the Lords and Commons were the audience—for whose better instruction the combat was to be conducted in English.

The subjects of controversy were—

1. The use of prayer in a tongue unknown to the people.
2. The right of local churches to change their ceremonies, if the edification of the people required it. And,
3. The propitiatory sacrifice for the quick and dead, said to be offered in the mass.

As a limit to diffuseness, the arguments were to be produced in writing: and to the catholics, in affected deference to their rank, was given the honour and the disadvantage of precedence. On their side were four bishops—White, Baynes, Scot, and Watson; with four doctors—Cole, who had preached at Cranmer's martyrdom; Harpsfeld, Pole's delegate, the inquisitor of Canterbury; Chedsey, Bonner's chaplain; and Langdale, Archdeacon of Lewes.

The Protestants were returned refugees; men who had kept prudently out of the way while their opinions were dangerous to themselves, but had reappeared with security. The true battle on these great questions had been fought and won at the stake. The Aylmers, the Jewels, the Grindals, were not of the metal which makes martyrs; but they were skilful talkers, admirable 'divines,' with sufficient valour for the sham fight in which they were required only to walk with decorum over the course. They had conviction enough—though Jewel at least had saved his life by apostasy—to be quite willing to persecute their adversaries; they were as little capable as the Catholics of believing that heaven's gate-keepers acknowledged any passport, save in terms of their own theology; and on the whole they were well selected for the work which they had to do.[1]

It had been contrived that throughout the controversy the Protestants should have the last word. The bishops either resenting the unfairness of the arrangement, or having as they said really misunderstood it, there was some confusion; and when the moment came they were unprepared to begin. After some hesitation however Cole was put forward to speak on the first point; and according to the account of Jewel conducted himself with no particular dignity. He stamped, frowned, raved, snapped his fingers, and if not convincing, was at least abusive. In argument he stated what was of course true, that at a time when there was no regularly-formed English language, the public service was conducted in Latin, and that in the first centuries of Christianity Latin liturgies had been used in the Latin churches, and Greek in the Greek; but the inference that either Latin or Greek should be used in a country where it was not understood scarcely followed.

The counter-statements of the Protestants were then read by Horne. They consisted of appeals to the Bible and tradition. The service of God was asserted to be a reasonable service of the mind and heart, and not a magical superstition. All rituals had a meaning, which

---

[1] The English names are well known to readers of English Church history. They are Scory, Grindal, Coxe, Whitehead, Aylmer, Horne, Guest, and Jewel.

was intended to be intelligible; and generally the position was maintained that words—human words—whenever used were meant to be understood.

With this the first day's proceedings ended; the discussion was adjourned till Monday; and the Catholics were requested to comply for the future with the prescribed form, that the second proposition might be argued more completely.

On Monday however things went no better. Bacon invited the bishops to commence. White answered that he desired first to reply on the argument of the preceding day. He was told that he might reply on the whole subject when the three propositions had each had their separate consideration. Watson said that they had mistaken the directions, and that on the first head his party had not been heard at all; Doctor Cole had spoken extempore, and had given only his own private opinion. The Lord Keeper regretted their misconception, but was unable to permit the prescribed order to be interrupted; and after some recrimination the bishops agreed to proceed.

But here another difficulty arose. They had been assigned priority, and they preferred to follow; they protested with some reason that it was not for them to prove the Church's doctrine to be true; they professed the old established faith of Christendom, and if it was attacked, they were ready to answer objections; let the Protestants produce their difficulties, and they would reply to them.

They did not and would not understand that they were but actors in a play, of which the finale was already arranged, that they were spoiling its symmetry by altering the plan.

The Lord Keeper replied that they must adhere to

their programme, or the performance could not go forward. He asked them one by one if they would proceed. They refused. He appealed to the Abbot of Westminster; and the Abbot of Westminster agreed with the bishops.

If that was their resolution then, the Lord Keeper said, the discussion was ended—and ended by their fault. They had refused to accept the order prescribed by the Queen, and they should not make an order of their own. 'But forasmuch as,' he concluded significantly, 'ye will not that we should hear you, you may perhaps shortly hear of us.'

Catholic bishops sent to the Tower.

From the first the Tower had been the destined resting-place for the Catholic prelates. The Bishops of Lincoln and Winchester were at once committed for contempt. The rest were bound in recognizances to appear daily at the Council Chamber, and to remain in London till further orders.[1]

The Supremacy Bill is passed.

The Parliament was then left to do the work by itself. The Houses met again on the 3rd of April, and business recommenced with a message from the Queen. Thanking them for the good-will which they had shown in the Supremacy Bill, Elizabeth refused, as she had promised de Feria, the title which was offered her, and desired that the rights of the Crown might be secured some other way. After so many alterations the Commons were unwilling to make fresh changes;[2] but a variation of phrase was all that was necessary; and the Act was then conclusively passed—the same essentially—though with its edge slightly blunted—which had originally severed England from the jurisdiction of Rome. The

---

[1] *Privy Council Register*, ELIZ., A° 1.—*MS.*
[2] De Feria to Philip, April 11.—*MS. Simancas.*

Crown became once more, 'in all causes, ecclesiastical as well as civil, supreme;' and the bishops and clergy were required to forswear obedience to the Papacy—no longer under the pains of high treason, but as a condition of admission to their benefices. The statutes of Henry the Fourth and Fifth against heresy, with the Act of Mary which revived them, were again repealed; and the Church authorities were forbidden to proceed against any person for any manner of opinion, except such as had been condemned by the first four General Councils, or by the plain words of Scripture, or such as might at a future time be declared heretical by Parliament and Convocation.[1]

Thus the broken idol which Pole had so laboriously replaced was once more flung down from its pedestal. Dagon had fallen at last for ever, and de Feria again applied to his master for instructions.

Touching first on other matters, he described the manner in which Elizabeth had received the news of Philip's marriage. 'She affected,' he said, 'one or two little sighs, and then with a smile observed her name was a fortunate one. I told her I was very sorry; but the fault was more with her than with your Majesty; she knew how unwilling I had been to accept her refusal. She admitted the truth of my words; but she said your Majesty could not have been so very much in love with her, or you would have waited three or four months. She did not seem to like it, though two or three of the council, she told me, were delighted.'

'Both she and they,' the letter continued, 'are alarmed at your alliance with France, and fear that it bodes no good to them. That pestilential scoundrel Cecil tried

---

[1] *Statutes of the Realm*, 1 ELIZ., cap. 1.

to persuade me that they would have liked nothing better than to go on with the war. I bade him say that to some one less well acquainted with the state of the country than I was. Lord Sussex heretic as he is has warned the Council that Ireland will rebel if they enforce the alteration of religion there; and the Welsh counties tell Pembroke to send no preachers across the marches, or they will not return alive. The Queen I think would now be glad if she had been less precipitate. Two of the bishops are in the Tower. By entreaties and threats I have delayed the catastrophe as long as possible; but the country is lost to us now body and soul, and it is time for your Majesty to see to it. You have made peace with France; you are at leisure and can do what you please.

'There are two sides to the matter. As to religion I do not pretend to measure your Majesty's obligations. I can merely say that the Catholics hold your Majesty responsible for the position in which they find themselves. But as a question of public policy you are aware of the just claims of the Queen of Scots; you know the defenceless state of the kingdom and the temptation presented to the King of France by the extreme facility of the conquest; and surely this is a catastrophe which you are bound to prevent. You have desired me to keep things quiet, not to quarrel with the Queen, and not to interfere in religion. I have obeyed your Majesty to the best of my powers; but it is still to be seen how far this can be done. Setting God's honour out of the question, each step forward which they take in heresy threatens the peace of the realm. The King of France you are aware will appeal to the Pope; the Pope will excommunicate the Queen, declare her illegitimate, and pronounce in favour of the Dauphiness; and your Majesty will be more perplexed than ever to know how to act. The French will enter England in the name of Holy Church: the Catholics will unquestionably join them: and how your Majesty can take arms against God— against justice, against truth—I confess myself unable to see. To allow them to succeed (and I am terrified to think how easy it will be for them) is politically ruinous to you; and to see these things as I see them, and yet to forbear to speak, would be treason against God and your Majesty.'[1]

So appeared England and England's chances to spectators not wholly led astray by Catholic sympathies, who nevertheless were mistaken in the one vital point. That which to them seemed a cause of weakness was in fact the secret spring of recovering life. Under the paralyzing grasp of spiritual tyranny the arm of England hung nerveless by its side. When the free blood was in her veins again she would renew her youth like the moulting eagle.

The doctrinal question came next. The commission for revising the Prayer-book had been busily at work, and on the 18th of April a proposal for its restoration was brought forward in the House of Commons.

The object had been so to frame the constitution of the Church of England that disloyalty alone should exclude a single English subject from its communion who in any true sense could be called a Christian; so to frame its formulas that they might be patient of a Catholic or Protestant interpretation, according to the views of this or that sect of the people; that the Church should profess and teach a uniform doctrine in essentials—as the word was understood by the latitudinarians of the age; while

[1] De Feria to Philip, April.—*MS. Simancas.*

CHAP I.
1559
April

in non-essentials it should contain ambiguous phrases, resembling the many watchwords which divided the world; and thus enable Catholic, Lutheran, Calvinist, and Zuinglian to insist each that the Church of England was theirs.

The Prayer-book and the Articles.

The 'Articles' were left in abeyance; and happy it would have been for the Church of England had they never been revived. The rubrics of Edward's second book were modified, allowing large latitude in the use of ornaments and vestments. In the communion service the words were restored which seemed to recognize the real presence, while the words also were not rejected which seemed equally to reduce the sacrament to a commemorative form.[1]

Thus altered the Prayer-book was presented to Parliament. The Genevan refugees clamoured that they had not been consulted, that 'fooleries were made of consequence,' and that ' truth was sacrificed to a leaden mediocrity.' At the heart of the matter it was they who were giving importance to what was of no importance; it was they who considered exactness of opinion a necessary condition of Christianity. They would have erected with all their hearts a despotism as hard, as remorseless,

[1] King Edward's second book appointeth only these words to be used when the bread is delivered at the Communion.—' Take and eat this in remembrance that Christ died for thee; and feed on him in thy heart by faith with thanksgiving;' and when the cup is delivered—'Drink this in remembrance that Christ's blood was shed for thee, and be thankful.' Whereas, in Her Majesty's book, on the delivering of the bread, these words must be said—'The body of our Lord Jesus Christ, which was given for thee, preserve thy body and soul unto everlasting life. Take and eat this, &c.;' and at the delivery of the cup, these words—' The blood of our Lord Jesus Christ, which was shed for thee, preserve thy body and soul unto everlasting life. Drink this.'—STRYPE, *Annals*, vol. i. part i. p. 224. The careful student of the Prayer-book will find the two lines of antagonistic thought represented in the alternative Prayers, which are left to the choice of the clergyman.

as blighting as the Romanist. Happily they found few among the laity to share their views, and they were not permitted to ruin their own cause. In the Commons there was no opposition; in the Lords the bishops still resisted, and they found a support which they had not met with on the Supremacy Bill. Lord Montague alone of the lay peers had opposed absolutely the separation from the Papacy. The old Marquis of Winchester, the Earl of Shrewsbury, and six other noblemen[1] voted against an alteration of the services.

The mass however was not to be saved. The Bishop of Ely who had returned from Cambray said that he would perish rather than see it put away;[2] but to no purpose. The Act of Uniformity[3] passed its three readings in three successive days,[4] and Cranmer's liturgy became again the law of the land.

The revolution was complete. The organization of the country resumed the solid and secular character by which, under Henry the Eighth, in the words of the statute of supremacy, 'the realm was kept continually in good order;' and the interests of England were no longer to be sacrificed to the passions of religious partisans. The vessel of the State though heaving dangerously in the after-roll was again on her right course, and began slowly to draw away out of the breakers.

Elizabeth when called on by de Feria to explain the doctrines which her people were to believe found a difficulty in making herself intelligible. She told him first that the Confession of Augsburg would be received in England, and when he expressed his surprise she told

---

[1] Lords Morley, Stafford, Wharton, Rich, North, and Ambrose Dudley, the Duke of Northumberland's eldest son.

[2] De Feria to Philip II.—*MS. Simancas.*

[3] 1 Eliz., cap. 2.

[4] April 26, 27, 28.

him it would not be precisely that confession: it would be something like it, and yet different: 'in fact' she said, 'she believed almost as Catholics believed, for she held that God was really present in the sacrament.'

'However,' de Feria continued,[1] 'she would not argue with me, and I was as little anxious to argue as she was; but I told her I should like to know what the religion was to be, for so far as I could hear there were as many opinions in England as in Germany; and I could not but be surprised that while other princes were laying down their arms and seeking leisure to compose these questions, she who had found her realm in good Catholic order had thrown it back into confusion. She had repealed the good and pious laws of your Majesty and her sister; and had there been nothing else to restrain her, the obligations under which she lay to your Majesty should alone have made her hesitate.

'She said that the laws which she had repealed had been made by her sister before her marriage; your Majesty knew from the first what her opinions were, and so did her sister.

'I assured her your Majesty knew nothing of the kind.

'She professed to be very angry at some comedy in which your Majesty had been insulted, and she said she would have the writer of it punished. Such things, I replied, were of small importance compared to the others; although both in jest and earnest she would do well to protect your Majesty from impertinence: and I mentioned by the way that I knew the plan of the comedy to have been furnished by one of her council. It was Cecil—she herself half admitted it to me. But

---

[1] De Feria to Philip II., April 29.—*MS. Simancas.*

religion, she went on, was a question of conscience, in which in life and death she meant to be constant. She wished she could have three hours' conversation with your Majesty; and she said in conclusion that she hoped to be saved as well as the Bishop of Rome.'

Chap. 1
1559
May

A few subsidiary measures now finished the work of legislature. Elizabeth's title was defended by a treason act; the monasteries which Mary had refounded were again dissolved; and on Monday the 8th of May, in the Queen's presence, the Lord Keeper thanked the two Houses for the patience with which they had discussed the grave and weighty matters submitted to them, recommended them to be as diligent in seeing the laws executed as they had been careful in framing them, and declared the Parliament at an end.

Distracted between his creed and his policy the King of Spain notwithstanding de Feria's urgency durst not interfere. He was persuaded firmly that without his help Elizabeth's throne could not stand; and he felt himself the responsible cause of the success of what he most detested. To avoid if possible the dilemma with which his ambassador had threatened him, he wrote to the Pope, making the most of Elizabeth's solitary act of virtue in refusing to be called Head of the Church, and requesting him to suspend his censures till other means had been tried.[1] He bade de Feria make Elizabeth feel the fresh obligations under which he had thus placed her, and press upon her the insanity of a course

Embarrassment of Philip.

---

[1] 'Me ha parecido que era tiempo de hacer oficio con su Santidad; y asi he mandado despachar sobre ello á Roma avisando á su Santidad del estado en que esta lo de ahí; y de la esperança que todavia se tiene del remedio; y lo que yo lo desseo y procuro, y que hasta ver lo que aprovecha de lo qual yo avisaré á su Santidad no innove cosa ninguna.'—*Philip to de Feria, May. MS. Simancas.*

which eventually would drive him from her side. Meanwhile since she had declined his own hand he had looked out another husband for her, and sent her the choice of his cousins Ferdinand and Carlos the Austrian Archdukes.

This last suggestion de Feria now warmly approved. He had discovered, he said, that Elizabeth was not likely to have children, and if the Archdukes were men, either of them might with the help which Philip would give him make himself master of the kingdom at her death.[1] He laid the proposal before Elizabeth, who affected to listen most graciously. He assured Philip that there was every prospect of success: his own relations with her however had become so constrained through these repeated differences, that he thought the negotiation could be better conducted by another hand: to recall him, he said, would be a significant and public censure on the revolution, and would confirm the constancy of the Catholics; while for himself he admitted that he found it no easy matter to deal with a woman whose humours were so uncertain, and who was surrounded by advisers too blind and stupid 'to comprehend their situation.'[2]

Sir William Cecil and his friends 'comprehended their situation' more entirely perhaps than de Feria himself. They were confident that so long as the only possible rival to Elizabeth was the Dauphiness of France, they might feel sure of Philip, let them do what they would. De Feria's request however was complied with. In an autograph letter full of warmth and friendliness Philip

---

[1] 'Si las espias no mi mienten, que no creo, entiendo que ella no tendra hijos; pero si el Archiduque es hombre, aunque ella se muera sin ellos, se podra quedar con el Reyno teniendo las espaldas de V. M^d.'—*De Feria to Philip II., April* 19. *MS. Simancas.*
[2] Ibid.

announced to Elizabeth that his ambassador's presence was required in Flanders; but that his place should be immediately supplied.[1] De Feria left London, and the Austrian marriage became immediately the all-absorbing topic of public interest in England, in the Low Countries, and throughout Europe.

To the English generally there was everything to recommend it. The house of Burgundy was traditionally popular. Whatever de Feria might dream, there could be no serious peril to English liberty from the younger son of an Austrian emperor; and the nation was feverishly anxious to see the Queen provided with a husband. Elizabeth herself felt and admitted its desirableness. There was but a 'little cloud, scarce bigger than a man's hand,' which shadowed de Feria's hopes. 'They tell me,' he wrote before leaving England, 'that she is enamoured of my Lord Robert Dudley, and will never let him leave her side. He offers me his services in behalf of the Archduke; but I doubt whether it will be well to use them. He is in such favour that people say she visits him in his chamber day and night. Nay, it is even reported that his wife has a cancer on the breast, and that the Queen waits only till she die to marry him.'[2]

Of the Lord Robert Dudley it is scarcely necessary to say much. As every one knows he was the younger son of the Duke of Northumberland, and was now about twenty-nine years old.

The wife spoken of was Amy daughter of Sir John Robsart, whom Lord Robert had married when little more than a boy. Though the ceremony had been public—at

---

[1] Philip II. to Elizabeth.—*MS. Hatfield.*
[2] De Feria to Philip, April 18 and April 29.—*MS. Simancas.*

the court of Edward the Sixth—it had been a love match of a doubtful kind;[1] and the marriage had not been a happy one. The lady lived apart from her husband, at a manor-house in Oxfordshire, and was never mentioned except as an obstacle to his rising fortunes; while he himself who had been Elizabeth's playfellow in childhood and had been a fellow-prisoner with her in the Tower, was now the chosen favourite of her prosperity.

Of his qualities so little can be said to his advantage, that were not the thing so common one would wonder which of them attracted such a woman as Elizabeth. If the Queen had a man's nature, Dudley combined in himself the worst qualities of both sexes. Without courage, without talent, without virtue, he was the handsome, soft, polished, and attentive minion of the Court. The Queen who had no one to guide or advise her selected her own friends; and in the smooth surface of Dudley's flattery she saw reflected an image of her own creation, which, because he devoted himself to her, she chose to believe that he resembled. Her daring, her intellect, her high conscientious devotion to duty, that great and sovereign nature which shone out in her grander moments, were dashed with a taint which she inherited with her mother's blood.

---

[1] Cecil, in a note on Lord Robert's character, spoke of it afterwards as *nuptiæ carnales*.

CHAPTER II.

THE Reformation was again the law of England. The Catholics sat still paralyzed by the rival interests of France and Spain, while the work of Mary and Pole faded away. The nuns and monks were scattered once more; the crucifixes came down from the rood-lofts, the Maries and Johns from their niches, and in Smithfield Market, at the cross-ways and street-corners, blazed into bonfires, as in the old days of Cromwell. Amidst bear-baitings and bull-baitings, May-day games and river pageants, London kept its feast of recovered liberty.

If here and there an ecclesiastic gave trouble, the Council were swift with their remedies. Harpsfeld at Canterbury swore impatiently that religion should not be altered. Sir Thomas Finch was sent to disarm his household.[1] The more dangerous of the bishops were in the Tower with some care for their entertainment there;[2] the rest were under careful surveillance; while commissioners went out to take the oaths of allegiance

---

[1] *Privy Council Register*, A° 2 Eliz.

[2] 'A letter to the Lieutenant of the Tower, with the bodies of the Bishops of Winchester and Lincoln, whom he is withal to keep in sure and several ward, suffering them nevertheless to have each of them one of their men to attend upon them, and their own stuff for their bedding, and other necessary furniture . . . and to appoint them some convenient lodging meet for persons of their sort, using them otherwise well.'—*Ibid*.

from the clergy, to superintend and enforce the alteration of the services, and to collect the subsidy.

In the country all was quiet. The subsidy commissioners were entreated to remember the difficulties in which the late Queen had left the realm, and to set an example themselves in returning the true value of their properties.[1] The result was on the whole satisfactory; there was no resistance or complaint, and the sum obtained was unusually large.[2]

The liturgy was accepted gradually, without enthusiasm yet without opposition, and in places even with pleasure;[3] but it was long before it came into general use. The vast majority of the clergy unambitious of self-sacrifice, or it may be acting under secret instructions, and with a dispensation for perjury when hard pressed, abjured the Pope, retained their benefices, and laboured in secret for the cause which they seemed to desert. Out of 9,400 persons holding cures of souls in various forms, less than 200 refused to the last to comply

---

[1] Letter to the Commissioners of the Subsidy, A° 2 Eliz.—*Domestic MSS. Rolls House.*

[2] Sir John Chichester to the Earl of Bedford.—*MS. Ibid.:* 'The entire sum collected for the first instalment of the subsidy of the laity (not including that of the clergy, or the 15th and 10th) was 137,414*l*. Among the counties, the return was highest from Kent, Essex, Norfolk, Devonshire, and Suffolk; being respectively, 9,015*l*., 7,576*l*., 7,465*l*., 6,863*l*., and 6,828*l*. Yorkshire returned only 5,000*l*.; Middlesex, 3,000*l*.; Lancashire, 1,000*l*.; Cumberland, Westmoreland, Durham, and Northumberland, desolated by Border wars, and charged with the constant expenses of the defence of the frontier, yielded but 24*l*. between them. Glamorganshire was apparently a desert—it was not charged at all. Of the towns, London and Southwark paid 18,658*l*. Norwich came next, at a vast distance, with 750*l*. York next, with 461*l*. Newcastle-upon-Tyne gave 5*l*. Bath, 12*l*.; Canterbury almost as much as York; while Chichester, Bedford, Buckingham, Poole, Aldborough, Harwich, Yarmouth, and Stafford, like Glamorganshire, produced nothing.'—*Subsidium a laicis,* A° 2 Eliz. *MS. Ibid.*

[3] 'The service in the churches is well received and done, for the most part of the shire (Devonshire). There wanted nothing but preachers.' —*Sir John Chichester to the Earl of Bedford.—MS. Ibid.*

with the statute, and resigned their livings. But several years passed before they could all be sworn. They evaded the visitation, or protected themselves in the house or behind the authority of some Catholic neighbour too powerful for the commissioners to meddle with. They absented themselves altogether from their parishes; they closed their churches rather than consent to read there what they considered heretical; and Elizabeth except in the towns where the Protestants were strong was compelled to bear with them till she sat more firmly on the throne. Of this more will be heard hereafter.

Meantime the bishops were less fortunate: the bishops were on the spot to be bent or broken; and professed themselves ready for martyrdom, of which however there was no present danger. On the 15th of May the whole body of the prelates fourteen in number were called before the Queen, and informed that they must swear allegiance or lose their sees. It was not now as when the oath was first offered, when More and Fisher chose the alternative of the scaffold, and Cuthbert Tunstall who believed as they believed dared not act as they had acted. The long debate in Parliament had left no axe for any recusant now to dread. Even the murderous Bonner had no worse fate to fear than some 'room befitting his condition' in the Tower or the Marshalsea, with the garden walls the limit of his exercise—such a fate merely as for 1,200 years the religious orders throughout Christendom had voluntarily chosen for themselves, in retiring from a world with which intercouse imperilled their souls.

The words of the oath were read over to them; and the Archbishop of York was first asked if he would swear. Instead of replying he addressed Elizabeth with a haughty admonition to remember her duty, to follow in the steps of her blessed sister who had brought back the country to the Holy See, and to dread the curse which would follow if she dared to be disobedient.

'I will answer you,' Elizabeth replied, 'in the words of Joshua. As Joshua said of himself and his—I and my realm will serve the Lord. My sister could not bind the realm, nor bind those who should come after her to submit to a usurped authority. I take those who maintain here the Bishop of Rome and his ambitious pretences to be enemies to God and to me.'[1]

The archbishop and the rest were allowed time to consider their final answer. Meanwhile there were found in Heath's house a number of letters and copies of letters which had passed between himself, several of the other bishops, Reginald Pole, and Mary, in Edward's time, containing evident proofs of treason. The Bishop of Ely on the other hand fresh from Cambray told Bacon that if the Queen listened to such advisers as him and Cecil she would bring the realm to destruction. The Bishop of Ely was suspected of being a party to the designs of the French, and his faint assurances of innocence scarcely satisfied the friends of Philip.[2] The situation became more dangerously complicated when the judges also refused the oath—which the court did not dare to resent;[3] and it was even reported that Bacon

---

[1] STRYPE, *Annals*, vol. i. pp. 107, 208.

[2] 'Soy certificado que la Reyna tenia entendido que el Rey de Francia Henrico trataba de quitarla este Reyno. Yo pensaba que el obispo de Ely tuviese parte en esto por ciertos indicios que tuve; pero el dice que no sabe nada cierto.'—*De Quadra to Philip II., June*, 1559. *MS. Simancas.*

[3] 'Los jueces que llaman de Inglaterra los quales han venido aqui á los terminos, no han querido jurar, y so han ido á sus casas sin que los hayan osado apretar en ello.'—*Ibid.*

had offered to resign the custody of the Great Seal, from the animosity with which the leading lawyers regarded him.[1]

Elizabeth attempted to temporize. Heath was told that he might be spared the oath and retain the revenues of the archbishopric if he would name a vicar-general; and the same or a similar offer was made to the rest. Kitchin of Llandaff however, 'the shame of his see,' was the single member of the bench with whom either entreaty or menace could prevail. Kitchin yielded in spite of the efforts of the Catholics to keep him firm.[2] Tunstall might have yielded as he yielded before had the question been merely of the supremacy; but he informed Cecil that he could not 'agree to be a sacramentary, or receive or allow any doctrine in his diocese other than Catholic.'[3]

Supported as they avowedly were by the King of Spain, scarcely affecting to conceal that they looked to him to reinstate them if they were deprived, encouraged by Philip's representative to expect an immediate revolution under his master's auspices, the bishops stood their ground fiercely and doggedly, and Elizabeth for a moment hesitated. De Feria was gone, and in his place had come a bold subtle and dexterous Spanish ecclesiastic, Alvarez de Quadra Bishop of Aquila—sent to England with a special commission to watch over the interests of the Church of Rome, to keep the Catholics true to Philip and themselves, to prevent them from rebelling prematurely, to hold them in hand ready

---

[1] De Quadra to Philip II., June, 1559.—*MS. Simancas.*

[2] 'El obispo de Llandaff que es un viejo codicioso y poco letrado anda vacilando. Yo le envié á visitar y á consolar lo mejor que puede, pero no ha sido bastante esto por sostenerle.' —*Ibid.*

[3] Tunstall to Cecil. — *Domestic MSS.*, Eliz., Rolls House.

to rise at the fitting moment, should other means fail of bringing Elizabeth to reason. Had there been any other candidate for the throne than Mary Stuart his task and Philip's task would have been easy: but the word had gone out that Mary Stuart was not to be thought of; and after a short uncertainty Elizabeth felt herself safe in the equilibrium of the Catholic powers. Their rivalries if they could not protect her from invasion saved her from the danger of mutiny among her own subjects, and she determined to dare all consequences. Among the refugees a sufficient number survived of those who under Edward had been called bishops, to maintain a semblance of the apostolic succession; and the Marian prelates one by one were brought up again for question, deprived of their sees and committed to the Tower or to private custody, there to wait till Philip either by force or by marriage could recover the erring Queen to the Catholic sheepfold.

The chief hope of the King of Spain was in the Austrian prince. To provide against contingencies however he was manœuvring to get into his hand a second card, if the first failed him, in the person of Lady Catherine Grey, who has been seen already in correspondence with de Feria. Encouraged it seems by de Feria's fair words to her, and exasperated at the coldness with which she was treated at Court, Lady Catherine had broken out at last into arrogant and unseemly words against Elizabeth. She had been banished from the royal presence, and was ready to lend herself to any desperate scheme. Philip offered to reward any one who would bring her away 'with three times as much as he or she should lose in England;' and the Countess of Feria, Lady Montague, Lady John Grey, Lady Hungerford, and even Lord Arundel himself, were thought of as likely to lend their assistance—so utterly precarious appeared Elizabeth's tenure of the throne. Finally a pretended Catholic refugee, in reality a spy of Cecil's, was selected as the fittest person. He was sent for by Alva, intrusted with the secret, and directed to manage the flight in concert with the Spanish ambassador.[1] The next post of course put Cecil on his guard, and Lady Catherine was watched too closely for the future to permit her evasion. But the spy added in a postscript to his letter the significant warning—'Be you most assured that there be at this day many eyes over England; and as her Grace doth match herself in marriage, so shall she see things fall out which yet are hidden; and, to make a lewd comparison, I may liken England to a bone thrown between two dogs; for many times I do hear that I will not speak of, and suffer that my heart will not bear.'[2]

The state of parties in England, the Court intrigues, the plans and schemes of the Catholics, the political aspect of the situation, when the Acts of Parliament were passed and the Queen had finally committed herself to the Reformation, will be seen most clearly in the correspondence between the Spanish ambassador in London, Philip the Second, de Feria, the Duke of Alva, and the Bishop of Arras.

DE QUADRA TO THE DUKE OF ALVA.

London, May 10, 1559.

'Parliament has risen, and the Queen has confirmed the Acts. It is uncertain whether she will eventually be Head of the Church; at present she calls herself

---

[1] —— to Sir William Cecil.—*Flanders MSS., 1559;* endorsed in Cecil's hand, from Antwerp.—ELIZ, *Rolls House.*
[2] Ibid.

Governor—declining the higher title, that she may give it to her husband when she marries. The difference is only in the name. The Holy Sacrament was taken away yesterday from the royal chapel, and mass was said in English. The bishops who will not swear will lose their sees; and when they have been all deprived the Queen will go on progress and institute their successors. Clergy refusing the oath are to lose their benefices. Clergy and laity alike who speak against the Queen's doctrines, for the first offence forfeit their properties— for the second their lives.[1] Infinite numbers would fly the realm were they permitted, and I am not sure that the Queen gains much by keeping them. Lord Sussex spoke at length before the Lords on the need of enforcing the statute. In the Commons the Queen was compared to Moses—sent by God to deliver his people from bondage. Neither the heretics of our time nor the persecutors of old ever ventured on so complete a piece of devilry; never I think was so monstrous an iniquity committed. To force a man to do a thing against his will may be unjust; but there may be some reason in it: but to force a man to understand a thing in the sense in which the sovereign understands it, is too absurd to be called either just or unjust.'[2]

---

[1] The bishop exaggerates and mistakes. To refuse the oath involved merely the loss of offices, of the tenure of which the oath of allegiance was and remains a condition. 'To maintain by writing, printing, teaching, or preaching,' that any foreign power, prelate, or person had authority or jurisdiction in the Queen's dominions, was punishable for the first offence by the forfeiture of personal property; and in the case of the clergy, by the forfeiture of their benefices. A second offence incurred Præmunire. It was not till a man had been twice convicted, and offended again, that he was to be held to have committed treason, or deserved death.—1 ELIZ. cap. 1.

[2] Yet de Quadra would have had no objection to sit as an inquisitor, and burn a man who would not believe what the Church told him to believe. Considering who the writer

THE BISHOP OF ARRAS TO PHILIP II.

Brussels, May 10.

'The most pressing danger at present is that the Queen of England's obstinate blindness may provoke an insurrection there, of which the French will take advantage to invade.

'Your Majesty knows better than I that if this happens it will be quite fatal to us. Should the Catholics rise, and should your Majesty refuse to help them, they will unquestionably turn to the French; and the French I think would have tried a descent on the Isle of Wight before this, had you not given them to understand so clearly that you would not permit it.'[1]

DE QUADRA TO THE COUNT DE FERIA.

London, May 29.

'The Queen says she has vowed never to marry a man that she has not seen—that she will not trust painters—with more of the same sort. Just now they affect to be especially polite to me. They tell me that had it not been for the relationship, the King would have been the very man for them.'

DE QUADRA TO PHILIP II.

London, May 30.

'The Constable Montmorency, with a number of French noblemen, have come over to ratify the treaty. On Corpus Christi day they were all at the royal chapel. The Queen placed herself close to the altar, and made

---

was, the words are so remarkable, that it is worth while to give them in the original:—' Forçar á un hombre, que quiera o no quiera, hacer una cosa tiene ya forma aunque injusta. Pero forçar le á que entienda ó no entienda una cosa como la entiendo el Rey es cosa de disparate, y no tiene forma ninguna justa ni injusta.'—*MS. Simancas.*

[1] GRANVILLE *Correspondence*, vol. v.

Montmorency and his companions sit by her side—much to the scandal of the Catholics to see them in such a place.

'Some English prayers and psalms and I know not what, were read; after which were to have followed some chapters; but as the chaplains began one chapter after another the Queen cried out—"Not that! I know that already; read something else." Afterwards I had a conversation with Cecil and the others about the Austrian marriage. I gathered from what Cecil said—though he did not actually use the words—that the Queen suspected that there was some plan in connection with it to force her back into the Church. He assured me however that he would much have liked her to marry your Majesty. He distrusted the Pope's dispensing powers.

'I answered as temperately as I could. I said that no doubt the changes which they had introduced appeared to your Majesty violent and ill-timed. I trusted however that ere long God would give us either a general council or a good Pope who would correct abuses, and then all would go well. I could not believe that he would allow so noble and Christian a realm as England to break away from Christendom and run the risk of perdition.

'There is a Swedish ambassador here who says that the Queen ought to marry his master because he was her suitor in her misfortunes. The King of Sweden, he says, will meddle with no man's religion; as far as he is concerned every man may believe what he pleases. I am not so much appalled at the expression of such monstrous views as at the fact that a man could be found to hold them.[1]

---

[1] Eric of Sweden was not a creditable representative of these principles. He was the greatest ruffian among the crowned heads of Europe.

The Council tell me they will not have the Archduke Ferdinand. They hear he is a bigot and a persecutor. They think best of Charles, only Cecil says he is not wise, and that he has as big a head as the Earl of Bedford.

'The Emperor's ambassador has had an interview. The Queen told him her fool had said that he was one of the Archdukes in disguise, who had come over to see her. She spoke warmly of the Emperor, calling him a good and upright man; and Maximilian,[1] she said, was a friend of the true religion. She ridiculed Ferdinand; she was told, she said, that he was a fine Catholic, and knew how to tell his beads and pray for the souls in purgatory. Of Charles she seemed to know nothing; but she declared she would never have a husband who would sit all day by the fireside. When she married it should be a man who could ride, and hunt, and fight.

'The Council are in an agony to have her married to some one, and Cecil and his immediate friends wish her to choose at home; the rest are frightened at the attitude of the Catholics—they apprehend a revolt, and prefer Charles: that is if they can be assured that he will conform to the Queen's views. If a Catholic prince come here, the first mass which he attends will be the signal for a rising.

'The behaviour of the Catholics themselves is beyond praise. It can hardly be but that she will flinch before their constancy and numbers. If she does not join them she will be forced to leave them in peace unless she means to be destroyed. She will find it a hard task, for she must restore what she has robbed them of; but whoever marries her will find incomparably more difficulty in going on with heresy than in turning back to the truth.'

---

[1] King of the Romans, the Emperor's eldest son.

The close of the letter anticipates the order of the story, but it must retain its place.

'Scotland is in insurrection, and the flame will soon spread here. The Protestants and Catholics hate each other more than ever; and the latter, in their exasperation with the Queen, say openly that she is not their lawful sovereign.

'The King of France, it is said, will send an army to Scotland, and the worst consequences are apprehended. The leader of the insurrection is a heretic nobleman, who it is thought will be the person after all that the Queen will marry.[1] They are to expel the French between them, and establish heresy all over the island. Such is the programme, which I regard myself as a chimera. But the spirit of the woman is such that I can believe anything of her. She is possessed by the Devil, who is dragging her to his own place.'

THE COUNT DE FERIA TO DE QUADRA.

Brussels, June 15.[2]

'I comfort myself with the certainty that the Queen and her council will soon have their deserts. If God will but strike in His own cause, the Devil may fly away with me; I care for nothing else.'

DE QUADRA TO PHILIP II.

London, July—.[3]

'I am compelled to tell your Majesty that the leading Catholics are amazed to see the Queen permitted to go forward in this course of recklessness, careless of the interests either of England or of adjoining realms. In

---

[1] De Quadra makes a confusion between the Duke of Chatelherault and his son, the Earl of Arran, who had not yet returned to Scotland.
[2] *MS. Simancas.*
[3] *Ibid.*

the six months that she has been on the throne she has
brought heresy to life again, and fed it up into strength
and spirit, when it was all but dead. I am well aware
that your Majesty does not forget these things; but it is
necessary that you should know what is said here. First
they looked to your Majesty to help them; then they
looked to France; and if France does nothing they say
it will be your Majesty's fault. Parties however are fast
shaping themselves. There will soon be neither French,
nor Spanish, nor Burgundian, but only Catholic and
heretic. In spite of all, it is your Majesty to whom the
good look with hope and the evil with terror.

'The Irish chiefs have communicated with me. They
request your Majesty to receive them as your subjects.
You have but to say the word and the country is yours.

'As for this woman, you must expect nothing from
her. She is possessed with a false opinion of her own
resources, from which she will never awake till she is
ruined. Heresy has been ingrained into her from her
cradle, and she so hates the truth that she thinks of
nothing but how to destroy it. If your Majesty were to
save her life a second time she would be no more faithful
to you than she is now. If she can spread the poison,
and set your Majesty's Low Countries on fire she will do
it without remorse.'

PHILIP II. TO DE QUADRA.

Brussels, July 9.[1]

'I have seen what you have written. It concerns me
deeply to hear of the increasing injuries done to religion
and of the risk to which the Queen is exposing both
herself and her realm.

'Seeing that neither the good offices which she dare

---

[1] *MS. Simancas.*

not deny that she has received from me, nor my demonstrations of brotherly affection, nor the warnings of the Count de Feria, have availed anything, I have resolved to address her in another tone. Don John de Ayala who is going over for the Countess of Feria is instructed to speak roundly to her. On his arrival you shall accompany him to her presence. You shall say to her that she knows well my feelings towards her, and that my regard obliges me to warn her that she is running a perilous course, that she has put her throne in danger by the changes which she has introduced, and that I require her to look better to her ways.

'You shall tell her that by what she is doing she is disturbing my affairs as well as her own, and that if she does not alter her proceedings, I shall have to consider what it will be necessary for me to do. I cannot suffer the peace of these estates to be endangered by her caprices, as I see plainly that it now will be.

'Say this to her from me.'

DE QUADRA TO PHILIP II.

London, July—.

'Thomas Randolph has come in haste from France to say that the Dauphin, after having publicly assumed the royal arms of England, is about to be proclaimed King of Scotland, England, and Ireland.

'The Queen, when she heard it, said that she would take a husband who should make the King of France's head ache, and that he little knew what a buffet she could give him. The Earl of Arran is in England and near London; Cecil has gone secretly from Greenwich to see him, and we shall soon hear more. She would not have received him here with the certainty that she was

---

¹ *MS. Simancas.*

giving mortal offence to the French if it were not a settled thing that the Earl was to be more than a guest. I have my spies about the Queen's person; I know every word that she says; I know the exact sum of money which Cecil took with him. The discontent grows and spreads. The northern counties refuse the new Prayer-book. Rebellion is not far off.'

A fortnight later the Earl of Arran was to meet the Queen in the garden at Hampton Court, and the interview was to decide whether in grasping at the English crown Mary Stuart had not lost her own. To explain the meaning of this sudden introduction of the name of Lord Arran, it is necessary to go back over the ground, and tell what in the last few years had been done in Scotland.

The causes which had merged into one the seven Saxon kingdoms, which had led gradually to the annexation of Wales and the absorption of the Palatinates, had been long working towards a similar effect on either side of the northern border. The wisest statesmen, both in England and Scotland, deplored the miseries which, till they ceased to be divided, the two countries would continue to inflict on each other; and the Scots, though uncertain, intractable, and passionately jealous of their national liberties, had again and again allowed the question to approach the edge of solution. James the Fifth was to have married the Princess Mary, Prince Edward was to have married Mary Stuart. Both schemes had fallen through at the last moment; yet, except for the disastrous victory of Pinkie Cleugh, which opened the wounds of centuries and united Catholic and Protestant Lowlander and Highlander in defence of their common freedom, the friends of England would have continued to increase, the French alliance would have grown weaker, and the daughter of James the Fifth at all events would have remained at home and grown to womanhood with a Scotch heart like her father.

But of all powers of evil in high places there is none equal for the mischief which it can produce to incapacity. Somerset who disgraced the Reformation in England flung Scotland back into the arms of France; Mary Stuart was brought up amidst the political iniquities of the Court of Catherine de Medici; Mary of Guise governed as Regent in the interests and under the direction of her brother; and the Catholic faction which had all but perished with Beaton recovered life and vigour.

Not indeed that the persecution of the Protestants was again ventured on to a severe extremity. The government was too weak, the temper of the public too dangerous, and the fate of the Cardinal of St. Andrew's a too recent warning. The French court too, so long as the war lasted with Spain, found its interest in toleration; seeking its allies among the Lutheran princes; courting Edward the Sixth while Edward lived; and during the Marian cruelties holding out its hand to Protestant conspirators. The Regent ventured on an occasional edict, but was encountered by armed deputations with steel bonnets and swords; and Scotland drifted on as it were in uncertain neutrality till the Queen should come of age and be married to the Dauphin.

Of special instruction in the reformed doctrines there was but little. Knox remained in England till Edward's death, and retired with the exiles to the Continent; the other preachers, suspected as they were of English sympathies, were obliged to hide themselves till the recollection of Pinkie Cleugh had cooled.

But though ill-informed in the new creed, the young generation grew to manhood in an inability to believe the old. The Earl of Arran, next heir after his father to the Crown should the Stuart lineage fail, the young Lord of Lorn afterwards Earl of Argyle, Lord James Stuart the Queen's brother, Glencairn, Maitland of Lethington, Henry Balnavis, and Kirkaldy of Grange who had assisted at the killing of the Cardinal—young men all of them between nineteen and nine-and-twenty, were passing into the new era unshackled with the memories of superstition, and for the most part with a noble desire for some faith in which they could live as honest men. As time passed on the humours of the people quieted down, and in the autumn of 1555 Scotland was again open to John Knox. The Marian persecutions had just commenced south of the Border; antagonism to England assumed the unusual form of toleration; and Knox who had fled for his life from London was able to present himself in Edinburgh.

His life in exile had been still disturbed and dangerous. The refugees had formed a community at Frankfort, where Knox's thoroughgoing honesty frightened the Anglo-Catholics. To gain favour with the Emperor, and perhaps with their own Queen, the respectable English 'divines,' Jewel, who had apostatized, Coxe, Sandys, and others, took advantage of some blunt expressions about Mary and Philip, and denounced Knox before the Frankfort magistrates. To save his life he escaped to Calvin at Geneva, and thence a few months later returned to his own country.

The Congregation in his absence had fallen under worldly temptations. To avoid open quarrels they had bowed in the house of Rimmon, and humouring the unavowed toleration of the Regent they had kept their opinions to themselves, and complied outwardly like the English with the Catholic forms.

But in England the Reformation was more than half-political. The hatred of priests and popes was a more predominant principle than speciality of doctrine. The movement had been under the guidance of the government, and the more violent factions had, except at intervals, been under control. What kings and Parliament had done in England, in Scotland had to be done by the people, and was accompanied therefore with the passionate features of a revolt against authority. In England the lives of the higher Catholic clergy had been outwardly decorous; in Scotland the bishops and archbishops set an example of the most enormous profligacy. Cardinal Beaton passed the night which preceded his murder with his mistress. Archbishop Hamilton succeeded to Beaton's vices with his power: he lived in notorious adultery, and at successive sessions of the Scottish Parliament obtained letters of legitimization for his children. The mass was no longer a mode of Christianity which serious persons could defend, but a Paphian idolatry, identified with the coarsest forms of licentiousness. To plain eyes unjaundiced by theology it resembled too nearly the abomination of the Amorites or the accursed rites of Thammuz; and the northern reformers saw in their first study of the Old Testament the antitype of their own history. They construed literally the order to keep no terms with idol worship, and in toleration or conformity they found the rock on which the chosen people had make shipwreck.

Penetrated to the heart with this conviction, John Knox became thus the Representative of all that was best in Scotland. He was no narrow fanatic who, in a world in which God's grace was equally visible in a thousand creeds, could see truth and goodness nowhere but in his own formula. He was a large noble generous man, with a shrewd perception of actual fact, who found himself face to face with a system of hideous iniquity. He believed himself a prophet, with a direct commission from heaven to overthrow it, and his return to Scotland became the signal therefore for the renewal of the struggle. He preached for some months in Edinburgh, Lothian, and Angus, where his steady will and distinct purpose carried all before them. Lord James Stuart, Argyle, and Glencairn became the most earnest of his followers; and even the brilliant William Maitland, after a long battle with him on the lawfulness of outward compliance with things established, yielded at last, saying that 'such shifts would serve nothing before God, when they stood in so small stead before men.'

John Knox returns to Scotland.

The Congregation therefore withdrew from the Church. Knox himself administered the communion in the Genevan fashion, and the bishops again prepared to interfere.

Knox was summoned to appear before them in Edinburgh, and replied with his once famous letter to the Regent. Moderate, if we consider his humour, generous, for with as much sincerity as St. Paul, he said he would himself gladly be accursed from Christ if he could convince her, he implored the Queen-mother—not to abolish idolatry—that, he admitted, she could not do—but to refuse to assist the bishops in their intended persecution, with the support of the secular arm.[1]

Appeals to conscience are not always comprehensible to the intellect. To the polished and acute Mary of Guise the words of Knox were but as the raving of the wind. Cultivated, as the times went, in worldly know-

---

[1] CALDERWOOD, vol. i. p. 308, &c.

ledge, steeped from her childhood in political intrigue, and bold as she was dexterous, the Frenchwoman regarded religious innovators with a contemptuous impatience, and tossing the letter when she had read it to the Bishop of Glasgow, said, 'Please you, my lord, to read a Pasquil?'

'If,' wrote Knox again to her when he heard of it—'if ye do no more esteem the admonition of God's servant than cardinals do the scoffing of Pasquils, then He shall shortly send you messengers with whom ye shall not be able to jest in that manner.'[1]

But the times were not ripe for a rising. Tyranny in its most horrid form was dominant in England, and the Regent had France at her back. Lord Argyle promised to protect Knox if he would stay in Scotland; but an entreaty from the refugees at Geneva came opportunely to give him an excuse for retiring. He was summoned again, and outlawed when he did not appear. The bishops burnt him in effigy at Edinburgh, and he himself withdrew once more to Calvin, with a promise to return with better days.

Four years passed. The Catholics used their triumph moderately. The Archbishop of St. Andrew's in 1558 burnt Walter Milne, an old man of eighty; but a severe persecution was still inconvenient for the policy of the French. The Queen Regent gave a general promise of toleration; and it was not till the peace of Cambray and the rejection of his advances by Elizabeth, that Henry the Second abandoned himself finally to an ultramontane policy. Then it was that he determined to crush his own Huguenots with fire and sword; uniting ambition with orthodoxy, to proclaim his daughter-in-law Queen of England; and with the Pope's sanction as the

---

[1] CALDERWOOD, vol. I. p. 317.

leader of a crusade annex Great Britain and Ireland to the Crown of France.

That this, or something like this, was a design really entertained by the court of Paris, was no mere creation of Elizabeth's or Cecil's fears—no excuse invented to justify their policy. The Spanish and Flemish statesmen were as uneasy as the English. Francis and Mary openly assumed the titles of King and Queen of England, Scotland, and Ireland. They engraved the arms on their seals and plate; they adopted the style in their official documents. The army of Italy was recalled on the peace, but it was not disbanded. Troops were assembled in Normandy; Calais and Havre were crowded with transports; while the French forts on the north bank of the Tweed were not dismantled, as the treaty required. Fresh companies of French troops were sent over to the Regent. Even Montmorency, the most unlikely of all the advisers of Henry the Second to flatter the ambition of the Guises, declared 'for the Queen Dolphin's title.'[1]

---

[1] Throgmorton to Cecil.—FORBES, vol. I. p. 136. Among the *Domestic MSS.* at the Rolls House, there is 'a brief note,' dated August, 1559, in Cecil's hand, 'to prove the French evil meaning towards England.'

'Their pretence for their false title appeareth—

1 'By their practices with the Burgundians at Cambray.

2. ' By their practices at Romo for Bulls; by their usurpation of the arms of England in jousts, plate, hangings, and seals.

3. ' By the special speech of the Scotch Queen; by the consultation for the style of the French King; by the usurpation of the style of England and Ireland, sent in a great seal to Scotland.

4. 'By their practices with Ireland. George Paris passed to the old Queen of Scotland with writings from the Lords of Ireland.

' Three thousand Frenchmen in Scotland.

5. ' Their preparations by sea and land. The Marquis d'Elbœuf. The Duc d'Aumale.

' In Alemannia, the Rhinegrave. The Duke of Saxe in Denmark.

' No other quarrel but England. At peace, and that by marriage, with the king Catholic.

'The old hatred of the House of Guise. Their authority at this present. Their private respects to advance their Queen's title to Scotland and England.'

With the Scotch nobles it was thought that the pride of giving a sovereign to their old rival would be motive sufficient to insure their co-operation. The only interest which would sway them in the other direction was Protestantism. The first step therefore towards the conquest of England was to destroy once for all the rising 'Congregation,' and for this purpose, so soon as the peace of Cambray had been finally concluded, France prepared to place an adequate force at the disposal of the Regent.

The Protestants, encouraged by the revolution in England, and perhaps at the private instigation of Cecil, had petitioned the Queen for a reformation. On the occasion of the burning of Walter Milne, they protested against those 'cruel oppressors and bloodthirsty tyrants the bishops,' and with a meaning menace had declared that if there was a rebellion in the country for religion, the fault should not be imputed to them. It is unnecessary to suppose, with Knox, that because the Regent refused to listen to demands couched in such language, she must have been possessed with the devil. She answered haughtily that if this was the style in which she was to be addressed 'she would drive the ministers from Scotland, though they preached as truly as ever did St. Paul.' The French reinforcements might be expected any day; the Regent grew more peremptory, the Protestants more uneasy. An interview of the reforming lords with her in May ended only in an interchange of menaces. Fortunately for them the question was not one of doctrine merely: the gaunt and hungry nobles of Scotland, careless most of them of God or devil, were eyeing the sleek and well-fed clergy like a pack of famished wolves.

The tinder was dry and a spark sufficed to kindle it.

The citizens of Perth opened the drama by declaring for 'the Gospel.' They took possession of the churches, and read the service from Edward the Sixth's Prayer-book.[1] Lord Ruthven as Provost was required to stop the 'disorder,' and oblige the people to attend mass. Ruthven replied that he could not cause them to 'act against their consciences.' The example of Perth was followed at Montrose and Dundee; and the Protestant preachers were summoned to appear before the Regent at Stirling on the 10th of May, and answer for their conduct. They prepared to go, but to go accompanied by five or six thousand armed men; and thus attended the Regent refused to receive them.[2]

At this crisis, and while they were waiting for the next step, John Knox reappeared. The 'better times' had come.

Immediately on the news of Elizabeth's accession, he had attempted to return to England; but unfortunately he had employed his leisure at Geneva in writing a book which Elizabeth could not forgive. The Catholic Queen Regent in Scotland, the Catholic Queen Mary in Eng-

---

[1] At a meeting of the Congregation on the 3rd of December, 1557, it was agreed that 'the Book of Common Prayer' should be read weekly on Sundays and festival days. Presbyterian writers have endeavoured to prove that it was not Edward's Prayer-book, but the Genevan which was here intended. The question is set at rest by a letter of William Kirkaldy to Sir Henry Percy, written on the 1st of July, 1559—'As to parish churches, they cleanse them of images, and all other monuments of idolatry, and command that no masses be said in them. In place thereof, the Book set forth by godly king Edward is read in the same churches.'—*Scotch MSS. Rolls House*.

[2] Protestant writers say that the Regent desired them not to appear, and then outlawed them for disobedience. This is scarcely the truth. Sir James Crofts, writing from Berwick to Cecil, says—'The Regent commanded the preachers to appear before her at Stirling, and they being accompanied with a train of five or six thousand persons, the Regent dismissed the appearance, putting the preachers to the horn.'

land, had chafed his imagination into a belief that a female sovereign was a monster, forbidden by the laws of God. He had already blown 'the first blast of his trumpet,' as a summons to rebellion against the unlawful authority of a woman, when Mary Tudor's death too late brought repentance and a changed opinion. Neither repentance nor change could earn his pardon from Elizabeth. The government of women had not been really odious to him, but only the government of this and that particular woman; and when times were altered he could remember Judith and Deborah. But he had allowed his argument to lead him to conclusions which he could not wholly disavow; and Elizabeth would not accept a half apology, in which she was permitted to reign as an exception to a rule. He had shot an arrow into a mark which he would most have desired to miss; and although she would admit his letters, respect his character, and accept his services, he could not be allowed to set foot in her dominions. In April he wrote an unavailing protest from Dieppe to Cecil; and on the 2nd of May he landed in Scotland. The ship in which he crossed carried a seal to the Regent engraved with the arms of England, and carried with it also in himself the person who, above all others, baffled the conspiracy and saved Elizabeth and the Reformation.

Still under sentence of outlawry, he spent two nights at Edinburgh; and then, supposing that the preachers would 'keep the day' at Stirling, he hastened on to Perth, 'intending himself also to be present, by life, by death, or else by both, to glorify God's holy name,' and desiring the prayers of his friends 'that he might not shrink now when the battle approached.'[1]

---

[1] Knox to Mrs. Anne Locke.—CALDERWOOD, vol. L p. 440.

He arrived to find the summons withdrawn, and the
'Congregation' waiting for the Regent to make the next
move. Within a day or two the Laird of Dun brought
word that the preachers were outlawed, and that the
Master of Maxwell had been arrested and imprisoned
for threatening to take their part.

On Thursday the 11th of May there had been
service in the church, and Knox had preached a
sermon passionate as the time invited. The congregation
was still undispersed, when a priest, encouraged
perhaps by the proclamation, came in, went up to the
altar, opened the tabernacle, and prepared to say mass.
A boy who was present said something insolent; the
priest struck him; and the boy snatching up a stone,
flung it at the crucifix, which fell broken to the ground.
The common instinct shot through the gathered crowd;
altar, ornaments, images, in a few moments lay in ruins
on the chancel floor. The saints were flung from their
niches; the storied windows dashed in atoms. Then the
cry rose, 'To the Grey Friars!' and in an hour or two,
the poor monks, started from their noonday dinner, were
adrift upon the world, and their homes going up in
smoke and flame into the sky.

'It was the work of rascals,' says Knox, 'who cared
nothing for religion;' and what Knox did not defend,
the Regent may be pardoned for having resolved to
punish. With the Grey Friars had perished the Charterhouse,
sacred as the burial-place of the first of the
Stuart kings. The French troops were sent for from
Leith; and Argyle, Chatelherault, and Lord James Stuart
were called upon to save their country from anarchy.

The Lords were willing to suppress a riot; they
were not willing that the riot should be made an excuse
to confirm the sentence against the preachers; and they

suggested a conference, like that at Westminster, where the reformers and the bishops might discuss their differences. But the Regent, with the instructions which she had received from France, was in no humour for conferences, and was resolute to use the opportunity which the riot had given her.

The gauntlet was thrown down. The Congregation finding that there was no escape for them, met defiance with defiance. They wrote to the Regent to say that they would fight for Christ and the Gospel sword in hand. D'Oysel the French ambassador was supposed to be doubtful in religion. They implored him to prevent the outbreak of a quarrel which, if once opened, would never be healed; while to 'the bishops—"the pestilent prelates"—"the generation of antichrist," they insisted and declared, that if they proceeded in their cruelty they should be treated as open enemies to God and mankind; the Lords of the Congregation would begin the same war with them which God commanded Israel to execute against the Canaanites.'

The word went out speeding like the fiery cross, for the friends of the Gospel to rally to Perth. In vain Lyon Herald at Glasgow bade the people 'sit still.' While the crowd was hesitating, young Glencairn exclaimed, 'Others may do as they will, I will go to my brethren at St. Johnstone, though I go alone with a pike on my shoulder.' Boyd and Ochiltree sprang to the side of Glencairn; and presently all Glasgow, Kyle, and Cunningham, were up in arms. Fife followed, and Angus and Dundee: and over all hills and all bypaths, north, south, east, and west, the steel bonnets came streaming in to the rescue of the preachers.

The French force was still small; the promised reinforcements had not yet arrived; and both the Regent and d'Oysel were uneasy at the scattering of Huguenots among the troops which at present were at their disposal. On the 24th of May she sent Argyle and Lord James, who still remained with her, to arrange some sort of terms. Knox bade them return and tell her she was fighting against God; if she wished for peace she must give up persecution once and for ever, and repent of her sins.

Argyle carried back the message, and with it an account of the strength of the Congregation. For himself, he said, he would support the Queen if she would make certain concessions; but when he named them, they were scarcely short of what Knox would have himself demanded—indemnity for the past and toleration for the future—toleration of what would itself tolerate no rival.

The Queen, fearless and resolute, at once advanced with all the force she could collect. Ten miles from Perth a deputation met her from the Protestants. She promised to forgive the riot, to allow liberty of conscience—every Scot to profess what creed he pleased. The citizens stipulated that they should not be required to receive a French garrison—and she consented to this also. Knox still distrusted her; but Argyle and Lord James became securities for her good faith, and signed a bond with the Western leaders to join them if she proved treacherous.

The terms were equitable, had there been on either side a full acceptance of them. The Regent, however, was only protracting the time till the troops in Normandy could be sent over; and the Protestants understood by toleration the right to prohibit Catholics from saying mass. The bands of the West dispersed; and the Regent entered Perth with d'Oysel, Chatelherault, Atholl, and the Archbishop of St. Andrew's.

A scuffle began—no one knew how—as they passed the gates; shots were fired, and a child was killed. Still it seems there was no immediate intention on the Regent's part of breaking the compact. The French were taken by surprise by the fierceness of the demonstration—they had not calculated on the combination of influences which would tell against them. The Church was rich, and the Scotch lords, like the Irish—even the good Catholics among them—were anxious for plunder. D'Oysel said he could not tell friend from foe; Lord Huntly, the best Catholic in Scotland, deserted him, and Chatelherault drifted with the stream. It is incredible that in such a position the Regent would have courted extremities could she avoid them; but circumstances were too strong for her. She had mass said in the church at Perth the Sunday after she entered it; it led to a fresh commotion, and when she returned to Stirling she left four hundred Scots there to keep order. There was an instant cry that she had broken faith: Argyle, Ruthven, Lord James Stuart, and Monteith, gathered their trains together and rode away with Knox to St. Andrew's, where they again sent out orders for the gathering of the Congregation. The Regent followed, uncertain what to do, as far as Falkland; and Archbishop Hamilton, supposing the Protestants to be as yet in small numbers, dashed on to St. Andrew's with two hundred men-at-arms—swearing that if Knox preached in his church 'a dozen bullets should light upon his nose;'[1] and that he would bring him dead or alive to the Queen.

But St. Andrew's was too strongly held for the archbishop to venture into it. He had to fly for his

---

[1] Knox to Mrs. Anne Locke.—CALDERWOOD, vol. i. p. 464.

own life—leaving his pulpit to its fate; and Knox, who ten years before hanging tired over his oar in the French galley, saw the white steeple of St. Andrew's rising out of the sea in the mist of the summer morning—and forlorn and helpless as he then seemed—prophesied that in that spot he should again preach to the glory of God —kept his word amidst the army of the Calvinists. As a fierce close to the wild service, the roods and vestments were heaped into a pile and burnt.

To sit still was now to abandon all: a lost battle could scarcely be worse than inaction; and on the 13th of June the Regent pushed forward from Falkland to Cowper Muir, with d'Oysel and Chatelherault. But 'the Duke's men were of the same opinion with the preachers.'[1] The Protestants had gathered so thick 'that men seemed rained from the clouds.' They had cannon with them, as well as the advantage of numbers; and d'Oysel, after a survey of their position, felt that to risk a fight would be mere waste of valuable life. He complained that 'he knew not whom to trust;' 'those who were with him in the morning were his enemies in the afternoon.'[2] The Regent was induced—perhaps compelled—to consent to an armistice; and under cover of a suspension of arms for eight days, the French withdrew to Edinburgh, and thence to Dunbar, where for a time their condition was unpromising. The army chest was empty; the Queen had spent her last shilling; the wages were unpaid; and the men, unable to buy provisions, were driven to plunder to save themselves from starvation. The Huguenots mutinied and came in bodies of two and three hundred at a time, demanding food or dismissal. Unless he was

---

[1] Sir James Crofts to Sir H. Percy, June 14.—*Scotch MSS. Rolls House.*
[2] D'Oysel to Noailles.—TEULET, vol. i.

immediately relieved, d'Oysel feared that he would have to return with them to France.¹

Thus the Congregation were left for the moment absolute; and they made haste with their opportunity. Perth was relieved of its garrison; Scone was sacked and burnt; Stirling threw open its gates; and the abbeys there, even to the very gardens, were destroyed in the presence and by the order of Argyle and Lord James.² The mass was everywhere put down. By the end of June the lords were in Edinburgh; and the entire fabric of the Catholic Church over the whole Lowlands had fallen.

'The manner of proceeding is this,' wrote Kirkaldy to Sir Henry Percy; 'they pull down all manner of friars' houses, and some abbeys which willingly receive not the Reformation; as to parish churches, they cleanse them of images and all other monuments of idolatry, and command that no masses be said in them; in place thereof, the book set forth by godly King Edward is read in the same churches. They have never as yet meddled with a pennyworth of that which pertains to the kirk; but presently they will take orders through all the parts where they dwell that all the fruits of the abbeys and other churches shall be kept and bestowed upon the faithful ministers, until such time as other orders be taken. Some suppose the Queen, seeing no other remedy, will follow their desire; which is that a general Reformation be made throughout the realm—conform to the pure word of God, and the Frenchmen sent away. If her grace will so do, they will obey and serve her, and annex the whole revenue of the abbeys to the Crown. If her grace will not be content, they will hear of no agreement.'³

---
¹ The Queen Regent to the King of France, July 1.—TYTLER, vol. i.
² Ibid.
³ Kirkaldy to Sir H. Percy, July 1.—*Scotch MSS. Rolls House.*

The supposition that the Regent would give up the struggle might be believed by those who considered only what was passing under the eye. To Knox, however, who knew the designs of France on England, and to every one else who was not blinded by the passion of the moment, it was plain that no such fortune could be looked for. Unencumbered with war elsewhere, and with a large army set free from work, Henry the Second was not the man to sit still while his daughter's kingdom was overrun with revolution, even had he no ulterior object. Whatever might be their immediate triumph, the clear-sighted among the Protestants knew that they would have to reckon sooner or later with the whole power of France. In the flush of success therefore they turned to England, confident that for her own sake Elizabeth could not allow them to be conquered: and they caught at the occasion as an opportunity for the union of the realms in the bond of a common creed, upon terms which would at once give them the safety which they desired, and gratify their national pride.

'If their imaginations hold,' Sir James Crofts wrote to Sir Henry Percy,[1] 'they mean to motion a marriage you know where.' The Earl of Arran had been thought of in his childhood as a fitting husband for Elizabeth, by Henry the Eighth. The King's desire had been to link the royal families together by as many ties as possible; and while seeking Mary Stuart for Edward he had selected the nobleman next in succession for his second daughter. Arran was now four-and-twenty, two years younger than the Queen of England. He was known to be an earnest Protestant. The character or ability which might lie behind his creed, time and op-

---

[1] June 14.—*MS. Rolls House.*

portunity were required to show. He had grown up in honourable captivity on the Chatelherault estates in France, where he had been sent as a security for his father's loyalty. On the first news of the insurrection in Scotland he was ordered to Paris; and as he did not obey, M. de Mompesat was despatched with orders to bring him 'quick or dead' to the court.[1] When de Mompesat arrived at Chatelherault the bird was flown, and he returned empty-handed to Paris, to be received with a burst of passion by the Dauphiness, who told him he could do her no better service than use her cousin as a traitor wherever he met with him.[2] Arran meanwhile, after hiding for a fortnight in the woods of Poitou, escaped to Geneva; and the anticipation of the world pointed instinctively to the step expected next to follow. If the Queen of Scots sent the French to conquer her subjects, she might be held to have forfeited the crown. 'You,' said an emissary of the Congregation at Paris to Sir Nicholas Throgmorton, ' have a queen, and we our prince the Earl of Arran, marriageable both, and chief upholders of God's religion. This may be a means to unite England and Scotland together, and there is no foundation nor league durable nor available but in God's cause.'[3]

In the face of the known intentions of the French court, Elizabeth would have been but defending herself legitimately if she had seriously entertained a project which would cut the knot of so many difficulties. To unite England and Scotland in a common cause and a common belief was perhaps the safest as well as the boldest course before her. 'It is certain,' wrote the Bishop of Aquila to Philip, 'that a part of the council have recom-

---
[1] Throgmorton to the Council.—Forbes, vol. i. p. 144.
[2] Ibid. p. 146.   [3] Ibid. p. 147.

mended this marriage to the Queen.'[1] Her own expression, that she would take a husband who would make the King of France's head ache, made de Quadra fear that she was herself deliberately contemplating it.

The difficulty was to get Arran safely to London. The French, the Austrians, the Spaniards, alike desired to prevent a catastrophe which would defeat all their schemes. The whole Continent was watched for him.[2] After a short correspondence with Sir Nicholas Throgmorton, Elizabeth's dexterous ambassador at Paris, Cecil selected Henry Killigrew and one of the young Tremaynes of Cornwall 'as the fittest persons to be trusted with so difficult an enterprise,' and dispatched them with instructions to bring the Earl through Germany to Emden, and thence to cross to England.

The Scots meanwhile continued to urge their own cause; intimating, without direct mention of Arran, that it might be of importance to 'both realms' 'that the Queen's marriage should not be hasty,' and pressing to know what Elizabeth would do if a French army were landed in Scotland. 'If ye suffer us to be overthrown,' Kirkaldy wrote to Cecil,[3] 'ye shall prepare a way for your own destruction; if you will advisably and friendly look upon us, Scotland will in turn be faithful to England to defend the liberties of the same.' Knox at the same time sent a second apology for his unhappy book, saying that he had long looked 'to a perpetual concord

---

[1] De Quadra to Philip, Aug. 13.—MS. Simancas.

[2] 'The safe convoying of the Earl of Arran hither seemeth here a thing profitable and needful. It must be done secretly, as well in respect of the Emperor's subjects and friends, and the King of Spain's, as of the French; and herein haste, so it be with discretion, is thought most necessary; and to take shipping at Emden, in Friesland, rather than at Antwerp, is thought more safe.'— Cecil to Throgmorton, June 1559. CONWAY MSS. Rolls House.

[3] June 13.—Scotch MS. Rolls House.

between England and Scotland as the happiest prospect for both of them; that the occasion had arrived if the Queen would embrace it; and begging to be permitted to repair to her presence.'[1]

It is impossible to believe that Cecil in so serious a matter would have ventured to act without the Queen's approval. He replied to Kirkaldy through Sir Henry Percy, thanking him for his communications. He said 'he had imparted the matter in such secret manner, and to such parties as thereto was behoving'—that is unquestionably to the Queen herself—and 'that they had very good liking thereof.' He was requested to demand however some more explicit information as to their plans, their resources, and the amount of help which they would look for; and to ask further, in case England consented to assist, 'what manner of amity might ensue, and how the same might be hoped to be perpetual.' Answers to these questions were desired with convenient speed; meantime Sir Henry Percy might assure the Congregation 'that rather than that realm should be with a foreign nation and power oppressed, and the nobility and such as sought to maintain the truth of the Christian religion should be expelled, the authority of England would venture with power and force to aid that realm against any foreign invasion.'[2]

Four days later Cecil wrote again to Sir James Crofts at Berwick, desiring him to let the lords know that the Earl of Arran was on his way to England; that he had certain intelligence that the French king had determined to send over an army; and repeating his assurances that

---

[1] Knox to Cecil, June 28.—*Scotch MSS. Rolls House.*

[2] Cecil to Sir Henry Percy, July 4, endorsed in Cecil's hand, 'My letter to Sir H. P. returned to me.'—*Scotch MSS. Rolls House.*

England 'neither might nor would see their ruin, so as the same might be assured of acquittal in some good friendship.'

Nay, so resolute was Cecil,[1] that he concluded by saying to Crofts:

'In any wise endeavour to kindle the fire—for if it should quench, the opportunity thereof will not arise in our lives—and that which the Protestants mean to do should be done with all speed: for it will be too late when the French power cometh.'[2]

So far all was going well. Arran's name had been barely mentioned—but the allusion was none the less intelligible. The letter to Percy, and the message sent through Crofts, were communicated to the lords at Edinburgh, who replied to it by an open address to Elizabeth herself.

The union of the realms, they said, had been an object for which the wisest men in Scotland and England had long laboured ineffectually. An opportunity now offered itself such as never had occurred before. They had themselves enterprised battle against the Devil, against idolatry, against 'that sort of men' who had throughout been the friends of France and the enemies of England; and their overthrow would only be the 'entry of greater cruelty.' For the sake of Christ therefore, and for the sake of His glorious Gospel, they implored the Queen and the English people to stand by them; 'and whatever conditions her Majesty or her Majesty's council could reasonably require should on their part not be denied.'[3]

---

[1] Again, it is idle to suppose that he was acting without Elizabeth's sanction.

[2] Cecil to Sir James Crofts, July 8. Autograph draft endorsed, 'to be put in cipher.'—*Scotch MSS. Rolls House.*

[3] The Lords of the Congregation to the Queen of England, July 19.—*Scotch MSS. Rolls House.*

The petition was signed by Argyle, Glencairn, Ruthven. Lord James Stuart, Boyd, and Ochiltree. It was accompanied with a letter to Cecil, in which they said that their object was truly and sincerely to advance the gospel, to put down the tyranny of the clergy, and defend the liberties of Scotland. How they should accomplish it. they did not know—they trusted only that He that had begun the good work would perform it to His glory. But they asserted with the utmost emphasis that there was no fear of their again falling away to France. There was no earthly thing which they so much desired as 'the joyful conjunction of the realms;' and they 'prayed God' that 'they might be the instruments by which the unnatural debate between them might be ended.'[1]

At this crisis an accidental thrust of a Scotch lance in Paris seemed for a moment as if it had spared Elizabeth the necessity of further anxiety. The excuse for the interference on which she had resolved was the unconcealed design of the King of France against herself. On the 11th of July the news arrived in London that the King of France was dead.

In honour of the marriage of his daughter with Philip of Spain, Henry the Second held a gorgeous tournament. The insurrection of the Protestants had only precipitated a purpose in which he believed the King of Spain would now be compelled to acquiesce; and with special and ostentatious significance, the English arms were embroidered over the hangings of the throne, over the galleries, and on the breasts and sleeves of the heralds. The display was understood as the public declaration of the Queen of Scots' pretensions, and of his own determination to support them. The King himself took his

---

[1] The Lords of the Congregation to Sir William Cecil.—*Scotch MSS. Rolls House.*

place in the lists. On the last day of the festivities he was running a course with the Count Montgomery de Lorge, captain of the Scotch Guard, when de Lorge's lance striking full upon Henry's casque, tore it away from the helmet; the point broke short off, and the ragged staff pierced the king's forehead above the eyes, bearing him senseless to the ground. The surgeons at first believed that there was no danger; but a splinter had reached the brain. He lingered ten days, and died; and Francis and Mary Stuart were King and Queen of France. Whether with him had departed the vision of the conquest of England would depend on the persons on whom the administration of the kingdom devolved. Francis himself was a fœble child. If Catherine de Medici, the Constable, and the King of Navarre could seize the control, the world would fall into its old grooves, and England would be safe. If Mary Stuart had influence enough to give the direction to her uncles, there was more danger than ever.

About this there soon ceased to be a doubt. Less than a week after King Henry's death Throgmorton wrote that the Guises and the Queen of Scots ruled all in Paris. The defence of Metz and the capture of Calais had made the Duke of Guise the idol of the populace. Mary Stuart herself, though but nineteen, was dexterous and energetic beyond her years. The ultra-Catholic party, of which the Guises were the especial chiefs, was for the moment in the ascendancy; and of the five brothers, three at least—the Duke himself, the Marquis d'Elbœuf, and the Cardinal of Lorraine—were men of large ability and high grasping ambition. On the accession of Francis a question rose immediately whether the English quarterings were to be introduced into the great seal of France. After some discussion, and probably in some fear of Spain, it was decided that the young king himself should use only the usual arms; but Mary Stuart might keep the title which she had assumed, and in all her public acts thenceforward should style herself Queen of England.

'The present King,' de Quadra wrote from England to the Emperor, 'will go forward with the enterprise more eagerly than his father. The army for Scotland is ready, and when Scotland is quieted will come England's turn.'[1]

'England,' said the Count de Feria to Sir Thomas Chaloner, 'will be another Milan to set the princes by the ears. You see who rule about the young King—the greatest enemies you have—only the House of Guise.'[2]

From France itself the warnings came thicker and ever thicker.[3] Could the Guises succeed in the conquest of England they would gain a hold in France which nothing again could shake. Their passionate orthodoxy gave them a claim on the regard of Philip. If he could tolerate the enterprise at all it would be in their hands, and they would be quick about it, for the health of Francis was precarious. The Queen-mother dreaded them. The King of Navarre and the Prince of Condé hated them. They would not wait for the possibilities of the future, they would make for port while the tide was at its flood.

Two courses were open to Elizabeth. Marry the Archduke Charles, said the Spanish ambassador, the Duke of Norfolk, Lord William Howard, and the English Conservatives: marry Charles, leave alone the revolutionary Scots and the new doctrines; and Spain will

---

[1] De Quadra to Ferdinand, August, 1559.—*MS. Simancas.*

[2] Sir T. Chaloner to Elizabeth, Aug. 13.—*Spanish MSS. Rolls House.*

[3] Letters of Sir N. Throgmorton to Elizabeth, July and August, 1559. —FORBES, vol. L

remain your friend, and you will have nothing to fear. Marry Arran, said the ultra-Protestants. Declare that if the French invade Scotland the Queen will forfeit her throne; accept the offers of the Congregation; unite the realms in a single kingdom; and with the whole island you may defy the world. Practise with Huguenots in France; practise with the disaffected in the Low Countries; and you will find these Catholic kings work enough at home, and they will be in no hurry to meddle with you.

Such in effect were the alternatives of the situation. Elizabeth herself appeared to have small desire to choose either. The Austrian marriage was safe but inglorious; reports were unfavourable of 'Charles with the large head;' and Spanish interference would come back with Spanish protection. The other plan was bold and grand, but there was many a doubt to be solved before she could venture a step so desperate; she had to be assured of the character of Arran whom she had never seen, and of the constancy of the Scots of which, in spite of the vehemency of their asseverations, she had reason to feel uncertain. How passionately they had set their hearts upon the Arran marriage will be seen hereafter; but Elizabeth did not know it. In their present fear of conquest they were ready to throw themselves into the arms of England; but there was a French faction among them, the creation of an alliance of centuries. There was a habit of looking to France as their guardian against English intrusion, which the capricious fever of national pride might at any time warm into life again; and the Queen might fly in the face of the public feeling of Europe to find herself left to bear the consequences alone. Sir N. Throgmorton himself, while advising her not to allow the French to oppress the Scots, added a warning that she must not trust them too entirely;[1] and even their present attitude and present condition were not promising. The insurrection had blazed up furiously, but it had burnt out like a fire of straw. In the beginning of July the Congregation were at Edinburgh many thousands strong; and d'Oysel was cooped up with a few hungry mutinous companies at Dunbar, expecting to be driven into the sea. But the popular army scattered as swiftly as it had collected. The people had come from their homes with a few days' provisions in their wallets: when it was eaten they could but disperse or starve.

'If these proceedings go forward,' wrote Sir James Crofts to Cecil, 'the principal doers must have relief. They be all poor, and necessity will force them to leave off when all they have is spent.'[2]

Nor was this the worst. Grand as was the cause, the hearts of many engaged in it were lukewarm, and French crowns had weight with too many an empty purse.[3] Even Kirkaldy hesitated to declare himself openly. He was owed money by the Regent, which he feared to lose.

In the midst of such symptoms Knox did not improve Elizabeth's humour. As she had not replied to his message through Cecil, he wrote to herself. She was angry with him, he said, for his book; but his book did not touch her unless she deserved it. If she would continue to defend God's truth God would defend her, and he and God's friends would pray for her.

'But consider deeply,' he rashly went on, 'how, for fear of your life, ye did decline from God and bow to

---

[1] Forbes, vol. i. p. 181, &c.
[2] Crofts to Cecil, July 10.—*Scotch MSS. Rolls House.*
[3] 'Some of our number are poor, and we fear corruption by money.'— Kirkaldy to Cecil, July 17. *MS. Ibid.*

idolatry. Let it not appear a small offence in your eyes that ye have declined from Christ Jesus in the day of His battle. God hath preserved you when ye were most unthankful, and hath raised you from the ports of death to rule above His people, for the comfort of His kirk. It appertaineth to you to ground the justice of your authority, not upon that law which from year to year doth change, but on the eternal providence of Him who, contrary to nature, and without your deserving, hath thus exalted your head. But if you begin to brag of your birth, and to build your authority upon your own law, flatter you whoso list, your felicity shall be short.

'Interpret my rude words as written by him who is no enemy to your Grace. By divers letters I have required license to visit your realm; not to seek myself, neither yet my own case or commodity—which if you now refuse or deny, I must remit myself unto God, adding this for conclusion: that such as refuse the counsel of the faithful, appear it never so sharp, are compelled to follow the deceit of flatterers to their own perdition.'[1]

Prophetic rebuke was not calculated to work favourably on Elizabeth; nor was it recommended by the proceedings with which it was accompanied. Kirkaldy, inviting Cecil to the proposed alliance, said that 'all Europe should know that a league formed in the name of God had another foundation than factions made by man for worldly commodity.'[2] Elizabeth would have been contented to have heard fewer words about God could she have found more genuine fear of God, or even more human firmness and resolution. The lords and commons of Scotland all united in arms, might

---

[1] John Knox to Queen Elizabeth, July 20.—*Scotch MSS. Rolls House.*
[2] Kirkaldy to Cecil.—*MS. Ibid.*

have disposed of a few hundred half-starved, mutinous Frenchmen, with no particular difficulty; yet not only were they unable to drive them from Dunbar, but after three weeks' respite, and after the first fierce heat had passed off, d'Oysel contrived to pacify his own troops, to win back Huntly and Chatelherault, and though without a single crown or an additional man, to make himself strong enough to take the field again. On the 23rd of July he occupied Leith. Erskine, the governor of the castle of Edinburgh, declared for the Queen, and threatened to fire on the Congregation if they refused to make terms; and Logan of Restalrig went over from them to the French. So swiftly the fire had burnt down. The next day the Protestants accepted conditions which they did not even profess to expect that the Queen would observe. Under pretence that the coin was debased, they had taken possession of the mint stamps. These they were made to return. They bound themselves to disturb no more monasteries and to alter the services in no more churches till the next Parliament; they would evacuate Edinburgh, and leave Holyrood for the Queen to reoccupy. On the other side, the citizens of Edinburgh stipulated for liberty of conscience; and the Government gave a general promise that no one should be troubled or prosecuted for the part which he had taken in the insurrection.

A clause was added by the Congregation in the first draft of the engagement, that the French troops should be sent out of the country, and that no more should be introduced without the consent of the Scotch parliament. Kirkaldy even represented to Cecil that it was one of the conditions to which the Queen Regent had agreed.[1]

---

[1] Kirkaldy to Cecil, July 24.—*Scotch MSS. Rolls House.* COTTON *MSS.* CALIG. B. 10.

But the Protestants had been too divided and too weak to insist upon the single point which would have guaranteed their safety. In vain the more determined among them pleaded that 'their cause was not yet so desperate, that they need grant things unreasonable and ungodly.' Intrigue, distrust, and lavish promises of money had done their work. The agreement was signed, Huntly and Chatelherault making themselves securities for the Queen;[1] and the few in the Congregation who were really in earnest, withdrew beyond reach of danger. The Lords who had written to Elizabeth, signed a bond to stand by each other through good fortune or evil; and they then dispersed, some to the Western Highlands, some into Fife.

It is no matter of surprise that a change so sudden should have increased Elizabeth's perplexity. She had distrusted their ultimate resources, but she had not looked for so complete and so immediate a breakdown. She had allowed Cecil to commit himself to a correspondence with unsuccessful rebels, and furnished the French with a pretext for declaring war against her, which the Spaniards would be forced to recognize. Argyle and Lord James sent explanations and apologies. They had been outnumbered at Edinburgh, three times over, they said; the Castle was against them; and a multitude was always hard to persuade into a revolt.[2] If this were so, it was the less safe to entangle herself with so fickle a people. John Knox went in secret to Berwick to talk to Sir James Crofts. The English commander told him he did not see how Elizabeth could interfere, while the

---

[1] D'Oysel to Noailles.—TYTLER, vol. I.
[2] Argyle and Lord James Stuart to Sir James Crofts, August 6.—*Scotch MSS. Rolls House.*

Protestants were thus disorganized, and had no recognized authority among them. Knox said that 'they would elect from among themselves whatever leader her Highness thought meet;' when Arran came to England she could see what he was made of; if Arran was not man enough, there was Lord James Stuart.[1] Crofts gave him still but a cold answer; and so little confidence had Knox in the stability of the cause, when left only in Scottish hands, that he wrote after leaving Berwick, that unless 'the English council were more forward,' they would utterly discourage the hearts of all their friends. 'If the Protestants could not have present support, they would not trifle, they would seek the next remedy to preserve their own bodies. He did not mean that they would return to France; but they would give up the struggle, leave the country to the enemy, and the English might make their account of what would ensue towards themselves.'[2]

Here was but a frail foundation on which to defy the Catholic world. Cecil wrote an enigmatic letter to Knox, expressing a wish, if possible, to see him. A few days earlier he had written to the Lords, recommending the course which had saved the Reformation in England, and had proved a better security for men's consistency than exaggerated and inflated phrases.

'Ye know,' he said, 'your chief adversaries the Popish kirkmen be noted wise in their generation, and they be rich also whereby they make many friends; by their wit, with false persuasions; by their riches, with corruption. As long as they feel no sharpness nor offence,

---

[1] Crofts to Cecil, August 3.—*Scotch MSS. Rolls House.*
[2] Knox to Sir James Crofts, August 6.—*MS. Ibid.*

they be cold; but if they be once touched with fear, they be the greatest cowards. In our first Reformation here in King Henry the Eighth's time, if the prelatry had been left in their pomp and power, the victory had been theirs. I like no spoil, but I allow to have good things put to a good use; as to the enriching of the Crown, to the help of the youth of the nobility, to the maintenance of ministry in the Church, and of learning in the schools.'

Cecil added that three thousand French were on the point of sailing from Havre; and he could not but wonder that the Scotch should seek for help from England, while they took so little pains themselves to secure their harbours, and prevent the invaders from landing. England would do what it could to save them, but the difficulties of the times were great, and it was a serious thing to begin a new war with France.[1]

So far Cecil, not unreasonably. But it was necessary to determine promptly what should be done; and according to his usual habit, he drew a sketch of the situation, with the arguments for and against an active interference in Scotland—arguments which had either been urged between himself and the Queen, or between himself and other members of the Council, or as an account merely of what had passed in his own mind.[2]

The greatest happiness for Scotland, he said, was either to be 'at perpetual peace with England,' ' or to be made

---

[1] Cecil to the Lords of the Congregation, July 28.— *Scotch MSS. Rolls House.*

[2] 'A memorial of certain points meet for the restoring of the realm of Scotland to its ancient state,' written by my Lord Treasurer's own hand, August 5, 1559.'— COTTON *MSS.* CALIG. B. 10. SADLER *Papers,* vol. ii. p. 375, &c.

one monarchy with England, as they two should make but one isle.' So long as Scotland was under the influence of the French, they would use it as an instrument of their designs on England; and therefore, as far as possible, it ought to be governed by the Scots themselves. The Queen being childless, the Hamiltons as next in succession had a right with the consent of the nobility, to keep watch over the liberties of the country. If they pleased they might insist on a Reformation both in the Church and in the administration; and if the Queen refused to consent, or if it were likely that she would refuse, then 'was it apparent that Almighty God was pleased to transfer from her the rule of the kingdom,' and Scotland once free, 'might consider what means could be devised to accord the two realms.'

Such being in Cecil's opinion the general bearings of the case, the question was, whether England should assist the Congregation to expel the French troops.

Against it was the natural impropriety of assisting subjects in a revolt against their Sovereign; the danger and expense of war; the possibility that after the Queen of England had fatally committed herself, the French and Scots might make up their quarrel, and combine to support Mary Stuart's pretensions to her crown; with the further possibility that Spain might make common cause with France to prevent Scotland and England from forming a united Protestant power.

On the other hand, self-defence was the first law of nature. All persons public and private, 'might use the same manner of defence as the adversary used in offence;' and there was sufficient justification for interference on these grounds, if Elizabeth chose to venture it.

It was not a simple case of helping insurgents—for the Queen claimed feudal sovereignty over the Scots, and was legally entitled to protect them. The intentions of the French were notorious to all the world. They had challenged the English crown at Cambray; they had applied to the Pope to pronounce for their right; and the Queen of France had assumed the English arms. The Guises aspired to immortal honour by annexing England aswell as Scotland to France, 'through the same woman, their cousin:' and they were only waiting for their opportunity. If the Scots could have kept the field there would have been no danger; but without money they could not hold together for more than a few days. They would be conquered in detail; and England would then have to contend with the power of both countries. It might be thought more prudent to wait to be attacked, but a large costly army would have to be maintained on the borders—and how unequal England was to such a burden ' was pitiful to understand.' The old generals Norfolk, Suffolk, and Northumberland, were dead; the people were decimated by famine and pestilence, and their temper was uncertain; the French had the trained armies of Italy; the Rhingrave had raised 5000 Germans for them; the King of Denmark had sent transports: and should they sit still at home, ' that would soon happen which would move and stir all good English bloods—some to fear, some to anger, some to be at their wits' end.'

Cecil's conclusion therefore was in favour of immediate action; and to this for a time he brought Elizabeth to consent. If possible, he would limit himself however to sending money, which it would be easy to deny. The necessary help might be given, and yet formal offence be avoided. Elizabeth, though in broad questions she desired to act uprightly, was without the minor scruples which embarrass timid consciences. The correspondence of the Lords with Cecil had been suspected though not absolutely discovered, by the Queen Regent. The French ambassador Noailles laid a complaint before Elizabeth; and putting a bold face upon the matter, she replied herself to Mary of Guise, in a letter which, after the part which she had played and was prepared to play, it must have required some courage to write.

ELIZABETH TO THE QUEEN REGENT OF SCOTLAND.

'Right High and Right excellent Princess, our dear sister and ally, we commend ourselves to you most cordially. We understand from the ambassador of our good brother the King of France, that certain of our officers on the frontiers have held intelligence with the rebels late in arms against your authority. We cannot but find it very strange that any of our subjects, and much more that persons in positions of public trust, should of their own accord, and regardless of our displeasure, have sought means to meddle with any such people. Forasmuch however as at present we know no particulars of these things—but, on being well informed, will proceed to punish the offenders—we must entreat you to specify more exactly what you complain of, and let us know the entire truth, to the end that after examination and proof, we may give orders for the chastisement of such as shall be found to have offended—which you may assure yourself we will not fail to do; being as we are most desirous to show you that good will and friendship which we owe you as our neighbour, and to maintain those good relations which at present exist between us.'[1]

---

[1] 'Très haute et très puissante Princesse, nostre chère sœur et alliée, nous nous recommandons très cordiallement à vous. Nous estant

The day after the date of this letter, Sir Ralph Sadler, whose experience in Scottish diplomacy had been long and tried, was sent down to the northern Border. He carried with him 3000*l.*, to be distributed among 'the rebels' at his discretion; Elizabeth herself giving him his commission 'to treat in all secrecy with any manner of persons in Scotland for the union of the realms,' and referring him for special instructions to a memoir which he would receive from Cecil.[1] The memoir directed Sadler, 'as his principal scope,' to nourish the factions between the Scots and the French, 'so as the French might be the better occupied with them, and the less with England.' The King of Spain did not govern Brabant and Flanders by Spaniards, nor had he thrust Spaniards into government in England. Chatelherault, in like manner, should insist that Scotland should be governed by Scots. It would be well also, if possible, to have d'Oysel arrested as a hostage for Arran.[2] And finally, Sadler was in-

donné entendre par l'Ambassadeur de nostre bon frère le Roy de France ici résidant que puis naguères aucuns de nos ministres des frontières auroient eu intelligence de vostre dernier troublement avec les rebelles et autres parties à vous désobéissans, ce que nous ne pouvons trouver que fort estrange que aulcun de nos sugès et plus nos officiers et ministres publiques ayants charge des places deussent de leur teste cognoissant quel desplaisir nous est et doibt estre, aller chercher tels moyens de se mesler avec telle sorte du peuple ! Pour autant que à présent nous n'avons encore entendu les particularités d'iceux nous avons pencé estre bon de vous prier de nous faire apparoistre les causes plus amplement, et nous donner entendre la vraye vérité et les particularités zertaines autant que en ce se peult cognoistre, et véritablement prover que enfin nous pouvons donner telle borde pour le punissement de ceux qui seront trouvés coupables et fauteurs.

'Ce que pouvés bien estre assurée nous ne ferons faute de faire pour le désir que avons de monstrer extérieurement le zelle et bonne amitié que portons à la bonne voysinance et maintenir l'amytié présente qui est entre nous. Donné soubz nostre signet, etc, le vii. de Aoust, le 1ᵉʳ an de nostre regne.'—TEULET, vol. i. p. 341.

[1] Elizabeth to Sir Ralph Sadler, August 8, 1559.—SADLER *Papers*, vol. i. p. 391.

[2] And yet, unless de Quadra was wrongly informed, Arran had been at this very time several days in

structed to find out whether 'Lord James Stuart did mean any enterprise towards the Crown of Scotland for himself; and if he did mean anything—and 'if the Duke were found cold in his own cause'.—' whether it would be amiss to let Lord James follow his own device, without dissuading or persuading him anything therein.'[1]

Meanwhile, what had become of the Earl of Arran? He came to England at the end of July—within a day or two of the despatch of Sir Ralph Sadler. He was concealed in Cecil's house in London, where the Spanish ambassador discovered that Elizabeth saw him.[2] The first impression was said to have been favourable. De Quadra feared from what he heard that the marriage would go forward; and in that case, he said, 'that the Queen would pursue her heretical intrigues in France as she had done in Scotland—neither fear nor conscience would stop her; when France was in flames, the turn of the Low Countries would come next; at that moment she was welcoming every heretic that came over to her.'[3]

'Her position,' de Quadra wrote at the same time to the Emperor, 'is so perilous that one would have thought she would have caught at the marriage with the Archduke to save herself; but she is so passionate in these matters of religion, she has so preposterous a

---

England, and Cecil had seen him. It is difficult to follow the intricacies of diplomatic byplay.

[1] Instructions to Sir Ralph Sadler, August 8.—*Scotch MSS. Rolls House.*

[2] De Quadra to Philip, August 13.—*MS. Simancas.* Cecil, writing to Throgmorton on the 29th of August, mentions the fact of Arran having been in his house, and of the Queen's interview with him, but does not mention the day.—CONWAY *MSS. Rolls House.* Jewel tells Peter Martyr in the following February, that 'Crito' (the name by which Arran was known) had been to Athens, and won the good graces of Glycerium.—ZURICH *Letters*, p. 68. Cecil's letter fixes the date to August, de Quadra's letter to the beginning of August.

[3] De Quadra to Philip, August 13.—*MSS. Simancas.*

notion of her own strength—of which it is impossible to
disenchant her—that I have little hope that she will do
anything good.'[1]

The interview with Arran however had not produced
the effect which de Quadra feared. The Queen saw him
again for some hours at Hampton Court; but although
she was forced to conceal what she thought of him—to
conceal, so far as possible, the fact of his having been in
England at all—it seems that she discovered him at once
to be the half-crazy fool which he proved to be, and resolved irrevocably that, whatever else she might do, in
that direction there was no road open to her.

Nor was the state of Scotland becoming more satisfactory. There were fewer signs than ever of self-reliance
among the Protestants, or of steadiness of purpose. Before
Sadler arrived they were growing more and more impatient of Elizabeth's slowness to help them. Chatelherault
wavered. Argyle and Lord James wrote to Cecil to demand
proofs of good-will more tangible than words. Mary
Stuart had written privately to each particular nobleman
to bribe, to flatter, or menace them back to their allegiance.
Throgmorton reported from Paris that a correspondence
of some kind was passing between Lord James and his
sister, that the French intended to promise the Scots
toleration in religion, if the Scots would support their
designs against Elizabeth.[2] It was understood that the
Queen of Scots and her husband 'would spend the crown
of France' rather than yield; and John Knox again gave
Cecil distinct notice that he would not answer for the
consequences, unless the Congregation 'saw greater for-
wardness to their support' in the English Government.[3]

---
[1] MS. Simancas.
[2] Sir N. Throgmorton to Elizabeth, September 10.—Forbes, vol. I. p. 226.
[3] Knox to Cecil, August 15.—Scotch MSS. Rolls House.

There was this strange feature in the attitude of the Scots, that if not the hearty allies of England, they would be the equally hearty enemies of England. If the new passion of religion could not be gratified, the passion of nationality, and the bitter memories of Flodden and Pinkie Cleugh would be revived. They were capricious friends and dangerous foes. The long-delayed French reinforcements were beginning to arrive. Two thousand men were landed at Leith at the end of August —the advanced guard of the Marquis d'Elbœuf, who was to follow with the main army. De Feria, who seemed to know all that passed in England, even to the whispers in the Queen's closet, warned Chaloner of the close approach of the catastrophe, and more than hinted that Philip would interfere to protect Elizabeth only as the wife of the Archduke Charles.[1]

While Sir Ralph Sadler on the Border therefore was secretly encouraging the Congregation, Elizabeth at home maintained more than ever an appearance of indifference to them. The Earl of Arran, after a last interview with her, went north on the 1st of September, in the company of Thomas Randolph.[2] Their passports were made out in the names of de Beaufort and Barnabee; and Sadler's instructions were to see the Earl safe over the Border; yet in such a manner that his own hand should be undiscovered, and that the fact of Arran having been in England, though it might be suspected, should be incapable of proof.[3]

---

[1] Chaloner to Queen Elizabeth, August 13.—*Spanish MSS. Rolls House.*
[2] Cecil to Sadler, August 31.— SADLER *Papers*, vol. i. pp. 417, 418.
[3] The secret had been so well kept from the French, that although known to de Quadra, it was only discovered by the French ambassador, Noailles, at the beginning of October. —*Noailles to d'Oysel*, October 12. TEULET, vol. i. p. 361.

On the same 1st of September, the French ambassador again spoke to Elizabeth of the correspondence between the Congregation and the Governor of Berwick. Elizabeth ventured to reply that although she could not answer for her ministers, some of whom might have been foolish enough to exchange letters with the insurgent Scots, yet that the Congregation deceived themselves if they expected assistance from her in their foolish enterprise. She had written nothing and had promised nothing. Her handwriting was well known. If the Queen Regent could find it, she might produce it.[1]

On the 5th, Noailles assured the King of France on Elizabeth's word that she would take no part in Scotland.[2] On the 6th, little knowing the nerve which he was touching, he spoke to her of Arran's escape from France, and required her, if the Earl came to England, to arrest him and send him to Paris—as by the treaty of Cambray she was bound to do. Elizabeth gravely avowed that she had heard nothing of Arran. Should it be in her power however, she would not fail to do what her good brother desired.[3] Again Noailles spoke of the communications with Berwick. Again she protested that she was not a

---

[1] 'Neantmoints que ceulx de la dicte Congrégation se trouveroient grandement déceux s'ilz espéroient aucune faveur d'elle en leurs folles entreprinses, et qu'elle ne leur avoit rien escript ny promis. Estant son signet bien sçeu a congnoistre pour estre monstré s'il s'en trouvoit.'— *Noailles to the Queen Regent of Scotland, September* 1. TEULET, vol. i. p. 341.

[2] Sadler's instructions were 'to lend the Protestants money as of himself, taking secretly their bonds of them to render the same, so as the Queen should not be a party thereto.'— *Cecil to Sadler, Sept.* 11. SADLER *Papers*, vol. i. pp. 438, 439.

[3] 'Le Roy désiroit qu'en vertus des tractas elle le luy voulust rendre comme son rebelle. A quoy la dicte Dame après plusieurs propos de ce fait m'asseura ne scavoir aulcunes nouvelles de luy, et quand il seroit en son pouvoir elle en contenteroit le Roy et satisferoit en cela à son désir.'—*Noailles to d'Oysel, September* 6. TEULET, vol. i. p. 347.

person to say one thing and do another. If bad stories were blown over the Border, she could not help it.

The coolness of her self-command only half deceived Noailles. She laughed too much. 'There is more dissimulation in her,' he said, 'than honesty or good-will; and few people living can play that game as well as she.'¹ Yet so cautious had she been that even members of her own Council knew but half the truth. Lord William Howard swore that he would lose honour and life if the Queen in any way whatever was a party to the Scotch rebellion.²

Count Cavour in 1860 encouraged Garibaldi's expedition to Sicily, while in public he denied all knowledge of it. The political exigencies of Cavour's position were but slight compared to those which drove Elizabeth into falsehood. Even among the Scots themselves the more cautious preferred secret help to an avowed alliance, which would give the French an excuse for sending troops among them; while the Spaniards, dreading in all its forms Elizabeth's advocacy of the Protestants, yet dreaded more a conquest of England by France; and their chief fear was of some open breach of treaty which would enable the French to require them to stand neutral.

Obligations of the Spaniards to defend England.

'If we would escape our own ruin,' the Bishop of Arras wrote to Philip, 'we must do as much to defend England as we should do for Brussels. The Queen will be our destruction if she openly assist the Scots³ in

---

¹ 'En tous ses propos je cuyde y avoir plus de dissimulation que de certitude et bonne volunté, estant, ce dict g ch: n. mieulx a se pour jouer ce personage que mil autres.'— *Noailles to d'Oysel.* TEULET, vol. i. p. 357.

² 'Il repondit avec grand serment qu'il vouloit pendre la vie et l'honneur, si elle y entendoit jamais.'— *Noailles to the Cardinal of Lorraine. Ibid.* p. 557.

³ 'Si a la descubierta ayuda à los Escoceses.'

favour of the Earl of Arran. The French will then have good ground to tell us that we are bound by the treaties not to assist her, seeing that she herself will be the attacking party.'[1]

Meanwhile Lord Howard's words and the decisiveness of the Queen's own denials succeeded in perplexing Noailles, if not in wholly deceiving him.

'The truth,' he wrote, 'will appear at last; and we shall know one day whether she has meddled in these affairs or not. If the war go on we shall take prisoners; and they, if there be a secret, will let it out.'[2]

Elizabeth was but defending herself with the weapons with which she was attacked—and so far she had scarcely exceeded the permitted bounds of diplomatic concealment. Her next step was more audacious. It was necessary to humour the hopes of the Spaniards, and to play with the Austrian marriage. It is just possible that after the sight of Arran she may have for a time seriously turned her thoughts toward it.

On the 7th of September—six days after Arran's departure—Lady Sidney,'[3] who was in attendance on the Queen at Hampton Court, sent a message to de Quadra to say that if the Archduke's suit was pressed it would be listened to favourably. The bishop who had ceased to hope, contrived to see Lady Sidney to inquire the meaning of so sudden a change. Lady Sidney told him a very strange story. She said that there had been a plot to murder the Queen and Lord Robert at a banquet which was to be given at Lord Arundel's. The frightfulness of the danger, coupled with the disturbances in

---

[1] The Bishop of Arras to Philip II., December 5.—*MS. Simancas.*
[2] Noailles to the Cardinal of Lorraine, Oct. 28.—Teulet, vol. i. p. 363, &c.
[3] Lord Robert Dudley's sister, wife of Sir Henry Sidney, and mother of Sir Philip.

Scotland, had so alarmed Elizabeth that she had positively determined to marry. Sir Thomas Parry and Lord Robert were the only persons as yet aware of her intention; but it was with the Queen's knowledge that she was now speaking to him. He might assure himself she would not risk her life in such a matter by telling an untruth; and de Quadra had but to take the first opportunity of speaking to the Queen himself, to be satisfied of the sincerity of her intentions.

Lord Robert Dudley confirmed his sister's story, and offered the ambassador his good offices. Parry told him that the Queen found the peril of her position too heavy to endure; and that only the evening preceding she had called Lady Sidney and himself into her closet, and after a long conversation had ended with saying that there was no alternative, and that by this marriage alone could she save either herself or the realm.

The very wildness of the story seemed a guarantee for its truth; no one would have invented anything so improbable. But the bishop perplexed and suspicious knew not what to think. He could discover nothing about the conspiracy beyond a whisper that Lord Robert was to have been killed and the Queen poisoned. Strange tales were flying about Montague, Dacre, and the Catholic bishops, as being concerned in it; and de Quadra feared some contrivance of the French. He sent a detail however of what had passed to the Duchess of Parma, de Feria, and Arras;[1] and a few days later wrote at length to Ferdinand, telling him of Elizabeth's attempt to revolutionize Scotland with her scheme of marrying Arran and uniting the realms; but saying that he believed really she had lost confidence in the Scots.

MS. Simancas.

She knew that the French had but to send over an army for the Catholics to rise, and that her only resource was to do as Lady Sidney had said. 'She did not wish to marry; she would escape it if she could, or if she dared; but circumstances were too strong for her, and she would make the venture.' So at least he thought.[1]

'You ask me to be frank with you,' said Elizabeth herself, when de Quadra spoke to her, as Lady Sidney bade him do. 'If the Emperor would have me for a daughter-in-law, let him send over his son to see me. I am a Queen and a lady. I cannot ask a man to come to England and marry me. I would die a thousand deaths first. Others marry for interest; I if possible would marry for affection.'

'His Highness cannot come,' replied de Quadra, 'without some assurance that it will not displease your Majesty.'

Elizabeth smiled.

'England,' she said, 'is free to all the world to come and go. If he has no fear but that, he may come when he will; but I am afraid he may not be contented with me.'

'A person so gifted by nature as your Majesty,' said the smooth bishop, 'need have no alarm on that score.'

'I mean,' replied the Queen, with some embarrassment, —'I mean, he may hear things said of me which may not please him.'

'Let not your Majesty trouble yourself about that,' said de Quadra. 'We know too well what really passes in this court to be moved by idle rumours. Had we given credit to the talk of the world, we should not have desired to see the Archduke here.'

---

[1] De Quadra to the Emperor Ferdinand, Sept. 12.—*MS. Simancas.*

CHAP II
1559
September

The Archduke Charles invited to England.

Elizabeth affected to be pleased. She was afraid, it appeared, that the Archduke might take advantage of the scandal which could not fail to reach his ears on his arrival in England, and should he not marry her after all, her honour might suffer. De Quadra regretted that she should have allowed her peace to be disturbed by so unworthy a suspicion. Married or unmarried, he assured her that the Archduke would never behave otherwise than as a courteous gentleman.[1]

Immediately on this conversation Elizabeth wrote to Philip, saying that it would give her pleasure if his cousin would come to England. She had always shrunk from marriage, as he was well aware; and she could not say that her aversion was diminished. The Archduke nevertheless would be welcome to the Court; and she herself would be glad to see and know him.[2]

The words were cautious, yet in connexion with her language to de Quadra could be interpreted favourably; while mutual assurances passed between the ambassador and Cecil—Cecil expressing his own earnest hope that the affair might go forward, his conviction that nothing else could save the Queen, and his confidence that the King of Spain would not forsake her in her necessities; de Quadra undertaking that when the marriage was once concluded the King his master would do more for her than she could ask.[3]

Nor was this all. The Queen seemed to accept the conditions which the marriage would imply and oblige; and as if to separate herself distinctly from the Protestant party she gave orders for the restoration of the crucifix in the Chapel Royal. Angry words were exchanged

---

[1] De Quadra to the Emperor, October 3.—*MS. Simancas.*
[2] Elizabeth to Philip II., October 5.—*MS. Ibid.*
[3] De Quadra to Philip II., October 5.—*MS. Ibid.*

between the Council and the chaplains; Bedford spoke with bitter surprise to Cecil, and the order was suspended for a day or two; but on the Sunday following service was performed with the altar in full costume, and the priest in orthodox vestments.[1]

If she failed in persuading the Catholics that she was likely to return to them, she succeeded in exasperating the Protestants to the furthest extent which the bishop could desire. The preachers raved at her from the pulpits; the people were distracted. She herself, if she was acting a part, was doing it so well that she deceived her own party; and de Quadra congratulated himself on seeing the difficulties of her position growing deeper every day.

After this last step it was thought that the Archduke had only to appear, and the Queen would find herself unable to escape. The Duke of Norfolk, Lord William Howard, the whole peerage, with but a few exceptions, were in favour of the marriage; while scarcely a man of note or interest would oppose it. And beyond the public and political reasons which made the connexion desirable, her best and truest friends on other grounds were anxious to see her under the shelter of a husband.

With or without cause, her relations with Lord Robert Dudley were attracting increasing remark. Norfolk, who detested and despised the whole Dudley clan, commented in public on the favour which was shown to Lord Robert; and Lady Sidney's strange story of the

---

[1] 'La Reyna mandó que se pusiese en el altar un crucifijo y unas velas por lo cual hubó tanto ruido entre sus capellanos y los del consejo que dejó de hacerse lo que la Reyna mandaba aquella tarde. El Sabado á vesperas fué hecho, y el Domingo hubó vestimientos y clerigos en vestidos como nosotros usamos.'—De Quadra to the Bishop of Arras, October 9. 'Bedford desbonró estos dias á Cecil sobre lo del crucifijo.'—De Quadra to de Feria, October 17. MS. Simancas

conspiracy was perhaps but a distorted and exaggerated account of some real menace expressed against a man who was putting in peril the Queen's honour.¹

More at his ease than with his royal correspondent, de Quadra wrote freely all his thoughts to de Feria.

'It is the devil's own business here. But the Catholics grow stronger daily, and the heretics are quarrelling with one another so bitterly that they have forgotten their other enemies.

'Bedford has insulted Cecil about the crucifix; the Queen has quarrelled with him—for what cause God knows; and the heretic bishops preach against her, and scream about the revenue of their sees. The harvest is ready if there were a hand to grasp the sickle; but I know not where the reapers are to come from unless from heaven.

'If the Queen were a woman with either sense or conscience, something might be done about the marriage. But she is so reckless, I know not what to think. Her embarrassments are all that we could wish. They could not be greater than they are. One step more and swords will be drawn. But this I conclude his Majesty wishes to prevent. The chief advantage of the match, could we bring it about, would be that the French would at once give up their enterprise. It would also tend to quiet the minds both of Catholics and heretics; each of whom believes that the Archduke will be on their side.

---

¹ 'No hay hombre que no habla dello y le amenaza. Esta motin tiene por caudillos al Duque de Norfolk y al Conde de Sussex; y á todos los principales que favorecen al Archiduque; y el de Norfolk ha dado mucho que pensar estos dias á la Reyna y á Roberto, hablando en sus liviandades y mal gobierno publicamente.'—*De Quadra to the Duchess of Parma*, Oct. 19. *MS. Simancas.*

The heretics however will let him be a Catholic if he will leave them alone; and so will the Queen, who is already tired of the fine doings in which she was tempted at the beginning.

'She talks to me in a marvellous manner; but I give her as good as she brings; and I can do much more with her than I could at first. She has discovered that all clergy are not such sheep as her own.[1] There are ten or twelve ambassadors of us, all competing for her Majesty's hand; and they say the Duke of Holstein is coming next, as a suitor for the King of Denmark. The Duke of Finland, who is here for his brother the King of Sweden, threatens to kill the Emperor's man; and the Queen fears they will cut each other's throat in her presence.'[2]

The letter to Philip might have served as a sufficient invitation for the Archduke; yet before the Queen had ascertained whether he was coming or not, she was playing with another suitor. The King of Sweden was the next favourite. Lord Robert, who had been so fervently imperialist, deserted his colours, and went over with the change of wind; and de Quadra, who had but half believed in the sincerity of the first advances, resolved to cross question her.

'Two causes influenced me,' he wrote to Philip. 'Lady Sidney finds her brother so changed that she has quarrelled with him. She remains true to us. He has passed over to the Swede. But this is not all. I have

---

[1] 'La Reyna anda muy mas á mi voluntad de lo que soliamos despues que ha visto que los clerigos no son todos orejas como los de su tierra.'
[2] De Quadra to de Feria, October 29.—*MS. Simancas.*

CHAP II
1559
October

Lord Robert
Dudley and
his wife.

learnt from a person who usually gives me true information, that Lord Robert has sent instructions to have his wife poisoned; and that all the dallying with us, all the dallying with the Swede, all the dallying which there will be with the rest, one after the other, is merely to keep Lord Robert's enemies in play till his villany about his wife can be executed. I have learnt also certain other things as to the terms on which the Queen and Lord Robert stand towards each other, which I could not have believed.

'From this, and from Lady Sidney's uneasiness, I resolved to come to an understanding with her. I told her that the Archduke was already perhaps on his way to England, and I desired to know how he was to be received.

'She evaded my question, and said something vague and general; but seeing this would not satisfy me, she said that although at present she did not wish to marry, she might perhaps change her mind when she saw him.

'I reminded her of what Lady Sidney and Sir Thomas Parry had said to me at her desire, and I told her that I could not have recommended the Emperor to send his son over unless with some tolerable expectation that good would come of it.

'She said that no doubt Lady Sidney had intended well; but she had spoken without any commission from her.

'I burst out at this. It was perfectly certain that she, and no one else, had been at the bottom of it. I told her that I should let the Emperor know what she had said, and it would be for him to decide whether on such conditions the Archduke should visit England.

'She was very ill pleased at being forced so far to declare herself. Lord Paget tells me that there is no escape for her, and that she must accept this marriage.

And yet, considering what Lady Sidney said to me, I think I did right in pressing her to say something definite.

'The Duke of Norfolk is the leader of Lord Robert's enemies, who are in fact all the greatest persons in the realm; and the Duke says Lord Robert shall never die in his bed unless he gives over his preposterous pretensions. I let him know what had passed between myself and the Queen. He sent me word in answer that if the Archduke was to come he would find the weight of the country on his side, and that for himself he would forfeit his rank if he did not secure him the votes of every man of influence or birth. For myself, I do not believe she will ever take the Archduke, whether he come or not; but her disorderly ways may bring some disaster upon her; and in that case the Lords might perhaps offer the Archduke the Crown, and marry him to Lady Catherine Grey.'[1]

To attempt to discover Elizabeth's intentions from her language is wasted labour. Deliberately, or in spite of herself, she was doing what she was compelled to deny; and she was either playing with the Spaniards, or else humouring her own subjects, or else providing herself with a reserved scheme on which she could retire in extremity, or else—but it is idle to speculate. It is certain only that on the one hand she was distinctly doing what as distinctly she said she was not doing; and on the other that she was holding out hopes which, if she could help it, she never meant to fulfil.

Her assertions of innocence with respect to Scotland, Sir William Cecil found it necessary to endorse. He even

---

[1] De Quadra to Philip, November 15.—*MS. Simancas.*

took the initiative in complaining to the French ambassador of the charges against her. He assured Noailles that, so far from helping or encouraging the rebels, she had refused them assistance when they applied for it; and he insisted with an oath that nothing should be done on her part to endanger the friendship between the King of France and herself.[1] Each day made assertions like these more difficult; but each day they were repeated with louder emphasis.

The Earl of Arran was met at Berwick by an emissary from the Congregation; he was carried over the Border into Teviotdale by Sir James Crofts and Sadler; but the intended secrecy could not be maintained. Spies informed the Queen Regent, the Queen Regent wrote to Noailles, and Noailles spoke to Elizabeth. Elizabeth, in full possession of the circumstances—having herself given the order for Arran's reception by the English commander, and having received from him a detailed account of what had been done—replied at first by saying that it was impossible; and next, by assuring the French ambassador that she had required Sadler to confess on his allegiance whether he had or had not assisted the Earl of Arran, and that she had been informed that the story was untrue. Her confidence in the honour and good faith both of Sadler and Sir James Crofts was unbounded; and she was therefore satisfied that the Queen Regent had been deceived.[2]

---

[1] 'Voulant asseurer et juror pour elle qu'elle ne produyroit jamais occasion à son endroit qui peult seullement altérer les amitiez du Roy et d'elle.'—*Noailles to d'Oysel*, Oct. 12. Teulet, vol. I. p. 362.

[2] 'Les quelz luy avoient respondu par lettres signées de leurs mains, qu'il n'estoit rien du tout de ce que la Reyne Regente luy en avoit fait dire et remonstrer, dont elle vouloit bien adjouster tant de foy à ces personnes qu'elle m'avoit asseuré que ladicte dame avoit esté mal advertie.'

Meanwhile, the money which she had sent down, the personal exertions of Sadler, and the non-arrival of the French reinforcements, had again rallied the Congregation. The prospect of church plunder counterbalanced among the hungry noblemen the promises of the Queen of Scots. Even Lord Erskine in Edinburgh, although he had threatened to fire on the Protestants, refused to admit d'Oysel's troops; and Arran on his arrival found the reforming leaders in eager consultation at Stirling.

He had brought with him from London a fresh supply of money, which assisted in deciding the waverers. The whole body adjourned the next day to Hamilton Castle, where Arran's father signed their bonds; and as heir presumptive and guardian of Scottish liberty, he headed with his name the subscription to a petition to the Regent, requiring that the fortifications which the French had commenced at Leith should be discontinued.[1]

Mary of Lorraine replied that she had as much right to build at Leith as the Duke at his house at Hamilton. The Lords, quickened into courage again by the support which Elizabeth denied so emphatically that she was giving, agreed to meet at Edinburgh on the 15th of October, when, if the Regent persisted in her present attitude, she was to be pronounced deposed.

The day came. Chatelherault, Arran, Argyle, Glencairn, Ruthven, Lord James Stuart, Boyd, Ochiltree—

—*Noailles to the King of France, November* 9; TEULET, vol. I. p. 369, &c. Cecil sent to Throgmorton an account in cipher of Arran's return to Scotland, and as a blind in case his letter miscarried, he added conjectures in his ordinary hand as to whether the Earl of Arran was still on the Continent or not.—*Cecil to Throgmorton, October* 1. CONWAY MSS. *Rolls House.*

[1] Knox; Calderwood.—*Arran to Cecil, September* 25. MS. COTTON, CALIG. B. 10. *Balnaves to Cecil,* MS. *Ibid.*

all those who had originally assembled at St. Andrew's, with the greedy crowd which flocked where there was a chance of plunder—were again together. Erskine would not come down from his crag, but his guns were silent. The Regent fled from Holyrood into the lines of Leith, and the action commenced. Elizabeth had declared that she could not make open cause with them so long as they had no settled organization. After a brief discussion, Mary of Lorraine, having conspired against the liberties of Scotland by the introduction of foreign troops, was declared to have forfeited the regency; and the government, till further orders, was vested in a council composed of Chatelherault and the young Protestant leaders.

The next step was to get possession of Leith, and to do it promptly—for d'Elbœuf's army might arrive any day, and they themselves would scatter as they were scattered before. For the moment they had 15,000 men, all more or less armed, and all accustomed to hand-to-hand fights: but the Scots, like the old Spartans, 'could scale no walls;' of war as a science they were absolutely ignorant; while they had neither money to pay trained troops with, nor provisions to feed them. Conscious of their deficiency, the Scottish leaders had applied for a thousand men from the garrison at Berwick. 'It is free for your subjects,' wrote the Master of St. Clair to Crofts, 'to serve in war any prince or nation for their wages; and if ye fear that such excuses shall not prevail, ye may declare them rebels to your realm, when ye shall be assured that they be in our company.'[1]

Something of the same kind was suggested by Knox. But the defences of Leith could not, it was thought, have

---

[1] St. Clair to Sir James Crofts.—COTTON MSS, CALIG. B. 10.

been carried far in so short a time. To send troops—
under whatever pretext they might seem to go—was an
open act, on which it was perilous to venture. So far
Elizabeth was proceeding without the support—perhaps
without the knowledge—of the majority of the Council.
Cecil himself ciphered and deciphered all despatches;
and Sadler and Crofts at Berwick, and Throgmorton at
Paris, seem alone to have been admitted into full possession of the secret. Money, Cecil wrote in reply, they
should have; for want of money they should not 'quail.'
Powder too might be conveyed to them from Berwick;
and if the French sent more troops than the Scots could
deal with, 'they should be impeached.' The rest the
Scots must do themselves.[1]

Yet Elizabeth was at times restive under the false
part which she had to play; and she was bringing herself to face the necessity of more decisive action. On
the 3rd of November, the date of Cecil's last letter, a
tournament was held at Greenwich, in which Lord
Robert and Lord Hunsdon held the lists against all
comers. The French ambassador was in Elizabeth's
box. She asked him if there were news from Scotland.
Noailles said his master was about to send an army
hither to suppress the rebellion.

'You do well,' she replied with sudden sharpness—
the truth bursting out. 'Look you to your affairs, and
I shall look to mine. Those armies and fleets of yours
in Normandy are not meant for Scotland only; your
troops already at Leith are a match for the Scots.'

'Your Majesty's mistrust is without cause,' Noailles
replied; 'the King my master means only well. I
will take my oath upon it he will observe the treaties.'

---
[1] Cecil to Sadler, November 3.—SADLER Papers, vol. ii.

'It may be so,' she said; 'but I find it well to be prepared. In times of danger it is the custom of England to arm. If we are well prepared you will be the less tempted to meddle with us.'

She had acted before she spoke. Silently and swiftly she had refilled the empty treasury; the second payment of the subsidy had been anticipated. The revenues of the vacant bishoprics had been appropriated, the Protestants nominated to the sees being left to whine in expectation. The first-fruits had been demanded again; the lands given by Mary to the new abbeys were disposed of, or made otherwise available. Sir Thomas Gresham had emptied the shops of the Antwerp armourers. and sent over ship-loads of guns, corslets, and saltpetre. Twenty ships were lying in Gillingham Harbour, manned for sea, and ready to sail at a moment's notice. The Isle of Wight was garrisoned under the command of Edward Horley the conspirator of Arundel's; and the young band of adventurers who had risked life and limb for Elizabeth in the bad times, were now, one way and another, engaged all in the public service—effective, brave, unscrupulous, ready by land and sea; ready to fight for England on shore, if needed there; ready to rove the seas at their own cost, and sack the towns and plunder the gold ships of the enemies of the truth.

Lord Grey went down to the Border with 2000 men nominally to reinforce the Berwick garrison; but at first with large latitude of action, and an opportunity of recovering the laurels which he had lost at Guisnes. Amidst her 'practices' and diplomatic

---

[1] Noailles to the King of France, November 9.—TEULET, vol. i.

subtleties, the Queen had steadily prepared for the time when it might be necessary to cross the Border.

CHAP II
1559
November

Unhappily, every post brought increasing evidence of the feebleness of the Scots—a feebleness too marked and extraordinary to be explained by mere incapacity. They had professed to expect that on the first menace the Regent would fly to Dunbar, and that the French would withdraw to their ships or to Inchkeith. But the Regent stayed quietly in Leith, and the French showed no signs of moving. An attempt scarcely deserving the name, was tried with scaling-ladders. The Edinburgh churches had been used as workshops to make them, and the Calvinists, shocked and disheartened by the sacrilege, were already beaten before the attack.

For a few days they waited in helpless expectation of impossibilities, and then another disaster happened—and a very serious one. An additional three thousand pounds which Elizabeth had sent down, had been committed to the charge of the Master of Ormeston to convey to Edinburgh. Intelligence of the treasure was carried to the Earl of Bothwell, who had a private feud with Ormeston; and snatching at the opportunity of doing service both to himself and to the Queen Regent, the young earl lay in wait in a wood, intercepted the convoy, cut Ormeston down, and carried off the booty to Crichton Castle.

Money for the Scots taken by Bothwell.

Arran and Lord James went from Edinburgh at daybreak the next morning with four hundred horse, to recover it; but when they reached Crichton they found Bothwell had gone a quarter of an hour before, taking the money with him; while during their absence 1500 French made a sudden sally from Leith, carried off two cannon—all which the Scots had that was serviceable, cut their way into the Canongate, penetrated almost through the whole length of Edinburgh, and retired only when Erskine began to fire on them from the castle.

The Regent followed up the success by a renewed offer to observe the conditions agreed on in the summer. The lords, believing that she was temporizing only till d'Elbœuf's arrival, replied 'that they had found her so false and unnatural, that they would never trust her nor have to do with her nor France but by the sword.'[1] The sword however served them ill. Five days later a number of provision carts were going into Edinburgh. The French again sallied out from Leith to cut them off. A sharp action followed, in which the Scots were again defeated. Three hundred were killed, two hundred were taken prisoners, and the rest escaped destruction only through the devotion of Alexander Halyburton, who sacrificed himself and a few gallant men who stood by him to cover their retreat within the walls.

A force held together by so loose a bond could not survive misfortune. In the universal panic every one cared only to shift for his own safety. The scene of the summer was re-enacted. One day the whole force of Scotland appeared united against a mere handful of foreigners; the next they were a rabble of fugitives. The Protestant leaders found themselves deserted as before, and almost alone. In a hurried council on the 7th of November, it was decided that they must again leave Edinburgh. William Maitland of Lethington— the younger Maitland as he was called, to distinguish him from the old laird—undertook to go to London to beg for larger assistance. The rest dispersed into their

[1] Intelligence from Scotland, November 10.—*Scotch MSS. Rolls House.*

own countries, and the Regent returned to Holyrood once more absolutely victorious.

Notwithstanding all their talk about God, it had come to this. God had as much interest in them as they had themselves courage, energy, capacity, understanding, and perseverance—so much precisely, and not more. That either through want of will or through want of ability the Scots were unequal to what they had undertaken was now certain. If defeated in the open field by 3000 French, they would be absolutely powerless before 20,000.

The commission of the Marquis d'Elbœuf was already made out as lieutenant-general of Scotland and England. His arrival was daily looked for, 'to strike while the iron was hot;'[1] and when Scotland was settled, an account could be demanded of Elizabeth. The money taken by Bothwell was damning proof against her. In vain Sadler and Crofts bade Randolph 'colour the matter,' telling him to say that the money was Ormeston's or their own.[2] In vain, afterwards, Sadler and Cecil took the guilt and the responsibility upon themselves. 'You will tell the Queen what we have discovered,' wrote d'Oysel to Noailles: 'she will disavow it all I suppose; but you will not on that account believe what she may say to you. Look her well in the face and she will blush however great be her assurance.'[3]

Randolph who had remained in Scotland with Arran, brought news to London of these combined disasters. A decisive resolution was now necessary; and at once

---

[1] D'Oysel to Noailles, November 12.—Teulet. vol. i.
[2] Sadler and Crofts to Randolph, Nov. 5.—Scotch MSS. Rolls House.
[3] D'Oysel to Noailles, November 12.—Teulet, vol. i.

Elizabeth submitted her position to the assembled Council. Opinions were widely divided. Day after day they sat through the second week in November, and 'could not come to any perfect resolution.'¹ Randolph indeed was sent back to the Border with money to replace what Bothwell had taken. The Protestants were urged not to shrink from their enterprise, and were 'animated with assurances' of assistance in case of extremity; and there was a talk of sending the fleet into the North Sea, and of offering the command of the Border to the Duke of Norfolk—on the principle on which his grandfather had been sent by Henry to Yorkshire, in the Pilgrimage of Grace. The Catholics would be paralyzed, or at least embarrassed, by the presence of their own natural leader at the head of the royal army.²

Norfolk, however, it was feared, would refuse to go. He spoke openly against interference. To him the marriage with the Archduke was the natural remedy. Lord Robert Dudley dared to tell him that whoever advised the Queen to marry a stranger was no good Englishman; high words passed; and Norfolk threatened to leave the Court and withdraw to Framlingham.*

In the midst of these discussions arrived Maitland and Henry Balnavis. They brought with them a brief letter from Arran, excusing the disaster at Edinburgh, and accrediting Maitland both as the representative of his party and of Arran's own private interest. Knox also had used the opportunity to send these few striking words to Cecil—'If you mind to join with us in the common cause, let not your support be so long delayed,

---

¹ The Council to Sadler and Crofts, Nov. 14.—Scotch MSS. Rolls House.
² Ibid.

* 'Lo que contienen tres cartas del Obispo de Aquila, November 13, 18, 27.'—MS. Simancas.

as the enemy may plant himself among us; that, after his having opposed such as would here resist him, he may attempt greater things. To drive time with France may appear to some to be profitable unto you; but as before I have written, so yet I fear not again to affirm, that nothing hath been, is, nor shall be more hurtful to both, than that ye dissemble your favour towards us. The godly here are and shall be so oppressed, that after they cannot be able to serve. Friends do fail and fall back from the enterprise. The whole multitude—a few excepted—stand in such doubt they cannot tell to which party they shall incline.'[1]

The Congregation proposed formally through Maitland the union of the two crowns. Sacrificing independence, throwing over once and for all Mary Stuart, France, and all their national traditions, they desired that Scotland and England should be merged in a common country, to be called henceforward 'by the ancient name of Great Britain.' Inviting Elizabeth to be their sovereign,[2] they had not even stipulated for her marriage with the Earl of Arran; although on both sides it must have been understood as a condition, when the terms of union should come to be arranged.

To accept such an offer or anything like it, would of course involve an immediate open and desperate war with France. Was England equal, single-handed, to such an encounter? what part would be taken by the Spaniards?

---

[1] Knox to Cecil, November 18.—*Scotch MSS. Rolls House.*

[2] 'Ils ont pensé au différent qui pourroit sourdre sur la préférence des deux couronnes, et que, pour l'éviter on pourroit supprimer le titre de l'une et de l'aultre pour redonner à toutes deux ensemble le nom ancien de la Grande Bretaigne.'—*Mémoire baillé à M. de la Muthe, December* 20. TEULET, vol. i.

From Brussels Sir Thomas Chaloner had reported an ever-increasing ill-feeling towards Elizabeth. After a conversation with de Feria in August, Chaloner had written to warn her that next to God she had only her right hand to depend on. On the 10th of November, he bade Cecil tell her 'so only to trust the Spaniards as first and best to trust herself.' 'He meant that she should arm and exercise her subjects.'[1]

On Maitland's arrival, it became necessary to learn distinctly what the Spaniards were prepared to do. Elizabeth told de Quadra formally that she had been driven to take arms in self-defence. She instructed Chaloner to ask the Bishop of Arras whether in event of war she might look to Spain for assistance.

The Bishop of Arras admitted at once without reserve or hesitation[2] the designs of Mary Stuart on Elizabeth's crown. 'The Cardinal of Lorraine had claimed it in her name in a conversation with himself at Cambray:' and 'the preparations in France were all made with a view to this one object.'

'The King of Spain,' he said, 'had done his best in Elizabeth's interests. He had saved her life when her sister would have destroyed her; he had offered her his own hand in marriage; he had continued to advise her when he found himself rejected; but she had paid no attention to his opinions. She had done everything which he had most advised that she should not do; and

---

[1] 'So,' he added, 'I shall trust, in mine old days, to toast a crab by the fire.'—*Chalmer to Cecil, November 10. Flanders MSS. Rolls House.* Sir Thomas Chaloner was an old friend of Charles the Fifth. He was with him in his disastrous expedition to Algiers. In the storm which shattered the Spanish fleet he was knocked overboard disabled, and was saved by a rope which he seized in his teeth.

[2] A letter from Arras himself to de Quadra, which is among the *Simancas MSS.*, confirms word for word the report of Sir T. Chaloner.

now he had only to provide for his own safety as best he could.

'Is it not strange,' Arras continued, 'that ye believe the world knoweth not your weakness? I demand what present store either of expert captains or good men of war ye have; what treasures; what other furniture of defence? Is there one fortress or hold in all England that is able one day to endure the breath of a cannon? Your men are hardy and valiant; but what discipline have they had these many years? and the art of war is now such that men be fain to learn anew at every two years' end. And if you had discipline, what should it avail when one draweth one way, another another? Suppose you we know not? The most part of the counties removed from London are not of the Queen's religion. Are there not of your nobles, trow ye, that repine at her proceedings? We are not ignorant how certain of them conspired of late, misliking the too much favour borne to some one.[1] Your weakness is well known; and when division reigneth, each will kill and betray others, to the ruin of the whole. The decree of the sequel pertaineth not to me.'

To the words of Arras, de Feria, with whom Chaloner afterwards dined, added a message to Elizabeth:—

'Commend me to your Queen,' the Count said; 'and bid her look to herself, and remember the Spanish proverb—"The cock may scrape in the dunghill till he uncovers the knife to cut his own throat." I mean not religion, or other such perilous attempts—but your wilful provoking of the war with France, to whom by sending money to Arran and the rebels you have given so just a

---

[1] Lord Robert Dudley.

colour and excuse to the world to break with you; as otherwise ye might well know they looked but for an opportunity.'

Chaloner, in obedience to orders from home, attempted feebly to lay the blame on Cecil.

'Tush!' de Feria said with a contemptuous laugh; 'we know the truth as well as you. What means your Queen? Is this a time to move war? Is Arran's persuasion worth such adventures? You will be torn in pieces, and other princes will fall out about your garments.'[1]

Alarm of the Spaniards at the supposed weakness of Elizabeth.

Words like these, though no answer to Elizabeth's questions, were of evil augury. The real opinion of the Spanish ministers on the situation will appear from a letter of Arras to Philip, written apparently on the day of his conversation with Chaloner:—

THE BISHOP OF ARRAS TO PHILIP II.

'If the French see signs of hesitation in us, they will at once set upon the English, and for our own sake we must take as much care of England as of the Low Countries. If therefore for their sakes we have to go to war again with France, we shall engage in the struggle on more favourable conditions if we first occupy England and restore religion there, than if we wait till this woman have destroyed herself and the French are in possession of the realm. While therefore I would let France understand plainly that we mean to protect England, we must put a bit in the Queen's mouth; we must make her fear that she will find us on the side of her enemies; we must tell her in clear terms that we do

---

[1] Chaloner to Cecil, December 6.—*Flanders MSS. Rolls House.* The Bishop of Arras to the Bishop of Aquila, Dec. 15.—*MS. Simancas.*

not mean to run into trouble ourselves merely that she may play her vile tricks at her leisure; leaning, as she supposes, on the shoulders of your Majesty.'[1]

With the storm thus gathering around them on all sides, the English Council was called on to decide what the Queen should do. The situation in Scotland remained unaltered. On the 10th of December, fifteen French vessels passed Berwick on their way to Leith, where they landed stores and troops—raising the force there to four thousand. On the other hand, an attempt made by them on Edinburgh Castle failed. Erskine intimated to Lord James Stuart that with 2000*l.* to feed and pay the garrison, he could hold out till the spring. The 2000*l.* was provided by Sadler, and Erskine's charge was preserved. But the real difficulty was the evident lukewarmness of the Scots themselves. Much might be done short of accepting the full offer of Maitland. Money might be privately sent; even troops might go as volunteers; but so long as Elizabeth hesitated to take some open step, the mass of the Scottish nobles refused to commit themselves. To do a little was as dangerous as to do all, while it failed to attach the nation to an English policy—and might lead in the end to a hostile union of Scotland and France, with the consummation of the dreaded invasion. Thus the Council sat from day to day and week to week, and could arrive at no conclusion. Two incidents of the discussion alone remain—one, a speech of the Lord Keeper, the other, a remonstrance of the Duke of Norfolk.

Cecil the great adviser of the war, had failed to persuade into the approval of it even his own brother-in-law.

---

[1] The Bishop of Arras to Philip II., December 5.—*MS. Simancas.*

CHAP II
1559
Dec 15

Sir Nicholas
Bacon de-
clares
against the
war.

'With the country so poor,' 'the nobility exhausted,' 'the middle classes discontented,' 'the spiritualty beggared,' Bacon argued that a war with France was too dangerous to be risked. Plague and famine, he said, had so reduced the population in the few last years, that there were scarcely men enough left to till the ground; while to employ foreign mercenaries, as the Protector had done, was pernicious in itself, and impossible without more money than the Queen possessed. Allies in such a quarrel they could have none except the Scots, who were so feeble that they could not even encounter three thousand French. At home the people were unsettled divided and dangerous. Some were disaffected on account of the change of religion; some because they had lost the influence in the State which they had enjoyed under the late Queen; while every man, whatever his party, class, or creed, was opposed to war.

War turned industrious labourers into idle vagabonds; war crippled farmers, embarrassed landlords, ruined merchants; while in this particular instance, the cause was so doubtful and so peculiar, that the soldiers would never understand it, and never fight for it heartily.

To join the Scots against the French was to help subjects in rebellion against their Sovereign. To break the public peace without provocation was a crime.

True, there were good answers to these objections—but they were not of a kind which soldiers could comprehend; they were not of a kind which the world would comprehend; while France was larger, more populous, and better prepared than England; the Pope would be at its back; and assistance from Spain was evidently not to be looked for.

All this might be granted—and yet it might be said

there was no alternative. France was determined to insist on the pretensions of her Queen, and England must make a virtue of necessity. At present the French in Scotland were but few: if attacked at once by sea and land they could be expelled; if they were left to be reinforced, the Scots would forsake England, believing that England had forsaken them.

Bacon admitted the argument, but he preferred notwithstanding to trust to time. He would continue to send money; and with money the Scots could keep the field. England would not be meddled with till Scotland was first conquered—and how effectually Scotland could resist invasion had been proved by the experience of Edward the First. Edward struggled for thirty-four years, and failed at last. Flodden and Pinkie Cleugh had been great victories, but they had not advanced the conquest. Wales had resisted for generations. Ireland was still unsubdued. The inhabitants of an invaded country fought for freedom, life, family—all that men held dear—and were unconquerable. At all events time would be gained. Money could be raised, factions quieted, the people made to understand the question. The French Queen might die; the House of Guise might be overthrown. The Queen of England might 'match herself in marriage,' and end the controversy so. Bacon therefore urged delay—delay for a year at least—unless opportunity should offer meanwhile for any notable success 'by wind or wave, or chance of war, or otherwise.'[1]

The same day, before or after Bacon's speech, the Duke of Norfolk was offered the command of the army on the Border. De Quadra had foretold that he would

---

[1] Speech of Sir Nicholas Bacon before the Council, December 15, 1559.— Harleian MSS., p. 398.

refuse. He said shortly that he thought the war would be gratuitous, and declined to meddle with it. 'The Council'—Bedford, probably, and Cecil—said that if peace could be had otherwise, they would sue for it on their knees; but they saw no second road open to them. The Duke replied that he was sorry, but he must adhere to his own opinion. The Queen then sent for him. He supped with de Quadra in the evening, and gave him an account of the interview. The Queen, he said, had entreated him not to desert her in her danger. He had told her that he neither doubted that danger nor the French designs; but there was a safer and surer course both for her own interests and those of the realm: let her marry the Archduke Charles; and the King of Spain, who had befriended her before, would not fail her in her present difficulties.[1]

The Duke of Norfolk had but expressed what many others were feeling. The timidity of Bacon on one side, and Norfolk's refusal of the command on the other, gave an impulse to the reactionary party; and in the end a majority of the Council advised the Queen to leave the Scots to their fate. The language in which they expressed themselves is as remarkable as the substance of their opinions; and other changes which they pressed upon Elizabeth implied that the Protestants were for the moment silenced and driven from the field.

The Lords said that the assumption of the English arms by the French Queen, the preparations for war in Normandy, with the undoubted information which had reached them from many quarters, permitted them to feel no uncertainty of the intentions of their enemies. 'The French Queen, as long as she lived, would pre-

---

[1] De Quadra to the Duchess of Parma, Dec. 18.—*MS. Simancas.*

termit no occasion to advance her pretended title;' and when Scotland was subdued—which in their opinions would be easily done—the invasion of England would follow. France being 'established with a State military,' and England 'being ordered for peace,' the Queen could resist only with a chance of success on her own soil. If she met the enemy elsewhere, and failed to gain a victory, her danger 'would be too dreadful to think upon.'

The Council therefore advised—

First, that the Queen should before all things 'seek the honour of Almighty God,' and seek it not by encouraging the reforming preachers, not by establishing 'the Gospel,' but by 'seeing the State ecclesiastical duly placed, and the care of all things thereto belonging remitted to the clergy, as in all her progenitors' time had been.'

Secondly, that the Queen should make an honourable marriage. The Archduke obviously being the person whom she was desired to choose.

Thirdly, that her Majesty should send an ambassador to King Philip, not only to procure his friendship, but to understand what she might trust to.

A single trace of the influence of the Reformers appears in a clause recommending her to seek the alliance of the Protestant Princes of Germany, to prevent the French from recruiting their armies there.

The last article, 'the foundation of all the rest,' was that she should raise a hundred thousand pounds by loan at Antwerp without delay.[1]

---

[1] The paper is written throughout in Cecil's hand, and is endorsed by him 'Opinion of the Council, not allowed by the Queen's Majesty.'— *Domestic MSS.*, ELIZ., *Rolls House*.

CHAP II
1559
December

Though the hand in which these advices are written is Cecil's, they did not express Cecil's opinions. Cecil would pluck safety only from among the nettles of danger. The times were critical, and it was dangerous to speak the truth before the world; but in private at Sir Thomas Parry's house, in the presence only of Sir Abraham Cave and Sir Richard Sackville, Cecil 'durst say what was fearful to be thought of, and what he would not speak commonly.' If the Queen waited to be attacked in the northern counties of England, and if she were to lose a battle there, as she might lose it, 'there were there hollow and discontented hearts which would find their time to break out, and yield to the title of France.'[1]

Steadily Cecil clung to this conclusion, and true to the oath which he swore when admitted her Secretary, steadily urged it on Elizabeth, whose constitutional irresolution shifted to and fro under the alternate pressure. Her convictions went with Cecil, but the weight of advice on the other side far preponderated, and the responsibility of choice was terrible.

Once, if not more than once, she gave way in earnest, determining to yield to the stream which she could no longer resist. And it was probably at the present crisis that Cecil, finding his influence gone, declined to act further in the matter, or to be the instrument of any policy but his own.[2]

---

[1] Memoranda of words spoken in Sir Thomas Parry's house, December 28, 1559. In Cecil's hand.—*MSS. Domestic*, ELIZ., *Rolls House*.

[2] 'With a sorrowful heart and watery eyes, I, your poor servant and most lowly subject, and unworthy secretary, beseech your Majesty to pardon this my lowly suit: That considering the proceeding in this matter for removing the French out of Scotland doth not content your Majesty, and that I cannot with my conscience give any contrary advice, I may, with your Majesty's favour and clemency, be spared to intermeddle therein.'— *Cecil to Queen Elizabeth* (without date). LANSDOWN *MSS*. Printed by Wright; vol. i. p. 14.

But Elizabeth's braver nature rallied again. Her own nobler qualities, which danger raised to their due pre-eminence—perhaps, too, the dread of her marriage, which was to be the condition of the King of Spain's assistance—brought her back to Cecil's views. The advice of the Council was 'not allowed.' And once more she determined to go forward—forward, though still in the tortuous course in which alone it seemed as if she could move with comfort to herself.

Orders went to Gresham to borrow, not one, but two hundred thousand pounds. Guns, pistols, and powder-barrels were sent over faster than ever. In a fatal confidence that the defeat at Edinburgh would keep Scotland quiet till the spring, d'Elbœuf had lingered in France. If he crossed now it should be only over the wreck of the English fleet. Sir William Winter, the young admiral, sailed from Gillingham with fourteen well-appointed vessels. He was charged with a trifling convoy to Berwick, and his orders were to proceed thence into the Frith of Forth, and watch for the coming of the French squadron. If they attacked him he was to sink and destroy them. If they attempted to pass him he was 'to understand that the principal point of his service was to impeach the access of any more succour from France into Scotland, and to frustrate any departure thence towards France.' 'If therefore he found himself strong enough, and if there was a convenient opportunity, war or no war, attacked or not attacked, he might destroy any armed French vessels that he should fall in with.' 'He might provoke a quarrel if he did not find one. He might challenge the right of the French commanders to carry the English arms, and tell them that as an Englishman he would not endure it. The French were a brave people, and he could not well fail of opportunity.' He was to allow no French vessel whatever to pass in or out of the Forth; and if on board any that he might arrest he found powder or guns, he should seize them for his own use. One only condition he was strictly to observe—he was not to profess that he bore the Queen's commission. If challenged, 'he was to say that he was acting on his own responsibility.'[1]

Were the admiral to lose an action, and be taken prisoner under such instructions, he would make himself liable to be hanged as a pirate. But Elizabeth expected these minor sacrifices from her subjects.

The moderate party, finding their opinion unaccepted, behaved like loyal subjects; and still hoping that the worst might be avoided, threw no difficulties in the Queen's way. The Bishop of Aquila learnt, to his mortification and surprise, that Norfolk consented after all, against his judgment, to command the army; while Elizabeth, though aware that she was committing herself to the course which the King of Spain most deprecated, seemed to face the consequences with much equanimity. Religious persecutions had commenced in the Netherlands; and Flemish Protestants with their families were taking refuge in multitudes in England. When de Quadra remonstrated, she said they were all welcome—as many as chose to come to her; 'if the Spanish troops in Flanders could be sent to toast themselves in their own Indies or Castile, religion would flourish there as well as in England; and the sooner, they were gone the better.'

---

[1] Commission to Sir William Winter, Master of the Ordnance, sent with fourteen ships, armed, to Scotland.—*Domestic MSS., Rolls House.* The commission was drawn on the 16th of December; but owing to the hesitation of the Council, Winter did not sail till the end of the month.

'At this rate,' de Quadra wrote, 'she will revolutionize all the world. She is already practising in France, and her "Gospel" is making too much progress there.'[1]

Hints were given through the western counties that privateers who would 'adventure' at their own cost would not be closely inquired after; and thirty piratical vessels, heavily manned, were swiftly hovering about the Channel. That the sea and all that floated on it was English patrimony was the tacit belief of half the people who lived within sight of the salt water.

Two letters of de Quadra, written on the 27th of December, will add as much as can be known of Elizabeth's humour, and of the views of the different parties, in England and out of it, on the approaching struggle.

DE QUADRA TO THE BISHOP OF ARRAS.[2]

London, December 27.

'The Queen said to me that she understood the King of Spain refused to take arms in her defence.

'I replied that his Majesty looked on the reopening of the war as a European calamity, which if possible he was bound to avoid. He trusted that her difficulties might be remedied more easily by her marriage with the Archduke Charles.

'Chaloner's account of his conversation with you troubled her so much that she was ill for two days with it. The Duke of Norfolk begged me to harp incessantly on the marriage string. He said that Cecil had placed her in a position from which he feared it would be impossible to extricate her; and so he said that he had

---

[1] De Quadra to de Feria, December.—*MS. Simancas.*
[2] *MS. Simancas.*

himself told Cecil. Since the war has been determined on, the Duke has been pointedly attentive to me. I tell him that the King my master will watch over the true interests of the Queen; but it will be with a strong hand, and in a fashion which she will not like. They think of sending Lord Paget to Spain. He will not go unless he take with him a commission to conclude the marriage—so at least he has assured me. Words are no longer of any use with the Queen—we must act. Preservative medicines are too late when the patient is down with the plague. The King our master cannot say that he has been left in ignorance of the state of things here. If he hesitate now it will cost him dear; and he will find himself compelled to protect a wicked woman in an unjust and ungodly cause. I do not mean that we may not interfere for her if she will consent to the marriage—we could then care effectively for the spiritual interests of the realm. But if she go on in her present career she deserves nothing at our hands. You would be astonished to know the things which take place here; but the less they are spoken of the better: I will not write of them.'

DE QUADRA TO THE COUNT DE FERIA.

London, December 27.

'This woman is possessed with a hundred thousand devils; and yet she pretends to me that she would like to be a nun, and live in a cell, and tell her beads from morning till night. If we do not determine what to do swiftly we shall repent of it. A certain person has informed me that if troops cross from the Netherlands to England, the most convenient place for them to land is Lynn, in Norfolk; there is a good harbour there, which can be easily fortified. Let his Majesty do what

he will, he cannot save this true daughter of a wicked
mother. And on my honour I believe those of her
own religion will rise against her even sooner than the
Catholics. For the love of God do not forget things
here! never was there a fairer opportunity to set them
straight.'[1]

The King of Spain, during the war with France, had
concentrated a large Spanish force in the Low Countries.
On the return of peace the Estates afraid of their
liberties had insisted that it should be withdrawn; and
Philip, who had intended to maintain a standing army
there for the preservation of 'order,' had been compelled
after an angry altercation to give way.

Philip himself had sailed for Spain at the end of
August, and was keeping his Christmas with the
heretics at Seville and Valladolid. He had promised
that the troops should follow as soon as means could
be provided for transporting them; and since they could
not remain in Flanders, what better destination could be
found for them than England? Six thousand Spaniards
thrown upon the Norfolk coast; all Catholic England
rising to welcome them; and Elizabeth obliged to retrace
her steps, restore the Catholic bishops, marry Carlos,
and live as a satellite of Philip—this was the scheme
which filled the imagination of the Spanish ministers,
and which faded away only when the Queen surprised
friend and foe by rising triumphant over her difficulties
by her own energy and skill.

In the midst of these grave matters, a little scene
had taken place in Lambeth Chapel, which must not be
entirely forgotten. To some persons it has appeared an

---

[1] *MS. Simancas.*

CHAP II
1559
December

event of great, and even transcendent moment—the re-adjustment of the ladder between earth and heaven by which alone Divine grace could descend on the inhabitants of these islands. To more secular minds it has seemed altogether secondary—a thing merely of this world—a convenient political arrangement.

A Catholic bishop holds his office by a tenure untouched by the accidents of time. Dynasties may change—nations may lose their liberties—the firm fabric of society itself may be swept away in the torrent of revolution—the Catholic prelate remains at his post; when he dies, another takes his place; and when the waters sink again into their beds, the quiet figure is seen standing where it stood before—the person perhaps changed—the thing itself rooted like a rock on the adamantine basements of the world. The Anglican hierarchy, far unlike its rival, was a child of convulsion and compromise: it drew its life from Elizabeth's throne, and had Elizabeth fallen, it would have crumbled into sand. The Church of England was as a limb lopped off from the Catholic trunk; it was cut away from the stream by which its vascular system had been fed; and the life of it, as an independent and corporate existence, was gone for ever. But it had been taken up and grafted upon the State. If not what it had been, it could retain the form of what it had been—the form which made it respectable, without the power which made it dangerous. The image, in its outward aspect, could be made to correspond with the parent tree; and to sustain the illusion, it was necessary to provide bishops who could appear to have inherited their powers by the approved method, as successors of the apostles.

Three pairs of episcopal hands at least were required to communicate the stream. Five of Edward's hierarchy,

English and Irish, had survived the Marian persecutions. The Bishop of Llandaff had apostatized. Out of these six, four were selected to supply in numbers the uncertainty of their qualifications; and, omitting Kitchen, whose character did not bear inspection, and Bale, who was a foul-mouthed ruffian; the others—Barlow, who had been Bishop of Bath; Scory, who had been Bishop of Chichester; the venerable Miles Coverdale; and Hodgekins, late suffragan Bishop of Bedford—were summoned by royal letter to Lambeth, on the 17th of December, to consecrate Matthew Parker Archbishop of Canterbury.

The choice of Parker was in every way a fortunate one—unless indeed to the Archbishop himself, who accepted the charge with the utmost unwillingness, and in allowing it to be forced upon him felt that he was sacrificing his peace. It was not easy however—perhaps it was impossible—to find another man in England with at once character and ability for so dangerous a post. Parker's name alone redeems the first list of Elizabeth's bishops from insignificance. He had borne himself through the changes of the preceding years with consistent probity and moderation. When first ordained, he had been one of Anne Boleyn's chaplains; afterwards he was Master of Corpus, at Cambridge, and Dean of Lincoln. On Edward's death he lost his preferments; and Mary, could she have discovered where he was, would have sent him to the stake. But he lived concealed with his wife, and his hiding-place was not betrayed till times had changed; and then Cecil laid hands on him as the one sensible man within his reach who was religious without being a fanatic, and a Christian without being a dogmatist.

The consecration was duly accomplished; the installation followed; there was an Archbishop of Canterbury once more. Rapidly one after the other the remaining sees were filled up; and the new order of English bishops settled down to their work, shorn of much of their wealth, shorn of their privileges, but still peers of the realm, and with sufficient provision for the appearance which they were expected to maintain. The estates restored by Mary were reappropriated; their judicial powers were transferred to the courts of law; their first-fruits were converted into harquebusses and powder, but if their courts had continued to sit, and if the Queen's armouries had been left unprovided, their tenure of office would have been brief.

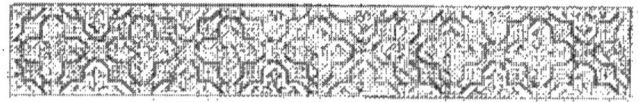

CHAPTER III.

THE English fleet had sailed for the Forth; the first step was taken; but the irresolution was not ended, nor the distrust which the hesitation of the last fortnight had created in the Scots. They had been encouraged to rebel: English agents, under the special direction of Elizabeth, had 'kindled the fire;' yet the English Council could gravely propose to leave them to their fate, and Elizabeth herself had scarcely resisted the temptation. In Edinburgh and London, in Brussels, Paris, Madrid, there was nothing but uncertainty, anxiety, and fear.

'The Queen of England,' the Duchess of Parma wrote to Philip, ' is compromising all of us. She herself is nothing. If she be destroyed, she will but reap the fruit of her own rashness. But if the French once establish themselves in Scotland, England is theirs; and with England they will have the Low Countries. In possession of both shores of the narrow seas, they will isolate us, and cut us off from support; and when we are overrun you must judge yourself how it will fare with Spain and the Indies.

'And yet, if it be our political ruin to allow France to conquer England, it will be our spiritual ruin to allow that woman to go her own way. If she annex Scotland and establish the Protestant religion throughout the island, you know the humour of the Netherlands—you know the peril of the example.'[1]

Whether policy or orthodoxy would prove the stronger motive, neither England nor France could tell; and as little was Elizabeth able to comprehend the Scots. Maitland told her that they were unanimous; but how different a unanimity was it from the fierce enthusiasm with which, age after age, they had combined against the invasion of the Southrons! When an Edward or a Henry sent their armies over the Border—the whole nation sprung to arms at the call of the fiery cross. Douglas and Gordon, Hamilton and Stuart, Highland chief and Lowland laird, buried their feuds in a greater hatred, and crowded to the field. Defeat could not break their spirit; bribes could not soil their patriotism; and had Flodden been followed by an attempt at conquest, it would have been soon avenged in a second Bannockburn.

How different was it now! Three thousand men had chased the Congregation from the field. They had scattered to their homes, earl, lord, and chieftain, threatening to make terms with the Regent unless an English army would enter Scotland to rescue them. The English were their 'auld enemies;' the French were their traditional allies. What security had Elizabeth for their truth, except the assurance of a few inexperienced youths? How lightly might the temptation of giving a sovereign to England win back the rest to the schemes of the Guises and Mary Stuart!

Thus from hour to hour the Queen's humour shifted. She told Noailles she would not begin; but whoever would might fling the first stone.[2] Throgmorton came

---

[1] The text is an epitome of three letters from Margaret of Parma to Philip, written on the 7th and 21st of December, 1559, and the 6th of January, 1560.—*MS. Simancas.*

[2] Noailles to D'Oysel, December 21.—FORBES, vol. 1.

over from Paris to hasten her decision; he was at first directed to return with a message to the King that England could not regard the Scottish nobility as rebels; and that for her own sake the Queen could not allow France to conquer them.[1] Sadler and Randolph received what they understood to be final instructions from London; and made arrangements with the Congregation to meet the English army in Cockburn Path, between Dunbar and Berwick, on the 10th of January.

But the orders were no sooner sent than they were repented of. Throgmorton was detained in London. The Duke of Norfolk, who having consented to command, was disposed to act with vigour, was forbidden to advance. The Queen wrote to him on the day on which Throgmorton's commission—which amounted to a declaration of war—was dated, that certain respects obliged her to forbear for one or two months from moving further; the matter might be otherwise arranged; she was unwilling to spend money needlessly; and the levies might be suspended till further orders: the Duke and Sadler could ascertain from the Scots whether the assistance of the fleet would not be sufficient; whether, if supplied with English engineers, cannon, and powder, they could not do the rest of the work themselves;[2] while Winter, she insisted again and again, whatever he did, must do it as of his own accord, pleading no directions from herself.

Meanwhile the French—afraid of Spain, and alarmed for the troops in Scotland, should the English army cross the Border—had affected a desire to negotiate. M. de la

---

[1] Commission to Sir N. Throgmorton, December 30.—CONWAY MSS.

[2] The Queen to the Duke of Norfolk, December 30, 1559.—BURLEIGH Papers, vol. i.

180   *History of England.*

Chap III
1560
January

Marque was sent over to assure Elizabeth of the innocency of the intentions of the King and Queen; to insist that they had no object beyond the pacification of Scotland, and by every artifice of diplomacy to gain time.

Elizabeth declines to interfere.

Elizabeth received their advances with courtesy and almost cordiality. She expressed the greatest desire for a peaceful termination of the crisis; she declared distinctly to de la Marque, and she declared to Noailles—who watched her face while she spoke—that she did not mean to break the peace, and had no intention of interfering.¹ 'Her acts are of one kind, her words are of another,' said Noailles. He knew not what to think of her; yet, unable to disbelieve so positive an assurance, he wrote to the Queen Regent, to tell her that he believed she had nothing to fear from England;² and with this letter, and with the promise to himself, de la Marque set out on the 2nd of January for Scotland.

The fair weather did not continue. As soon as he was gone an altercation rose between Cecil and Noailles. The French ambassador accused Cecil of lighting a fire which would never be extinguished. Cecil answered that 'the French had lighted it, and were every day heaping it with fresh fuel to make the blaze the hotter.'³

De la Marque was scarcely over the Tweed, than he and his despatches fell into the hands of the insurgent Scots. In all likelihood his capture was his own work, for he was able to inform the Congregation of the words in which Elizabeth had disclaimed them. The letter of Noailles confirmed his story. Sadler at the same time

---

¹ 'La Marque museth not a little what moveth the Lords of the Congregation to hope for succour out of England, and reporteth that the Queen of England promised the contrary by her own mouth unto Noailles and him.'—*Randolph to Sadler, Jan. 11. Scotch MSS. Rolls House.*

² Noailles to the Queen Dowager, January 2.—*Scotch MSS.*

³ Noailles to the King of France, January 4.—Teulet, vol. i.

was obliged to announce to them that the advance of the army was postponed indefinitely; there were still no signs of the fleet, and after so many changes they ceased to expect it; they believed themselves deliberately betrayed; and in a passion of fear and disappointment, Chatelherault wrote to Francis and Mary—to make his submission, to implore their pardon, and to offer to send Arran and his other children to France as hostages for his future behaviour.[1]

Taking courage from Elizabeth's uncertainty, d'Oysel had resumed the offensive. After another ineffectual attempt on Edinburgh Castle,[2] he had ventured to divide his force; and leaving Leith garrisoned, had marched on Christmas eve leisurely to Stirling, scattering the lords who were assembled there. Thence gathering increasing confidence, he passed down into Fife, the stronghold of the Protestants, intending to occupy St. Andrews and fortify it into a second Leith.

D'Elbœuf was daily and even hourly expected. He was to sail at latest at the end of December, and at any moment his transports might be looked for. Maitland wrote to Cecil, that 'delay was most dangerous;' he could not believe, he said, that the Queen, after what she had said to him, could have altered her mind.[3]

---

[1] 'Sire,—La fiance qu'il a pleu à la Royne Regente me donner de vostre bonté et clemence m'a faict prendre la hardiesse de vous escripre pour vous supplier très humblement de me recepvoir et les myens en vostre bonne grace, et vouloir oublier et pardonner les choses passées avec quelques articles dont je vous faix requeste. Apres avoir eu vostre response si me le voulez mander j'envoyerai mes enfans en France. De Glasgow, le 15 jour de Janvier, 1560. Votre très humble et très obéissant serviteur, James.'—TEULET, vol. i. p. 206.

[2] Lord Erskine refused to recognise any authority but Parliament. He would not admit within the walls either the Congregation or the French, and threatened to fire on Holyrood if he was attacked.—*Randolph to Crofts and Sadler, December. Scotch MSS.*

[3] Maitland to Cecil, January 10.—*Scotch MSS, Rolls House.*

Norfolk who had protested against the enterprise till Winter sailed protested equally now against the weakness of affecting to withdraw from it. In reply to the Queen's order to delay the invasion, he said that the Protestants were powerless without the neutrals, and the neutrals would not move till they were assured of England. The Scots, he said, could not expel the French unassisted: if the Queen tried their patience too far, she would make the Scots her enemies also. She had gone too far to recede, and it would be impolitic, dishonourable, and dangerous to disappoint now the hopes which she had raised.[1] Concealed assistance was impossible. If Winter lay in the Forth and prevented French vessels from going in or out, the world would never believe he was acting without instructions. For himself he thought it would be better if the Court would 'no more seek to hide that which on the Border was so manifest;' Leith, in the absence of the French, was unguarded and might easily be surprised; the only safety was in boldness.

Arran and Lord James Stuart had meanwhile made a stand at Kinghorn; but d'Oysel had defeated them with loss. Each day the little band of the Congregation grew thinner by desertion; and though they continued to hover in the field, the number of men with them diminished in a week from eight hundred to two hundred. The French commander pressed steadily forward along the shores of the Forth, with provision vessels and store ships attending his march; and Arran wrote piteously that although the Protestants would hold out as long as twenty horse could keep together, yet that the whole country was weary, discouraged, and desperate of help.

---

[1] Norfolk to Cecil, January 24.—BTALZIEH Papers.

And yet Elizabeth never really meditated forsaking the Scots; she disliked only parting with money; she tried to persuade herself that the difficulty might be escaped in a less violent manner; and she was one of those people who insist on quarrelling with the course which notwithstanding they have resolved to follow, and who therefore halt and hesitate over each successive step which they are compelled to take.

'The Queen,' wrote de Quadra on the 15th of January, 'is the same as ever. Cecil who is the heart of the business, alone possesses her confidence, and Cecil is obstinately bent on going forward with his Evangel till he destroy both it and himself. I have tried hard to gain him over, for we are the best of friends; but he is possessed with the chimerical notion of uniting Scotland and England under one creed and government; and I might as well talk to a deaf adder as try to move him.

'If there be any other who knows the Queen's purpose, it is my Lord Robert, in whom it is easy to recognise the king that is to be; and either I am deceived and know nothing of the English people, or they will do something to set this crooked business straight. There is not a man who does not cry out on him and her with indignation.

'She tells me that the Scots expect her to marry the Earl of Arran as a condition of the union. She will as little marry Arran as she will marry the Archduke; she will marry none but the favoured Robert.'[1]

Left to her own self-guidance, Elizabeth would scarcely have worked the ship out of the breakers. But Cecil

---

[1] De Quadra to de Feria, and to the Bishop of Arras, January 15, 1560.—MS. Simancas.

was ever at her ear, and the invisible powers were on her side.

A few days before Winter sailed d'Elbœuf had started from Dieppe. Had the weather been fair he would have been in Leith before the English fleet had cleared the Thames, and would have thrown a force into Scotland which would have changed the course of history.

Northerly winds however delayed his heavy-laden transports, and with the new year they blew wilder and more wild. The English admiral was scarcely in the Channel than he was driven by a gale into Lowestoft Roads and was kept there for a fortnight motionless. D'Elbœuf less fortunate was caught at sea by the tempest. In all directions the storm must have blown: half the fleet was dashed in pieces on the Holland flats—sailors, troops, horses, all perishing. Some vessels foundered at sea and the drowned bodies were washed up upon the Norfolk coast. De Martigues, d'Elbœuf's colleague, after beating for days in the North Sea, found his way at last into Leith with a hundred men; d'Elbœuf's own vessel recovered Dieppe; but out of the entire fleet those two ships alone seemed to have survived.[1] In one fatal day and night the laborious preparations of the autumn were annihilated; and with France growing every day more agitated with religious passions, with the Prince of Condé and the Huguenots avowedly sympathizing with the Scotch reformers—months must now elapse before d'Oysel could hope to be relieved.

'The Spaniards at Brussels,' wrote Sir Thomas Cha-

---

[1] 'La perdida de los naos del Marquis d'Elbœuf se entiende que ha sido muy grande por el gran numero de muertos que ha echado la mar á la costa de Norfulk.'—*De Quadra to the Duchess of Parma, January* 11.—*318. Simancas.* Compare Chaloner to Cecil, January 13 and January 15.—*Flanders MSS. Rolls House.*

loner, 'be sorry for the news. The loss is esteemed of
no less moment than an overthrow by land. If hope
might allow men to sit idle, we might suppose the
French undertake this enterprise *diis malis*. Nevertheless let us provide as if every Frenchman were two;
so the best will save itself: and trust we none but God
and ourselves.' 'For if I were God,' Chaloner continued
in his peculiar way—' I would swear by myself that I
believe our trust is in God's defence only, and by Him,
in our foresight; so our professed enemies and faint
friends instead of cartels of defiance will send us solemn
letters of congratulation.—Otherwise *vœ victis!*'[1]

All this while Winter had been riding out the gale.
He had suffered little loss, save that most of his ships'
boats were washed away; and when the weather moderated he pursued his way to the North. On Monday
the 15th he was off Flamborough Head. The wind rose
again and drove him back into the Humber; but ignorant of d'Elbœuf's fate and impatient of delay he again
put to sea the following day. On Saturday morning he
was off Berwick, where Norfolk sent out to him a few
hundred 'hackbutters;' and after waiting two days there
for the slow sailers in the fleet to rejoin him he passed
on to the Frith of Forth.

And now let the reader imagine the storm over—a
cloudless January morning, and the grey calm of the
Forth lined at intervals with the faint ripple of an air
just sufficient to give the vessels steering way. The
young English admiral was drifting slowly with the tide
along the coast of Fife, just outside Kinghorn. Beyond
the point in front of him lay Burnt Island where the

---

[1] Chaloner to Cecil, January 15.—*Flanders MSS. Rolls House.*

French had mounted a few guns. In the middle of the Channel was Inchkeith which they occupied in force. Close in under the Fife shore were two large armed vessels with a number of lighters, hoys, and barges. A boat with two men in it pushed out from a cove, and presently Robert Kirkaldy, Sir William's younger brother, with one of the Hamiltons, climbed up the side of Winter's ship and told him that d'Oysel with three thousand men had slept the night before in Dyssart. That morning they had burnt his brother's house; and having seen the ships in the offing, and supposing them to be d'Elbœuf's transports, they were then in full march towards St. Andrew's. The vessels under the shore contained their military stores and provisions. The country people had carried off their corn and cattle, and d'Oysel drew his whole supplies from the sea. If the barge could be destroyed he would have to subsist his troops on water; while the two large ships contained a rich prize of cannon, powder, and pioneers' tools for the intended works at St. Andrew's.

The Admiral's resolution was immediately taken; he continued his languid advance till he had brought his ships under the guns at Burnt Island. He showed no colours. The French flag was flying on the fort; but he did not condescend to salute it. The French commander sent off to know who he was; he gave no answer. A shot was sent across his bows; he paid no attention to it. His quiet insolence produced the effect which he desired. The next shot was fired into him: the French had commenced the attack and he was at liberty to defend himself.

In an instant every vessel which could be brought to bear replied with a broadside. The few guns on the island were silenced and dismounted; the fort was blown up; the two ships were seized and carried off; the transports and provision boats were driven ashore, where they were sacked and burnt by the people: and d'Oysel discovered his mistake only to find the English admiral in command of the Forth, his communications cut off, his troops without food, in the one county in Scotland where he was without a friend, and with no retreat open to him save by the tedious circuit over Stirling Bridge.

If the Scots had had a force in the field, if Elizabeth's changes had not disheartened and distracted them, d'Oysel at this time could have been destroyed or compelled to surrender. Not more than six hundred men remained in Leith; and Winter sent an express to Norfolk to say that if he and Grey would advance at once from Berwick with the troops already collected there, the work would be done.[1]

The advance of Norfolk however would have committed Elizabeth to the sanction of what she had resolved beforehand to disavow. In the face of her instructions the Duke could not move; and indeed he might reasonably have expected that the Scots could now dispose of the business for themselves. Queen's Ferry was commanded by Winter. There was a bridge at Alloa, but William Kirkaldy promptly broke it: and so satisfied were the Congregation that d'Oysel could not escape, that they left him as they believed to starve, and proceeded at their utmost leisure to call their men about them to receive his surrender.[2]

The French had now an opportunity of showing what disciplined troops could do in the face of tremendous dif-

---

[1] Winter to Norfolk, January 25.—*Scotch MSS. Rolls House.*
[2] Arran and Lord James to Sadler, January 26.—SADLER *Papers*, vol. II.

ficulties. They were beyond the Leven when they discovered their situation. In their first consternation they rested for a night in the field.[1] In the morning, wet, chilled, and hungry, they commenced their rapid retreat. Not a loaf of bread could they hope to touch till they had crossed the water. The tempest broke again, and the western gale drove the rain into their faces as they struggled across those melancholy moors. On the evening of the third day they reached Alloa to find the bridge gone, and the river it is likely pouring down in a winter flood.

Escape of the French army.

D'Oysel was a man of prompt expedients. In an instant the nearest parish church was unroofed; the timbers were dragged to the water-side, and laid across the piers of the broken arches. The army itself brought the news of its escape to Stirling—and once there, they were safe. The Congregation were loitering at Glasgow, congratulating themselves over a victory which they had allowed to slip through their hands. D'Oysel refreshed his famished but gallant little force, and fell back at his leisure into Leith.

Well might Elizabeth distrust the allies whose cause she had undertaken. Had an English army been so cut off, not a man of it would have come back to tell the tale.

Meanwhile the Queen Regent had sent a herald to Winter to know for what purpose or by whose order he was levying war in the dominions of the Queen of Scots.

---

[1] 'Suddenly comes Master Alexander Wood, and assured M. d'Osel that thai were Ingliissmen who were send for the support of the Congregation. Thain mycht have bein seine the ryveing of a baird, and mycht have been hard sucho dispyte as cruell men use to spew forth, quhile as God brydellis thair furie. —Knox, *History of the Reformation*. Laing's Edition, vol. ii. p. 13.

'My answer was,' wrote Winter—false to truth, and true to his mistress—'that I was sent to conduct divers ships loaded with ordnance and cannon to her Majesty's fort of Berwick; and there being no sure anchorage there, I determined to seek the Forth, knowing no other but good peace between my said sovereign and all other princes: and as I was running into Leith Roads, the French forts at Inchkeith and Burnt Island shot at me; and I being therewith moved, and hearing the great cruelty which the French used against the Congregation of Scotland, I determined with myself to give all the aid I might to the Congregation, and to let the French from their wicked practices as far as I might; and that hereof the Queen's Highness my mistress was nothing privy.'[1]

The Duke of Norfolk supported this mendacious story. A dispatch from Berwick was written to the Queen, accepting and repeating the written report, for the benefit of foreign ambassadors. Lord Dacre and Lord Westmoreland who had not been admitted to the secret gave their unsuspecting signatures—being even allowed to add conjectures of their own that the two ships taken had been intended to act against Ayemouth.[2] It pleased Elizabeth to seat herself in the midst of a web of illusions, and to expect her subjects to have as little scruple as herself in disavowing what it was inconvenient to confess. It may be doubted however whether falsehood so extremely transparent was of real service to her.

---

[1] Winter to Norfolk.—*Scotch MSS. Rolls House.*

[2] 'The which I was well contented withal for their better contentation; wishing, indeed, that the matter should rather burst out by little and little, than to make all here, with the suddenness of the things, in a hurly-burly. —*Norfolk to Cecil, January* 19. BURLEIGH *Papers*, vol. I. pp. 232, 233.

'Such a mask,' the Queen Regent wrote to Noailles, 'is too easy to strip off. As if it were likely or credible that a subject and an officer should have had the will, far less the power, of making war without the consent and against the orders of his sovereign. Speak openly to the Queen. Bid her remember how God avenges unjust dealings. If she persist in her disavowal, tell her to write me a letter which I can show. Let her prove plainly that she means to punish these breaches of the peace—if indeed they have been ventured on without her knowledge.'[1]

It is hard to think that honesty would not have been as much more beneficial at the time, as it would have looked fairer on the page of history. Yet it must be remembered that France too all this time was affecting the most profound sincerity; that the King of Spain had said that he would take part against that power—whichever it was—that first openly broke the peace. If Philip dreaded the ascendancy of Protestantism, he dreaded equally a French conquest of Great Britain; and as long as war was not actually declared in the name of the English Government, he might perhaps regard Winter's indirect hostility as no more than a legitimate act of defence, which tended to prolong the situation, and left the field open to mediation, or perhaps to armed interference. There are 'practices' in the game of politics which the historian in the name of morality is bound to condemn, which nevertheless in this false and confused world statesmen till the end of time will continue to repeat.

At all events there was now breathing time. The

---

[1] The Queen Regent to Noailles, January 28.—TEULET, vol. I.

English fleet lay in Leith Roads. The ships' boats watched the mouth of the harbour day and night.[1] The weather continued foul; the sailors were ill supplied with winter clothes; the service was 'cruel;' but the admiral was able to say that the Frenchmen, if asked their opinions, 'would not deny but he had kept them waking.' Could the Scots have been as diligent on land, the garrison must have been soon straitened and eventually starved. They had before declared that they would not act without English assistance: the assistance had come; yet they seemed as unwilling or as helpless as before: a blockade by land was not so much as attempted. Recovering from his first alarm, d'Oysel reoccupied Edinburgh, the castle only excepted; while Erskine gave the protection of its walls to the Regent and her train. Knox on the 6th of February flung in the teeth of Chatelherault that the English had been fifteen days in the Forth, 'and had never received comfort of any man, Lord James Stuart only excepted, more than they had lyen upon the coast of their mortal enemy.'[2] A little after, d'Oysel and de Martigues took the field again, wasted the country to the gates of Glasgow, and swept the corn and cattle which they could seize inside the walls of Leith.

Both France and England now turned to Spain. On the part of Elizabeth, Sir Thomas Chamberlain and Lord Montague were despatched on a special embassy to Madrid. Montague was selected as the one Catholic nobleman who had opposed every one of Elizabeth's

---

[1] Winter to Norfolk, February 12, 1560.—*Scotch MSS. Rolls House.*

[2] *History of the Reformation*, vol. ii. p. 41. This was an exaggeration, however. Winter said that he was well supplied by the Scots with wine, barrelled salmon, cod, and herring.—*Winter to Norfolk, Feb.* 12. *Scotch MSS. Rolls House.*

reforming measures, and who therefore would be the most welcome to Philip; Chamberlain went as a check upon his companion, and—in Montague's own opinion —as a spy upon him. There was perhaps a secret reason for a choice from which so much danger was to be feared; the Queen may have desired that in the event of a rising of the Catholics their principal leader should be out of the way. He went unwillingly. Before his departure he attempted secretly to communicate with de Quadra, but sent a message to say that it was made impossible for him. De Quadra wrote to Philip that Montague would have something to tell him in secret which it would be to his advantage to hear.

The terms of the message with which the ambassadors were charged had been long discussed and often changed. The first drafts of it contained a list of complaints against the French, with a request for help under the treaties should England be invaded. In its ultimate form Elizabeth apologized for having despatched the fleet without Philip's consent. She undertook to 'reserve to her good brother's wisdom her further proceedings;' she promised 'to remit to him any advantage which God might give her to the detriment of France;' and was 'content to accept his Majesty as a judge in the quarrel;' 'trusting that his Majesty for honour, and zeal to common peace, would not refuse to take that office on him.'[1]

The French were scarcely less submissive. In the general uncertainty the Guises had taken alarm at trifles.

---

[1] 'Notes of matter to be reported to the King of Spain, from Sir Thomas Chamberlain and Lord Montague, January, 1560.'—*Spanish MSS. Rolls House.*

The Princess Elizabeth had gone to Spain to join her husband. So slight a matter as the inscription over the door of the house in which she was received at Guadalajara sufficed to rouse suspicion.[1] The Bishop of Limoges hastened to represent to the most Catholic King that the Queen of England was the enemy of the faith; that she had encouraged the Scotch rebellion only for the overthrow of the Church; that she was pursuing the same insidious policy in France with no less fatal success; and that his interest as a European sovereign and his obligations as a Christian prince alike forbade him to assist her.[2]

The dilemma was pressed home; but Philip imagined that he had discovered a possible escape from it. Alva replied to the representations of the Bishop of Limoges, that the Queen of England could not tolerate the presence of a large French force in Scotland. When the Bishop asked if a sovereign was not to put down an insurrection of her subjects,—Alva said that the French King and Queen had given Elizabeth just cause of suspicion; she could not be expected to hold her crown at their will and pleasure, nor could the King of Spain look on passively at an aggression which might next endanger himself. But Alva was ready with an alternative. A heretic rebellion was not to be passed over with impunity; and what neither England nor Spain could allow the French to do, his master, in his high generosity, and in his zeal for God's honour, would do him-

---

[1] 'Audi filia et vide et inclina aurem tuum, et obliviscere populum tuum et domum patris tui, et concupiscet Rex decorem tuum.'—Hearken, oh daughter, and consider; incline thine ear, forget also thine own people and thy father's house, so shall the King have pleasure in thy beauty.

[2] Intervention de l'Espagne. Negociation de l'Evesque de Lymoges, —TEULET, vol. ii.

self. The transports were lying ready in the Zealand harbours for the removal of the Spanish troops. If the King of France had really no ulterior object, his master's army would co-operate with d'Oysel. Elizabeth would have then no excuse for alarm. Her fleet she would be compelled to withdraw; and, safe under the Spanish flag, the French Government might send their reinforcements and supplies to Leith.[1]

Most ingenious offer! which would give the Spaniards the footing on British soil which they so coveted, as a prelude to a Catholic rising. The jealousy of the French happily served to shield Elizabeth from Philip — as Philip's anxieties protected her from the Guises. The presence of the Spaniards, if fatal to the English Reformers, would have been no less disastrous to the pretensions of Mary Stuart. But the probability of such a movement had been considered in Elizabeth's cabinet. De Feria had distinctly told Sir Thomas Gresham that Philip would not allow her to separate Scotland from France.[2] She was securing herself in the only way in which security was to be found; and was arming to the teeth. Guns and powder were shipped in such quantities from the Low Countries, that the Zealand customhouse officers at length refused to let them pass, 'marvelling what the Queen's Majesty meant to arm herself in such sort.' But the embargo could not be sustained; and Gresham on his own responsibility shipped a hundred thousand weight of copper — 'wish-

---

[1] Teulet, vol. ii.
[2] 'I do well remember the communication that the Count de Feria had with me long past, and that was — Doth the Queen of England think the King my master would suffer her to win Scotland from his brother, the French King? No, no, said he, they be abused.' — *Sir T. Gresham to Cecil, February 18, 1560.* — *Flanders MSS. Rolls House.*

ing he was able to persuade the Queen to make out of hand thirty or forty cannon.' 'What a terror that would be to the enemy to see them in good order, he referred to Cecil's judgment.'[1]

In England all the world was mustering, drilling, and practising. Elizabeth herself, on a Neapolitan courser, exercised every day with the train bands in St. James's Park; and even de Quadra could not withhold his sarcastic admiration from her.[2]

A sharp watch was kept upon the Catholic embassies. English subjects found attending mass at the Spanish or French chapels were threatened with arrest; and the menace was more than once carried into execution—not without disturbances at the doors. The Queen, while she was severe, would have attempted to conciliate; and could she have had her own way, she would have restored the crucifixes in the parish churches, as she had already done in the Royal Chapel. She was encountered by an opposition too strong for her. Cecil's policy was in the ascendant; yet there were signs of weakness in the ground under his feet: at any moment it might split open and swallow him in the same destruction which had engulphed Cromwell before him. Arundel reproached Clinton in the Queen's presence for the arrest of the Catholics; and Elizabeth herself could scarcely prevent them from coming to blows. 'Those,' Arundel exclaimed, 'who had advised the war with Scotland were traitors to their country!'[3]

---

[1] Sir T. Gresham to Cecil, January 27, 1560.—*Flanders MSS. Rolls House.*

[2] 'Su Majestad sale cada dia al campo en un courrier de Napoli o un ginete à exercitarme por esta guerra, sentada en un sillon destos que aqui se usan; que es muy buena cosa de ver. En fin aqui todo es armas y recogitos de guerra ahora.'—*De Quadra to the Count de Feria,* February 11. *MS. Simancas.*

[3] De Quadra to Philip, February 19.—*MS. Simancas.*

Chap III
1560
February

So the world drove forward—the horizon growing every moment darker. Yet the form in which the storm would break was still uncertain. After the news of d'Elbœuf's disaster, and the arrival of Winter in the Forth, the French offered to withdraw all their troops except four hundred, if Elizabeth would cease to interfere. In the middle of February, M. de Sèvre came over to supersede Noailles, to amuse Elizabeth with a repetition of de la Marque's assurances, and to pretend that the assumption of the English arms and style by the Queen of Scots had been forced upon her by her father-in-law. But Throgmorton warned Cecil to agree to nothing short of complete evacuation. If four hundred men were left in Scotland they would be a nucleus which could be increased again at a more convenient time; and the French faction would be kept alive. The Guises—let them say what they pleased—had relinquished no iota of their purposes; and if the present opportunity was passed over it might never return.[1]

Elizabeth replied to de Sèvre that she could not believe in his explanation. The Queen of Scots, in her public deeds and private letters, still styled herself Queen of England. 'She would not suffer her estate to be thus neglected in the open sight of the world;' and as to the Scots, whom the French called rebels, they seemed to her to be wise and natural subjects of their own crown. If in the absence of their Sovereign they allowed the kingdom to be 'evicted out of the hands of their own nation,' and to be sacrificed to the Cardinal of Lorraine and the Duke of Guise, all Europe would cry shame on them. Even the Queen of Scots herself, if she outlived

[1] Throgmorton to Cecil, February 4, and February 16.—Forbes, vol. i.

her husband, 'would have occasion to condemn them as cowards and unnatural subjects.'[1]

Meanwhile the English troops lay idle at Berwick, while Leith grew stronger and the Protestants weaker and more dispirited. If assistance was to be granted at all, prudence required a decisive step to be taken before it was prohibited by Spain. A conference therefore was arranged between Scotch and English commissioners to fix the terms on which the Queen would allow her troops to march; and on the 25th of February, Lord James Stuart, Lord Maxwell, Lord Ruthven, Young Maitland, and Henry Balnavis came to Berwick.

Elizabeth required to be satisfied how, if she expelled the French garrison from Leith, the Scots proposed to prevent them from returning at a future time. She could not be expected to keep a fleet in the Forth in perpetuity; and as France would probably declare war against her, she must know how far she might depend upon them if she was invaded. Further, she had to enquire whether they had any project for a durable alliance between the two realms of such a kind as would promise a final peace and dispense with the irritating necessity of the border garrisons.

The last question, involving the delicate and doubtful arrangement of the Arran marriage, was allowed to stand over. After two days' discussion a formal agreement was concluded—signed on one side by the Scotch Lords, on the other by the Duke of Norfolk.

Elizabeth, in consideration of the attempt to annex 'Scotland to the French crown, for the preservation of its ancient liberties ['*as a Christian realm in the profes-*

---

[1] 'Words to be said to the French Ambassador in the name of the Queen, February 17.'—COTTON MSS. CALIG. B. 10.

sion of *Christ's true religion*,[1]] took that realm under her protection, together with the again penitent Duke of Chatelherault, and promised to assist the Duke and the nobility in driving out the foreign invaders.

The Scots on their side, and Elizabeth on hers, bound themselves to agree to no peace till both were satisfied. The Scots—and this was one of the most serious features in the treaty—being the subjects of the French Queen, offered hostages for their fidelity to another sovereign. The English undertook to build no fortresses in Scotland unless the Lords desired them to do so. The Scots engaged to provide an army at their own expense to assist Elizabeth if the French retaliated by invading England.

The agreement concluded with a declaration that nothing was intended by it in prejudice of the lawful authority of the Scottish Queen. The object was the defence of the constitutional and hereditary liberties of Scotland, and that only.

Another step, it might have been thought a final one, had thus been taken. The 25th of March was fixed as the day on which the English army would cross the Border; the Lords returned to make their preparations to meet it; and Maitland went on to London to communicate in private with Elizabeth and Cecil.

The arrangement was satisfactory on all points except the one which was of most grave moment. The Congregation confessed that the force which they could bring into the field would be but small. The people

---

[1] The words in Italics appear in the draft of the agreement, which is found among Cecil's *Papers*, vol. i. p. 153. They are absent from the version of it given by Knox, and also from that in Rymer's *Fœdera*. It is almost certain that the paragraph was struck through, to enable Elizabeth to rest her interference on political grounds only.

generally, if not hostile, were not with them; and the
work, if done at all, would have to be done by the
English alone—an intimation certain to strengthen the
hands of the opponents of the war, who were still urging
on Elizabeth the alternative of the marriage with the
Archduke, and who dreaded the complications in which
her connexion with the French and Scotch revolutionists
threatened to involve her. The conditions of the Austrian alliance were still being canvassed. Elizabeth still
from time to time professed a desire to see her suitor.
Count Helfesteyn had come from Vienna with formal
proposals from Ferdinand, and as yet had received no
answer.

The position of this, with the other great questions
of the hour, can be seen again with the help of de
Quadra:—

DE QUADRA TO PHILIP II.

London, March 7.

'The French have offered to recall all their men from
Scotland, except three or four hundred, on condition that
England withdraws her fleet, and the insurgents submit
and disperse. The arms and style question they will
refer to a mixed commission of French and English; and
if the decision is unfavourable they will abandon them.
The Queen however says she will not compromise her
right by referring it to any one; and Throgmorton tells
her to believe nothing that they say. They are only
watching their time to take her at a disadvantage, and
she, I am confident, is determined to drive them from
Scotland.

'The French are working hard to make a party here as
well among the Catholics as the heretics; and the weakness of the Scotch insurgents disturbs the Queen; but
she says she can take care of herself, and she is scraping

up money, fitting out ships, and fortifying the coasts in all directions.

'The French King professed surprise to Throgmorton that the Queen should be trying to make a religious revolution in France; and their ambassador here said the same to herself. It is reported that there are five or six gentlemen of note who can produce proofs against her. The expectation in London is that the Pope will declare her illegitimate, and will lay the kingdom under an interdict. She is afraid that your Majesty will then separate yourself from her; and therefore to me she has been affecting a desire to have a General Council. She pretends that she is not the friend of the new theology which I suppose her to be, with much more that would impose upon a person who did not know her. But it is all words.

'Should any disaster befall her, I am told that the Catholics would choose for their King the son of the Countess of Lennox;[1] my informant is ———,[2] so that the story has foundation. Both the boy and his parents are good Christians. The Queen professes to intend to nominate Hastings;[3] but Hastings himself thinks the Tower his more likely destination. The Queen's proceedings provoke so much complaint that I am only surprised she has kept her place so long. It will not be the fault of the French if something does not happen soon.

'The French ambassador says that all this trouble has arisen in Scotland because his master and mistress refuse to consent to the change of religion there. The Queen declares that as far as she is concerned religion

---

[1] Lord Darnley, now just fourteen.
[2] The name is in cipher—perhaps Lord Paget.
[3] Afterwards Earl of Huntingdon.

has nothing to do with it. Not a word has passed between herself and the Scots on the subject.

'The Scotch party are making great efforts here. The obstacle is the natural enmity between the two nations. On the other hand, your Majesty's name is held in general veneration. The Queen and the heretics about the court are exceptions; but the people generally look to you as the first object of their desire. I think it right that your Majesty should know this.

'The French ambassador tells me that if she will not come to terms with them, he believes that the Pope will be brought to declare against her; and he wishes to know what your Majesty will do in that event. I have evaded the question, saying merely that in just causes the princes of Spain have been never wanting in devotion to the apostolic see. The Queen herself believes you will forsake her if the Pope venture such a step. It was but yesterday that she was talking over her situation with me; and coming to this point, she said that however things went on, though she might break, she would never bend.[1] She is straining every nerve; she has eight or ten additional ships ready for sea; and——[2] thinks that the game is up here for the present; and if it were not for leaving his family he would be glad to go and serve your Majesty in Spain.[3] Count Helfesteyn is in good spirits about the prospect of his affair, and is all for the Archduke Charles coming over. Once here, he thinks the Archduke will find so many friends that she will be obliged to consent whether she like it or not.[4]

---

[1] 'Me dixó que como quiera que fuese ella queria mor victa sed non supplex.'

[2] Name again in cipher.

[3] '.... 'Me ha dicho que esto esta perdido á su parecer y que si no fuese por no dexar su casa quisiera hree a servir á V. M^d. en España.'

[4] 'Sir Thomas Gresham was most anxious for this marriage. 'For my

CHAP. III.
1560
March

Nothing can be worse than to let her go on as she is going. The present difficulties are wholly due to the practices of the heretics. They have ruined religion in Scotland, and they will do yet worse in France, unless they are checked. Two thousand families of Flemish Protestants are established in England, and every renegade Spaniard is received with open arms. There will be small difficulty in remedying all this: the state of feeling here is so generally Catholic, and the Queen has so small a force at her command. Lord Montague and his companion are gone to your Majesty to invite you to renew the treaties, and to blind your eyes about religion and the Archduke. The real meaning is this: if the Queen and Cecil can expel the French from the island, and either by marriage or religion make a union of the realms they think they can do without your Majesty. If they fail they would have a resource on which to fall back.

'The Catholics cannot believe that you will make any fresh treaty without stipulating for the restoration of religion; and Lord Montague, in secret, hopes the same. Doctor Cole sent two days ago to tell me in the name of his party that if your Majesty deserts them they will apply to the French—they will apply to the Turks if necessary—sooner than not get the better of the heretics. Montague was not allowed to speak with me alone. He said that if it were not to kiss your Majesty's hands, and to give you information about England, he would have lost his head before he would have gone on a service for the Queen.

The English Catholics threaten to go over to the French.

part,' he wrote to Cecil, on the 17th of January, 'I pray God to bless her Majesty, and to strengthen her hands to it, for that all nations like and hold with that marriage—both Protestant and Papist as they term them. They say that marriage will both augment her Majesty's estate, and keep her Majesty and her realm in peace for ever.—*Flanders MSS. Rolls House.*

'The Catholics are jealously watched. The Court are uneasy about Shrewsbury and Northumberland.

'A few days ago the Queen despatched a noted heretic named Tremayne into Brittany, with a message to the Huguenots. I have just learnt that there is something going on there of extreme importance.'[1]

DE QUADRA TO THE COUNT DE FERIA.

London, March 7.

'I have just been with the Queen. She has treated me like a dog.[2] The youth[3] must have been complaining to her of a message which I sent him three days ago. I laughed it off, and asked her why she was so melancholy. She knows I suppose that her case is desperate unless she makes terms with the French; and even if she does, I do not see that there is much hope for her.

'You will see what I have written to the King; I have sent a copy of it to the Duchess of Parma. The Scotch rebels distract the Queen. Instead of growing stronger their numbers diminish daily, and the people here neither like to help such a set of wretches, nor can venture to desert them—knowing that they are lost if the French become masters of Scotland. They would make peace if they could tell how to make it with safety or with honour. And all this time the garrison at Leith are taking in the stores which they so much needed, and the neutrals are only waiting to see them fully provisioned to declare for France. Every rebel will then

---

[1] *MS. Simancas.* — Endorsed in Philip's hand—'Mirad en lo descifrado una palabra que no esta descifrada y monstrad luego á la mañana al Duque de Alva, que contiene lo ves luego por lo que ha de hablar al Embajador de Francia si no lo ya ha hecho hoy.'

[2] 'La qual me ha tratado como á un perro.'

[3] Dudley.

submit, the French King will offer a general pardon, and the Queen will have to shift for herself.

'God knows how it will end—we shall soon see. The French ambassador seems to wish it to be understood that the Guises will not let themselves be deterred by fear of any one from insisting on their right, and carrying out their enterprise. He came one night to talk to me. He found the Council, he said, more reasonable than they had been of late—probably for the same reason that the Queen was so sad. He said he would lose his head if she did not marry the Archduke—necessity would compel her to it. The French King, he said, would be well enough satisfied, provided it is understood that if the Queen die without children the right goes to the Queen of Scots.

'The sum of it all is, that if the King our master neglects to interfere here much longer, England will be as completely French as Scotland is, and we shall then be driven to do what now we will not do. If his Majesty will act now, he will not only do God service, gain honour for himself and save everything, but he can have a king here of his own nomination—English or foreign as he pleases. It will cost him no more effort than it costs him now to keep this woman here—far less indeed—for he cannot trust her; and she sits so insecurely on her throne, that any day may witness her fall; while he may bind to him by obligations another person whom the English people may like better than they like this one.

'I say nothing of religion, nothing of honour, nothing of the injuries which she has done to us. I leave out of sight the danger which the neighbourhood of these heretics causes in the Low Countries; that is too notorious to require mention. What I mean is that, unless his

Majesty resolves quickly, there will come a day of convulsion and revolution; and either the kingdom will fall to the French, or we shall have to take up arms in the most ignominious and shameful cause which Christian prince ever sustained. That, and nothing else, it will be to maintain this woman against God, against right, against the wishes of all her subjects, Catholics and Protestants, and against the commonwealth of the whole Christian world.

'Now is our time to do what we ought to do. If we are to throw our shield over such a business as this is—God have mercy on us!—such an opportunity as we have now will never return; we have the good will of all parties—even of the heretics themselves.

'Lord Robert is the worst young fellow I ever encountered. He is heartless, spiritless, treacherous, and false. There is not a man in England who does not cry out upon him as the Queen's ruin.'[1]

Happily for Elizabeth, England was not the only country in Europe which was troubled with religious differences, and the game of revolutionary intrigue was one which all parties could play, and which she could play unusually well. At the moment when in de Quadra's eyes she was tottering to her fall, the conspiracy of Amboise broke over the heads of the Guises. How far Elizabeth had encouraged it was a question which she would have answered with proud facility. Throgmorton had been the very focus of the plot; and the Queen herself had been in close correspondence with Condé and the Colignys. It failed—as is well known—failed in its immediate object of destroying the Duke of

---

[1] *MS. Simancas.*

Guise; and the scaffold, the rack, and the wheel, were the rewards of the Huguenots' forlorn hope. But as the threads of the conspiracy were followed up, it was found to be no mere outbreak, as it was first supposed to be, of a few unsupported fanatics, but the first scud before a storm which was about to deluge France with blood. Whichever side they looked the Catholic leaders saw black gulphs of uncertainty and suspicion opening round them; and brave as he was, Guise was appalled at the sudden peril in which he was standing.

'They know not where to turn,' wrote Throgmorton. 'He that all trust to-day, to-morrow is least trusted. You can imagine your advantage. Spend your money now, and never in England was money better spent than this will be. Use the time while you have it.'[1]

A war with England in the face of internal dangers, it was for the present essential to avoid. Monluc, Bishop of Valence—the same person who nine years before had been in difficulties in the castle of the Irish chieftain—hurried over to London, affecting a readiness to agree to anything which could be demanded. Elizabeth sent orders to Winter to suspend the blockade, and to Norfolk to postpone for three days longer the entrance of the army—to give the French an opportunity of proving their sincerity by commencing the evacuation.

Monluc caught of course at the opportunity to sow distrust again among the Scots. To the Scots he contrived to intimate that the Queen was aiming at a separate peace. To her he represented the inaction of the

---

[1] Throgmorton to Cecil, March 15; Throgmorton to the Queen, March 21.—FORBES, vol. I.

Scots as deliberate treachery; and de Sèvre produced
the letter in which the unlucky Chatelherault had made
his submission to Francis and Mary.

Chatelherault however, putting a bold face upon his
cowardice, denied his handwriting. He offered to prove
his innocence on the body of de Sèvre, either in his own
person or with the sword of any one of a hundred Hamiltons.[1] He sent Randolph to assure Norfolk, 'upon his
honour and faith to God, that there was no such thought
in his head.' If the Queen still doubted him, 'he would
put his eldest son in state of his lands, and yield himself
into her Grace's hands to live and end his life where it
should please her Highness to assign.'[2]

Stuart, Arran, and Balnavis, while they admitted the
alarm which had been created by the first postponement
of the invasion, protested that they were never more
resolute than at that moment. Norfolk himself thought
it would be dangerous to delay beyond the time when
the French promised to commence the evacuation of
Leith; and Elizabeth told de Quadra that the Scots
were so anxious for the union of the Crowns and for her
own marriage with the Earl of Arran, that she had
ceased to dread a change of purpose in them.

Every post brought some new communication more or
less disturbing. While feeling his way towards more
decisive action, Philip wrote a hurried letter to Elizabeth, entreating and almost commanding her to take no
further step. The Earls of Westmoreland and Northumberland were believed to be disloyal. Norfolk doubted
Lord Dacre, and requested Cecil to have him removed

---

[1] Chatelherault to de Sèvre, March 11.—BURLEIGH *Papers*, vol. i.
[2] Credit committed to Sir Randolph by the Duke of Chatelherault, March 15.— *Scotch MSS. Rolls House.*

from his office of Warden of the Marches; while it was uncertain how far Norfolk could be depended on himself, against the declared wishes of the King of Spain. A letter from the Cardinal of Lorraine to the Queen Dowager fell into the hands of the Scots—which again raised doubts among them of Elizabeth's firmness.[1] And Elizabeth herself was as uneasy as ever at the prospect of war.

'She has but 8000 men,' wrote de Quadra; 'she cannot depend on the musters of the northern counties, where they are all Catholics; and the transport of troops from the south and west of England is difficult and expensive.

'Randolph thinks so ill of the Scots themselves that he fears the English enterprise will fail, and regrets that it has been undertaken. The Queen suspects Norfolk, and repents of having given him the command of the expedition. Too many of the nobles look to him as their leader, and he is popular with the army.

'Cecil says that the differences of religion forbid her marriage with the Archduke; and Paget tells me that so obstinate are both she and those about her in their

---

[1] 'The King of Spain will help us against the Scots with as many vessels, men, and victuals as we will, and so hath written to the said Queen; so that it seemeth she repenteth to have gone so far in the matter. We think that your rebels will be far from their reckoning if they make their account of the said lady's protection, or else there is much dissimulation.'

The closing sentences of this letter mention the conspiracy of Amboise—

'Within these twelve or fifteen days there has been a conspiracy to kill us both, and take the King, and give him masters and governors to bring him up in those wretched doctrines. Great numbers of persons assembled, not without the favour and comfort of some great ones. Except for the help of God, and intelligence which we have had from all parts of Christendom, and also of some of the conspirators that have disclosed it, the matter should have taken effect.—*Translation of an intercepted letter of the Cardinal of Lorraine to the Queen Dowager, March. Scotch MSS. Rolls House.*

heresy, that to save the realm she will not consent to it.

'The general desire here is to have the son of Lady Margaret Lennox for king. Not only would all sides agree to choose him were the Queen to die without children, but the Catholic lords, if an opportunity offers, may declare for him at once; and at all events they will never again endure a female sovereign.

'Things are in a strange state. The Catholics look only to your Majesty. Lord Robert says that if he lives a year he will be in another position from that which he now holds. Every day he presumes more and more; and it is now said that he means to divorce his wife.

'Your Majesty may rely upon it they will make religion a pretext to keep the world in hot water. The heretic ministers cry from their pulpits that, having now a sovereign on their side, they will leave preaching, and take the sword as a more effective weapon with which to smite Antichrist.'[1]

There was heavy risk any way; yet on the whole it seemed less dangerous to advance than to retreat. The Council, after the arrival of Philip's letter, reconsidered the whole question, and concluded in an opinion which professed to be unanimous, that they had, as Norfolk said, gone too far to recede, and that they must now go forward at all hazards. 'The Queen of Scots, her husband, and the House of Guise, were the mortal enemies of the Queen's person;' 'so long as her Majesty and the Queen of Scots were alive, they would never permit her

---

[1] De Quadra to the Duchess of Parma, March 15; de Quadra to Philip, March 27.—*MS. Simancas.*

Majesty to live in assured peace;' and unless the French were driven wholly out of Scotland, she 'and all those who defended her title would be in continual danger.' The excuses, explanations, and promises which the French had offered, the Council 'disallowed, as false, foolish, and absurd, and not worth the hearing;' while the Guises' present difficulties were England's opportunity. The Scots if they were deserted after the engagement at Berwick would never more trust English promises. A French army would soon be reassembled; and when a general invasion was attempted on the northern Border —as without question it would be attempted—Elizabeth's advisers were obliged to say plainly 'they knew not how it should be repelled.' There was no real ground for suspecting the Scots of bad faith; they were ready to give hostages; and England could now obtain the object of its long desire in 'the assured and enduring alliance of the whole Scottish people.'[1]

Once more for a time indecision was at an end. A paper of measures was sketched by Cecil for the national defences, the first of which—characteristic of his simple piety—was 'to see the realm set in order with a clergy that the ire of God light not upon the people.'[2] Final orders to march were sent down to Berwick. The Queen in a brief proclamation explained the motives which had caused the step which she was about to take. She was still at peace and still intended to remain at peace, both with France and Scotland; she

---

[1] The Council to the Queen, March 23.—COTTON MSS. CALIG. B. 10. It is noticeable that a passage in the Address, describing the Scots as 'professing the same religion' with the English, is struck through with a pen as before. The handwriting is Cecil's.

[2] Memorial of matters to be considered, March 25.—Domestic MSS. Rolls House.

desired her subjects to commit no act of hostility against the French nation by land or sea; her quarrel was with the House of Guise, who in the minority of the King had persuaded their niece to usurp her title, and intended to crush the liberties of Scotland as a prelude to an attack upon herself. She had demanded redress, but she was unable to obtain it; and she was now driven to use force to compel the withdrawal of the French troops from Scottish ground.[1]

Monluc, should he be unable to prevent this decisive step from being taken, was instructed to go down to Scotland, and there, with bribes, entreaties, and threats of Spanish occupation, to work division among the Protestants; to gain time by an affectation of a wish to negotiate, and to direct d'Oysel to hold out till relief could reach him. As soon as he knew that the last orders were gone, Monluc hurried to Elizabeth to assure her that his Government would make larger concessions than any which had been yet proposed; if but a handful of troops might remain to save their honour, it would be enough: he said that he was empowered to arrange terms with the Regent, and he begged for a passport to go to her.

Catching at the thread of hope, Elizabeth sent him forward to the Border. She wrote again to Norfolk to settle the matter if possible without bloodshed—'being content, if the bishop spoke truly, to qualify her demand for an absolute evacuation.' The army should advance; and if force had to be used there should be no delay about it; but all other means should be tried first; and she added—not meaning it perhaps but only being in an ill-humour—that Winter's fleet had remained long

---

[1] Royal Proclamation, March 24.—BURLEIGH *Papers*, vol. I.

enough in the Forth; and that she was about to recall him.[1]

The Queen could scarcely have been unaware that the siege of a fortified seaport town by a land army unsupported by a fleet was the most unpromising of all undertakings.

The English army enters Scotland.

Meantime the English had entered Scotland. Norfolk and Sadler remained with the reserve at Newcastle; on Thursday the 28th of March, Lord Grey, accompanied by Sir James Crofts, Lord Scrope, Sir Henry Percy, and Maitland, crossed the Tweed with 6000 foot and 2000 horse. Keeping the old sea road which eleven years before he had travelled with Somerset, Grey moved on by easy marches. The country people received him with seeming welcome. 'Victuals' were brought into the camp 'as good and cheap as at Berwick.' There was a slight skirmish on Sunday with a party of French who were at Dunbar, but no one was killed; and the general reported that night 'that he had brought the army so far without loss of man, woman, child, horse, hag, or baggage.'

On the 4th of April the Congregation joined him at Preston Pans. He was more annoyed than surprised to find that they had engaged their men for but twenty days' service; that of these twenty days, dating from the day originally fixed for the English to enter, twelve had already expired; and that in a week the Scottish contingent would be reduced to a few noblemen and their household servants.

Grey proposes to seize Edinburgh Castle.

His heavy guns which were coming round by sea had not yet arrived, and while waiting for them he proposed to utilize the Scotch force by seizing Edinburgh Castle,

---

[1] The Queen to Norfolk, March 29.—BURLEIGH *Papers*, vol. i.

where the Queen Regent had taken refuge with Erskine. She was not expecting to be attacked; he believed the enterprise an easy one; and he sent back to Norfolk for advice. As to Leith, it was a large place, he said, elaborately fortified, with a garrison of 4000 men in it. As he had nothing to depend upon except his own troops, he found that he would require a stronger force, and he must have money also; he had hardly enough for himself, and 'all the Lords wanted to borrow.'[1]

The short supplies of money had been already made matter of remonstrance by Norfolk and Sadler. 'What,' wrote Sadler, 'is 20,000*l.*, more or less, in comparison with the enterprise in hand, and the union of the realms? What dishonour if the army return *re infectâ!*' 'Send money,' Norfolk wrote; 'English troops will not fight if they are not fed; if they are not paid their wages they must live by plunder and make enemies of the country people.'[2]

Far different had been the humour of the Scots when Grey last stood on the slopes of Preston Pans. There was no haggling then over terms of service when 30,000 men had sprung to arms to drive back the Saxon invader. The Saxon had come now as an invited friend, and they stood by—cold, doubting, and suspicious—ready to accept the service which England might do for them, and that was all.

Norfolk durst not sanction the scheme for taking the castle without the knowledge of Elizabeth. Elizabeth, to the disgust of Norfolk, who believed that Mary of Guise 'did more hurt than five hundred French,' forbade Grey

---

[1] Grey to Norfolk, April 4.—*Scotch MSS. Rolls House.*
[2] Sadler to Cecil, March 31.— SADLER *Papers*, vol. ii. Norfolk to Cecil, March 31.—DOMLEIGH *Papers*, vol. i.

to think of it.[1] The English commander was painfully contemplating Leith, and comparing it with the force which he had brought with him—when to increase his perplexity the order reached him which Elizabeth had sent with Monluc—either to compose matters without force or bloodshed, or else to finish the work at once, 'for the navy could not be suffered to remain.' He had come as a soldier to recover the honour which he had lost at Guisnes. It seemed likely that he would fail a second time, and more fatally than the first.

'The matter is confused,' he said, 'to proceed in this manner with force and treaty, and if the navy go, it had been better the army had never come to Scotland.'[2]

His spirits revived slightly the next day. He had sent a herald from Preston Pans with a demand in form for the dismissal of the French garrison. He had received no answer, and he moved forward to Restalrig a mile from Leith. The French horse came out and a skirmish had begun, when a tardy message came from the Castle intimating a desire to treat. Sir James Crofts and Sir George Howard went with a safe conduct to the Regent, and Grey rode forward to stop the fighting; he was received however with a volley of musket balls: there was a cry of treachery; the English cavalry charged led by young Tremayne who had come back from France for the campaign; and after a brilliant hand-to-hand fight the French were driven into Leith leaving a hundred of their number dead on the field.

Grey perhaps never prayed more heartily for any

---

[1] Norfolk to Cecil, April 19.—*Scotch MSS. Rolls House.*
[2] Grey to Norfolk, April 6.—*MS. Ibid.*

gift or grace than he prayed now that the blood drawn might end the talk of treaties. But his evil genius would not have it so. Sir George Howard had been a page of the old Duke of Guise and a playfellow in childhood of Mary of Lorraine; Crofts was secretly opposed to the war and half disloyal; the Regent understanding perfectly that her business was to gain time persuaded them that terms could be arranged; and Elizabeth's last orders seeming imperative, an armistice was agreed upon till Howard could go to London for instructions and return. The English army lay on their arms at Restalrig, and the question which had appeared at last to be coming to a clear issue was resumed into the dreary atmosphere of diplomacy.

CHAP III
1560
April

An armistice.

The eight days of the Scots' services were wasted in absolute inaction; the English troops lying idle became dissolute and careless; the French court was notoriously straining every nerve to equip a second expedition; while alarming reports were circulated among the Scots, that Philip's menaces had proved too strong for Elizabeth's courage. No sooner was Howard gone than Maitland—by far the most clear-sighted man in Scotland—thought it necessary to warn Cecil of the danger of an uncertain policy.

'The mark I do always shoot at,' Maitland wrote, 'is the union of these two kingdoms in perpetual friendship. There is no good in mine appearance to be wrought in this cause that doth not tend to that end. If we for fear of being destituted of your aid be enforced to any other appointment than this, in my opinion we be undone. Her Majesty hath proceeded too far if now anything make her Highness leave off. The treating doth stay a number of noblemen who were determined to join with

Irritation caused by Elizabeth's uncertainty.

us. I dare not write nor speak all I think in this case; but if the army should fail in the purpose they came for, or you should drive us to a doubtful appointment, I would wish her Majesty had not so far proceeded in it.'[1]

In the same spirit and with equal vexation Norfolk wrote that 'for every pound her Majesty saved by her present proceedings she would by and bye have to spend ten.' The work having been once undertaken must be gone through with, 'or the Lords of Scotland would be left as a prey to the enemy;' they would make the best peace they could for themselves, and 'in such sort as they with the French would needs become both enemies to England.'[2]

On arriving in London Sir George Howard found Elizabeth's humour changed again. The wish for a peaceful settlement had passed away, and she was ready to fight all Europe in the cause which she had undertaken.

Mission of the Seigneur de Glasion.

Following up his letter Philip the Second detained the English ambassadors in Spain, while he despatched to London the Seigneur de Glasion a Flemish nobleman and one of the Duchess of Parma's council to communicate his final pleasure. De Glasion was instructed to inform Elizabeth that the King of Spain was astonished and pained at her proceedings; that if her troops had crossed the Border she must immediately recall them, and she must abstain for the future from any kind of intervention in Scotland; while he himself would send an army there to restore order and deprive her of all excuse for uneasiness. If she refused she would be left to her fate.

---

[1] Maitland to Cecil, April 9 and April 10.—*Scotch MSS. Rolls House.*
[2] Norfolk to Cecil, April 10.—*MS. Ibid.*

If the French declared war against her, she must expect no support from him. He would perhaps feel it rather his duty to give open assistance to the Queen of Scots.[1]

Philip had contrived ingeniously to touch the chord which was certain to rouse Elizabeth to fury. To argument she was ready, often too ready, to listen; menace drove her at once into the course from which it was intended to deter her; while on the other hand if Philip's language was peremptory, the hand with which it was written was far from firm, and the ambassador who brought it far from acquiescent in its import. The Flemish ministers cared much for England and little for orthodoxy; and jealous of their own liberties, they were scarcely more anxious to see England occupied by Spanish troops than to let it become a prey of French ambition.

'M. de Glasion,' writes Cecil in his diary, 'came and joined with the Bishop of Aquila to move a revocation of the army out of Scotland, but Glasion privately to my Lord Admiral and me the Secretary counselled us to the contrary.'

Glasion's private advice was but an illustration of the uncertainty, distrust, and treachery which was under-running European diplomacy. To the old worldly-wise practitioner Doctor Wotton, Philip's conduct appeared 'very strange.' The greatness of the House of Burgundy he thought had risen from the steady preference of its princes for the English alliance, and if the King of Spain now intended to surrender England to France, he 'showed marvellous want of wisdom and he bore England no good will.'[2]

---

[1] Instructions to the Seigneur de Glasion, March 27.—TEULET, vol. ii.
[2] 'By likelihood, King Philip would be ready enough to maintain a good cause against us, that is so ready to pick this quarrel with us.'— *Wotton to Cecil, April,* 1560. *MSS. Rolls House.*

Philip's object however was not to help France, but to outwit both France and England; and France saw through his schemes, and on his own terms had no intention of accepting his assistance. Philip himself was haunted with the dread that when he had struck in and declared himself, the old Liberal party in France would recover their power and join England and the Reformation; while de Glasion warned de Quadra in secret 'that the Low Countries would in no wise endure a quarrel with England.'

'M. de Glasion is so suspicious of the French,' the Bishop said, 'that any excuse from these people seems to satisfy him, although he knows their bad hearts and corrupt intentions, and understands the dangers to which those provinces are exposed so long as this woman remains Queen.'[1]

De Sèvre, in a conversation with de Glasion and de Quadra, admitted that the French King and Queen had really intended to strike for the English Crown, that a plan had been formed to throw 12,000 men on the coast or across the Border; and although he pretended that the scheme had been abandoned, Philip's ministers concluded that it was only postponed, that the French would not listen to Spanish mediation, and that the presence of a Spanish force in Scotland would be utterly unwelcome.[2]

---

[1] De Quadra to the Bishop of Arras, April 13.—*MS. Simancas.*

[2] 'Ce qui nous fait ainsy juger, veu qu'ilz ne nous monstrent avoir volunté d'eulx ayder de l'assistance et faveur que sa Majesté leur a presenté, ny de nostre offre plusieurs fois à eulx fait, d'estre moyenneurs pour les accorder; demonstrant avecq le dict de Sèvre qu'il n'estime gueres nostre intervention et qu'elle luy est peu agréable; de sorte que ny l'ung ny l'autre des dictes parties ne feront rien par nostre moyen; dont il fait à douter que les affaires se conduiront de sorte que sa Majesté se pourroit cy

Elizabeth knew what the French felt, and gathered confidence from their embarrassment. She told de Glasion in his first interview that she 'regarded the Scotch insurgents as the best friends to their country.' She was convinced that whatever might be Philip's wishes he would be forced to leave his menaces unexecuted, that he was not the man to venture on those bold strokes of policy which are either ruinous or splendid successes.

It was still possible however that Alva and de Feria might overbear their master's timidity. The attempt might be made though it seemed unlikely; and it was necessary to resolve what to do. If a Spanish fleet should appear after all in the Forth, were the English to oppose the landing of Philip's troops? Cecil consulted Wotton, and Wotton showed by his reply that he felt the reality of the peril.

'If the Spaniards were once on shore in Scotland,' he said, 'the neutral Scots, already cold, would forsake England wholly,' and the cause of the Reformers would be lost.

If they came at all they would come 5000 or 6000 strong. If the English fleet attacked them it would probably be defeated; the army without the fleet would be lost, 'and what would ensue from that was easy to be considered.' Supposing the fleet victorious, 'it would not be without great bloodshed on both sides, the Spaniard being a brave and a superb soldier.' 'King Philip in anger and despite would declare open war, whereunto he would lack no council in Spain;' and with

---

après trouver bien empeschée pour les remedier; ou du moings qu'ils s'accorderont sans nous.'—M. de Gla-sion et l'Evesque de Aquila à la Duchesse de Parma, April 27. TEULET, vol. ii. p. 113, &c.

England already inclined to mutiny, 'the danger seemed so great that it was little wisdom to counsel the Queen's Highness to attempt it if by any other tolerable means it might be avoided.'[1]

Yet from private conversations and public discussions the improbability of any such step being taken by Philip became more and more apparent. Cecil threw in the 'Calais question,' which was certain to divide further the Flemings from the Spaniards. He suggested next that a joint commission of the three nations should be chosen to treat with the Scots. Forty days at least would be required to obtain the necessary powers for the commissioners; and in the mean time the siege of Leith could be continued and probably finished. De Glasion played up into the hands of the English ministers, and de Quadra poured himself out in distraction to Arras.

Troubles of the Bishop of Aquila.

'Be assured that the one object of these people—I have always warned you of it—is to embroil us with the French. I pray God that they may not succeed, and that their plot may not cause the destruction of the little that remains of Christendom. The French are growing angry and desperate. It is unlikely that they can come to terms with England; yet I do my best to avoid irritating them. This Queen has forty ships at sea well armed. The French fleet is getting ready, and should it unite with the English, Flanders is poorly defended. The farther this business goes the more difficulties multiply.'[2]

With the assistance of these glimpses into the inner

---

[1] Minute endorsed by Cecil to Doctor Wotton, touching the Scots, April, 1560.—*MS. Rolls House.*
[2] De Quadra to the Bishop of Arras, April 13.—*MS. Simancas.*

minds of men, the formal answer of the English Government to de Glasion becomes intelligible. Elizabeth's ministers had made up their minds to dare Philip to do his worst—being satisfied that the worst would be nothing very terrible—and the ambassador was invited to receive their final resolution.

Refusing to perceive the hostile tone of Philip's message, the Council said they were satisfied that he had been actuated by the kindest intentions, but that he was misinformed on the facts of the case. The French were aiming at England more than at Scotland, and at Elizabeth's Crown rather than at the maintenance of the Queen of Scots' authority in her own country. England could not wish that Spanish troops should interfere; the Queen of Scots required no foreign assistance to make her people loyal and obedient; they desired nothing beyond the mere observance of the laws of their country. King Philip's army, if transported thither, could not always remain. When it was withdrawn, the French would come back, and the difficulties would recommence. If England was to be secure, England must expel them; and the King of Spain's desire for the recall of Winter and Lord Grey could not and might not be complied with.[1]

Glasion accepted the reply which he had possibly assisted to frame; and de Quadra—distrusting both England and France and in turn by both distrusted, distrusting his colleague to whom he dared not communicate the views which he had urged on his master—was compelled to content himself with verbal protests. Monluc, who had been detained at Berwick out of respect to the remonstrances of the Scots, was allowed to go forward

---

[1] Reply to M. de Glasion.—FORBES, vol. I.

to the Queen Regent and do what he could to make peace; but meanwhile orders went down to press the siege.

De Sêvre had no commission to declare war; the French Government durst not venture it. He was instructed only if nothing could be done to protest to the Queen against the injustice of her proceedings; and he desired de Quadra and de Glasion to accompany him to her presence and witness the delivery of the message. The ministers of Philip might not countenance France without their master's leave—de Sêvre went alone—and Elizabeth, who was in one of her violent humours threw off the last affectation of concealment. Once more the weary ground of the Queen of Scots' misdoings was trodden over; then bursting out, she said,—

'You complain of the fleet and army which we have sent to Scotland. What were we to do? Have we forgotten, think you, your treachery at Ambletue, when our brother was king? You challenge our Crown; you deny our right to be Queen. You snatch the pretext of a rebellion to collect your armies on our Border; and you expect us to sit still like children. You complain that we sent our fleet to intercept your reinforcements. It is true we did so; and the fleet has done its work; and what then?

'Those cannon, those arms, those stores, which you sent to Leith were not meant only or chiefly for Scotland; they were meant for us. You tell us we are maintaining your rebels—we hate rebels; but the Scots are none. These men whom you call rebels are the same who fought against England at Pinkie Cleugh. It is you who are in fault—you who stole the rule of their country from them, overthrew their laws and sought to govern them with foreign garrisons. You have seized their fortresses, you have corrupted their money, you have filled their offices of trust with greedy Frenchmen, to rob and pillage them: and they endured all this till they saw their sovereign the childless queen of a foreign prince—herself an absentee—and their country, should she die, about to become a province of France.

'With these facts before us we are not to be blinded with specious words. We know what was intended for ourselves—some of your own statesmen have given us warning of it. Your Queen claims our Crown; and you think that we shall be satisfied with words. You say you recalled d'Elbœuf. The winds and the waves recalled him; and our fleet in the Forth frightened him from a second trial. You have given us promises upon promises; yet our style is still filched from us and your garrisons are still in Leith. We have forborne long enough. We mean nothing against your mistress's lawful rights: but events must now take their course.'[1]

Brave words, could they have been resolutely acted out; but it was a hard matter to carry on a war without declaring war, and to step out boldly in so dense a diplomatic mist.

Still however Spanish interference was declined, menace or no menace; and Philip was left to seek his remedy where he could find it.[2]

The siege of Leith was immediately to be pressed; and

---

[1] 'Responsum ad Protestationem quam Orator Regis Galliarum, nomine ad Principis Serenissimæ Angliæ Reginæ obtulit, April 15, 1560.' —TYTLER, vol. ii. p. 21, &c. The reply is very long, and I have condensed it much in the translation.

[2] To the delight of the English Protestants, who could not praise Cecil's firmness sufficiently. The most influential advocates of a Spanish policy were Lord Paget and Sir John Mason. 'The object of this letter,' wrote Lord John Grey to Cecil,

the complete departure of the French was again demanded, with the deposition of Mary of Lorraine from the Government, and the transfer of the regency to Chatelherault and a Council of the Lords. Cecil warned Lord Grey to beware of 'French enchantments,' and commended him to his work. Elizabeth desired Norfolk to pacify the Scots and assure them that she had never thought of making separate terms for herself.

The Scots distrust Elizabeth.

Unfortunately the contradictions in the Queen's language—her deliberate deceptions at one time—her indeliberate changes of purpose at another—had produced so deep a distrust in the Scots that until they saw Leith actually attacked they would not believe her. They were afraid—and perhaps justly—that if she could wrest from Mary Stuart a recognition of her own rights, she would not insist on the points which to them were of vital moment; and the permission to Monluc to go to Edinburgh neutralized the effect of the seeming firmness of her resolution. Maitland wrote to Cecil that the 'very talk' of a treaty paralyzed the energy of the people. He 'feared more deceit by treaty than the worst that could otherwise fall out;' and, so long as peace continued to be spoken of, the Scotch nobles would continue to believe that the Queen intended to betray them.[1] Even in the English

---

[1] 'Is to make you understand the good opinions which godly Protestants have conceived of you, in your stout and wise standing for the maintenance of God's cause, the defence of your country and the surety of your sovereign. God confound all Pagetyan devices with Mason and all his fellows. Such arch-practicians against God and their country were never bred in any country; and be you well assured cousin Cecil that neither the Queen's Majesty you nor never an honest-minded man in England shall have his head on his shoulders if those practices may take place.'—*Lord John Grey to Cecil, April, 1560. Domestic MSS. Rolls House.*

[1] Maitland to Cecil, April 17.—*Scotch MSS. Rolls House.*

army itself, there were men who considered they could best please Elizabeth by inaction—who were jealous of the Scots, or opposed to the policy of supporting them. Sir James Crofts, who was afterwards found 'to have gone as near the edge of treason as a man might do without falling into it,' wrote that the Congregation were careless of England; that they would play Elizabeth false unless she would promise to marry the Earl of Arran; and that if she was prudent she would shift for herself.[1] The Duke of Norfolk forwarded Crofts' letter to London, with copy of his own answer;[2] and entreated Cecil to procure a direct 'forbidding of the treaty,' and an immediate order to assault Leith. It was not so hard to win: 'Winter's sailors had said that if they might have the spoil, they would enter it or die there for.'[3]

It was time for something to be done. The inactivity among the leaders had already produced dangerous carelessness among the English troops. The French force was divided. A hundred and sixty men with seventy

---

[1] Crofts to Norfolk, April 26.—*Scotch MSS. Rolls House.*

[2] 'As you, Mr. Crofts, have written unto me your mind concerning your treaty, so will I requite you with the like, being of a quite contrary opinion unto you; for whereas by your letter it doth appear that you think the treaty most convenable to us, for my part I think it most to be eschewed; for we may hope for no long amity if either the Scots suffer the Queen Dowager to be Regent, or else to have any number of French in any one fort there. I cannot induce myself to think but that the French, if they have once footing in Scotland, will soon have out of France as many as they list, when we neither shall nor dare help. The matter with delaying cannot amend. We shall never have the French at such advantage again.

'Therefore, good Mr. Crofts, hasten your business, which shall be far more honourable and surer for the Queen's Majesty and both the realms, and banish yourselves out of that cursed deanery of Restalrig, which keeps you so long from coming into the camp. Let not Martigues brag and say the Queen's army is come to besiege Restalrig.' — *Norfolk to Crofts, April,* 1560. *MS. Ibid.*

[3] Norfolk to Cecil.—*MS. Ibid.*

women and boys were in Inchkeith, cut off by Winter's fleet from the mainland. They had nothing to eat but the fish which they could catch from the rocks, and the oysters and periwinkles which they gathered at low water; and as famine would soon compel them to surrender, the Admiral would not squander valuable life in assaulting them. Another detached company in Blackness capitulated on Easter Sunday the 14th of April. A few hundreds were isolated in Dunbar. The main body, French and French Scots, amounting together to 4000 men, with d'Oysel himself, Labross, and de Martigues, were shut up within the lines of Leith. Though blockaded effectually by sea, they had gathered provisions which were calculated variously as likely to last till June, July, or August, and by July at latest Mouluc had promised them relief.

The fortifications were a mile in extent, and were drawn according to the best engineering science of the day. There was an ample supply of heavy guns, collected gradually with a view to the campaign in England, and there were other military stores in abundance, intended for the army which d'Elbœuf had failed to bring over. The French part of the garrison were choice troops who had been seasoned in the Italian wars.

The English army lay in what Norfolk called 'the accursed deanery of Restalrig,' under Arthur's Seat, and with Leith at a mile's distance immediately below them. The siege guns were mounted as they arrived; and shots at long range were exchanged from day to day; but in general, a spirit of languor had taken possession of the scene. The English soldiers believed that they had been sent to Scotland rather as a menace than for work. There was little discipline among them; they lounged about unarmed in the streets of Edinburgh; they passed their time over dice and cards, 'calling upon God with nothing but swearing.'[1] The very neighbourhood of an enemy seemed to have been forgotten—so entirely were the commonest precautions neglected. A rough lesson brought them to a recollection of their position. On the 14th of April a party of French disguised as women entered the English works, and walked over them and round them; they killed a sentinel who had perhaps discovered them, and carried off his head as an ornament to a pinnacle of Leith church. The next day the garrison poured out in a swarm, cut up the pioneers in the trenches, spiked the cannon, and took Sir Maurice Berkeley—who was the first to come to the rescue—prisoner. Arthur Grey, Captain Vaughan, and others, each as they could collect their companies, rushed to the front in time to save the guns; but the French would not retreat till half the English army was brought into the field. 'It was one of the hottest skirmishes ever seen.' Arthur Grey, who in his haste had not taken time to put on his corselet, was shot through the shoulder; Sir Bryan Fitzwilliam was badly wounded; and the English themselves admitted a loss of a hundred and sixty men.

'I hope,' wrote Norfolk, in his report of the affair, 'that this will be a lesson to them that have the charge there to keep their men out of Edinburgh.'

Close on this surprise followed letters from Elizabeth, ordering the more active prosecution of the siege; and the discovery of Monluc's double dealing brought the talk of negotiation at last to an end. Monluc had told Elizabeth that it was England which he desired to satisfy. In

---

[1] Norfolk to Cecil, May 15.—*Scotch MSS. Rolls House.*

Scotland, his only effort had been to work on the distrust of the Scots. The Queen Regent in concert with him offered the lords all that they could desire; she promised to send away the French; she would guarantee them liberty of conscience; she herself would soon cease to be an obstacle—confinement and anxiety had done their work upon her—she was sickening of the dropsy, and her days in this world she well knew were numbered; the regency therefore would present no difficulty; but she insisted that they should abandon the English alliance; the Queen of Scots could not suffer her subjects to be in league with a foreign power.

It was to the credit of the Scots that they refused these overtures. Chatelherault, Maitland, and Lord James Stuart, at the close of a long conference, consented only to refer the alliance to the Parliament. The Bishop's temptation failed. He withdrew to Berwick; and the knot was then so hard drawn that it could be cut only by the sword.[1]

At last therefore Lord Grey was free to exert himself. The treaty which had lain upon his energies like lead was at an end.

On Tuesday the 16th of April 3000 additional troops under Sir Ralph Sadler arrived from Berwick; a second siege train was landed from the ships; the lines were pushed forward 'on the east side of the town;' and

---

[1] 'The Bishop is gone. The parley broke up on the Article of the League with England, for that they would not revoke their hostages. They would have put the matter to the Parliament. They are gone so far they cannot go out of it; whereof I will make my profit and will not fail to publish it. I am still lame, and have a leg that assuageth not from swelling. If any lan his finger upon it, it goeth in as into butter; you know there are but three days for the dropsy in this country.'— *Intercepted Letter from the Queen Dowager to d'Oysel*, April, 1560. *MS. Rolls House*.

notwithstanding incessant sallies of the French, a battery was placed within six hundred yards of the walls.

St. Anthony's steeple on which guns had been mounted was brought rapidly to the ground. Unable from want of numbers to enclose the whole French lines, Grey threw up works at intervals along the south and south-west. The main body of the army moved from Restalrig to the southern angle—virtually completing the blockade. Boats could still creep into the harbour on dark or stormy nights; but the supplies which could be thrown in thus were inconsiderable. When the stores within the walls were exhausted, d'Oysel if unrelieved must surrender.

Skirmishes went on daily, in which the English were generally successful, penetrating occasionally into the French defences. Grey's spirits rose with success. He complained that with the exception of half a dozen Protestant noblemen, he could find no Scot to serve with him even for wages; but the fall of the town he considered certain and not distant.

Elizabeth after Monluc's departure changed her mind about Edinburgh Castle, and sent word that if Grey still wished it, he might attempt its capture; but the opportunity was passed. The siege of Leith having now been begun in form, must be finished before anything else was undertaken.[1]

Day and night the English batteries flashed and roared. On the evening of the 30th the town was observed to be on fire. Fanned by a fresh breeze, the blaze rose into the sky, lighting up the masts and spars of Winter's fleet, and throwing its red glare on the walls and chimneys of Edinburgh. The English skirmishers to assist

---

[1] Grey to Norfolk, April 30.—*MS. Rolls House.*

the confusion, attacked the enemy's lines; and amidst the shouts of action and the roar of the artillery, Grey sat in his tent writing an exulting despatch to Norfolk. A third part of Leith was in ashes ere he closed his letter. The flames shot up again as he was writing the last words, and an eager postscript added—'Yet it burns—yet—yet.'[1]

The French however rose above their difficulties with a spirit which was beyond praise. When day broke the next morning, as if to mock the hopes of the besiegers, there were Maypoles standing on the walls, and May garlands festooned above the trenches. The English guns tore open breaches; but the defences rose again as if by magic. Elizabeth impatient of the expense believed that the soldiers were intentionally dilatory, and wrote in anger and impatience; yet the longer Grey looked at the French works, the less he liked the prospect of assaulting them. He preferred to trust 'to spade and mattock:' 'his powers were far too weak;' should he attempt to storm and fail, he 'saw not that he should be able to make a second trial,' and might be forced to raise the siege with dishonour.

But the blockade though sure was slow and costly. Even Norfolk was inclined to think that there was a want either of energy or of skill. 'My Lord Grey's service,' he wrote to Cecil, 'doth consist but upon courage without conduct; every man that can lead a band of horsemen is not fit for so great an enterprise.'[2] It was remembered that Grey had lost Guisnes; and to himself the Duke wrote even more painfully, almost accusing him of timidity—and taunting him with being delayed

---

[1] Grey to Norfolk.—*MS. Rolls House.*
[2] Norfolk to Cecil.—*MS. Ibid.*

so long before a sandbank. Grey himself was perhaps in fault, yet not as Norfolk supposed; and there were other and far worse offenders. Systematic fraud was carried on in the army, particularly in Sir James Crofts' division. The numbers were not what they were pretended to be: the soldiers had deserted by hundreds; to conceal their carelessness, a false return was sent in by the captains—and wages continued to be drawn for more than three thousand men who had left the camp.[1]

A competent commander should have detected so large a deficiency; but there were so many crooked influences at work, so many cross purposes, such shifting orders, such vacillation of policy, that a plain blunt soldier like Grey might well have been perplexed into worse mistakes.

Driven forward however by Elizabeth's reproaches, and stung by Norfolk's taunts, the general found himself compelled against his judgment to run the risk of an assault. The weather had been foul, the nights wet cold and stormy. The English troops which were young and unused to exposure, had suffered heavily from the extended trench duty to which their numbers were unequal. Even for the blockade they would now require reinforcements, while a *coup de main* might perhaps succeed and end the siege. On the 6th of May the batteries seemed to have broken an available opening in the works. A general storm by land and sea was resolved on in a council of war for the following morning. In the evening, after all had been settled, Sir Ralph Sadler, William Kirkaldy, and Crofts, went

---

[1] 'Your Majesty is charged at this time for 8813 footmen, and there are not 5000 serving in the camp; so that your Majesty is monstrously robbed.'—*Report of Sir Peter Carew, May 28.* BURLEIGH *Papers*, vol. i.

CHAP III
1560
May

The English attempt to storm Leith and are repulsed.

forward to examine the ground. It was dusk, but as well as they could see the breaches were extremely dangerous if not wholly impracticable. They agreed that the attack must be deferred; and Sadler and Kirkaldy went to their tents, leaving Crofts going as they supposed to Grey to report their opinion.

For some reason which was never known, the original order was maintained. A thousand Scots had been brought in the day before by the Earl of Argyle, whom it was perhaps thought well to make use of before they scattered again; and in the morning twilight between two and three, the whole English line advanced.

On reaching the point where the breaches ought to have been, they found themselves encountered by a deep broad trench, beyond which stood a stone wall scarcely injured, with the approaches swept by flanking towers.

Careless of the works which they saw before them, the men leaped into the ditches and attempted to scale, but the ladders were six feet too short. Scrambling helplessly on the upright masonry, they soon found that they were trying an impossibility, and as they fell at the foot of the wall, they were overwhelmed with shot, stone, and blazing pitch. 'The Frenchmen's harlots'—Scotch women of the town—swarmed on the battlements, loading the guns, rolling tar-barrels or carrying scalding water. So ill had the arrangements been made, that though Sir James Crofts was responsible for the assault, he did not himself come to time, and his division was not present. For two hours the storming party struggled desperately, at the mercy of enemies whom they could not reach. Some few even found their way into the town and persuaded themselves that if Crofts had done his duty they might after all have succeeded; but more probably it was a mismanaged and entirely hopeless business from the first.

The dying Mary of Lorraine had been carried from her bed to the walls of the Castle to watch the fight. As the sun rose out of the Forth, she saw the English columns surge like the sea waves against the granite ramparts, and like the sea waves, fall shattered into spray.

After half the officers engaged had fallen, and eight hundred men lay dead and wounded in the trenches, the bugles sounded a recall and the unavailing carnage was ended.

All was now panic. The Scots in Edinburgh made haste to wash their hands of allies of whose success they now despaired; they refused even to give houseroom to the wounded and left them to die in the streets.[1] 'The soldiers were so feared,' that at once to check desertion ten days' pay was advanced throughout the camp. At first the number lost was thought to be terrible, for the delinquent captains caught the opportunity to cover their frauds, and reported men as dead who had not existed save on the muster-roll. A few days shrunk the estimate below a thousand; yet so far from feeling equal to a second attempt, Grey doubted whether he could continue in the field, and it was even proposed to send the siege guns for safety on board the fleet.

Norfolk, when the news reached Newcastle, on his own responsibility sent off two thousand men—the whole of his reserve—and wrote to the Court, pressing for instant reinforcements, 'or the matter would quail.' One only comforting symptom was reported: the French were running short of food, and if the blockade could be sustained, success at last might still be hoped for.

---

[1] Sir George Howard to Norfolk, May 7.—*MS. Rolls House.*

Grey therefore clung tenaciously to his ground, dreading only that he might be driven from it before assistance could reach him, or that the army might rebel and insist on a retreat.

Weakness of the English army.

'If the French knew how weak we are,' wrote Sadler, 'it might be dangerous to us. Many fall sick, many daily and nightly steal away, or run from us. Those which remain are so wearied with watch and ward, that they and their captains murmur and grudge at it; and it is rather to be feared that they will mutiny and leave us in the field, than to be hoped that any good service is to be looked for at their hands.'[1] The cowardly inhumanity of the Edinburgh citizens was supposed to foretell the general apostasy of the Congregation; and the Regent again offered them every concession which they could ask, if they would relinquish the English alliance. Maitland happily supported by Lord James Stuart and Ruthven, had influence enough for the present to keep his party true to their promises;[2] and a day or two later the two thousand men sent from Newcastle arrived, to allay the panic and restore order and confidence.

But how would Elizabeth endure to hear that her army had been defeated, that the assault which she had insisted on in her impatience of the expense had failed, that she must now either increase her force and submit to an indefinite protraction of the enterprise, or recede with dishonour upon the support of her Spanish brother-in-law?

Amidst the cross purposes and intentional falsehoods, with the difficulty of distinguishing between the Queen's

---

[1] Sadler to Norfolk, May 11.—*MS. Rolls House.*
[2] Maitland to Cecil, May 14.—*MS. Ibid.*

own views and those expressed in letters which were written in her name under Cecil's influence, her personal opinions are throughout hard to discover. She was still so young, her temperament was so singular a compound of self-confidence and irresolution, the position itself was so difficult, and the opinions of her most experienced advisers were so widely divided, that she must have yielded from the first with some reluctance to Cecil's guidance. Nay there is reason to think that even before the defeat her mind misgave her, and that her purpose had required to be sustained by a restatement of the grounds on which the Scotch expedition had been attempted.[1]

When the bad news came, her Majesty 'renewed the opinions of Cassandra.'[2] 'God,' wrote Cecil to Throgmorton, 'trieth us with many difficulties. The Queen's Majesty never liketh this matter of Scotland; you know what hangeth thereupon—weak-hearted men and flatterers follow that way.'[3] 'She mindeth,' Cecil continued in his ordinary hand, 'she mindeth so earnestly as nothing shall be spared: order is given to send both men, money, and artillery, with all possible speed!' But he added in cipher, 'I have had such a torment herein with the Queen's Majesty as an ague hath not in five fits so much abated me.'[4] A week later her humour was not improved. On the 22nd of May Cecil again wrote that

---

[1] There is a paper in the Rolls House, endorsed in Cecil's hand, 'A Memorial for the Queen's Majesty,' and dated the 5th of May, in which the arguments for the war were drawn out with great power and clearness.—*Domestic MSS.*, ELIZ., vol. xiii. There was nothing in these however which had not been said many times before, and it is difficult to guess why such a memorial should have been required.

[2] Killigrew to Throgmorton, May 13.—FORBES, vol. i.

[3] Lord Robert Dudley especially, who dreaded Arran's rivalry.

[4] Cecil to Throgmorton, May 13 1560.—FORBES, vol. I.

'she was so evil disposed to the matter, that it troubled them all.'[1]

Fortunately the Council whatever their general policy, were unanimous in determining that it was now impossible to recede, and that every effort must be made to repair the disaster. Norfolk, the most unwilling to consent to the expedition, was the loudest to insist on supporting it. The old Marquis of Winchester, who was more than half a Catholic, concluded that 'worldly things would sometimes fall out contrary, but if quietly taken could be quietly amended;' it was idle to lament for what could not be recalled, and 'misfortunes should increase the Queen's courage to apply the revenge.'[2]

Lord Clinton reminded Cecil that 'the French were a nation of soldiers,' who of course 'would stand to their defence for a first assault.' Their expulsion out of Leith could not be effected without loss of men; and if the Queen was irritated, she must be told the truth. 'If the French have the upper hand in Scotland,' he said; 'if that come to pass which God defend, then all the wars and plagues that ever were to this realm in our days and our fathers', will be found but a fleabiting in comparison of the dangers and griefs that will be felt in all good Englishmen's hearts.'[3]

Clinton went down to Portsmouth to hurry the reserve fleet to sea. Orders were sent round the shore to call out the musters, trim the beacons, and draft contingents for the northern army. Ten thousand men in a few weeks would assemble at Newcastle, and Norfolk undertook to lead them in person to Edinburgh. To

---

[1] Cecil to Throgmorton, May 22.—FORBES, vol. I.
[2] The Marquis of Winchester to Cecil, May 12.—*Domestic MSS. Rolls House.*
[3] Clinton to Cecil, May 12.—*MS. Ib.*

prevent disturbance at home the ex-bishops were ordered into stricter confinement; the notorious Catholic families were placed under stricter surveillance; Sir James Crofts was deprived of his command and sent to London to answer for himself; and courage was restored in the camp.

Better news too came from Spain. On the first reception of Elizabeth's answer, Philip had talked loudly of the necessity of sending a Spanish force into Scotland; the French asked for them, he said, and he had no excuse for refusing. A singular story too, whether true or false, reached the ears of the English ambassadors: the Emperor's minister at Madrid gave them warning that another conspiracy was on foot to murder Elizabeth and Lord Robert Dudley; while to end all quarrels, Don Carlos was to marry a sister of the French King, and the British Isles were to be partitioned between France and Spain.[1]

But the acute and suspicious Philip could scarcely have conceived as yet so wild an enterprise; and the French, although they desired the promise of Spanish assistance as something which might frighten Elizabeth, yet dreaded the reality as much as the English themselves.[2] So far as Philip had a distinct intention—it was to revolutionize England; and in proposing to land an army in Scotland, he spoke truly when he said they

---

[1] Montague and Chamberlain to the Queen, April 29; decipher.—*Spanish MSS. Rolls House.*

[2] 'Franceses han trabajado y trabajan por cuantas vias pueden sirviendose de la fama de Nra asistencia y teniendo muy poca gana de usar della.'—*De Quadra to the Count de Feria, May 23.*

Even Spanish mediation was not really welcome.

'Nous presupposons bien que vostre Majesté sorra aussi advertie que les Françoises en nulle sorte du monde ont intention de traicter et vult appointer effectuellement avec ladicte Royne par le moyen et intercession de vostre Majesté.'—*De Quadra and de Glasion to Philip II., June 7. MS. Simancas.*

would act as much against the French as for them. The Duke of Alva angrily told the English ambassadors that as the Queen had made her bed, so she must lie on it; she had been warned 'against innovations, either in religion or otherwise, to the misliking of the world;' but she would listen to no advice, and must take the consequence of her folly. But when Chamberlain pressed for his secret opinion, the Duke briefly quoted the Spanish proverb—'If thy enemy be in water to the girdle, lend thy hand to help him out; if he be in to the shoulders, hold on him and keep him down;'—meaning, as the ambassador understood him, 'If the Queen be strong enough to drive the French out of Scotland, let her do it without asking further counsel or aid.'[1]

The Spanish army is recalled from the Netherlands.

Such uncertainty as might remain on the proceedings of the Spaniards was soon at an end. In the beginning of June news came that the Spanish fleet in the Mediterranean had been destroyed by the Turks; and Philip, whose object was to restore his[2] ruined finances, recalled his army in the Netherlands to Spain, and relinquished for the moment the thought of interference in the British Isles.

'Let her Majesty proceed,' wrote Sir Thomas Gresham, 'and her Highness will bring her subjects and the realm in like estimation as heretofore hath been. A God's name, put to with all the powers ye may, recover the name and credit that England hath had in times past, and that was that England had the best men of war by land and sea that was in all Christendom, for the which

---

[1] Montague and Chamberlain to the Queen, May 19.—*Spanish MSS. Rolls House.*

[2] 'Where her Majesty oweth one million of ducats, King Philip and the French King oweth each of them twenty millions.'—*Gresham to Sir T. Parry, June 16.—Flanders MSS. Ibid.*

all princes feared England. King Philip sends the
Queen word that he will help the French King to subdue
the Scots. They urge another way here and say that
King Philip shall be fain to seek to her Majesty for succour, saying that God is such a God; and they say
openly that God hath blessed her Majesty for her religion's sake, and plagues all other princes for their papistry
and idolatry.'[1]

Everywhere notwithstanding the defeat events were
working in favour of England. The Guises went about
in daily fear of murder. The Cardinal of Lorraine
travelled in a coach mounted with falconets. Thirty
thousand Huguenots were expected to rise in open
rebellion, 'to put down the House of Guise or lose their
lives.' Sir Nicholas Throgmorton had dug his mine
below the schemes of the Queen of Scots and her kinsmen, and instead of leading a victorious army to London
they were soon to have a struggle for existence at their
own doors.

No aid from France could reach the doomed garrison
at Leith, for all their gallantry; and as the English
lines once more closed up, M. de Randan came over to
London to be joined in commission with the Regent,
Monluc, d'Oysel, and Labross, to make the best terms
they could. De Randan's instructions were vague; his
powers were not openly avowed; he was still if possible
to cause divisions between the English and the Scots; he
was forbidden at all hazards to recognize their alliance
as legitimate; engineers came in his train disguised as
his servants, to survey the works of Berwick, and to
assist at Leith. Yet in case of extremity he was em-

---

[1] Gresham to Cecil.—MS. Rolls House.

powered to surrender the town and agree to a peace, reserving only the allegiance of the Scots to the daughter of James the Fifth.

On the 17th of May the Regent wrote to d'Oysel to inquire how long he could hold out. The letter was written in cipher on the pocket-handkerchief of an adventurer who attempted to steal with it through the English lines.[1] Failing to communicate with him thus, Mary of Guise professed to desire medicine from a physician who was in Leith. She sent her application to Grey, and requested him to forward it. Grey held the letter to the fire. The invisible ink turned black, and the real contents appeared. He threw it into the fire, bidding the messenger 'tell his mistress that he would keep her counsel, but that such wares would not sell till a new market.'

The French in Leith grow distressed.

The neutrals, seeing the English determined, began to perceive what the end would be, and to declare themselves more decisively. The French troops were reduced to sixteen ounces of bread for each man daily, with a slice of salt salmon. The conclusion in spite of their victory could not be far off, and de Randan found that he would be compelled to negotiate in earnest. The raising of troops in England was not intermitted for a day. The terms which could be exacted depended on the strength of the new army of reserve.

As the war had been Cecil's, Cecil was appointed commissioner to end it. Cecil, Sadler, Wotton, Sir Henry Percy, and Sir Peter Carew were chosen to meet de Randan and the Bishop of Valence at Newcastle; if the French ministers required the assistance of the Regent and d'Oysel, they were to go on in a body to Edinburgh.

---

[1] Intercepted Letter of the Queen Regent.—*MS. Scotland*, ELIZ.

Reluctant to leave London, yet unable to refuse, Cecil accepted his nomination with painful misgiving. Had he felt sure of Elizabeth, he would have gone with confidence, knowing that no one could do better than he what the Queen's service required. As it was, 'the journey,' he said, 'appeared to him very strange.' 'He feared the success, because the Queen's Majesty was so evil disposed.' 'His friends in the Council thought it convenient that he should go;' his friends abroad 'thought that he was betrayed to be sent from the Queen's side.' He was obliged to warn Throgmorton 'to write circumspectly, for how he should be judged of in his absence he knew not;'[1] while Sir Henry Killigrew wrote that 'the worst interpretation was placed on Cecil's departure;' Pembroke, Clinton, and Norfolk were true to him, but 'other friends he had none;' 'I know,' Killigrew added significantly, 'I know that none can love their country better than Mr. Cecil: I would the Queen's Majesty could love it so well.'[2]

The management of the treaty, and the responsibility of the treaty alike were left to him. The defeat still weighed upon the court and the courtiers. In one of many ways, the object for which he was contending was expected to be snatched from him, and his disgrace would follow on his failure.

The conditions which he intended to demand were limited to the points which Elizabeth's safety required. The English and French troops alike should withdraw from Scotland: a handful of French might remain, but no more. He meant to ask for the restoration of Calais, on the plea that the treaty of Cambray had

---

[1] Cecil to Throgmorton, May 22 and May 27.—FORBES, vol. I.
[2] Killigrew to Throgmorton, May 28.—Ibid.

been broken; but he did not mean to insist upon it. He would require the Queen of Scots to relinquish the arms of England, and to signify formally that she abandoned her pretensions to Elizabeth's throne; yet even here he was so anxious to secure the essentials of peace that he would content himself with something general and vague. The government of Scotland might be settled between the French and the Scots; with that he did not propose to interfere; but he should require the King and Queen of France, as an absolute condition of the treaty, to promise liberty of conscience to their subjects.[1] Liberty of conscience would follow necessarily on the departure of the French army.

To secure these objects, Cecil, sick at heart for what might happen in his absence, set out on the 30th of May for the north. One more article he was prepared to require, which would be the hardest of all to extort. He would agree to no treaty in which the alliance between England and the Lords of the Congregation should not in some form or other be recognized; while de Randan privately assured de Quadra that sooner than admit the right of their subjects to make a league with a foreign prince, his master and mistress would lose Scotland altogether.'[2] The French would make any concession however extravagant to the Scots themselves, if they could separate them from the English, and save their

---

[1] In the first draft of 'the articles to be demanded,' 'The English,' it was said, 'shall intercede with the French to grant liberty of conscience in Scotland, and suspend the action of the laws.' Cecil altered this in his own hand into—

'The English Commissioners shall press for liberty of conscience; and if it is refused, they shall break off the treaty.'—*Instructions to Sir William Cecil. Scotch MSS.* ELIZ., *Rolls House.* Though the articles are in the form of instructions, they appear to have been determined by Cecil himself from the changes which he felt himself authorized to introduce into them.

[2] De Quadra to Philip, June 7.—*MS. Simancas.*

Queen from the ignominy of admitting Elizabeth to a share in her subjects' allegiance.

No sooner was Cecil gone than the influences which he most dreaded were brought to bear upon Elizabeth. Incessantly on the watch to assail her in her weaker moments, the smooth-tongued de Quadra was charged with a message to her from the Pope. It had been resolved at a meeting of the Cardinals to treat her errors with paternal kindness, instead of letters of interdict and excommunication to send the Abbot of St. Saviour's who had been one of Pole's chaplains, to confer with her; and de Quadra was commissioned to win a promise from her to receive him. How the message was accepted, with much else on the Queen's general humour, the ambassador tells for himself.

Margin: CHAP III. 1560 May. De Quadra desires Elizabeth to receive a nuncio from the Pope.

DE QUADRA TO THE BISHOP OF ARRAS.[1]

London, June 3.

'The commissioners are gone. The Queen expects that the French cannot relieve Leith, and that famine will force the garrison to surrender. The French on their side are as confident as she. They believe that they can make terms with the insurgents, and go on with their other projects. For myself I think the chances are with the French; the garrison I know is in difficulties; but they will have leisure to arrange their quarrel with the Scots, and will offer them separate conditions which they will accept. It is in fear of this that Cecil has been sent. I spoke to the Queen two days ago, and she could not conceal her uneasiness from me. She was neither so bitter nor so suspicious as I have lately found her. If she succeed in her wild projects of embroiling us

---
[1] *MS. Simancas.*

with France, and of making one monarchy out of this island, she will care nothing for us; but in case she fail she desires to keep on terms with our King, who if her Catholic subjects rebel, may be able to pacify them for her.

'These last she is arresting right and left. I told her she was treating them cruelly and wickedly. She said they were conspiring to make a revolution: she could show me proofs of it; and those who had appeared the most sanctified were the worst.

'It has become too plain that neither menace can terrify her nor kindness win her confidence. I employ a tone with her therefore in which I can point out her mistakes, and show her the mischief which may rise from her chimerical policy, without driving her into a passion. I do not blame her: I lay the fault on her advisers. I have told her that at the beginning of her reign she ought to have strengthened herself with a prudent marriage; she should have looked for alliances abroad, she should have attended to her revenues, and have engaged officers to train her subjects in the art of war.

'She thought I was alluding to that first great offer of ours which she refused. She said she was well aware of the greatness of the King our sovereign; the world had not another such match to offer; but she had no wish to marry — she hated the thought of it; her greatest happiness would be to live and die a virgin. As to the Archduke, she had given the Count Helfestcyn an answer with which he ought to have been satisfied; and the person in fault in this matter was the old gentleman,[1] who would not let his son come to England.

---

[1] 'Aquel viejo'—meaning the Emperor.

'I told her she must be perfectly aware that I could
not believe that. I knew too much about the Earl of
Arran and her scheme for the union of the realms.

'She pretended to be very angry, and protested that
she had no intentions of the kind.

'Speaking of the war, I said she had been wrong in
quarrelling with the French; she knew that she might
have perfect confidence in his Majesty; and his Majesty
—as M. de Glasion had told her—was ready to send
troops of his own to Scotland, to spare her every reason
for alarm. The Scots were a miserable bankrupt people,
engaged in a scandalous rebellion, and inveterately hostile to England.

'We talked long. I silenced her; but she remained
unconvinced and unchanged. At last she said the past
could not be cured.

'Her object in pressing matters to extremity has been
to divide us from France. If she fail, she leaves a door
open to recover her seat and her stirrups with the help
of his Majesty. She is now aware that she cannot light
up a continental war again; but she still hopes to expel
the French from the island, and to unite the realms;
and till she is undeceived on this point also, she will
never confess the truth. Her conviction is that the
Low Countries will not endure to be at war with England, and that his Majesty for his own sake will be
forced to continue her friend.

'Leaving these matters we talked of the mission of
the Abbot of St. Saviour's from the Pope. She seemed
surprised, and remembering the humour of the Catholics
even alarmed.

'I said his Holiness being a wise prince and a loving
father to all his children, could have no object save to
give her paternal admonition and advice. I thought

perhaps the mission had originated in a suggestion of the King our sovereign, who always hoped that a woman so gifted and so wise would find a way to reunite her subjects with the Universal Catholic Church. His Majesty I knew had expressed this conviction to the Pope, to obviate the designs of the French; and the Pope perhaps wished to ascertain her real feelings.

'She was evidently pleased; she was afraid that his Majesty had withdrawn his support from her at Rome, and a declaration of the Pope against her at this moment, she knows would be most unseasonable. For this reason she went on to tell me that she was as good a Catholic as I was. She called God to witness that her belief was the belief of all Catholics in the realm.

'I said that if this was true she had done wrong in dissembling against her conscience on a question of so vast importance. She had committed a crime against her poor subjects, who had been led by her example to desert their religion. Her very honour was touched by it.

'She replied that she had been compelled at the time to act as she did, and that if I knew how she had been driven to it she was sure I should excuse her.

'I said nothing could excuse her; or if circumstances were conceivable which might palliate such conduct, they had not existed in her case. As the realm stood when she succeeded to the crown, she might have kept religion as her sister left it, with far less trouble and danger to herself.[1]

---

[1] 'Consolóse mucho á esto, porque cierto ella temia que su Mag'd hubiese alzado la mano de su proteccion en Roma, y sabe que le vendria muy á mala sazon cualquiera declaracion que el Papa biciese en su negocio..... y con este placer vinó a decirme que era tan Catolica como yo, y que hacia á Dios testigo de que lo que ella creia no era diferente de lo que todos los Catolicos de su Reyno creian.

'Dijela que como disimulaba en

'In the end I pretended to believe what she said; and I made much of it, that she might find a difficulty hereafter in extricating herself from her words, which assuredly she will try to do when her present alarms are over.

'I brought her to say that the nuncio which the Pope was sending should be welcome, and that it should not be her fault if the Church was not united again.

'If I had pressed for a more distinct promise, I believe she would have given it; but her words are not her thoughts. I am as convinced as ever that her real intentions are what I have before described them; but I am astonished at the effrontery with which, on such grave subjects, she will say whatever is convenient for the moment.

'After all however she is a woman and inconstant; and she may one day be compelled to do what now she pretends to be willing to do.

'I affected to believe her and even to appear in some degree satisfied with her. Had I shown her that I saw through her, I should have driven her to animosity and obstinacy. We parted better friends than usual. It is idle to threaten; I may not go beyond my commission; and by keeping up appearances with her however false, and by pretending to be her friend, I am able to tell her

---

cosa desta calidad contra su conciencia y contra la de los pobres subditos que por su ejemplo dejaban la religion verdadera y contra su honor proprio que padeceria grandemente haciendo mudanzas en cosa en que no se sufria hacerla la menor del mundo.

'Respondióme que era forzada al tempus, y que yo supiese lo que á esto la habia forzado que sabia que la tendria por escusada.

'Dijele que yo sabia bien que ninguna cosa podria escusarle en tan importante negocio, pero que aunque pudiese escusarse yo sabia que el estado de las cosas de este Reyno era tal que con mucho menos peligro y trabajo pudiera conservar la religion que halló en el tiempo que murió su hermana.'

things which she does not know, and which her ministers keep concealed from her. Your Grace in this will not disapprove my conduct.'[1]

Was Elizabeth, as de Quadra supposed, simply a practised diplomatist? was she, a young woman of twenty-seven, already so careless of truth, so skilled in the artifices of state-craft? In the crooked policy of the last twelve months she had been compelled often to equivocate, and sometimes deliberately to lie. Yet the language of Cecil and Killigrew pointed rather to some uncertainty in herself—to some infirmity of purpose in a mind but half made up. A Protestant, in the sense that Cecil was a Protestant, Elizabeth never to the last became. It is more natural to believe that she had many humours, many partially-formed views, by which she allowed herself in turn to be influenced.

To return to the northern commission.

Before Cecil reached Newcastle, the engineers had been discovered in de Randan's train,[2] Papal emissaries were reported to be busy in the families of the Scotch nobles. The women as usual were on the side of conservatism romance and the Catholic faith; and Randolph wrote that 'too many of the lords kept their promises only so far as their wives would have them.'[3] The most cheering feature was the increasing famine in the Leith garrison. Sir Henry Percy had been able to tell Norfolk on the 6th of June, that d'Oysel finding that no help could reach him from France and that a second English army was ready to advance, had admitted that he must be

---

[1] De Quadra to the Bishop of Arras, June 3.—*MS. Simancas.*
[2] Cecil to Norfolk, June 4.—*MS. Rolls House.*
[3] *MS. Ibid.*

overpowered, and had expressed a wish to treat with Percy rather than 'taste the cruelty of Lord Grey.'[1] There was as yet no actual starvation 'except among the superfluous people;'[2] but famine was in the town with fever in its rear, and it was advancing.

The first conference at Newcastle resulted only in an adjournment to Edinburgh. Before the commissioners were over the Border, the French party had lost for ever their presiding spirit.

Shut up in Edinburgh castle, cut off from her friends and half a prisoner under the cold neutrality of Erskine, the mother of Mary Queen of Scots had sunk from day to day, her body swollen with dropsy, the visible shadow of death fast closing over her; yet to the last going through her daily work with the same cheerful resolution, cool, clear and dauntless as became a daughter of the House of Guise.

Her position was forlorn and even tragic; religion had not many consolations for her; her confessor was an abandoned debauchee, whose ministrations must have been a mockery, and it was over late to learn a new creed. But she came of a race who could bear the goods and ills of fortune with an even pulse, nor was she a person at any time to believe that much depended on nice precision of opinion. In May she had seemed better; at the beginning of June the worst symptoms returned. On the 6th she was reported 'very ill and like to die.' On the 8th she sent for Chatelherault and Lord James Stuart; her hands and feet were then grow-

---

[1] Percy to Norfolk, June 6.—*MS. Rolls House.* Possibly however, this too was 'practice.' Percy might be suspected of sharing the opinions of his brother, the Earl of Northumberland; and d'Oysel might hope to make a party in the English army.

[2] Cecil to the Council, June 8.—*Burleigh Papers*, vol. i.

ing cold; she knew that she was dying, and though scarcely able to speak she said she was sorry for Scotland and sorry for her own share in Scotland's sufferings. 'Her mind' seemed 'well disposed to God.' Lord James whose earnest Calvinism made him anxious for her fate asked if he might send for Willock the preacher—Knox's colleague in Edinburgh. She made no objection, and Randolph in a letter to Norfolk said that Willock at the moment when he was writing was at the Queen's bedside.[1] She heard him probably with but a languid sense of what he said, for her mind was wandering; she received the last sacraments as a Catholic, and desired the two noblemen not to leave her while she breathed; at midnight, between the 10th and 11th of June, she died.

So ended Mary of Lorraine, once Mary Duchesse de Longueville, the wittiest brightest fairest ornament of the Court of Francis the First, whom Henry the Eighth had desired as a bride; now closing thus her nineteen years of widowhood and exile in the land of the stranger.

To her had been committed the hopeless task of fighting the Reformation and holding together the friends of France, at a time when another destiny was marked out for Scotland, and the alliance with France was perishing to revive no more. From Solway Moss to the siege of Leith her retrospect was a strange one—her child's

---

[1] Knox may be pardoned the triumph with which he describes the scene:—'Quhowsoever it was, Christ Jesus got na small victorie over sich an enemy. For albeit before sche had avowit that in despyte of all Scotland the preacheris of Jesus Christ sould ather die or be banischeit the realm, yet was sche constrainoeit to heir ane of the principell ministeris within the realm, and to approve the chief heid of our religion.'—KNOX, *History*, vol. ii. p. 71.

birth and her husband's death; the harrying of Scotland
by Henry's armies; the murder of Beton, and the vain
carnage of Pinkie Cleugh—through it all she had clung
fast to the helm—tempest-tossed yet with firm front
and heart undaunted; and now at length her cause like
herself was in its death-throes.

Her body remained in the castle—to be carried back
to France when opportunity allowed; and was treated
meanwhile with decorous though Puritan solemnity.[1]
With her the worst enemy of England was gone; and
the chance if chance there had been of prevailing on the
Scotch nobles to make a separate peace with France had
departed with her. The news gave increased resolution
to the English Council. A letter followed Cecil on the
15th, telling him that if de Randan and Monluc took
advantage of the Queen's death and pretended inability
to proceed, he might 'let them go' and 'take order for
as vigorous a use of force as might be;' 'her Majesty
being determined to go through with expelling the
French without longer delay.'

The commissioners on both sides reached Edinburgh
on the 16th. There had been no fighting since the
failure of the 7th of May; but the blockade had been
sustained rigidly by sea and land. On the 18th an
intercepted letter from de Randan to d'Oysel informed
Cecil that no relief could be sent from France before
August at the soonest. De Randan said he intended to
agree to withdraw all the French except a few at
Dunbar and Inchkeith; but he was instructed to agree

---

[1] 'I saw the Dowager's corpse in a bed, covered with a fair white sheet, the tester of black satin, and the bed hanged to the ground with the same. It is determined she shall have all solemnities fit for such a personage, save such as savour rather of superstition than of Christian piety.'— *Randolph to Killigrew, June 20. Scotch MSS. Rolls House.*

to no clause by which the Queen of Scots should abandon her claim on the English Crown. He might promise that the King of France would use his influence to induce her to relinquish the arms and style, but his commission went no further.[1]

Cecil was thus in possession of two valuable secrets, and knew for what he was to look and how far he might dare to insist. Meantime there had been a general reform of the army; the strutting in gay dresses had been a vice of the English officers; 'some captains carried twenty, some forty soldiers in their hose.' Extravagance had led to fraud, and fraud to worse mischiefs. Sir Peter Carew had come from London with summary power from the Queen to punish delinquents and to set crooked things straight. With Carew's assistance discipline had been restored, and the troops were reported to be 'doing truly and worthily like good men of war.'[2] Of Lord Grey, Winter, and Randolph, Cecil could not speak in too high praise: 'My Lord Grey,' he said, 'is a noble, valiant, painful and careful gentleman; Randolph worth more than I fear our time will well consider, and no poeler nor robber. Of Mr. Winter all men speak so well I need not mention him.'[3]

Norfolk with the army of reserve reported himself from Berwick as ready to come forward should the French prove intractable. It was evident that embarrassed at home and in dread of Philip, the French Go-

---

[1] Decipher of an intercepted letter to M. d'Oysel, June 18.—*Scotch MSS. Rolls House.*

[2] Report of Sir Peter Carew.—FORBES, vol. I. Cecil to the Queen. June 19.—*MS. Rolls House.* Cecil had an especial aversion to the fine dresses. 'Your Majesty,' he said, 'will think me a great enemy to sumptuous apparel, that neither can spare my speech at it in London nor in Edinburgh.'

[3] Ibid.

vernment did not mean to declare war. De Randan's solitary hope was of working upon the Scots.

The Scots themselves felt their advantage and were inclined to make the most of it.

'Although,' wrote Cecil, 'the lords of Scotland[1] hate the French and be devoted to England, yet some be for one respect and some for another. Many questions be moved to me whereunto I cannot answer. As for making a peace here, I think we may sooner do it than the Scots would have it.'

The Scots desired to have the benefit of both connexions; they wished to keep the pensions and lands which many of them held in France; they desired to use the assistance of England to insist on points which the English themselves most desired to see abandoned; they were impatient for the conclusion of the Arran marriage on which Elizabeth had been ominously reserved. From Maitland, Argyle, and Lord James, Cecil derived his most real help. Maitland, he said, 'was disposed to work all the minds of the nobility to allow anything which the Queen of England might determine.' Maitland was 'most in credit for his wit' of any in Scotland, and 'almost alone sustained the whole burden of Government.' 'Next him was Lord James, not unlike neither in person nor qualities to be a king's son.' 'Argyle was a goodly gentleman universally honoured of all Scotland.'[2]

The conference opened on the 17th. An armistice was allowed for a week; and the armies had leisure to exchange courtesies. The French and English officers met at a sort of picnic on Leith sands, 'each bringing

---

[1] Cecil to the Queen, July 19.—*MS. Rolls House.*
[2] Cecil to the Queen.—*MS. Ibid.*

with him such victuals as he had in store. From Grey's camp came hams, capons, chickens, wine and beer. The French produced a solitary fowl, a piece of baked horse, and six delicately-roasted rats; the last, they said, was the best fresh meat in the town, but of that they had abundance.[1]

The Gospel also became fashionable with the improvement in its chances of success. The Scots had adopted the Genevan 'discipline.' Many persons confessed their sins before the Congregation at sermon time in Cecil's presence, and Lady Stenhouse the mistress of the Archbishop of St. Andrew's and the mother of his children was ordered to do penance on the following Sunday.[2] Among the first difficulties in the conference were the extravagant pretensions of the preachers, to whom mere toleration seemed now utterly inadequate. Had it not been for Maitland 'whose credit and capacity was worth any six others,' 'their folly would have hazarded all.'[3] In general however the French conceded everything which the Congregation demanded. It was agreed that 'they might remain in their religion, as a thing the French dared not meddle withal.' Of the whole French army fifty soldiers only would remain at Inchkeith and fifty at Dunbar; the number was not to be increased; they were to be 'answerable to the justice of Scotland;' and should be withdrawn wholly if the Scotch Parliament on its next meeting should so desire. All seemed going well. In his anxiety for peace and his uncertainty how far he would be supported at home, Cecil had been even inclined to pass lightly over the

---

[1] Randolph to Killigrew, June 22.—*MS. Rolls House.*
[2] Ibid.
[3] Cecil to Norfolk, June 25.—*Hatfield MSS.*

more difficult points of the treaty with the Scots, and the title to the English Crown. Calais had not been so much as mentioned; and peace was on the point of conclusion when a difficulty arose from an unexpected quarter.

Elizabeth, finding her Cassandra prophecies unfulfilled, had passed to an extremity of confidence. Encouraged by 'the rugged state of the French and their little power to annoy her,'[1] she desired to obtain some more substantial advantage from her outlay than Cecil had been prepared to demand. She had relinquished in her heart—if she had ever seriously entertained—the thought of marrying Arran and uniting England and Scotland; and she had therefore to look to indemnify herself in another quarter. Cecil had expressed his belief 'that if she had money to carry on the war for a year, she might so abase France as her posterity to the third generation might live quietly.'[2] She had suddenly discovered that she was both ready and willing. She sent orders to Cecil to exact a literal and formal admission of her right to make a treaty with the Scots; she required the Queen of Scots not only to engage to abandon her claim on the English Crown, but to signify to all the world by a formal act and proclamation, that she withdrew her pretensions; and further, she insisted that the treaty of Cambray was void, and that her right to Calais and to the old debt of the half-million crowns should be referred to the arbitration of the King of Spain.[3]

The 'new matter' put all in a hazard. A day or two later the Queen in a second letter demanded further that a clause should be added to the treaty, which the Scotch nobles should sign, binding themselves as parties for

---

[1] Sir T. Parry to Cecil, June 22.—*MS. Rolls House.*
[2] Cecil to the Queen, June 19.—*MS. Ibid.*
[3] Elizabeth to Cecil, June 26.—*MS. Ibid.*

whom their sovereign's signature did not wholly suffice, —to see its conditions fulfilled. If the French refused to consent the conference was to cease, and Norfolk should advance from Berwick and 'set on in God's name.'[1]

A survey of Leith had convinced Cecil that unless the French troops mutinied the capture of it would still be expensive and bloody. The garrison was not yet at its last extremity; the salmon were coming in from the sea, and were caught in numbers with boats and nets in the mouth of the harbour. Arrows were shot over the walls with notes attached to them telling the French troops that they were to be sacrificed, in the hope that with 'this practice' 'the town might be rendered.' Yet even a bare surrender Cecil hardly desired, feeling that if Leith fell without conditions, the pride of France would be touched too deeply and peace would be made impossible.[2]

The French commissioners had evidently reached the extent of the concessions which they were prepared to make. They would grant everything which the Scots asked for; they would yield nothing to the English. When Cecil in obedience to Elizabeth's orders brought up his demand for Calais, de Randan refused to entertain it. 'Rather than the house of Guise would deliver Calais,' he said, 'in minority of the King, being a conquest of theirs, they would suffer all those in the town to perish.' Neither he nor Monluc 'durst so much as enter into speech thereof, for fear of the loss of their heads.'[3]

On 'the arms and style,' they were at first equally

---

[1] Elizabeth to Cecil, June 28.—*MS. Rolls House.*
[2] Cecil to Norfolk, June 28.—*Hatfield MSS.*
[3] Cecil to the Queen, July 2.—*MS. Rolls House.*

unwilling to give way. Cecil offered 'to spend his blood in the quarrel upon any that would deny Queen Elizabeth's right.' At length, 'after vehemency and some threatening,' de Randan consented 'to have it confessed in words that the realms of England and Ireland of right appertained to her Majesty.'[1] But the league between England and the Scotch nobles, the French commissioners positively and decisively refused to recognize by word or deed. They said that they had 'special instructions which they could not disobey, not to mix matters of Scotland and England in one treaty, or dishonour their master with noting that he was forced by the Queen of England to observe anything towards his own subjects.' Cecil said that it might stand as 'a separate engagement;' but 'his travail was in vain;' while Elizabeth's letter to himself left him no discretion. The French could not yield a point which they were distinctly directed not to yield; and 'utterly against his will Cecil was forced to break off, and commit the matter to God.' The importance of the question to the Queen of Scots can be easily understood; the right of the Scotch nobles to make a treaty with the Queen of England was the first step in the transfer of their allegiance; while if the treaty was concluded without it, 'the French,' Cecil said, 'would soon find ground to quarrel again with the Scots;' by avoiding the mistake of resuming prematurely the arms of England, they would leave Elizabeth without a pretext for interfering a second time; and if the Scots were left without support, the friends of France among them would recover their ascendency.[2]

CHAP III
1560
June

The French will not recognize the league between England and the Scots.

---

[1] The confession thus extorted is in the clause beginning 'Cum Regna Angliæ et Hiberniæ ad dictam serenissimam Dominam Elizabetham jure spectent et pertineant.'—*Treaty of Edinburgh.* RYMER, vol. xv. p. 594.

[2] Cecil to the Queen, July 2.—*Scotch MSS. Rolls House.*

CHAP III
1560
July

The commissioners separated, and Cecil most unwillingly was about to direct the advance of Norfolk and the second army; a letter to the Court announcing the failure of the conference was written and sealed; when 'perplexed with the lack of peace' he sent a message to Monluc, which brought Cecil and the Bishop of Valence together again by themselves.

The difficulty is at last arranged.

Both had been anxious for an arrangement; both were disappointed at their ill success. A vague clause was suggested by which the King and Queen of France might promise Elizabeth to fulfil their engagements with the Scots.[1] It did not amount to a stipulation; it was not literally covered by the prohibitory order of the French Court; yet it recognized in Elizabeth the shadow of a right to interfere if those engagements were broken. De Randan consented, Cecil was satisfied, peace was concluded, and the treaty of Edinburgh was drawn and signed.

The Treaty of Edinburgh.

The substance of it was generally this:—The Scots obtained a general amnesty, the removal of the French army, with a promise that it should never return, the limitation of the officers of state to their own people, and a Government by a council of twelve noblemen, seven of whom were to be named by the Queen, and five by the Estates. Nothing special was said of religion; but it was left to be settled between the Queen of Scots and her own Parliament. The Scottish nobles were permitted to retain the pensions and estates which they held under the French Crown.

England obtained an admission of Elizabeth's right to her Crown, a vague and partial sanction of her relations

---

[1] The clause beginning 'Cum Deo optimo Maximo,' &c.—*Treaty of Edinburgh.* RYMER, vol. XV. p. 593.

with the Queen of Scots' subjects, and the disappearance
for ever of the threatening army of invasion on the
northern Border.

The names of the commissioners were affixed on the
6th of July. It was but just in time. On the 7th
another letter arrived from Elizabeth; she was exasperated at the success with which the Scots were securing
their own interests, and at the small profit which in
return for so much money spent she was likely to receive
for herself. If peace was concluded, she said, it need
not be disturbed again; if there was still time,—'the
Scots could not serve God and Mammon,'—Cecil must
tell them that they must be content to part with their
livings and pensions in France, which would breed
troubles; while for herself he was to stand to his demand for the restitution of Calais and the payment of
the half-million crowns, as an indemnity for the usurpation of the arms.[1]

The public letter was accompanied by another in
cipher addressed to Cecil. It is lost; but Cecil's answer
to it remains, to show the flight which Elizabeth's ambition was now ready to venture.

SIR WILLIAM CECIL TO THE QUEEN'S MAJESTY.

Edinburgh, July 9.

'It may please your Majesty; the sight of your most
gracious letter written with your own blessed hands,
before I had deciphered it, raised me up in such height
of comfort that after I perceived the sense thereof my
fall was greater into the deep dungeon of sorrow than
ever I thought any letter of your Majesty's should have
thrown me.

---

[1] Elizabeth to Cecil and Wotton, July 9.—BURLEIGH *Papers*, vol. L

'And yet after a season gathering my astonished spirits together, I am risen into this opinion and comfort of your Majesty's accustomed goodness towards me, and of my own clearness of mind and soul, that when it shall appear by our letters sent from hence the 6th of this month how far we were proceeded, and that also it shall be well weighed in all parts how honourable and necessary this peace is, and how it could not be made any other way, your Majesty will not only take and allow our doings, but will think it a good luck that we had not these your letters before our conclusion; for so had no peace at all been gotten. For breaking off upon the matter of Calais, the French ambassadors would have departed and my Lord of Norfolk should have entered; whereupon must within ten days have happened one of these three things—either the loss of the town, and a perpetual dishonour of the realm—or a winning of it by assault to the effusion of a great deal of Christian blood —or a taking of it by composition—by any of which three ways wars still should have remained; and then by what means Calais could have been obtained I see not; nor by what means this manner of peace would have hereafter been obtained, I neither see nor can consider.

'As for the message brought by Tremayne,[1] God forbid that your Majesty should enter into that bottomless pit of expense of your force and treasure, within the French King's own mainland—being that manner of war to you more troublesome and dangerous than this of the French King here in Scotland; and yet this is his advantage, that the obedience of this is due to his

---

[1] There were two Tremaynes, one of whom was with the army at Leith. Both had been employed in carrying messages between the Prince of Condé, the Admiral Châtillon, and Elizabeth.

wife and cannot be lost; and there your Majesty should
have no more to further you but a devotion popular
upon opinions of religion; wherein the French King
rather than lose that country, would not stick to incline
to his people's request, and so your Majesty's purpose
could not then last.

'Indeed this I could and meant always to have
allowed, that if ye could not come to a reasonable accord with France, but that they would continue wars,
then your Majesty should have entertained that matter
of Brittany and Normandy—to have therewith offended
and annoyed the French King. But as to have taken
and kept any piece there, experience of Boulogne being
in sight of Dover teacheth us what to do; and when I
consider that for charges neither is Portsmouth your
own haven fortified, neither the town of Berwick—most
necessary of all others—finished; I should think it
strange to take Brest or any other town in those parts,
to keep longer than of necessity the French would maintain wars against your Majesty; which being now ceased,
and to your great honour, I think it a happy mishap
that your Majesty's letter came not before our conclusion. In which my opinion I most humbly beseech
your Majesty to pardon me, submitting myself to your
Majesty's reformation as becometh me.'[1]

It is plain that some communication had been made
to Elizabeth by the Huguenot leaders of France; some
offer to put her in possession, in return for her assistance, of a town or towns on the coast of Normandy or
Brittany; and that Elizabeth in her passionate anxiety
to recover Calais had listened to the temptation.

---

[1] *Scotch MSS. Rolls House.*

1560
July

General
results of
the war.

The fate of the project when two years later it was actually put in execution, the story in due time will relate. Meanwhile, her letter came a day too late. The objects for which the war had been undertaken were obtained. The French troops sailed away from Leith. The Scots were left to their own resources to go on with the Reformation. Elizabeth's crown was secured. The Catholics had seen their opportunity fade away amidst the diplomatic perplexities of Europe. The English Government which was supposed to be so weak that it would fall at the first breath of war, had proved strong enough to defy France and accomplish successfully a difficult military enterprise. The King of Spain was forced to feel that Elizabeth was no creature of his own, that she could choose her own course and carry through her own purposes, whatever might be his pleasure or displeasure.

Lord Clinton wrote to Cecil that 'no better service had ever been done to England;' he trusted it would be 'no less considered than it deserved;' and 'time would show the fruits of it to his great praise that had so discreetly travailed in the same.'[1]

It remained to be seen how far Elizabeth was prepared to go on with what she had begun, to fulfil the passionate wishes of the Congregation, and accept the hand of the heir presumptive to the Scotch crown.

I have pursued the story of these proceedings in Scot-

---

[1] Clinton to Cecil, July 13.—*Domestic MSS. Rolls House.* 'My Lord Pembroke,' Clinton continues, 'is your very good friend. Touching the matter of Scotland, he remaineth firm and sure as in the beginning without change or alteration, and hath hitherto stayed his going from the Court until he might hear of a final order of the matter of your commission which now he heareth to be such as is much to his contentation.'

At the foot of the letter Pembroke adds his signature to that of Clinton, who must have shown Pembroke what he had written.

land thus minutely, because they bring out with so
much distinctness the relations of the great powers of
Europe towards one another and towards their own subjects; and the characters at the same time of those
princes and ministers who were to work out among them
the problem of the future of the world. Had Elizabeth preferred her immediate ease and safety, she would
have married Philip's kinsman, and disclaimed all connexion with Scotch or French or Flemings struggling
for freedom. She would have left religion in England
unchanged, attempting to modify the fanaticism of the
Catholics by some practical toleration; and so have
drifted on in happy insignificance, till some fresh ascendency of ultramontanism and persecution had been followed by rebellion and civil war. To this issue it must
have come at last. The Catholics were constitutionally
intolerant, the Protestants constitutionally aggressive.
Even the strong hand of Henry the Eighth would have
failed eventually to hold an even balance between them.
Yet such a course promised better for the moment
for the political influence of England—better for peace
and quiet at home. The temptation of it to a common
nature would have been irresistible; and that Elizabeth
remained in essentials true to the great cause of the
Reformation to which she owed her birth and crown,
must never be forgotten when we are provoked to
condemn her inconsistencies. That she was without
distinct doctrinal conviction was rather her merit than
her fault. That she was irresolute—that she listened to
all sides—that she was unwilling to risk a throne in
defence of opinions with which she had but a moderate
sympathy—that she was irritable and impatient—that
she quarrelled with her truest friends—all this is plain
enough, but it is also reasonable enough. If she had

other faults, she was young—and she was a woman. It is sufficient praise that she perilled crown and life in a bold and noble policy.

One special ground of irritation the Queen had too, and special claim for sympathy. Of a nature most free proud and independent, she found her own person among the pieces of the diplomatic game. She was to be assigned to this suitor or that according to the projects of this or that political party. She knew that she might be compelled to endure what nevertheless appeared to her a degrading sacrifice: and while she was prepared to yield at the last extremity, the necessity exasperated her pride.

Beyond England the eye rests chiefly on the strange position of Philip of Spain. Charles the Fifth had bequeathed by will to his son two special injunctions—to destroy heresy, and to maintain the English alliance: and Philip found himself distracted between the incompatible obligations, with no middle course discoverable. If he interfered for France he gave the English throne to the French Queen. If he defended Elizabeth he was maintaining the most dangerous enemy of the Catholic faith. He could not allow the English Catholics to use the occasion of the Scotch war to rebel, lest they should cripple the Queen's power to resist France; and thus virtually he made himself her ally in carrying out a policy which he most dreaded and most deplored. He assisted in establishing the Reformation throughout the whole island of Great Britain, feeling even while doing it that the example in the dangerous neighbourhood might drag the Netherlands into the vortex. De Quadra clung to the hope that Elizabeth might still keep her promise and admit the nuncio; but he found, as he expected, that she had changed her mind with the change of fortune in Scotland. She objected personally to the

Abbot of St. Saviour's, as having been a friend and companion of the detested Pole. She endeavoured to persuade the Spanish ambassador that between Lutherans and Catholics there was no substantial difference, and that if he knew what she thought he would be sufficiently satisfied with her.

'I told her,' the bishop wrote to Philip, 'that knowing how she had been brought up I was surprised at nothing that she did. But to your Majesty I am forced in discharge of my conscience—and that I may not be wanting in my duty to your service—to say how deeply the Catholics here are hurt at the support which this Queen has received from your Majesty, and at the opportunity which you have afforded to heresy to strike its roots into the realm.[1] I am well aware of the efforts which your Majesty has made to divert her from her evil ways; but seeing that nothing avails, you have to consider whether you must not now alter your conduct towards her. The injury to your Majesty's estate in the Low Countries is but too certain. Ten thousand of your subjects are already here with their preachers and ministers, and those who are left behind will be soon infected.

'I see the Queen obstinate. I see the hearts of the Catholics alienated from your Majesty. Will your Majesty be pleased to think of these things, and to tell me what I am to do?'[2]

---

[1] In the margin opposite this passage Philip wrote 'á este capitulo es bien mirar.'

[2] De Quadra to Philip II., July 25.—*MS. Simancas.*

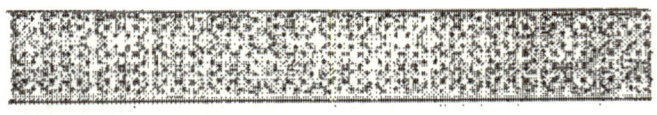

CHAPTER IV.

Unpopularity of Cecil at Court.

IF Cecil hoped for gratitude on his return to the Court his expectations deceived him. Clinton and Pembroke might express their private satisfaction; the Duke of Norfolk might think the 'agreement' so happy for England 'that the Queen could not have bought it too dearly;' he might wish 'that those who quarrelled with it might do their country as good service;'[1] but the Queen had set her heart on a more substantial result for the money which she had laid out. The favourites of the palace who hated Cecil, and had objects of their own at which they could arrive only through Cecil's fall, persuaded her that she might have covered herself with glory, and extorted the surrender of Calais; and knowing that the conclusion of the peace would bring with it the necessity of accepting the Earl of Arran, or of affronting the Scots by his rejection, she quarrelled with conditions which far exceeded her recent anticipations, and resented the close of a war which she had so unwillingly consented to undertake.

Could she have acknowledged a community of religious interest with the Scotch reformers, Arran or no Arran, she might have secured the attachment of one at least of the two great parties into which Mary Stuart's

---

[1] Norfolk to Cecil, July 29.—BURLEIGH *Papers*.

subjects were divided; but the clause which would have identified her faith with theirs had been expunged from the treaty with the Lords. The Reformation with which Elizabeth sympathized was the abolition of the spiritual tyranny which encroached on freedom. She hated Calvinism—she hated Knox. The heated zeal of the reforming preachers she wished to strangle with copes and surplices; and while the returned exiles were denouncing the man of sin, she had been herself coquetting, not in entire insincerity, with the Pope's proposal to send a nuncio to England. The Scots had been made formally to feel that she had interfered for them on political grounds alone. Was she prepared to accept the political conditions on which, in the absence of religion, the alliance could alone be secured?

For the Arran marriage the Scotch Catholics were as anxious as the Scotch Reformers, and the Lords of the Congregation cared more for it than for the Genevan gospel. To give a King to England, to end the long rivalry of Scot and Saxon in a union in which the descendant of the Bruce should sit on the throne of the Plantagenet, was a passion in which Scotland, divided on everything else, was eagerly and enthusiastically united.

'All the Lords,' Randolph wrote from Edinburgh, on the 27th of August, 'are bent on the marriage. They know the inequality of the match; but they hope that of the nobleness of her nature the Queen will consent. She will gain the hearts of the whole nation which neither money nor force could win. It is our daily and hourly talk.'[1] The suspicion that Elizabeth was unfavourable had—as Sir James Crofts truly said—been the chief cause of the lukewarmness of 'the neutrals.' The ultra-

---

[1] Randolph to Cecil, August 27.—*Scotch MSS. Rolls House.*

Protestants in England were no less unanimous.[1] Cecil indeed, when spoken to at Edinburgh about it, 'had shifted the matter, as unwilling to enter on it;' yet Maitland 'could not persuade himself that Cecil being so wise and well-affected towards his country did altogether mislike it.'[2] To Lady Cecil, under whose roof the Earl of Arran had lived while in London, Maitland addressed himself as confident of her support and aware of her opinion.[3] Nor were her husband's wishes in themselves doubtful. The union of the realms was the culminating point of his policy, and the marriage would be at once the final severance of Scotland from France, and the link of a league which would enable England to defy and despise the menaces of the Catholic powers. Cecil however understood too well his mistress's humour to feel confidence; and Arran, had there been no other objection, was a raw sullen half-crazy boy, who under the most propitious circumstances would have failed to find favour.

The time was come when the Queen would be compelled to declare her intentions.

As soon as the French were gone from Leith and the English army were over the Border, the Scotch Estates assembled at Edinburgh, and Knox and his friends proceeded to reconstruct the Church. Far different was the

---

[1] 'I hope and pray that all may be well with Crito and Glycerium. It is of the greatest moment that England and Scotland be united; and I trust only those may not hinder it who wish well neither to them nor to us.'—*Jewel to Peter Martyr.* ZURICH *Letters.*

[2] Maitland to Cecil, September 13. —*Scotch MSS.*

[3] 'Now, by Mr. Secretary's wisdom are we come to a good end of our troubles if promise be kept. Marry, now we shall begin to have most need of your help in the matter whereunto you know I most earnestly press. I believe time is not able so to overcome you that you will wax cold in it.'— *Maitland to Lady Cecil, July* 19, 1560. *Hatfield MSS.*

form assumed by the Reformation in the two kingdoms. In England it was the revolt of the laity against ecclesiastical authority; in Scotland the Calvinist elders desired to retain for themselves the supremacy from which the priesthood had been deposed. Religion north of the Tweed remained the basis on which civil society reposed; the elect ministers of God were the prophets by whom his will was made known; they were or sought to be the supreme rulers of a state of which their special theology was the law code, and where moral and spiritual sins were identified with civil crimes. At the opening of the session Knox 'preached from Haggai' on the rebuilding of the temple. A system of doctrine was prepared embodying in its first form the entire spirit of Calvin religious and political. A petition was presented by the Congregation for the abolition of the 'man of sin,' whose representatives—'those murderers, rebels, and traitors,' the Roman clergy—'passed their time in whoredom, adultery, deflowering virgins, and corrupting matrons;' the Congregation desired the establishment of pastors in their place, who would feed Christ's flock with the milk of the word.

That Knox represented in these views the wishes of the noblest of his countrymen the after history of Scotland may be taken to prove; but as yet there were many even of the moving party unprepared to submit to him; the foundation of the kirk was a great thing, but it was not everything; there appeared to be truths of earth, if not truths of heaven, which Calvin's formulas failed to reach; and the Reformation did not then mean simply a despotism of ministers in the place of a despotism of priests. 'Hey, then!' said Maitland, after the sermon, 'we may all bear the barrow now to build the House of the Lord.' 'The Confession of Faith,' as

CHAP IV
1560
August

it left the hands of its framers, contained a dangerous 'chapter on the obedience or disobedience which subjects owed to their magistrates.' When 'the magistrate' commanded what in the opinion of 'the minister' the word of God forbade, disobedience was represented to be the subject's duty. Maitland and Lord James considered that this 'was unfit matter to be entreated at that time;' 'the austerity of many words was mitigated,' and 'sentences' omitted 'which seemed to proceed rather of some evil-concealed opinion than of sound judgment.'[1]

The Confession of Faith.

Tempered however into the form in which it now stands upon the Scotch Statute Book, 'the Confession' passed unanimously, 'many offering to shed their blood for it.' 'The bishops' feeling the stream too strong against them 'were silent.' Old Lord Lyndsay, as he gave his vote, said—'I have lived many years: I am the eldest of this company of my sort; now that it hath pleased God to let me see this day when so many nobles and others have allowed so worthy a work, I will say with Simeon, *Nunc Dimittis, Domine.*'[2]

The mass was abolished: persons saying mass or hearing mass were made liable for the third offence to be put to death; and the Pope's authority was declared to be for ever at an end.

---

[1] Randolph to Cecil, September 7.—*Scotch MSS. Rolls House.*

[2] Among the visitors to Edinburgh on the occasion of this Parliament was an ambassador from Shan O'Neil to the Earl of Argyle. The chief—nothing less than a chief would have been sent on such an errand, and he was probably the ancestor of some living Irish peer—had come over *more Hibernico*; he 'had walked on foot out of Ireland.' 'His diet by reason of the length of his journey so failed him that he was fain to leave his saffron shirt in gage. The rest of his apparel such, that the Earl before he would give him audience arrayed him from the neck downwards. Cap he would have none.' Tall, gaunt, and shaggy, with his glyb shading his eyes, 'he lodged in the chimney,' 'his drink aqua vitæ and milk.'—*Randolph to Cecil. MS. Ibid.*

Whether Elizabeth expected more or expected less—whether she had desired the English model to be more exactly imitated—whether she was merely impatient with the Scots, and disposed to make faults if she did not find them—their proceedings did not please her. Cecil complained of the Confession of Faith; Randolph endeavoured to prevent it from passing;[1] and so angry was the Queen, and so anxious were the moderate Scots to gratify her, that Maitland promised if she would specify what she disliked to see it 'further altered or modified.'[2]

The Estates were ready to yield anything could they bring Elizabeth to consent to 'the other matter.' They had set their whole heart on her marriage with Arran, and they could not rest till it was brought about. The repeated visits of Maitland to England, his personal acquaintance with Elizabeth, and his intimate relation with the Cecils, enabled him to conjecture better than most of his countrymen her probable reluctance; and though himself as anxious as the rest, he knew that the subject must be approached with the utmost wariness. The Estates to his extreme vexation determined at once to make a formal proposal, and he was unable to prevent them. No sooner were the Church matters disposed of than the subject was brought under public discussion. A resolution was passed to send a special embassy to London.[3] All parties were so determined that they could not be restrained from the expression of their wishes; and Maitland could but send apologies to Cecil depre-

---

[1] 'If my poor advice might have been heard touching the Confession of Faith, it should not so soon have come into the light.'—*Randolph to Cecil, September 7. Scotch MSS. Rolls House.*

[2] Maitland to Cecil, Sept. 13.—*Ibid.*

[3] The resolution has been printed by KEITH, vol. ii. p. 6, and was mistaken by him for the petition taken to London by the commissioners—a very different document.

cating his displeasure, and obtain a brief delay from the Estates while he prepared the way by a private letter.

An immediate answer was naturally looked for, but no answer came. 'Never in my life was I so desirous to hear from you,' Maitland wrote again, 'yet I can learn nothing.'[1] Rumour only said that Elizabeth was in a worse humour than ever, and that she had been listening to complaints against the Scots from the Cardinal of Lorraine.[2] The symptoms were unfavourable, but the Estates were in earnest. Elizabeth knew their wishes, and had forborne at least to forbid the expression of them. They forced a favourable interpretation upon her silence, and drew up at length a formal address to the English Council, pressing the marriage as the only means to make the alliance between the two countries permanent.

The Estates request Elizabeth to marry the Earl of Arran.

'Other devices,' said the Estates, in this remarkable paper, 'may seem probable for a time, but we fear not for long. We wish the best, but many incidents which may fall out make us to fear the worst; but if this may take place, then are all doubts removed for ever. We have no King to offer you—the more sorry we; but we present unto you him who being in place next unto a King shall bring with him the friendship and force of a kingdom. We assure you with him of the hearts and good will of a whole nation, which you could never by riches obtain. We present no stranger, but in manner your own countryman—seeing this isle is a common country to us both, one that speaketh your own language, one of the same religion. You need not fear that by marriage of a King of Scotland unto a Queen

---

[1] Maitland to Cecil, September 7.—*Scotch MSS. Rolls House.*
[2] *Ibid.*

of England, the pre-eminence of England might be defaced, for that should always remain still for the worthiness thereof; neither need you fear any alteration of the laws, seeing the laws of Scotland were taken out of England, and therefore both these realms are ruled by one fashion. By these means Ireland might be reformed; and thus the Queen of England become the strongest princess upon the seas, and establish a certain monarchy by itself in the ocean, divided from the rest of the world.'[1]

The sincerity, the unanimity, the earnestness, with which the Scots were pressing their proposals, could not be disputed. Mary Stuart was far away—the childless Queen of a foreign realm, from which at that time there seemed no likelihood that she would ever return. Her sovereignty, by the expulsion of the French, had been reduced to a name. Could this marriage have been brought about, the shadow would soon have followed the substance. The opportunity for so complete a retaliation on the rival claimant of her Crown—the occasion freely offered of accomplishing without effort the passionately-cherished object of her father and grandfather—must have been a temptation to which Elizabeth could hardly have been insensible. Why then had Cecil been so long silent? Why when he wrote at last was he silent still on the subject nearest to every Scottish heart? and why did he say that he was about to resign his office, and retire from the Queen's service?

He had been working for her gratuitously. Elizabeth had not allowed him even the expenses of his journey to Scotland. Shortly after his return, at the beginning of

---

[1] *MS. Scotland, Rolls House.*

August she went on progress on which he had not accompanied her. She was entertained among other places at Basing House by Lord Winchester; and the old Marquis took the opportunity of the visit to write to Cecil of certain 'back counsels' about the Queen to which she was giving too easy credence, and of some influence which was especially unfavourable to Cecil himself.

'There shall never appear assured council,' Winchester said, 'until you have a smaller number, and perfect trust of the Princess in them; and the mean time all good councillors shall have labour and dolour without reward; wherein your part is most of all men's, for your charge and pain be far above all other men's, and your thanks and rewards least considered; and specially for that you spend wholly of yourself, without your ordinary fee, land, present, gift, or anything, which must needs discomfort you; and yet when your counsel is most for her Majesty's honour and profit, the same hath great hindrance by her weak credit of you, and by back counsel; and so long as that manner shall continue, it must needs be dangerous service and unthankful.'

The Lord Treasurer however recommended Cecil to bear with his treatment for the present, as well as he could; 'to pass things as he might, and take other doings in moderate part, till better help might come;' while he himself would 'play the part of a good subject,' and tell the Queen the truth.[1]

Three days later, Cecil was himself at Basing, brought thither perhaps by Winchester's letter. Of what passed while he was there, the only evidence is a letter written

---

[1] Winchester to Cecil, August 24; from Basing.—DUNLRIAN *Papers*, vol. i.

by him from thence on the 27th of August to Sir
Nicholas Throgmorton. He had urged on the Queen—
but urged in vain—that some small presents should be
made to those of the Scotch nobles who had done best
service in the war. It would 'have been good economy,'
he thought—'spending a thousand pounds to save
twenty;' but Elizabeth would not listen; nor were her
objections merely on the ground of inability, or of simple
unwillingness to bestow favours, since at the very time
when she was accepting the unpaid services of her ministers, and refusing to reward the exertions of Argyle
and Lord James Stuart, she was conferring on Lord
Robert Dudley the lucrative and mischievous privilege
of exporting woollen cloths free of duty.[1] In lamenting
her determination to Throgmorton, Cecil implied some
grave misgivings as to her general proceedings.

'I dare not write that I might speak,' he said. 'God
send her Majesty understanding which shall be her surety,
and so full of melancholy I wish you free from it, as I
doubt not but your fortune shall be to find you free. I
omit to speak of my comfort in service that in this journey have for her honour oppressed myself with debt and
have no consideration made me; I can bear it better for
myself than for others.'[2]

Irritated at this fresh mortification, resenting the neglect of his services, and distressed perhaps more deeply
by a cause which will presently appear, Cecil seems now
to have determined to withdraw from public life. On
the 29th of August, two days after his letter to Throg-

---

[1] LANSDOWNE MSS. 4.
[2] Cecil to Throgmorton, August 27; from Basing.—CONWAY MSS. Rolls House.

morton, he wrote to Randolph who was in Edinburgh with the Lords,[1] to say that he was about to resign his office.

'Your absence from Court,' replied Randolph on the 7th of September, 'if it so chance, will be more grievous unto some men than the loss of half their lives. I dare not as yet give them here any token thereof; and for mine own part I know that when you leave that place you occupy many will greatly doubt what will become of their cause.'[2]

A few days later Randolph wrote:

'The reasons why you should retire yourself are better considered on your part than coveted of your friends, who wish you would abide the consummating of the happy work that is now in hand.'[3]

Again a few days and Randolph wrote once more, in answer this time to some information which Cecil had sent him of an extremely agitating kind.

'Though my case be as miserable and as far from happy good fortune as any man's that ever travailed so far, or served prince with so willing and careful heart, yet I call God to witness I sorrow more for other men's misfortunes than I lament my own.

'The first word that I read of your letter of the 11th[4] of this present, conferring it with such bruits and slanderous reports as have been maliciously reported by the French and their faction, so passioned my heart that no

---

[1] The letter itself is lost, but Randolph's answer to it remains.
[2] Randolph to Cecil, September 7.—*Scotch MSS. Rolls House.*
[3] Same to the same, September 23.—*MS. Ibid.*
[4] Amy Robsart's death was generally known in London on the 11th of Sept.

grief that ever I felt was like unto it; I neither had
word to comfort, nor advice to give to my friends. We
measured our affection for our country and friends as
though we had seen that heart that you wrote with your
pen. The selfsame comfort that you stay yourself upon,
quod jactas curam tuam super Dominum, doth also relieve
us, and so we intend to moderate our cares. Both ——
and I thought it good for a time to keep your letters from
all; it is yet no time to cast such doubts.'[1]

These letters too simple too natural and too varied to
leave room for a suspicion of any intentional deception
practised by Cecil upon his correspondents, form an introduction to the following despatch from de Quadra. It
cannot fairly be doubted that Cecil at the end of August
was not in favour with the Queen, that he was much
dissatisfied at the state of the public service, and that he
thought of leaving it. It is equally certain that on the
11th of September he had communicated something of a
most distressing nature to Randolph.

DE QUADRA TO THE DUCHESS OF PARMA.[2]

London, September 11.

'Since my last letter to your Highness so many great
and unexpected matters have taken place here that I
think it right to give you immediate information of them.

'On the 3rd of this month the Queen spoke to me
about her marriage with the Archduke. She said she
had made up her mind to marry, and that the Archduke

---

[1] Randolph to Cecil, September 23. —*Scotch MSS. Rolls House.*

[2] When anything of unusual importance occurred in England, the Spanish ambassador wrote first to the Government at Brussels, as the nearest point from which he could receive instructions. The despatches were then forwarded to Philip.

was to be the man. She has just now told me drily that she does not intend to marry, and that it cannot be.

'After my conversation with the Queen, I met the Secretary Cecil whom I knew to be in disgrace. Lord Robert I was aware was endeavouring to deprive him of his place.

'With little difficulty I led him to the subject, and after many protestations and entreaties that I would keep secret what he was about to tell me, he said that the Queen was going on so strangely that he was about to withdraw from her service. It was a bad sailor, he said, who did not make for port when he saw a storm coming, and for himself he perceived the most manifest ruin impending over the Queen through her intimacy with Lord Robert. The Lord Robert had made himself master of the business of the State and of the person of the Queen, to the extreme injury of the realm, with the intention of marrying her;[1] and she herself was shutting herself up in the palace to the peril of her health and life. That the realm would tolerate the marriage he said that he did not believe; he was therefore determined to retire into the country, although he supposed they would send him to the Tower before they would let him go.

'He implored me for the love of God to remonstrate with the Queen, to persuade her not utterly to throw herself away as she was doing, and to remember what she owed to herself and to her subjects. Of Lord Robert he twice said he would be better in Paradise than here.

'I could only reply that I was most deeply grieved; I said he must be well aware how anxious I had always

---

[1] 'Y que el veia la perdicion de la Reyna manifiesta causada desta privança de Milor Roberto, el qual se ha hecho señor de los negocios y de la persona de la Reyna con estrema injuria de todo el Reyno, destinando casarse con ella.'

been for the Queen's well-doing. I had laboured as the King my master had directed me to persuade her to live quietly and to marry—with how little effect he himself could tell. I would try again however as soon as I had an opportunity.

'He told me the Queen cared nothing for foreign princes; she did not believe that she stood in any need of their support. She was deeply in debt, taking no thought how to clear herself, and she had ruined her credit in the City.'

'Last of all he said that they were thinking of destroying Lord Robert's wife. They had given out that she was ill; but she was not ill at all; she was very well, and was taking care not to be poisoned; God, he trusted, would never permit such a crime to be accomplished or allow so wicked a conspiracy to prosper.'[2]

'This business of the Secretary cannot but produce some great results, for it is terrible. Many men I believe are as displeased as he, especially the Duke of Norfolk, whom he named to me as one of those most injured by Lord Robert and most hostile to him.

'The day after this conversation, the Queen on her return from hunting told me that Lord Robert's wife was dead or nearly so, and begged me to say nothing about it. Assuredly it is a matter full of shame and infamy, but for all this I do not feel sure that she will immediately marry him, or indeed that she will marry

---

[1] Again this letter receives an accidental confirmation from another source. For some reason, the London merchants, in this month of September, refused a request of Elizabeth to them to pay 60,000*l*, which was due at Antwerp.—*Flanders MSS. Sept.* 1560. *Rolls House*.

[2] 'Por ultimo me dixó que pensaban hacer morir á su muger de Roberto y que ahora publicamente estaba mala, pero que no estaba sino muy buena, y se guardaba muy bien de ser avenenada, y que nunca Dios permitiria tan gran maldad, ni podria tener buen suceso tan mal negocio.'

at all. She wants resolution to take any decided step; and as Cecil says, she wishes to act like her father.

'These quarrels among themselves and Cecil's retirement from office will do no harm to the good cause. We could not have to do with any one worse than he has been; but likely enough a revolution may come of it. The Queen may be sent to the Tower, and they may make a king of Lord Huntingdon who is a great heretic, calling in a party in France to help them, because they know that when they aim at injuring religion they have nothing to hope for from his Majesty. I have my suspicions on both these points. It is quite certain that the heretics wish to have Huntingdon made king. Cecil himself told me that he was the true heir to the crown; Henry the Seventh having usurped it from the House of York. That they may have recourse to the French I dread, from the close intimacy which has grown up between Cecil and the Bishop of Valence. It may be that I am over-suspicious; but with such people it is always prudent to believe the worst. Certain it is they say openly that they will not have a woman over them any more; and this one is likely to go to sleep in the palace, and to wake with her lover in the Tower. The French too are not asleep. Even Cecil says *Non dormit Judas*. We can be sure of nothing except of revolution and change. If I made up to them they would trust me and tell me all; but I have no orders what to do, and until I receive instructions I shall listen to both sides and temporize. Your Highness will be pleased to give me directions. I show the Catholics all the attention in my power; and they are not so broken but what, if his Majesty will give the word, they will resist the machinations of the rest. It is important that his Majesty should know that there is no hope of improvement in the

Queen: she will be his enemy and her own to the last, as I have always told him.

'Since this was written the death of Lord Robert's wife has been given out publicly. The Queen said in Italian—"Que si ha rotto il collo." It appears that she fell down a staircase.'[1]

Many difficulties present themselves on reading this letter. It seems so unlikely that the cautious Cecil, if possessed of such deadly secrets, should have chosen the Spanish ambassador as the depositary of them, that de Quadra might be imagined rather to have invented the story for the Duchess of Parma's amusement, or Cecil to have been playing upon the bishop's credulity. Yet the ambassador can hardly be supposed in a matter which touched the interests of the Spanish Government so nearly, to have imposed upon the Regent of the Netherlands with an idle falsehood; while, although it is most strange that despondency should have carried Cecil so far, yet the substance of the bishop's communication falls in but too closely with what is known from other quarters of Cecil's state of mind; and it is impossible to believe that in mere practice or diplomatic trickery he would have compromised the Queen's honour.

Well might Randolph say that he had never felt grief like that which Cecil's letter gave him, if this was the mystery which it contained.

But to leave conjecture.

It has been seen that for fifteen months Lord Robert Dudley had been spoken of as the probable husband of the Queen. To him alone she had shown signs of personal attachment. That he had a wife already had not

[1] *MS. Simancas.*

been held an insuperable objection; and the expectations had been general that Lady Dudley would be disposed of by poison or divorce.[1]

Eleven years before when a boy of nineteen Dudley had married the daughter of Sir John Robsart. The ceremony was performed at the court, and is mentioned by Edward in his diary;[2] but it was a love match, and had not been a happy one.[3]

Lady Dudley appeared at no time in public with her husband, either in the eclipse or in the sunshine of his fortunes. From the date of Elizabeth's accession certainly, if not from an earlier period, she was living childless and alone at Cumnor Hall, three miles from Oxford, a clog on his ambition, an obstacle to the hopes which the Queen's marked favour encouraged him to entertain.

If either by Dudley himself or by dependants who hoped to benefit by his promotion, her murder was really contemplated, the pressure of the Arran marriage was an inducement to be quick about it. Certain it is that on the 8th of September at the time or within a day of the time when Cecil told the Spanish ambassador that there

---

[1] It must be particularly observed that these enunciations were not inventions subsequent to Lady Dudley's death, but are proved to have existed anterior to it. The story told by Parsons the Jesuit in *Leicester's Commonwealth*, copied by Ashmole in his *Antiquities of Berkshire*, and preserved by local tradition, is known to every one through Scott's novel. The charity of later years has inclined to believe that it was a calumny invented by the Jesuits against Leicester, whom they hated as the leader of the Puritans; and as it was not published till a quarter of a century after the crime—if crime there was—had been committed, it will not be relied upon in this place for evidence. The reader will judge for himself how far Parsons deserves credit.

[2] Diary of Edward VI., June 4, 1549.—BURNET'S *Collectanea*.

[3] 'Nuptiæ carnales in lætitiâ incipiunt, in luctu terminantur,' was the remarkable reference of Cecil to Dudley's first marriage, in a sarcastic paper on his qualifications to be the Queen's husband. In 1566, when the Archduke Carlos was again a candidate for Elizabeth's hand, and Dudley was again the

was a plot to kill her, Amy Dudley was found dead at the foot of a staircase.

Lord Robert was at Windsor.[1] It appears that before he was made aware that his wife was dead, he had heard difficulty, Cecil, *more suo*, sketched a table of the necessary points to be considered, and of the merits of the two suitors.

TO BE CONSIDERED IN THE MARRIAGE.

Convenient Person.	CHARLES.	EARL OF LEICESTER.
In birth	Nephew and brother of an Emperor.	Born son of a Knight, his grandfather but a Squire.
In degree . . .	An Archduke born . . .	An Earl made.
In age	Of — and never married .	Meet.
In beauty and constitution.	To be judged of	Meet.
In wealth . . .	By report 3000 ducats by the year.	All of the Queen, and in debt.
In friendship . .	The Emperor, the King of Spain, the Dukes of Saxony, Bavaria, Cleves, Florence, Ferrara, and Mantua.	None but such as shall have of the Queen.
In education . .	Amongst Princes always .	In England.
In knowledge . .	All qualities belonging to a Prince—languages, wars, hunting, and riding.	Meet for a courtier.
In likelihood to bear children.	His father, Ferdinando, hath therein been blessed with multitude of children. His brother, Maximilian, hath plenty. His sisters of Bavaria, Cleves, Mantua, and Poland, have already many children.	'Nuptiæ steriles.' No brother had children, and yet their wives have— Duchess of Norfolk. Himself married, and no children.
In likelihood to love his wife.	His father Ferdinando, *ut supra*.	Nuptiæ carnales a lætitiâ incipiunt et in *luctu terminantur*.
In reputation . .	Honoured of all men . .	Hated of many. His wife's death.

Notes in Cecil's hand.—*Hatfield MSS.*

[1] In accepting the correspondence between Dudley and Sir Thomas Blount, as giving a true account of the inquest, it is right that I should say what these letters are.

They are preserved in a volume of the PEPYS MSS., at Cambridge. They are not originals, but they are copies, all written in the same hand, and written out for Sir Thomas Blount himself, since they are signed by him alternately 'T. B.' and 'R. D.' In one instance, in the haste of signature, Blount subscribed one of Dudley's letters, by mistake, with his own initials; and wrote the 'R. D.' over them. There being no pains whatever taken to vary the handwriting of the letters themselves, or to imitate Dudley's real signature, it is obvious that

something which had alarmed him; for his cousin Sir Thomas Blount had left him before the news arrived to go down to Cumnor. A husband on receiving news of the sudden and violent death of a lady in whom he had so near an interest, might have been expected to have at least gone in person to the spot. Lord Robert however contented himself with sending a letter after Blount, desiring that the strictest inquiry should be made into the circumstances; that an inquest should be held immediately, and 'the discreetest and most substantial men should be chosen for the jury.' He prayed his cousin,

they could not have been intended as counterfeits; but there are circumstances connected with the production of them which suggest one or two questions.

In the same volume, and apparently forming part of the same set of papers, is an indistinct and mutilated letter from Blount to Leicester, written, it would seem, in 1566—at any rate, after Dudley was made Earl,—from which it appears that the question of Amy Robsart's death had been secretly revived by the Council in connexion with the appearance of fresh symptoms of a desire in Elizabeth to make Leicester her husband. Blount had been sent for by the Council to be cross-questioned. He was very sorry, he said, that he had not been able to speak with Leicester before he encountered his examination. It appeared that more than one of Amy Robsart's relations had been raising questions about her death; that they were secretly supported by several noblemen; that one of them, John Appleyard, her half-brother, had been offered a thousand pounds if he would come forward and give evidence; and that Leicester, in an

interview with Appleyard, had been so angry that Blount thought he would have run him through the body.

The Inquiry was so secret that except from this fragment, we know nothing of it. It is but a conjecture, but it is not an unlikely one, that the correspondence between Blount and Dudley was produced by the former in the course of the investigation, as evidence in Leicester's favour. But in that case, and in any case, it remains to ask why he produced copies of the letters if he was in possession of the originals, unless there was something in the originals which he was unwilling to show? How, if the originals were destroyed, was he able to bring forward those exact copies? or if we suppose him to have kept copies of his own letters at the time when they were written, why did he not keep the originals of those which he received from Dudley? These questions may admit of very simple answers, but they are sufficient to throw a shade of uncertainty over their value as witnesses in Dudley's defence. They are printed in PETTIGREW's *Enquiry into the Death of Amy Robsart*.

as he 'loved him and tendered his quietness, to use all devices and means for learning of the truth without respect to living person;' especially he begged Blount himself not to 'dissemble,' but to tell him faithfully and truly 'whether it happened by evil chance or villany.'

If this letter was really written by Dudley, and if it was not written to be seen by others, which there is no reason to believe, it is inconsistent with a consciousness of guilt in himself. Lord Robert affected no sorrow for his wife's death, but expressed the utmost alarm for 'the talk which the wicked world would use;' he suspected, to say the least, that there might have been a murder—of course in his own interest, for no other motive is imaginable—and he desired an inquiry as the only means to clear his own reputation. A postscript added that he had sent for his wife's half-brother John Appleyard, with others of her friends, to be present at the inquest.[1]

Blount replied on the 11th from Cumnor. He said that the coroner before his arrival had already called a jury, 'as wise and able men being but countrymen, as ever he saw.' The cause of the death so far as had then appeared was lost in mystery. The servants were all absent when it happened, at Abingdon Fair, where they had been sent according to their own story by Lady Dudley herself. They had gone in the morning—they returned to find their mistress dead. She had been in bad spirits; 'she had been heard many times to pray God to deliver her from desperation;' and there were other stories which showed she had been in 'a strange mind.' Blount suggested to one of her attendants that she had perhaps destroyed herself. But he was told she 'was a good and virtuous gentlewoman,' unlikely to

---

[1] Lord Robert Dudley to Thomas Blount, September 9, from Windsor.—PETTIGREW.

have taken any step of that kind; and the desperation, if it was true that she expected poison, could easily be explained.

On the 13th Blount wrote again to say that the jury were very active; 'whether equity was the cause or malice against Foster, 'he knew not.' They were very 'secret,' yet he could not hear that they had found 'any presumption of evil,' although he believed some of them 'would be sorry if they failed.' For himself, his own opinion was 'much quieted;' he could learn 'almost nothing to make him think that any man should be the doer of it.'[2]

A letter undated, but probably next in time, follows from Dudley to Blount, saying that the foreman of the jury had written to him—that although the inquiry was not yet over, for anything they could learn 'it was a very misfortune.' Dudley said that he was much relieved; but for better security, after the first jury had given their verdict, he wished that there might be a second, and the investigation be pursued further. He had desired another of the Blounts—Sir Richard—'a perfect honest gentleman,' to be present; and he understood that Appleyard was there also, as well as Arthur Robsart, Lady Dudley's own brother.[3]

If Dudley was dissatisfied with the inquiry, it became more than ever his duty to hasten in person to the spot; yet his conduct was not that of a person who had a crime on his own conscience. He knew that the world would believe him guilty, and he had the most serious misgivings that his wife had really been murdered; yet for his own sake he seemed to wish that there should be a

---

[1] Antony Foster, the owner of Cumnor Hall.
[2] Blount to Dudley, September 13.—PETTIGREW. p. 30.
[3] Dudley to Blount.—*Ibid.*

searching examination; and in sending her brother he appeared to be giving the best security for fair play.

There was something in the conduct of the proceedings which was not satisfactory, and whether the inquest had been adequate or not, the people in the neighbourhood did not think so. On the 17th of September, Lever the preacher wrote from Coventry to Cecil, that 'the country was full of dangerous suspicion and muttering,' and he entreated that there might be an 'earnest searching and trying of the truth, with punishment if any were found guilty;' if the matter was hushed up or passed over, 'the displeasure of God, the dishonour of the Queen, and the danger of the whole realm was to be feared.'[1]

In deference to the general outcry, either the inquiry was protracted, or a second jury, as Dudley suggested, was chosen.[2] Lord Robert himself was profoundly anxious, although his anxiety may have been as much for his own reputation as for the discovery of the truth. Yet the exertions to unravel the mystery still failed of their effect. No one could be found who had seen Lady Dudley fall, and she was dead when she was discovered. Eventually, after an investigation apparently without precedent for the strictness with which it had been conducted, the jury returned a verdict of accidental death; and Lord Robert was thus formally acquitted. Yet the conclusion was evidently of a kind which would not silence suspicion; it was not proved that Lady Dudley had been murdered; but the cause of the death was

---

[1] Lever to Sir F. Knollys and Cecil, Sept. 17.—BURLEIGH *Papers*, vol. I.

[2] On the 27th of September, Dudley wrote again to Blount—'Until I hear from you how the matter falleth out, in very truth I cannot be quiet. Yet you do well satisfy me with the discreet jury you say are chosen already.' This can hardly be the same jury which was sitting sixteen days before, and with whose foreman Dudley had been in correspondence.

still left to conjecture; and were there nothing more —were Cecil's words to de Quadra proved to be a forgery—a cloud would still rest over Dudley's fame. Cecil might well have written of him, as he did in later years, that he 'was infamed by his wife's death;'[1] and the shadow which hung over his name in the popular belief, would be intelligible even if it was undeserved.[2]

A paper remains however among Cecil's MSS. which proves that Dudley was less zealous for inquiry than he seemed; that his unhappy wife was indeed murdered; and that with proper exertion the guilty persons might have been discovered. That there should be a universal impression that a particular person was about to be made away with, that this person should die in a mysterious violent manner, and yet that there should have been no foul play after all, would have been a combination of coincidences which would not easily find credence in a well-constituted court of justice.

The strongest point in Dudley's favour was that he sent his wife's half-brother, John Appleyard, to the inquest. Appleyard some years after in a fit of irritation, 'let fall words of anger, and said that for Dudley's sake he had covered the murder of his sister.'[3] Being examined by Cecil, he admitted that the investigation at Cumnor had after all been inadequately conducted. He said 'that he had oftentimes moved the Lord Robert to give him leave, and to countenance him in the prose-

---

[1] BURLEIGH *Papers*, vol. i.

[2] 'Down stairs
Tumble—tumble headlong; so
The surest way to chain a woman's tongue
Is break her neck: a politician did it.'
—*Yorkshire Tragedy*, quoted by PETTIGREW.

[3] Note of the examination of John Appleyard, in Cecil's hand.—HATFIELD MSS.

cuting of the trial of the murder of his sister—adding that he did take the Lord Robert to be innocent thereof; but yet he thought it an easy matter to find out the offenders—affirming thereunto, and showing certain circumstances which moved him to think surely that she was murdered—whereunto he said that the Lord Robert always assured him that he thought it was not fit to deal any further in the matter, considering that by order of law it was already found otherwise, and that it was so presented by a jury. Nevertheless the said Appleyard in his speech said upon examination, that the jury had not as yet given up their verdict.'[1]

If Appleyard spoke the truth there is no more to be said. The conclusion seems inevitable, that although Dudley was innocent of a direct participation in the crime, the unhappy lady was sacrificed to his ambition. She was murdered by persons who hoped to profit by his elevation to the throne; and Dudley himself—aware that if the murder could be proved, public feeling would forbid his marriage with the Queen—used private means, notwithstanding his affectation of sincerity, to prevent the search from being pressed inconveniently far.

But seven years had passed before Appleyard spoke, while the world in the interval was silenced by the verdict: and those who wished to be convinced perhaps believed Dudley innocent. It is necessary to remember this to understand the conduct of Cecil.

When first he spoke to de Quadra, his dismay at the prospect had perhaps led him to believe more than was true, and he must have supposed the case to be desperate.

---

[1] Note of the examination of John Appleyard, in Cecil's hand.—HATFIELD MSS.

CHAP IV.
1560
September

What followed is full of obscurity.[1] That the Queen would attempt to marry Dudley now that he was free was the immediate and universal expectation. The London preachers who had set their hearts on her taking Arran, burst into a scream of indignation. The Dudleys were detested by the greater part of the nobility, and it was supposed that Arundel, Norfolk, Pembroke, and others would forcibly interfere.[2]

The Bishop of Aquila reported that there were anxious meetings of the Council; the courtiers paid a partial homage to Dudley; while Cecil and the Protestants, in dread of imminent convulsion, thought of pressing the Queen to declare Huntingdon her successor. Then again there was a compromise. Huntingdon, though no friend of Dudley's, was his brother-in-law, and the verdict at Cumnor seemed to bear him clear of crime. It was rumoured—seemingly on Lord Robert's own authority—that some private but formal betrothal had passed between the Queen and himself. Cecil, either in appearance

---

[1] De Quadra's letters for the six weeks which followed the murder are lost. There remain only at Simancas, abstracts of their contents, which tell the story most imperfectly. On my first perusal of them, I sent a hasty paper from Spain to *Fraser's Magazine*, in which there are several mistakes, which I take this opportunity of acknowledging. I have no excuse to offer, except that the paper was written in the first excitement of what appeared to me an important discovery. From the essential part of what I then wrote I have nothing to retract; but I admit fully that I misread the notes which refer to what took place at the Council, after Amy Robsart's murder. They consist of a series of unconnected propositions, loosely strung together, and to make mistakes in hurriedly reading a foreign language in manuscript, is not difficult. I subsequently took careful copies of these and all the MSS. from which I quote in this history.

[2] The saying of Arthur Guntur to George Cotton, that 'Ere this my Lord Robert's wife is dead, and she broke her neck. It is in a number of heads that the Queen will marry him. If she do you shall see a grand stir, for my Lord Arundel is sure of the Earl of Pembroke and the Lord Rich, with divers others, to be ready with the putting up of his finger; and then shall you see the "White Horse" (the badge of the Arundels) bestir him, for my Lord is of great power.'— September, 1560. HATFIELD MSS.

or in reality, consented to be reconciled to him;[1] and the reconciliation was in some way connected with the plan for the recognition of Huntingdon as heir presumptive.[2]

In the midst of the confusion, Lady Dudley was splendidly buried at St. Mary's, at Oxford—the gorgeousness of the ceremonial was intended to drown suspicion, and some members of the Council gave it the sanction of their presence.[3] For the rest, amidst imperfect reports themselves half composed of rumour, it is certain only that throughout September there was the utmost excitement and uncertainty. At last, in the beginning of October, the Queen told Cecil 'that she had made up her mind, and did not intend to marry the Lord Robert.'[4]

---

[1] This was certainly true. Cecil had perhaps discovered that things were not so bad as he had feared—he may really after the verdict have thought Dudley innocent of the murder; at any rate he visited him, and they parted apparently friends, as the following letter among the HATFIELD MSS. proves—

LORD ROBERT DUDLEY TO CECIL. (Endorsed in Cecil's hand) *Sept.* 1560.

'SIR,—I thank you for your being here, and the great friendship which you have shown towards me I shall not forget. I am very loath to wish you here again, but I would be very glad to be with you there. I pray you let me hear from you what you think best for me to do. If you doubt, I pray you ask the question, for the sooner you can advise me thither the more I shall thank you. I am sorry so sudden a chance should breed me so great a change; for methinks I am here all this while as it were in a dream, and too far—too far from the place where I am bound to be; when methinks also this long idle time cannot excuse me from the duty I have to discharge elsewhere. I pray you help him that seems to be at liberty out of so great bondage. Forget me not though you see me not, and I will remember you and fail ye not; and so wish you well to do. In haste this morning.

'R. DUDLEY.

'I beseech you sir forget not to offer up the humble sacrifice you promised me.'

[2] 'Que el designo de Cecil y de aquellos hereges de encaminar el Reyno al Conde de Huntingdon es certissimo porque el fin Cecil se ha rendido á Milord Roberto el qual dice que se haya casado con la Reyna en presencia de su hermano y de dos mugeres de su camara.'—*Abstract of* DE QUADRA'S *Letters. MS. Simancas.*

[3] Ibid.

[4] So Cecil himself told de Quadra, —'El obispo dice que le habia dicho Cecil que la Reyna estaba resuelta en no se casar con Milord Roberto, segun que de la misma lo habia entendido.' —*Note of a letter from de Quadra to Philip, October* 13.

But the next hour, or the next moment, she might again change her mind. The only real security was in another marriage, and to this Cecil addressed himself with all his energy. The people were in no humour to be trifled with, and insisted that they must have something to look to in case of her death. There was a fear that Philip might take up Lady Catherine Grey again, with an Austrian prince for a husband.[1] Lady Margaret and the Earl of Lennox proposed to de Quadra to withdraw to Flanders and place themselves at the disposal of Philip. The Huntingdon affair was probably found impossible; and the nation was justly impatient at what appeared to them Elizabeth's culpable trifling.

There were many suitors. The Scotch ambassadors were on their way; the King of Sweden was looked for daily in person; the Duke of Holstein was said to be coming, and there was a talk of the Duke de Nemours. Cecil's preference—if Arran was impossible—was for the Archduke Charles. The Queen herself, notwithstanding her declaration to the contrary, would marry if she might marry the person she cared for; and her unfortunate passion placed her truest friends in the position of requiring her to take a husband, and yet of refusing her the only man on whom her fancy had fastened itself.

Dudley too had his friends at the court—the ladies chiefly, or the mean intriguing eunuch race of the officers of the household; and even among the peers some one or two. Lord Sussex, to whom Cecil wrote for an opinion, viewed the question practically, and on physical grounds was inclined to let the Queen have her way. The Austrian alliance had its advantages; the union

---

[1] 'Temen que muriendo la Reyna V. Md. meteria aquel Reyno en su casa por via de Miladi Caterina.'—*Note of a letter from de Quadra to Philip.*

of Scotland and England would no doubt be of great political importance; but England's true and best security would be in the prince which 'God should give her Majesty of her body.' And therefore Sussex said—

'I wish not her Majesty to linger this matter of so great importance, but to choose speedily, and therein to follow so much her own affection as by the looking upon him whom she should choose, *omnes ejus sensus titillarentur*, which shall be the readiest way with the help of God to bring us a blessed prince which shall redeem us out of thraldom.

'If I knew that England had other rightful inheritors I would then advise otherwise and seek to serve the time by a husband's choice. But—seeing she is *ultimum refugium*, and that no riches, friendship, foreign alliance, or any other present commodity that might come by a husband, can serve our turn without issue of her body—if the Queen will love anybody, let her love where and whom she list, so much thirst I to see her love; and whomsoever she shall love and choose, him will I love, honour, and serve to the uttermost.'[1]

Love for Dudley Elizabeth probably did not feel; a strong fancy rather, which contradiction made more violent, and from which she turned away herself whenever those around her seemed disposed to yield. She proposed to make the favourite a peer, and the patent was drawn out; but when it was brought to her to sign she cut it in pieces with a penknife,[2] saying that 'the Dudleys had been traitors through three descents.' A

---

[1] Sussex to Cecil, October 24, 1560.—*Irish MSS. Rolls House.*
[2] 'The Queen's Majesty stayeth the creation. The bills were drawn for the purpose; when they were presented, she with a knife cut them asunder.'—*Jones to Throgmorton, Nov. 30.* HARDWICK *Papers*, vol. I.

lovers' quarrel followed. The lady half-relented. 'Robin was clapped on the cheeks with No, no, the bear and the ragged staff is not so soon overthrown;' and they 'were as great as ever they were.' But when the courtiers said, marry him then, the Queen would 'pup with her lips: she would not marry a subject;' 'men would come and ask for my Lord's grace;' and when they said 'She might make him a King,' 'that she would in nowise agree to.'[1]

Meanwhile the political clouds were gathering again. The treaty of Edinburgh was but a half-victory; the doubtful attitude of Philip and the conspiracy of Amboise had checked the enterprises of the Guises; but the Bishop of Valence and de Randan had not concealed their contempt for Elizabeth's pretensions to a right of interference in Scotland. The Duke of Guise had used his time well, and for the moment seemed to have trampled out the conflagration in France. The King of Navarre and Condé were thrown into prison; their followers were hunted down, hanged, shot, broken on the wheel, torn in pieces by horses; and the Catholics were watching their opportunity to renew the struggle with England.[2] 'If,' wrote Throgmorton on the 8th of September to Cecil, 'her Majesty do not provide to keep that which she has now obtained beyond the expectation of all men, it had been better to have stood in the mercy of your enemy.'[3]

The French Government said openly that the commissioners had exceeded their powers, and that they would never acknowledge that Elizabeth possessed rights over

---

[1] Sir Henry Neville to Throgmorton.—CONWAY MSS.
[2] 'Relacion de las cartas del obispo de Aquila al Rey, de 25 Julio y 3 Agosto, 1560.'
[3] CONWAY MSS. Rolls House.

the French Queen's subjects. Alva assured Sir Thomas Chamberlain that but for Philip a second French army would have been in Scotland before the end of the summer. The galleys were coming round from Marseilles; the dockyards at Havre and Brest were in full activity; and Mary Stuart proposed to lead in person the next expedition which should sail.[1] 'What thinketh your Queen?' Alva said. 'Hath the French King no party in England? Yea I assure you he hath a great party there; and I fear me I may say as great as the Queen or greater. Should he land 10,000 or 12,000 men at Dover or the Isle of Wight it will be a shrewd piece of work, and be found more difficult to remedy than all men would think.' The Guises pored daily over plans of the English harbours; they were again in communication with the Pope; and at Rome it was said openly that the articles concluded at Edinburgh were not would not and should not be ratified; the Pope would assist the French with 5000 men at his own expense.[2] At the first mention of ratification at Paris, Throgmorton was told plainly ' that the English treaty was part of the Scotch treaty ; that a treaty made by subjects without consent of their sovereign was void; and that the English treaty was therefore void.' Sooner than permit the league between England and Scotland to continue the King of France would ' quit all;' and as for the arms and style, they belonged of right to the French Queen, and she would not abandon them.[3]

If Elizabeth would neither marry the Archduke nor

---

[1] 'Advertisement from beyond seas.'—*Domestic MSS. Rolls House.* Sir Thomas Chamberlain to Elizabeth.—*Spanish MSS., Ibid.*

[2] John Shers to Cecil; from Venice, October 30, 1560.—*Venetian MSS. Rolls House.*

[3] Throgmorton to Chamberlain, November 21, 1560.—Wright's *Elizabeth*, vol. i.

admit the Papal nuncio, sooner or later the King of Spain would be against her; if she refused Arran it was likely that the Scots would turn against her. The rumour that she would marry neither of them, and that she intended instead to take Lord Robert Dudley, was caught at in the Court of Paris with passionate delight. In Paris there were no uncertainties how Amy Robsart met her end. Mary Stuart's wit gave expression to the popular feeling. The Queen of England, she said, was about to marry her horsekeeper, who had killed his wife to make a place for her;[1] and Throgmorton could only console himself with believing that the report was a calumny, and that while Cecil was in power so wild a step was impossible. Were it true, he could see nothing but instant ruin, and could but exclaim—

'Una salus victis nullam sperare salutem.'[2]

So he wrote to Cecil, and Cecil's answer was little reassuring. Elizabeth had contemplated a marriage with Dudley, perhaps was contemplating it still; and living in the focus of the European conspiracies against her, Throgmorton read too plainly in the exultation of her enemies the frightful danger in which she would involve herself. He at least refused to credit the Cumnor inquest. 'He knew not,' he wrote, 'what countenance to bear, the bruits were so brim of the marriage of the Lord Robert and the death of his wife.' 'He would rather,' he said, 'perish with honesty than live with shame,' and he flung into his remonstrance the whole energy that he possessed.

'If, Mr. Cecil,' he wrote, 'you think I have any small

---

[1] Dudley was Master of the Horse.
[2] Throgmorton to Cecil, October 20.—CONWAY MSS. Rolls House.

skill or judgment in things at home, or can conjecture sequels, I do assure you, the matter succeeding, our state is in great danger of utter destruction; and so far methinks I already see into the matter, as I wish myself already dead because I would not live unto that day.

'If the matter be not already determined, I require you, as you bear a true and faithful heart to her Majesty and the realm, and desire to keep them from utter desolation, in *visceribus Jesu Christi* I conjure you to do all your endeavour to hinder that marriage. We begin to be in derision already for the bruit only; if it take place we shall be *opprobrium hominum et abjectio plebis*. God and religion shall be out of estimation; the Queen our sovereign discredited contemned and neglected; our country ruined undone and made prey. With tears and sighs as one being already almost confounded, I beseech you again and again to set to your wits and all your help to stay the Commonwealth which lieth now in great hazard.'[1]

So desperate the situation seemed to Throgmorton that not contented with writing to Cecil he determined to address Elizabeth herself. First he proposed to send a letter to her, but remembering that he must write in cipher, and that his despatch would perhaps be deciphered by a second hand for the Queen's use, he sent his secretary with a verbal message, and a letter to Sir Thomas Parry, who was supposed to be the chief promoter of the Dudley marriage.

The secretary found Elizabeth at Greenwich, and was admitted to a private audience.

She asked why he had come over. He told her. She

---

[1] Throgmorton to Cecil, October 28, 1560.—HARDWICK *Papers*, vol. i.

said she thought as much, and he had better have stayed where he was.

But he was not to be daunted. He knew his mission was a perilous one and determined to go through with it.

He spoke of the antecedents of Lord Robert's family: of his infamous grandfather, his more infamous father Northumberland, and of the hatred felt for the race by the nobility.

'Her Majesty,' said the secretary in his report to Throgmorton, 'laughed and turned herself to one side and the other, and set her hand upon her face.'

The murder came next.

She said that 'the matter had been tried in the country, and found to the contrary of that was reported.' Lord Robert was at the court, and none of his [servants] at the attempt at his wife's house,'[1] and that 'it fell out as should neither touch his honesty nor her honour.'

But the Queen listened patiently to remonstrance; she was not displeased, and promised to tell no one what Throgmorton ventured to do. She looked ill and harassed. 'Surely,' the secretary said, 'the matter of the Lord Robert doth much perplex her, and it is never like to take place, as generally misliked but of the setters forth thereof.'[2]

Sir Thomas Parry, when he read what Sir Nicholas had written to himself, was not 'over-courteous' but 'was half-ashamed of his doings.' The very report and expectation had deranged the whole country. 'Religion was neglected; all were discontented; no man con-

---

[1] This expression admits that there had been an attempt of some kind, and by some one.
[2] Jones to Throgmorton, Nov. 30.—HARDWICK Papers, vol. i.

sidered.' 'The very captains' in the army were selling 'their harness.' 'Every man was for himself.' The secretary hoped 'Lord Robert's matter would not go forward, yet the favour was great which was shown him at the Queen's hands.'[1]

Meanwhile the Arran petition had at length arrived, brought by the Earls of Morton and Glencairn, and by Maitland, who, as he could not prevent it, thought it better to accompany the presentation.

In the Protestant part of the English Council the standing reasons which recommended the connexion were enhanced by the desire to save Elizabeth from Dudley. The apparent failure of the French Protestants and the menacing attitude of the Guises made the league with Scotland more necessary than ever, while the Scotch Commissioners did not conceal that if their request was refused, 'they would be constrained to save their necks, and win the French favour again.' They were entertained by Bedford and Pembroke with marked hospitality; and by these two and by all their friends the marriage was looked upon almost as 'a necessity.'

So strong was the feeling that Elizabeth durst not— perhaps she did not desire to—give a peremptory refusal. She delayed her answer, promising to take time to consider; and it is possible that public considerations might have outweighed after all her personal objections. There was a capacity in her for great self-sacrifice. Her weaknesses were wilful: she could shake them off at her pleasure. Conscious of her power over herself, she liked to dally with temptation; but she remained at all times mistress of her passions; and to steer the English nation in the midst of the breakers was a keener en-

[1] Jones to Throgmorton, November 30.—HARDWICK Papers, vol. I.

joyment to her than to listen to the soft dalliance of a Robert Dudley.

But at the crisis an event happened in France which destroyed Arran's hopes, and delayed the union of the crowns for half-a-century.

The French King and Queen were at Orleans holding a high court of justice on the heretics there. Condé was under sentence of death and was about to be executed; the Calvinists all over the country were marked for massacre; when the keystone was struck suddenly from the arch which sustained the Guises' power. At eleven o'clock at night on the 5th of December, Francis the Second after a short illness left the world. Mary Stuart was a childless widow; the Crown lapsed to the dead King's young brother Charles; and the government of the country fell during the minority to the Queen-mother and the princes of the blood. The King of Navarre and Condé passed from a prison to the steps of the throne.

At first all was uncertainty. The Duke of Guise was not expected to relinquish his power without a struggle. Mary Stuart who had watched dutifully by the sick bed was speculating before the body was cold on her next choice; and Throgmorton writing on the 6th of December to Cecil said with a side blow at Elizabeth, that 'so far as he could learn, she more esteemed the continuation of her honours and to marry one that might uphold her to be great, than she passed to serve and please her fancy.'[1]

But years at all events would have to elapse before the Guises would be in a position to renew their dream of conquest. It was more likely that they had fallen

---

[1] Throgmorton to Cecil, December 6.—CONWAY MSS. Rolls House.

for ever and that France would now follow England into a reformation, while Scotland was once more severed from the French crown. For the present the pressure was removed from Elizabeth, nor was the opportunity a fitting one to conspire against a widowed Queen.

She therefore dismissed the Scotch Commissioners with a reply which though not precluding the possibility of hope was in fact conclusive.

She was glad to find, the Queen said, that the Scots were not ungrateful for her kindness and that her money had not been wholly thrown away. With respect to their proposal of the Earl of Arran, she did not doubt that it was well meant—that the Earl was all which they described him, and that they were offering her the choicest person that they possessed. She was however indisposed to marry. A time might come when circumstances might oblige her to do what willingly she would not do; but that time had not yet arrived; and she would not ask the Earl of Arran therefore to postpone any other connexion which might appear to him desirable. As to the alliance between the two countries, the Scots were most interested in its maintenance. She warned them not to be led away by sinister influences; if they would do their part her own should not be wanting.[1]

Elizabeth had scarcely calculated perhaps on the effect of her answer, although warned what it would be. 'What motive the Queen of England had in this refusal we omit,' says Knox. 'There is such resentment at the rejection of the offer of marriage,' wrote Randolph, 'that the Scots hold themselves almost ab-

---

[1] KEITH, vol. ii. p. 9.

solved from all their obligations.' Arran himself who had set his idle heart on being King of England, unable to obtain his wish in one way, sought it in another, and wrote to offer his hand to Mary Stuart—not, one is surprised to read, without Knox's knowledge and consent.[1] Maitland on his return wrote that he had himself done what he could 'to keep the people still, in some hope that the matter was not impossible;' but 'all men's minds were stirring;' they had not forgotten their obligations to England; but the Queen of Scots would now be the inevitable object of their first attachment; she would probably return to Scotland, and they would 'perforce put themselves in her good graces.'[2] What Scotland would do however—what England would do—what Elizabeth would do—depended on the effect of the King's death in France.

Three parties were left there, almost equal in resources and power: the ultra-Catholics under the Guises supported by the Pope and Philip; the Calvinists under the King of Navarre, his brother, and the three Colignies; and between them the central Gallican or national party, represented by the Constable Montmorency, who had no sympathy with fanatics of either extreme—who were Catholics, but moderate and tolerant, and were disinclined to sacrifice the unity and greatness of France to the special interest of theology. The Queen-mother

---

[1] Since the King of France's death, Arran has written to the King of Navarre and the Constable, and, with Knox's knowledge and privity, designs if possible to marry with the Queen of Scots, supposing the Queen of England will not have him.' —*Randolph to Cecil, January 3, 1561. Scotch MSS. Rolls House.*

Knox himself mentions Arran's proposal, saying nothing of his own share in it; but he adds a sentence or two after, that 'at that time he had great intelligence with some of the Court of France.'

[2] *Maitland to Cecil, January 15.— Scotch MSS. Rolls House.*

Catherine de Medici—who in the late reign had seen
the honour of the throne given to the Queen of Scots,
and the power of the throne to the Duke of Guise
and his brothers—had wrongs of her own to avenge,
and untroubled with special opinions, intended to
play off party against party and rule herself by their
divisions. By the custom of France the Regency
would have fallen to Antony Bourbon King of Navarre.
Montmorency and the Calvinists equally pressed him
to undertake it; but he was a poor creature too small
for the opportunity; Catherine de Medici persuaded
him in private that the office would sit better upon
herself; while in return the charge of treason against
Condé was withdrawn, the prisons were emptied of the
Huguenots, and at a meeting of the States General
on the 13th of December, an edict was passed for general toleration. The Cardinal of Lorraine retired from
Paris taking Mary Stuart with him, after an ineffectual suggestion that she should be the young King's
wife. Navarre became Lieutenant-General; and for the
time the Catholic faction experienced in a violent reaction
the common fate of a despotic party suddenly deposed
from power.

Now was the time for Elizabeth to throw her weight
into the scale. The impending General Council, with
England, France, and Germany, united on the Reforming side, might be 'a free council,' which would give
peace to Europe; England might recover Calais, and
England's Queen be at the head of the Protestant world.

So thought Throgmorton; and he wrote earnestly to
her to seize the occasion—and to seize it promptly.
Time was everything. The English ambassador knew
too intimately the essential strength of the Catholics in
France, and the skill and popularity of the Guises, to

doubt that the tide would soon turn again, especially if the Queen of Scots recovered the allegiance of her subjects, and won them back, as he feared she might, to Rome and orthodoxy.[1]

Throgmorton had been one of those who had most desired the Arran marriage, which he believed would have closed for ever the political prospects of Mary Stuart. He understood the humour of the Scots and the effect upon them of the affront which they would suppose themselves to have received. It would be forgotten if Elizabeth would take the position which he desired for her; but she must stand there in a character worthy of the cause; he was profoundly dejected at hearing that the danger having passed away, she was returning to her unhappy project of marrying Lord Robert.

How in Throgmorton's opinion such a step would affect her—and affect with her the prospects of Europe —will be seen in the following letter:

THROGMORTON TO CECIL.

December 31.

'The House of Guise presently does seem here to bear small rule. The countenance and hope they have is of the King of Spain who for religion and other respects it is thought will help to stay their credit as much as he may.

'The principal managing of the affairs doth seem to be chiefly in the hands of the Queen-mother, the King of Navarre, and the Constable; and as the King of Spain will earnestly travail to suppress religion, so is it most

---

[1] Throgmorton to Elizabeth, December.—CONWAY *MSS.*

safe for her Majesty and her best policy to be as diligent to advance it.

'I do well see you will do the wise and good offices that are necessary to be done and that may be done. The true religion is very like to take place in France, and so consequently throughout all Europe where Christianity is received. I did of late address myself to the Admiral who for his virtue and wisdom is much esteemed. I do find by him that if the Queen's Majesty will put to an earnest mind and hand to this matter, it will be here well accepted and will work very good effect. We talked of many particularities. He thinks that the general council cannot take place, but that the King must assemble a national council, whereunto if her Majesty would send some learned men, he does not doubt but all shall be well.

'But *if her Majesty do so foully forget herself in her marriage* as the bruit runneth here, never think to bring anything to pass either here or elsewhere. I would you did hear the lamentations, the declamations, and sundry affections, which have course here for that matter. Sir, do not forget yourself as to think you do enough because you do not further the matter. Remember your mistress is young and subject to affections; you are her sworn councillor and in great credit with her. You know there be some of your colleagues which have promoted the matter. There is nobody reputed of judgment and authority that doth to her Majesty disallow it, for such as be so wise as to mislike it be too timorous to show it; so as her Majesty's affection doth rather find wind and sail to set it forward than any advice to quench it.

'My duty to her, my goodwill to you, doth thus move me to speak plainly.'

The letter went on to speak of a general league among the Catholic powers, the object of which was to destroy the Reformation.

The projected Catholic league.

'The parties,' Throgmorton said, 'which will have to do in the matter be these, and every one doth make his profit in the reckoning:—the Emperor, the King of Spain, the King of Denmark, the King of Sweden, the Pope, the Queen of Scotland, the Cardinal of Lorraine, the Duke of Austria, and the Duke of Guise. The matter is that the Duke of Austria shall marry the Queen of Scotland, the King of Denmark one of the Emperor's daughters, the King of Sweden another. If this alliance be made, you can consider what may happen.

'Sir,' the letter concluded, 'after I had written thus much the ambassador of Spain came to visit me; who did amongst other matters earnestly require me to tell him whether the Queen's Majesty was not secretly married to the Lord Robert; for said he, I assure you this Court is full of it; and whatever any man doth make your mistress to believe, assure yourself that there never was princess so overseen, if she do not give order in that matter betimes. The bruits of her doings, said he, be very strange in all courts and countries.

'I have presently written a letter to the Lord Robert Dudley the true copy whereof I have herewith sent you,' and also the copy of my letter to her Majesty[2] written of mine own hand; of both which I pray you take knowledge.'[3]

Throgmorton's proceedings, however well intended, were not well calculated for the end he had in view; for

---

[1] No found. [2] Not found.
[3] Throgmorton to Cecil, December 31.—CONWAY MSS.

Elizabeth was one of the many strong-willed people on whom perils and remonstrances operate only as a spur. Cecil was not so idle as his correspondent believed him; but he understood better the disposition with which he was dealing. His reply to Throgmorton's letter showed how dangerous his position was, and how difficult the course which he had nevertheless determined to follow. By 'practices,' by 'bye-ways,' as he afterwards described it, by affecting to humour what he was passionately anxious to prevent, he was holding his mistress under delicate control; and he dreaded lest his light leading-strings should be broken by a ruder touch.

CECIL TO THROGMORTON.

January 15.

'I have professed and do avow earnest friendship to you; and in respect thereof I must advise you not to meddle with the matters of this Court, otherwise than ye may be well advised from hence. What her Majesty will determine to do, only God I think knoweth; and in her His will be fulfilled. Writings remain, and coming into adverse hands may be sinisterly interpreted on the other part; servants or messengers may be reporters to whom they list, and therefore I cannot safely give you so plain counsel as I wish; but in one word I say contend not where victory cannot be had.'[1]

But if Cecil shared Throgmorton's alarm, he did not expose his feelings a second time to de Quadra. The bishop reported at the end of January that since the death of Francis a close correspondence had passed

[1] CONWAY MSS.

between the secretary and the Huguenot leaders. If the King of Navarre remained in power, he foresaw the same consequences for which Throgmorton was so anxious: England and France would draw together; Calais would probably be restored; and he 'prayed God that nothing worse might follow, and that so evil a union might not produce basilisk's eggs.' He was afraid 'that Navarre and Montmorency would cast their eyes on the Low Countries,' which the English would assist them to seize and thus limit the Catholic influence of Spain to the Peninsula.[1]

But comfort came to de Quadra from a quarter from which he least expected it. In spite of Cecil's influence and without his knowledge, Elizabeth, perhaps on the only occasion in her life, was really on the edge of an act of stupendous folly. The Spanish ambassador himself must tell his own story.

DE QUADRA TO PHILIP II.

London, January 23.

'There came lately to me Sir Henry Sidney who is married to Lord Robert's sister a high-spirited noble sort of person and one of the best men that the Queen has about the Court.

'After speaking generally on ordinary matters he came to the affair of his brother-in-law, and the substance of his words to me was this:—The marriage was now in everybody's mouth, he said, and the Queen I must be aware was very anxious for it. He was surprised that I had not advised your Majesty to use the opportunity to gain Lord Robert's good-will. Your

---

[1] Aquila to Arras, December 31.—*MS. Simancas.*

Majesty would find Lord Robert as ready to obey you
and do you service as one of your own vassals; with
more to the same purpose.

'I replied that all which I had heard about the business was of such a character that I had not ventured to
write two lines to your Majesty on the subject. Neither
the Queen nor Lord Robert had spoken to me about it;
and it was of no more importance to your Majesty to
gain the good-will of English sovereigns than it was to
them to gain your Majesty's. Your Majesty could not
divine the Queen's wishes; and she had shown so little
inclination to follow your advice when you had offered
it hitherto, that you could not be expected to volunteer
your opinion.

'He admitted this. He is evidently well acquainted
with what has passed, and he is not too prejudiced to see
the truth. But he added that if I could be satisfied
about Lady Dudley's death, he thought I could not
object to informing your Majesty of what he had said.
The Queen and Lord Robert were lovers; but they intended honest marriage, and nothing wrong had taken
place between them which could not be set right with
your Majesty's help.[1] As to Lady Dudley's death, he
said that he had examined carefully into the circumstances and he was satisfied that it had been accidental,
although he admitted that others thought differently.

'If this was true, I replied, things were not so bad as
I had believed. Had Lady Dudley been murdered God
and man would surely have punished so abominable a
crime. Lord Robert however would find it difficult to
persuade the world of his innocence.

---

[1] 'Aunque gran amores, iban endereçadas a casamiento, y no habia cosa
ninguna illicita en tal que con la autoridad de V. M. no pudiesen saldarse.'

'He allowed that there was hardly a person who did not believe that there had been foul play. The preachers in their pulpits spoke of it—not sparing even the honour of the Queen; and this, he said, had brought her to consider whether she could not restore order in the realm in these matters of religion. She was anxious to do it; and Lord Robert to his own knowledge would be ready to assist.

'I answered that your Majesty would gladly see religion restored in England as well as everywhere else; but it was not a thing to be mixed with concerns of the world. Whether married or wishing to be married, if the Queen was a Christian woman she would regard religion as between God and herself.

'He said that I spoke truly; but though ill-informed in such matters, he was satisfied that religion in this country was in a deplorable condition and that it was imperatively necessary to take steps to reform it. He mentioned a multitude of things most distressing; and he assured me on his solemn oath that the Queen and Lord Robert were determined to restore the religion[1] by way of the General Council; and he then went on to press me to write to your Majesty to forward the affair in such a form that Lord Robert should receive the prize at which he aims from your Majesty's hands.[2]

'I reminded him of what had passed between me and Lady Sidney in the affair of the Archduke Carlos, and how the Queen had deceived both her and myself. I said I could not write unless I received instructions from the

---

[1] 'La religion'—an expression which, as used to the Spanish ambassador, could only be intended to mean communion with the Pope.

[2] 'Apretando mas por persuadirme que yo quisiese escribir a V. M. y encaminar esto negocio de manera que de mano de V. M. M. Roberto recibiese este bien.'

Queen herself. In that case it would become my duty, and I would do it with pleasure.

'He said the Queen could not begin the subject with me, but I might assure myself she waited for nothing but your Majesty's consent to conclude the marriage.[1] In the mean time Lord Robert would speak with me, and would desire me to communicate to your Majesty what I should hear from him. He would offer your Majesty his services to the extent of his power in whatever your Majesty would be pleased to command; especially he would be ready to assist in restoring the religion, seeing clearly that it ought to be done and that it was this which had separated England from your Majesty and forfeited your protection.

'I said again that religion ought not to be complicated with matters of this kind. If Lord Robert desired to communicate with your Majesty on the subject, I would make no difficulty; but I thought that his conscience should be motive sufficient, when the course to be taken was so plain. If he desired to obtain your Majesty's good opinion, so much the more improper it seemed to me that he should stipulate for conditions.

'He then asked whether I thought it would be well for the Queen to send a special minister to your Majesty, to satisfy you on the points where your Majesty might look for fuller explanation, as to what you were to expect both from herself and from him. The ambassador resident in Spain was a confirmed heretic, and not a person therefore whom the Queen could trust in a matter which concerned religion.

'I said I would think it over, and I would tell Lord

---

[1] 'Dixó me que hablarme la Reyna en ello no lo haria, sino fuese comenzando yo la platica, pero que podia estar seguro que ella no esperaba ni deseaba sino el consenso de V. M. para concluirlo.'

Robert as soon as I had heard what he had to say. Sidney himself, I imagine, desires to go. He is a cousin of the Countess of Feria and would like to see her.

'This was the end of our conversation, and I now wait till he brings Lord Robert to me. I have related to your Majesty exactly what passed between us. For some days I had suspected that the Queen had something of the sort in her head. It is so bad a business that I durst not meet their overtures with cordiality; while nevertheless I thought it right to listen to them and report what they say to your Majesty. If we irritate them we may drive them into mischief. Your Majesty will consider the thing on all its sides and resolve what shall be done.

'I do not doubt that if there be a way by which the Queen can be brought to a better mind, either in religion or in her relations with your Majesty—so long at least as her present passion lasts—it will be by this marriage.

The Queen and the Dudley marriage.

'Of this I am certain, that if she marry Lord Robert without your Majesty's sanction, your Majesty has but to give a hint to her subjects and she will lose her throne: I know how this matter really stands and I know the humour of the people. But I am certain also that without your Majesty's sanction she will do nothing in public, and it may be that when she sees that she has nothing to hope from your Majesty she will make a worse plunge to satisfy her appetite. She is infatuated to a degree which would be a notable fault in any woman, much more in one of her exalted rank.[1]

---

[1] 'Podria ser que quando viese que no podia valerse del favor de V. M. se arrojasse á lo peor con que pudiese ejecutar su appetito del qual esta tan vencida que en ninguna condicion de persona dexaria de ser falta notable, quanto mas en una muger de su estado.'

'Cecil who was the great obstacle has given in, being bribed by a promise of the offices vacated by Sir Thomas Parry, who died a few days ago of mere ill-humour. I ought to add that this woman is generally believed to be out of her mind; and it is thought too that she can never have a child. Some say she is a mother already, but this I do not believe.

'Something ought to be done to secure a successor on whom your Majesty may depend. Your Majesty will be pleased to tell me what to do. The thing is of moment, and they will press for their answer.'[1]

De Quadra had occasion afterwards to lament that he had been unable to close with these strange advances at the moment when they were made. Spain was far off, and in the transit of the couriers to and fro the iron grew cool. Cecil had not 'given in' as the bishop supposed, and was as determined as ever to save his mistress if she would allow herself to be saved. He had discovered the intrigue, and with an affectation of acquiescence worked himself into its management. 'Howsoever the end is,' he wrote afterwards to Throgmorton, 'the way thereto was full of crooks; I found my Lord Marquis, my Lord Keeper, and my Lord Pembroke in this matter my best pillars, and yet I was forced to seek byeways so much was the contrary labour by prevention. The Bishop of Aquila had entered into such a practice to further the great matter here, meaning principally the Church matter and percase accidentally the other also, that he had taken faster hold to plant his purpose than was my case shortly to root up.'[2]

---

[1] De Quadra to Philip, January 22.—*MS. Simancas.*
[2] Cecil to Throgmorton.—CONWAY *MSS.*

CHAP IV.
1561
January

Cecil like an honest Englishman laid the blame anywhere rather than on his own countrymen. He was charging the bishop too hardly. A fair consideration of these letters, whatever attempts may be made to explain them away, leaves an impression which the sequel will confirm that Elizabeth's interest in the Reformation was eclipsed for an interval by her interest in Lord Robert Dudley. Stung by the reproaches of the Protestant preachers which in her heart she knew to be deserved, she was tempted to forsake a cause to which in its theological aspect she was never devoted. If Philip would secure her the support of his friend in making a husband of the miserable son of the apostate Northumberland, she was half-ready to undo her work and throw the weight of the Crown once more on the Catholic side.

Self-willed self-confident and utterly fearless, refusing to believe in her lover's infamy and exasperated at the accusations which she might have wilfully considered undeserved, she could easily conceal from herself the nature of the act which she was contemplating, and the palace clique might have kept her blind to the true feeling of the country. The bishop's story has not the air of an invention; and it is incredible that Sir Henry Sidney could have ventured to make a communication of such a character, unless he had believed himself to have the Queen's sanction.

But the bishop learnt afterwards that Elizabeth had consented with extreme reluctance, and only at the passionate entreaties of Lord Robert who had persuaded her that her life was in danger. Cecil's efforts then and always had been to divert her from the wrong course by forcing her to commit herself to another; and before Sidney was allowed to speak to de Quadra, the league

with the Huguenot leaders which Throgmorton had so
earnestly advised and the Spanish ambassador had so
anxiously dreaded, was already under consideration. On
the 19th of January Cecil had written to urge Calvin to
come boldly forward 'to stir the liberal noblemen in
France to suppress the tyranny of the Papists.' He had
advised Navarro to put forward into places of trust
'those who in fearful times were busy with their pens
and weapons.'[1] The Earl of Bedford had been appointed
special commissioner to the French Court. His instructions were drawn in harmony with the broadest liberal
policy and were but waiting the Queen's signature, while
she herself stood poised between two courses on neither
of which she could resolve. On the one side were freedom, truth, greatness, glory, and self-sacrifice; on the
other, bondage to Spain and the possession of the loved
Lord Robert.

The nobler side would perhaps at all events have
triumphed in the end. Whatever her struggles, her
temptations, her vacillations, her inconsistencies, Elizabeth was ever true in the main to the rough path of
greatness. But Cecil found an effective assistant in a
quarter whence he could least have looked for it. Lord
Paget at home and abroad had been an opponent of his
past policy. The old and worldly-wise diplomatist had
deprecated internal changes, and had been the steady
advocate of the Spanish alliance. Like Maitland he was
essentially a secular statesman and had little confidence
in transcendental revolutions. His creed was probably

---

[1] 'Such courage,' he said, 'will abash the Papists, so well I know their cowardice; I mean specially of the shavelings.'—*Cecil to Throgmorton, January 19.*—CONWAY MSS.

of the broadest; he hated fanatics; he believed in good order, good government, and a good army, more than in whitewashed churches, or in doctrines of justification however exemplary their exactness; and the course pursued by Cecil since Elizabeth's accession had been so different from what he would himself have advised that he had withdrawn almost wholly from public life. Once only he had come forward—to protest against the Scottish war; but his opposition like that of his friends had been overruled.

When therefore at this moment he is found again in confidential communication with Elizabeth, it is likely that he had been sent for to give the weight of his experience to the scheme which Sidney had opened to the Spanish ambassador.

Paget advises an alliance with the Huguenot leaders.

Invited or uninvited at any rate Paget in the course of the crisis was again in the Queen's closet; and the opinion which he gave exactly contradicted what was expected of him. It was one thing to advocate the Spanish alliance on open and avowed grounds of national policy—Lord Paget was too keen-sighted to believe and too honest to affect to believe that Elizabeth could safely fall back upon it in connexion with a scandalous love affair. The unlooked-for success at Edinburgh and the death of Francis the Second had changed the aspect of Europe. The Reformers were now the legitimate directors of the French Government with whom the Queen might honourably and safely connect herself, and at whose hands—far better than at Philip's—she might hope to recover the still passionately longed-for Calais; so that the Bishop of Aquila learnt to his disgust that when the Queen was apparently at the point of yielding to Lord Robert, Lord Paget had advised her to sanction

Bedford's mission, to make an alliance with the King of Navarre and the Calvinists, and to let Spain stand over till she could dictate her own terms.[1]

Winchester, Pembroke, and Bacon were on the same side. Beyond the palace walls, had Dudley's scheme been heard of, he would have been torn in pieces by the populace. Bedford's commission was signed on the last of January, and he started the next day for Paris.

Once more as we read his instructions we breathe the wholesome air of heaven after the sinister and stifling vapours of de Quadra's cabinet. The Earl was directed to establish close and intimate relations with the King of Navarre, the Prince of Condé, and the Colignies, to 'impeach' the intended general council by which Lord Robert and the Queen were to have restored religion; and to prevent the marriage of the Queen of Scots with any foreign prince.

To the Queen of Scots herself he was charged with an autograph letter from Elizabeth, who believed perhaps that as she was still young and was feeling keenly a sharp and sudden change of fortune, it might be possible to persuade her into cordiality.

Not indeed that the Queen of Scots had shown symptoms as yet of any desire to conciliate: on the one

---

[1] 'I have delayed so long to write again in the affair of Lord Robert because they have been long in making a second move in it; and because, so far as I can understand, the Queen will not place herself at your Majesty's disposal unless she is forced into it by Lord Robert's persuasions. He is well aware of the peril in which they stand. He sees clearly that without your Majesty's help they can scarcely hope to secure themselves from an insurrection in the realm, or to repress it should it break out. The Queen I believe would have done what Lord Robert presses her to do, had not Paget interfered, who, knowing her humour, has advised her to pause, and to make a firm peace and alliance with France; after which she can negotiate with your Majesty more to her advantage.' —*De Quadra to Philip, February 23. MS. Simancas.*

CHAP IV.
1561
February.

Relations between the Queen of Scots and her subjects.

hand, she had thought of marrying Don Carlos of Spain, and of persuading Philip to transfer his English patronage from Elizabeth to herself; on the other, an independent career was opening itself to her in her own country. She understood her subjects; she knew the angry disappointment which Elizabeth had provoked by rejecting the Earl of Arran. The ambition of giving a sovereign to England, which had made them her enemies in the summer, would now restore their allegiance to herself and their support to her pretensions; and so far from their pressing upon her the ratification of the treaty of Edinburgh, by which those pretensions were abandoned, she could calculate safely on their connivance—perhaps on their open support—if she refused to do it.

The first effect of the affront which the Scots had received was a proposal of marriage to her from the rejected Earl; the second was to bring over flights of the young Scotch noblemen to her feet—among them the bold and 'glorious' Earl of Bothwell, the one among them all who through good and evil had been faithful to her mother's fortunes.

She was not slow to understand her position or to profit by it. On the 31st of December the English ambassadors had demanded the ratification of the treaty. She said that her husband's death had required a revision of the terms in which it had been drawn; but she would refer it to a mixed commission of English and French; and as they should recommend she would act.[1]

But Elizabeth understood little as yet of Mary Stuart's character, and apparently as little of the game which it was open to her to play. The chief fear was of some fresh marriage like the last, which would again

---

[1] Mary Queen of Scots to Throgmorton.—COTTON MSS. CALIG. B. 8.

give a Catholic prince a pretext for interference in Scotland.

Lord Bedford was therefore instructed when he delivered Elizabeth's letter to avoid irritating topics; and to say merely that he was commissioned to give her advice, which Elizabeth if the case were her own would thankfully receive. Scotland was a free country; let the Queen endeavour to govern it by its own laws, by love rather than by force, and with the advice of her own Estates and subjects. She might possibly feel displeasure at the expulsion of the French from Leith; but in reality the service to herself had been as great as the service to England, and Elizabeth could honestly say that she had taken no advantage of the occasion to obtain any purpose of her own. She had annexed no Scottish soil; she had withdrawn no subject of the Scottish Crown from his allegiance; the country was now at peace, well governed, and in good order. Let the Queen keep it so; let her accept the hand which was offered her, and 'bury all unkindness;' and Elizabeth on her part would forget the injuries to herself and would believe that their past disagreements had been occasioned only by the French marriage.

If these advances were well accepted nothing more was to be said about the treaty. Elizabeth could afford to be generous; and if the Queen of Scots showed a desire to be on good terms with her, she would not insist on the letter of her rights.

If however either in words or manner Mary Stuart showed that she would not accept these overtures, 'the intended friendship and love would have to be altered to some other affection;' but 'the fault' would be with the Queen of Scots herself, and she in the end would have most cause of regret. In that case Bedford was to demand the immediate ratification, which there was no longer an excuse for refusing, and he was to warn the Cardinal of Lorraine and the Duke of Guise to be cautious in the advice which they should give to their niece. The Queen of England was ready to forget the past, but on condition only that she had no further cause for complaint or suspicion; and if Bedford ascertained that either a Spanish or an Austrian marriage was in contemplation for the widowed Princess, he was to entreat the Protestant chiefs to do all in their power to prevent it.[1]

Position of the Huguenots in France.

When these instructions were drawn, it was believed in England that the predominance of the Reformers in France was for a time at least secured; but the turn of affairs had proved less favourable to them than the first revolution promised. Catherine de Medici wavered between her dread of the Guises and her hatred of Beza and Calvin. Navarre had introduced Protestant preachers into the palace chapel. Montmorency swore that the King's faith should not be corrupted by men whom his grandfather thought worthy only of fire and sword.

The toleration edict of December had not only set at liberty the prisoners for religion, but it had permitted the reclamation of forfeited estates; and every provincial council was a scene of wrangling and confusion. Cardinal Châtillon Archbishop of Beauvais, the Admiral's brother, superseded his cathedral mass with a 'supper' in his private house, while the mob—there, as in Paris, fanatically Catholic—were howling for vengeance round the walls. The Huguenot congregations attended sermons with steel cuirass and hand on sword-hilt; and Cecil had miscalculated the humour of the 'Papists'

---

[1] Instructions to the Earl of Bedford, January, 1561.—CONWAY MSS.

when he said he knew their cowardice. The ancestors of the French of 1793, removed from them by little more than 200 years, were ready to fight for the faith of the Church with the infernal passions of a legion of fiends. The whole people were drifting fast into civil war; Montmorency and the Marshal St. André were determined that no compact should be made with England of which the surrender of Calais should be a condition; and thus after all Bedford's mission bore little fruit. He failed to persuade Catherine de Medici to refuse her sanction to the council which was about to reopen at Trent. He succeeded only in coming to an understanding with Navarre, Condé, and the Admiral, who foreseeing that they would soon be fighting for their lives again were ready to bid high for Elizabeth's support.

On the 15th of January the Scotch Estates met to receive in form Elizabeth's refusal of the Earl of Arran. Bothwell, Ogilvy of Findlater, Leslie of Auchtermuchty, and others, had returned from Paris to be present. They brought with them as many as three hundred letters from the Queen to different noblemen and gentlemen, containing fair promises that henceforth she would know nothing but Scotland, and study only the greatness of her own subjects; the French that were left at Dunbar and Inchkeith should be withdrawn, and if her subjects would receive her she was ready to return and throw herself without reserve upon their loyalty. To each nobleman she had found something special something gracious to say, something to lead him to believe that she had a peculiar interest in himself. She played on the passionate Scotch heart as upon an instrument of which she understood every note but one. She knew their feudal affection for their sovereign; she knew their national pride, their jealousy of England; she could appeal with the certainty of a response to her own position as a young and desolate widow; she comprehended all save the new hard insoluble element of religion; and so successful was she that the Estates began immediately to consider whether they would not invite her back among them. Randolph wrote that 'all men were going after her;' that if Elizabeth desired to preserve a party in Scotland she must see to it promptly; and that if Mary Stuart returned 'it would soon be a mad world.'[1]

Thus, when Bedford brought Elizabeth's offer of goodwill, he was received with sufficient courtesy to prevent him from producing the more disagreeable part of his instructions. The Queen of Scots could say with entire sincerity that she intended to be guided, as her good sister recommended, by the advice of her subjects. She answered Elizabeth's letter in a tone of the utmost seeming cordiality,[2] while she no longer spoke of referring the treaty to a commission, but desired only to consult the Scotch Estates.

With this very partial success Bedford returned to England, while Noailles went to Scotland to solicit a renewal of the old league with France; and Maitland informed Cecil that what he had foreseen was coming to pass; and that Elizabeth, if she wished to retain the good-will of the Scots, must conciliate Mary Stuart in earnest.

'I pray you,' he said, 'in any wise let means be found that the Queen our sovereign may be in friendship with

[1] Randolph to Cecil, February 26.—*Scotch MSS. Rolls House.*
[2] LABANOFF, vol. i. p. 92.

that realm, otherwise the intelligence betwixt us can for no time endure. You may easily judge what subjects professing obedience are able to do when the prince is bent a contrary way. If her highness may be induced by good means to embrace an equal league with that realm, then I trust the subjects of both shall long live in ease.'[1]

In a second letter, and more confidentially, Maitland described the condition of Scottish parties.

'Since,' he said, 'it had not pleased God that the realms should be united as he and Cecil had proposed,' every one was agreed 'that they must of necessity, so far as in them lay, procure the Queen their sovereign's benevolence towards them.' The neutrals who had hung back during the war were wholly for their own princess, and so were the Catholics. Chatelherault and the Hamiltons would have her return on condition that she would marry Arran; the remainder—'no small party, neither in humble degree nor power'—desired to have her among them with no conditions at all except that she would trust them and bring no strangers with her. All for the present was calm; but when the renewal of the league with France came again under discussion Maitland feared that although it might be delayed for a time resistance in the end would be found impossible.

'If,' he concluded, 'we could altogether refuse which I can hardly think—yea I think it will not be so—then besides the Queen our sovereign lady's displeasure we shall have France perpetually our enemy. It were a perilous estate for Scotland to break the league with France and so have the protection of no foreign nation, we being by a dry marsh joined to that realm which is

---

[1] Maitland to Cecil, February 28.—*Scotch MSS. Rolls House.*

so puissant. Although you be now our friends and like enough that you will so continue for a good season; yet seeing the means of perpetual friendship is desperate, it is to be thought that time may make you enemies, and then were we a facile prey for you being destitute of all friendship. I give you warning of all these matters beforehand and ere they come in question, that you may advise therewith in time.'[1]

Maitland also like Mary Stuart surveyed all the elements of the question but one. He too made small account of religion. How little he thought of it appears from his passing it over in silence. Yet it was this which alone political intrigue failed to disintegrate; it was this which was to determine the future of the Scotch nation, and the power of it was immediately to be visible in a signal instance. Noailles came, and with him the expected discussion on the terms of the Queen's return; and so sure had he and his friends felt of success that he had added a demand in Mary's name that the Catholic faith should be re-established, and 'the bishops and kirkmen' restored to the livings of which they had been deprived. So absolutely was political ingenuity at fault that Noailles' mission was instantly wrecked. 'The bishops' for whom he pleaded were called 'wolves, thieves, murderers, and idle bellies;' the Catholic Church was reviled as 'the congregation of Satan;' the league —the acceptance of which Maitland thought so certain—was flung back in the face of the French, and the Estates declared that after the services which they had received from England the English alliance should be preferred to all others. The Protestants might resent

---

[1] Maitland to Cecil, February, 1561.—*Scotch MSS. Rolls House.*

the slight which had been passed upon them, but their
creed was as dear to them as ever, and policy and national
pride might be powerful without being all-powerful.
The country divided itself into two sharply-divided
parties each professing loyalty to their sovereign and
each anxious to see her return to Scotland. Huntly,
Athol, Sutherland, Caithness, Bothwell, Seton, and the
Archbishop of St. Andrew's formed into a separate
convention for the immediate restoration of Catholicism.
They sent Leslie afterwards the famous Bishop of Ross,
to Mary, to invite her to land at Aberdeen, where
they would join her with 20,000 men and march on
Edinburgh. The Protestants sent Lord James Stuart
to bid her come to them in the name of the Parliament
which had passed the Confession of Faith, and
to rule by the law of which the reformed religion was
a part.[1]

If not mistaken in the feelings of her subjects, Mary
Stuart had been utterly premature. Victory over the
Reformation if not impossible was as yet far off; and
Lord James as a proof that the invitation to the Queen
was not intended as an act of hostility to England, went
through London on his way, taking with him from Randolph
as his credentials an assurance 'that Elizabeth
would find him such a man as the like was not in the
nation for wit and power to serve her Majesty.'[2]

Leaving the two commissioners to make their way to
France we return to Lord Robert who was busily engaged
in reconstructing his torn web. Elizabeth, if she
had escaped the immediate temptation, had by no means
parted with her hopes. The mission of Bedford had
borne less fruit than those by whom it was originated
had expected; and half-deceiving her lover half-led away

---

[1] Randolph to Cecil, March 18.—*Scotch MSS. Rolls House.* [2] Ibid.

herself, the Queen allowed him to continue his negotiations with de Quadra.

On the 13th of February, three weeks after Sidney's first interview, the promised meeting was effected between the Bishop and Dudley.

Lord Robert repeated the assurances which his brother-in-law had made in his name. He said that he believed that the Queen would marry him if the Bishop could assure her of the King of Spain's approbation; the King of Spain in return should find in himself at all seasons and in all services the most humble and devoted of his followers.

De Quadra had as yet received no answer from Philip, and replied that without instructions he could say nothing to the Queen of the desirableness of any particular marriage; but believing as he did that could Elizabeth be tempted to so rash a step she would be walking over the precipice down which he longed to see her plunged, he said he would press upon her generally the necessity of marrying some one, and if she mentioned Lord Robert's name he would recommend him to the best of his ability. A day or two after de Quadra saw Elizabeth herself, and in a letter to his master he thus described the scene:—

'I said she was well aware of your Majesty's desire to see her married; it was rumoured that she was seriously thinking of it; and I could not but tell her what pleasure the report had given me. Should she wish to consult your Majesty, I would use my diligence in communicating her wishes to you; and if I could not at that time be more precise it was because my commission did not allow me.

'She replied after much circumlocution that she would make me her ghostly father and I should hear her confession.

'It came to this, that she was no angel. She could not deny that she had a strong regard for the many excellent qualities which she saw in Lord Robert. She had not indeed resolved to marry either him or any one; only every day she felt more and more the want of a husband. She thought her own people would like to see her married to an Englishman, and she asked me what your Majesty would think if she married one of her household, as the Duchess of Suffolk had done, and the Duchess of Somerset whom she used to laugh at. To this I said I could not tell. I had never spoken on the subject with your Majesty; but if she would direct me what to say I would write and ask you. I was sure of this, that marry whom she would your Majesty would be pleased to hear of it, and that your Majesty well know the high character which was borne by the Lord Robert.

'With an air of much satisfaction she said she would speak to me again, and meanwhile she would promise to do nothing without your Majesty's sanction. She evidently wished that I should say more, but I refrained for fear of making a mistake, and because she is——what we know her to be. As there is danger however that carried away by passion as she is she may fly into some opposite extravagance, I would not leave her without hope. The heretics are full of energy: they have intelligence with Germany, France, and Scotland. Your own Low Countries are in no safe condition; and if we let this woman become desperate she may do something which may fatally injure us, although she destroy herself at the same time.'[1]

The next day Lord Robert again sought de Quadra.

---
[1] De Quadra to Philip, February 23.—*MS. Simancas.*

He told the Bishop that the Queen was delighted with her interview. She was but hesitating out of timidity: if he would press her a little further she would give way. For himself he would be Spanish heart and soul; and as to religion, not only should England send representatives to Trent, but if necessary he would attend the Council in person.

For decency's sake when religion was brought in question de Quadra protested. The King of Spain he said would no doubt be glad of Dudley's services; but he added that any return of Elizabeth to the Church must be matter of conscience rather than of condition: it must not be said that Spain had made a bargain to recover England to orthodoxy. In again writing to Philip however he pressed the necessity of prompt resolution. Double-minded and unstable as Elizabeth evidently was, he thought—though he spoke with diffidence—that Lord Robert had expressed her real feelings. The King of Spain must decide whether he would close with these proposals or assist the Catholics openly to make a revolution.

'Nothing can be worse,' he said, 'than to leave things thus to chance, which will breed some great disaster to your Majesty. You must pardon me if I go beyond my office in speaking thus; my duty makes me forget my prudence. I do not speak my own opinion only; every honest man in the realm uses the same language. The Duke of Norfolk is on the worst terms with the Queen and Lord Robert. Lady Lennox wishes to marry her son the Lord Darnley to the Queen of Scots, and as I understand, is not without hope of success.'[1]

---

[1] De Quadra to Philip, February.—*MS. Simancas.*

The introduction of Lord Darnley's name for the first time in connexion with Mary Stuart, requires a few explanatory words.

Eighteen years before, the Earl of Lennox had claimed against the Hamiltons the succession to the Scotch throne, in default of the royal line. Chatelherault then Earl of Arran and Regent of Scotland was a tool in the hands of Cardinal Beton; and Henry the Eighth had found in Lennox a convenient instrument for maintaining the English party. But the Earl had played his cards ill: he was driven out and took refuge in England, where he had remained ever since a discontented pensioner of the English crown. He had married with Henry's consent Margaret daughter of Margaret Tudor Queen of Scotland by the Earl of Angus her second husband; and Lady Lennox though unnamed in the line of succession in Henry the Eighth's will had been the favourite candidate of Queen Mary who had given her precedence over Elizabeth in the court. She had taken part in Elizabeth's persecution, and had used the opportunity of insulting her when she was brought from Hatfield as a prisoner to answer for her life after Wyatt's conspiracy.

Elizabeth on coming to the throne had repaid her impertinence by marked kindness; but the Countess could neither forgive the mortification of her own hopes nor endure her position as a dependent of a princess whom she hated. She was thus leading a restless life of feverish intrigue. She was a passionate Catholic, and her only son Lord Darnley she had brought up to be the hope of the Catholic party. In addition to her proximity to the English crown, she was as the sole child of Angus, the reputed heiress of the vast inheritance of the Douglases. The Hamiltons still kept from her husband the escheated lands of Lennox; and thus a wronged, angry, and ambitious woman, she was fishing ever in the troubled waters, and was now speculating on the match between Darnley and the Queen of Scots as a means of recovering her property and establishing a double claim on the English crown.

To the existing complications another was about to be added. Lord Robert had undertaken for Elizabeth that she would send representatives to Trent. Whether he had authority for what he had said, or had formed his expectations out of his wishes, was immediately to be put to the test. Paul the Fourth had died in August, 1559. The Cardinal de Medici had succeeded under the title of Pius the Fourth, with the joint consent of Spain and France; and peace between the great powers had given the opportunity for the revival of the Council which their quarrels had dissolved.

After much correspondence and some uncertainty, the French, Spanish, and Imperial Courts had again agreed upon Trent as the spot where it should assemble. Whether England would consent to be represented there was the great question of the day. Although Edward's Liturgies had been restored, the mass abolished, the Pope again deprived by act of Parliament of his spiritual supremacy, yet England had always expressed her readiness to submit to any Council which could represent freely and fairly the learning and piety of Christendom. This Council, like the last, was called in the name of the Pope—yet the Pope had not retaliated on Elizabeth by excommunication as the world had expected; it was understood that a temperate policy was to be the order of the day; and a nuncio was now on his way from Rome to invite the Queen of England to unite in the common interests of Christianity.

There was much to be said on the surface in favour of compliance. The Pope had shown forbearance where it was least expected of him. If the reformed countries refused to take a part in the Council, they left the field to their adversaries, and seemed to shrink from a tribunal to which church controversies had from the beginning been submitted: while as certainly those who had held aloof would be visited at the conclusion by interdict and excommunication—to which neither Elizabeth nor her ministers could affect to be indifferent. The majority of her subjects were under a prejudice which it was unsafe to disregard, that they were still members of the corporate Catholic Church. Lord Robert Dudley had caught the opportunity to identify his private ambition with a great cause; and knowing himself to be execrated by the Protestants, he was cultivating with partial success the gratitude of the orthodox.

On the other hand, to accept the invitation of the Pope was to admit in a sense his supremacy. In a Council under the Papal presidency, the Lutheran and Calvinist ministers would be fortunate if they were allowed to speak without molestation. The votes would be confined to the bishops; and with England the ugly question would rise, whether if the Pope's supremacy was admitted even by implication, the prisoners in the Tower were not the only bishops whom the Pope could recognize.

Lord Bedford when at Paris had laboured but laboured in vain to persuade Catherine de Medici to agree to a national council in France, or to a general council in Germany. Catherine had gone with her kinsman; and Trent and the Papal presidency were established certainties.

332   History of England.

Chap IV
1561
March

Immediately that the meeting and character of the Council was determined, the Huguenots disclaimed interest in it, denied its legality, and avowed openly that they would never submit to its decisions. The princes of the Smalcaldic league met at Nuremberg to answer the message of invitation which the Pope had sent them. They declined unanimously to send any minister in any capacity to a council so constituted. They invited England and Scotland to join them in their refusal; and here we are met by the singular phenomenon that at the very time when Lord Robert believed that he had secured Elizabeth for himself, for Philip and for the Pope, Cecil with or without her sanction was recognizing an identity of religious interests with the Scots which before he was forbidden to acknowledge. In desiring Randolph to express to the Lords of the Congregation the Queen's cordial regard for them, he bade him tell them that 'her Majesty saw daily no amity or intelligence betwixt one country and another so sure as that which was grounded upon unity and consent in religion.'[1]

Elizabeth admits a community of religious interests with the Scots.

Elizabeth's real state of mind was perhaps divined truly by de Quadra when he said that she was self-willed and detested dependence. She courted the Reformers abroad to free herself from the King of Spain; she was exasperated at the thraldom in which she was held by the heretics at home, who forbade her to marry Dudley; and when the yoke pressed hard she looked wistfully to Philip to emancipate her. In great things and small, in fact, like other people, she preferred her own way and was angry when she could not have it—and yet through

---

[1] Memorial to Randolph in the Queen's behalf, signed by Cecil, March 20, 1561.—*Scotch MSS. Rolls House.*

fear in the opinion of de Quadra, or as the reader may prefer to believe through the prompting of her nobler instincts, when the time came for action she yielded always to the direction of Cecil.[1]

The Bishop's chief anxiety and Cecil's chief fear was that she might be tempted into some position from which she could not be extricated. Very soon Cecil ascertained that the intrigue with de Quadra was on foot again. How far it had gone he could not learn; he was ignorant and was most anxious to ascertain whether either Elizabeth or Dudley had spoken to the Bishop alone.[2] He obtained a promise from the Queen however that she would do nothing without consent of Parliament,[3] and when Lord Robert fell ill with vexation, he seems to have contrived to obtain for himself the direction of the negotiation with de Quadra—promising to do his best in it.

Certain it is at any rate that Cecil went to de Quadra on Elizabeth's behalf, to speak to him about her marriage with Lord Robert. He understood, he said, that Sir Henry Sidney had wished the King of Spain to write to Elizabeth advising her to marry Lord Robert. He

---

[1] 'El deseño de la Reyna esta eximirse en cierta manera de V. M. que la tiene apretada de manera que no puede hacer en su Reyno todo lo que quiere viendo la confiança y afision que los Catolicos de aqui tienen a V. M. La summa es que Cecil y estos ereges quieren tener á la Reyna sujeta y atada á su voluntad y obligada á mantener sus eregias; y aunque ella vee que los ereges la tratan muy mal especialmente los predicadores y que Roberto esta peor quisto dellos que de los Catolicos, no osa hacer otra cosa que lo que Cecil le aconseja, porque piensa que luego se levantarian los unos y los otros contra ella.'—De Quadra al Rey, March 23.—MS. Simancas.

[2] Ibid.

[3] 'Me dixó Cecil que la Reyna estaba resuelta de no hacer nada en este negocio sin la voluntad y consentimiento de los de su Reyno, el qual tiene autoridad de gobernar los negocios publicos de su Reyno, y no era bien que en este la Reyna le prejudicase casandose sin consultando á ellos.'—Ibid.

thought it would be well if the King would write such a letter—but it should be a general letter recommending merely that she should marry an Englishman—such as could be laid before Parliament. He assumed as a matter of course that Lord Robert would be the person whom the Queen would choose.

De Quadra inquired whether he was to consider this language as a message from the Queen, which he was to report to his master.

Cecil said that the Queen being a lady could not enter on the subject of herself. It was not for her to invent contrivances to enable herself to be married. Her name must not be mentioned.

At this conversation Sir Henry Sidney had contrived to be present; he had been sent, the Bishop said, by his brother-in-law to keep watch on Cecil.

De Quadra turned to him and asked if he had anything to suggest.

Sidney answered coldly that Lord Robert would be grateful for any service which the King of Spain might do for him. In passing into Cecil's hands he was well aware that the scheme was at an end. De Quadra said that both Sidney and Lord Robert had endeavoured to persuade Elizabeth to shake off Cecil's tyranny and throw herself unreservedly on Philip, but they had not succeeded.

But this subject was not the only one on which Cecil had to speak to de Quadra. The Spanish ambassador was the medium of communication between England and the Catholic world; it was through him that the coming of a messenger from the Pope was made known, and Philip had sent by him a personal request to Elizabeth to admit the nuncio to her presence. This too was a delicate matter on which cautious fencing was necessary. 'That the Church of England itself should have been consulted on an occasion of such importance could have occurred to no one who was acquainted with the conditions of its existence; but Elizabeth's humour about it was dubious and as usual irresolute.

If the council was held in a place which the Kings of France and Spain considered satisfactory, the Queen of England, Cecil said, 'could not reasonably object; she would not refuse to allow the presidency of the Pope, provided it was understood that the Pope was not above the council but merely its head; and its decisions should be accepted in England if they were in harmony with Holy Scripture and the first four General Councils.' But he assumed—as if it was a point on which no difficulty could be raised—'that the English bishops, having been apostolically ordained, and not merely elected by a congregation like Lutheran or Calvinist heretics, would be admitted to sit with the rest.'

The ambassador said it should be considered hereafter, and parried Cecil's thrust with another. The General Council, he said, would probably be a failure after all, through the obstinacy of the Germans; was it possible that a national Council could be held in England under a Papal legate?

To this of course Cecil objected: de Quadra reminded him that the change in religion had been effected by Act of Parliament alone in the teeth of the entire ecclesiastical estate; but Cecil said peremptorily that the admission of a Papal legate was impossible; and firing a last shot as he took his leave, he added that if the Pope wrote to the Queen, he must address her as Defender of the Faith; if her titles were inadequately rendered the letter would not be received.

CHAP IV.
1561.
March

'I know not what to think,' the Bishop wrote in concluding his account of this conversation; 'things are so perplexed that they utterly confuse me: Cecil is a violent heretic; but he is neither a fool nor a liar, and he pretends to be dealing with me frankly and honourably.

'The points which he concedes about the Council are of great value.

'The Queen's position is a most difficult one; but although it is possible that the consciousness of her danger united with her passion for Lord Robert may make her really desirous to rejoin the Church, so it is possible that she may be playing a game to keep in favour with your Majesty, and to deceive her Catholic subjects with hopes which she has no intention of fulfilling.'[1]

A few days later arrived Philip's answer to Sir Henry Sidney's first proposals. The King of Spain was never in a hurry; the couriers were on the road a fortnight between London and Madrid; six weeks were spent in deliberation, and at the end of them Philip had concluded to consider Dudley's offer with favour. He was anxious for peace—anxious for the success of the Council; he shrunk from the rough methods of dealing with Elizabeth which were pressed upon him by de Feria, because he knew that if he encouraged an insurrection of the Catholics, he would embroil himself with France, and Europe would be once more in a conflagration. Thus, although he admitted that he had little confidence in Elizabeth—that many times before he had found that her smooth words meant only that she was in difficulty, and that when the difficulty passed her humour changed again—

---

[1] De Quadra to Philip II., March 23.—*MS. Simancas.*

he let himself believe that her present passion was more deeply rooted; and that if so, he might as well take advantage of it.

But before he would take any action, he required proofs of Elizabeth's sincerity. He must see a declaration in her own hand, and signed with her name, that she wished to be reconciled to the Church. She must release the bishops and others who were in the Tower for refusing the oath of supremacy; she must allow her Catholic subjects to use their own services freely till the conclusion of the Council. If she would satisfy him on these points, she might assure herself that he himself, and the Catholics in England and out of it, would support her in her marriage with Lord Robert Dudley.[1]

Could de Quadra have returned this answer when Sidney first spoke to him, something might perhaps have come of it; but it was too late. It was a misfortune of Elizabeth's stratagems that she deceived her friends as well as her enemies. From the first opening of the intrigue, she had treated de Quadra with marked attention; the apparent cordiality between the Court and the Spanish ambassador alarmed the Catholics into a belief that Philip was about to desert them; and to allay their apprehensions de Quadra told Heath and Montague that she had held out hopes to him that she would acknowledge the Council, and that negotiations were actually in progress which might lead to her return to the Catholic Church. Heath and Montague told their friends, and the news went through London like an electric shock.

At the beginning of April the Queen removed to

[1] Philip II. to de Quadra, March 17.—*Toledo MS. Simancas.*

CHAP IV
1561
April

Greenwich, where it was generally understood that she intended to receive the nuncio; and Lord Robert, when the contents of Philip's letter were communicated to him, could not conceal his imprudent exultation, and paraded his own and (as he represented it) the Queen's intention of 'restoring *religion*.'[1]

From the time that Cecil's hand had been in the matter, de Quadra had felt misgivings that Dudley was deceiving himself. The nuncio's arrival however would be a final criterion of the course which England would follow. If a messenger from the Pope was publicly received, Elizabeth's professions were sincere; if he was refused an audience, the bubble would break.

Unless Cecil was purposely deceiving Throgmorton, Elizabeth was really entangled;[2] yet already unfavourable symptoms were justifying the Bishop's uncertainty. By way of answer to Philip's demand for the liberation of the bishops, and to allay the alarm of the Reformers, Cecil had instituted a general search for Catholic conventicles. Sir Edward Waldegrave one of Mary's Council had allowed mass to be said in his house; he was sent, with Lady Waldegrave, the priest, and the congregation, to the Tower.[3]

---

[1] Elizabeth had given Lord Robert a fresh proof of favour. 'El discontento de Milord Roberto ha pasado; en que le ha mandado la Reyna dar un aposento en lo alto junto al suyo por ser mas sano que el que tiene abajo, y esta contentisimo. Le dije que V. M. se habia holgado mucho de haber entendido la determinacion que el tiene de procurar la restauracion de la religion en este Reyno. Respondiome luego y sin detenerse ni pensar en ello que era verdad que la tenia, y que la misma tenia la Reyna, la cual no desecha otra cosa que verse fuera destas disentiones y tener su Reyno quieto.' — *De Quadra to Philip, April 12.—MS. Simancas.*

[2] 'Here hath been no small ado to refuse this Popish messenger. The Bishop of Aquila had wou more with former practices than was easy to overtake.' — *Cecil to Throgmorton*, HARDWICK *Papers*, vol. I.

[3] Examination of persons arrested April 17.—*Domestic MSS. Rolls House.*

'When I saw this Romish influence toward,' wrote Cecil, 'I thought it necessary to dull the Papists' expectations by punishing of massmongers for the rebating of their humours.'[1]

CHAP IV
1561 April

Sir Henry Sidney received orders to repair to his presidency. Before he left London he told de Quadra that it was a pretext to get rid of him—he had been the first instrument in the negotiation, and his presence was inconvenient. The Queen had changed her mind, and would act like a woman, and the blame would be thrown upon Lord Robert.[2]

Sir Henry Sidney is sent out of London.

It appeared also that the Catholic nobles would be no parties to the intrigue. On the 23rd of April, at the annual meeting of the Knights of the Garter, Sussex proposed an address to the Queen, recommending Dudley

---

[1] Cecil to Throgmorton.—CONWAY MSS. Several curious circumstances were connected with these arrests. Sir Thomas Stradling of Glamorganshire, was charged with exhibiting a crucifix said to have been found in the heart of a tree that was blown down in his park, and it was thought worth while to send a commission from London to investigate the story.

The Bishop of London acted as Cecil's Inquisitor in the affair of Sir Edward Waldegrave; and wishing to do his work effectually, yet not venturing, as he admitted, to inflict a heavy punishment for merely saying or hearing mass, he discovered that the officiating priest had been concerned in making a 'love philtre.' Sorcery would be a safer ground for process. The Bishop applied to the Lord Chief Justice Catlin, to learn what the law was in such cases, and Catlin replied unexpectedly that it was an offence for which no provision had been made. The Church courts had hitherto claimed cognizance of all such cases; but they were now crippled and powerless, and the only precedent which he could find bearing on the case was one of the time of Edward the Third, thus entered on the roll:—

'Ung homme fut prinse en Southwark avec ung taste et ang visaige dung homme morte et avec ung lyvre de sorcerie en son male et fut ameane en banke du Roy devant Knyvet Justice mais nulle endictment fut vers lay, por qui les clerkes luy fierent jurement que jamais ne feroit sorcerie en apres, et fut delyvere del prison, et le teste et les lyvres furent arses a Totehyll a les costages du prisonnier.' —*Domestic MSS.*, ELIZ., vol. xvi.

[2] De Quadra to Philip, May 1.— *MS. Simancas.*

z 2

to her as a husband. Norfolk and Arundel refused their consent; Montague, to whom a few days before Lord Robert had in vain written a fawning letter, was equally unwilling, and there must have been some bye-action behind the scenes—like the game which had been played with de Quadra; for an address was presented, in the place of that proposed by Sussex, recommending marriage generally, but without Dudley's name, and the Queen replied in a passion that when she married 'she would consult her own pleasure and not that of her nobles.' The scheme was not progressing; it was plain that the Catholics would not purchase a change of policy at the price of accepting a Dudley as their King.[1]

In the face of such symptoms de Quadra foresaw too certainly the fate of his demand for the admission of the nuncio. It had been presented in the form of a personal request from Philip to the Queen, by whom it was submitted to the Council. The nuncio himself waited in Flanders to hear the result of their deliberation.

The points raised in the discussion were, first, whether under the statutes of Henry the Eighth a Papal emissary could legally be admitted into England; and secondly, whether, if the law could be evaded, the advantages to be gained would compensate for the possible inconvenience.

Premunire—that fatal spell before which spiritual pretensions sunk exorcised, mysterious as excommunication, and no less terrible in its vagueness—was again brought forward. The Council remembered that even Queen Mary had held at bay with it the legatine commission sent by Paul to the rival of Pole; while again 'the very sound'

---

[1] 'Relacion de las cartas del Obispo de Aquila á su Mag.'; Avril, Mayo, 1561.'—*MS. Simancas.*

of the coming of a nuncio had awakened dangerous hopes
and agitating rumours. Priests had 'conversed with
the devil,' to learn how long the Queen would live; and
the devil had answered—loyal citizens would hope untruly—'that she should not long continue.' Summer
was coming on, when 'the devil had most opportunity
to make trouble and tumults;' and if there were signs
of yielding to the Pope, bad subjects would rebel, and
good subjects 'would be cast down.'

The nuncio might offer to take an oath that while he
was in England he would do nothing prejudicial to the
realm—but prejudicial was a vague word; 'or he might
think it was no perjury to break faith with heretics.'

The Pope could not possibly mean well towards the
present constitution of the English Church; and the
nuncio's chief object would probably be 'to prepare the
discontented subjects for rebellion.'[1]

While the Council were thus deliberating, Elizabeth
sent for de Quadra, if possible to soothe him. She
attempted to persuade him that differences of opinion in
religion were not matters which need interrupt her good
relations with the Catholic powers; and she then asked
particularly what Philip had proposed to do about Lord
Robert and herself in case Catholicism was restored.

De Quadra replied sullenly that Philip had proposed
nothing. Overtures had been made by Sir Henry Sidney,
by Lord Robert, and by herself; Lord Robert had
declared expressly in his own name and hers that
England was to be brought back to the Church; and the
King of Spain, who was only anxious for the welfare of
the realm, had professed extreme pleasure at the news.

---

[1] Note of a consultation held at Greenwich, May 1.—*Spanish MSS. Rolls House.*

She said she could not believe Lord Robert could have made such large offers.

The Bishop replied that if she would send for him he would confess it in her presence; nay she had said as much in her conversations with himself; he reminded her of the times and places.

She could not deny her words; she said it might be so, but there had been conditions. The Bishop answered that he remembered nothing of conditions; and as a last hope, he implored her not to reject the opportunity which God had offered her of restoring order, and to admit the nuncio.

She said he would receive his answer from the Council, before whom he was presently after requested to appear. The deliberation was concluded; they were prepared to communicate their decision.

The nuncio cannot be admitted.

What that decision was de Quadra read in Cecil's face. He refused to hear it; he would take his answer, he said, from no one but the Queen. He was told that he might do as he pleased about that. The resolution would be read in his presence, and he might report it or not, as seemed good to him.

Politely and peremptorily the visit of the nuncio was declined. Neither directly nor indirectly could England recognize the authority of the Pope; and for sending bishops or ambassadors to the Council, as soon as any free and truly general council could be assembled by consent of all Christian princes, with guarantees for liberty of discussion, England would be willingly represented there; but for the Council to which they were now invited—called by the Pope as a continuation of the Council lately held at Trent—'where no manner of person might have voice or decision but such as were already sworn to the maintenance of the Pope's authority,' 'her Majesty could hope no good from it, as tending only to confirm those errors and those claims which had occasioned the disorder of Christendom.'[1]

That was their final judgment.

The Bishop coldly replied that for such a message they must use their own ministers. For himself he had been the bearer of a request from the King of Spain to their mistress, and he must learn from her own lips whether the words were theirs or hers.

He at once returned to her room.

'I found her,' he wrote in his report to Philip, 'embarrassed, confused, and evidently frightened. I had been told, I said, that the nuncio was not to be admitted. She had led me to expect a different result. I was sorry on public grounds; and for myself she had made me ridiculous in your Majesty's eyes.

'She pretended that when she had spoken to me of sending to the Council she had assumed that it would be a free Council.

'I said I knew nothing of assumptions: I had but reported to your Majesty her own words. But the chief loss was not mine. I knew how it was; and it rested only with herself to retrace her steps when she pleased.

'She spoke much in reply of her grateful devotion to your Majesty, and so I left her.'[2]

'Bitterly sorry am I,' the Bishop said in conclusion, 'that I could not close with Sidney's first advance to me before those practices had grown through Paget's means with the French and German heretics; but I have not ceased to show both the Queen and Lord Robert that

---

[1] *Spanish MSS. Rolls House.* De Quadra to Philip, May 5.—*MS. Simancas.*
[2] De Quadra to Philip, May 5.—*MS. Simancas.*

whenever they choose to turn to your Majesty they may take their own way, and marry without having to sue as mendicants for the consent of their subjects,'[1]

The nuncio then was refused. The Pope's offered hand was rejected; and in a manner more marked than ever England declared her confirmed hostility to the see of Rome. 'God, whose cause it is,' wrote Cecil, 'and the Queen's Majesty, whose only surety therein rested, hath—the one by directing, the other by yielding—ended the matter well; and if it may so continue I shall be in more quietness.'[2] Once more the Catholics saw their hopes fade away, yet not at least without a consolatory accident, which seemed to show that they were not wholly forsaken of Heaven. The spire of St. Paul's was the pride of English architecture. Five hundred feet it towered up into the then transparent air, dipping the gilded eagle which glittered on its summit into the lower strata of the clouds—the envy of the Christian world. On the 4th of June a thunder-cloud drew down over London. The sky grew black as ink, still as night, and almost as dark. About two in the afternoon the first flash broke, and amidst the roar of the thunder a pinnacle was struck from the tower of St. Martin's church, and fell through the roof into the nave, while a boatman from his wherry on the river saw a jagged line of light touch for an instant the highest point of the proud cathedral. For the moment it seemed to have passed harmlessly by—the slender shaft stood proud as

---

[1] 'No he dexado de proceder por la via que ha començado, que es mostrarles á ella y á Ruberto lo que han de tomar si quieren ganar la voluntad de V. M⁴. para con esto poder hacer la suya, que es casarse sin haber de mendicar ny comprar como hacen el consento de sus subditos.'—*MS. Simancas*.

[2] Cecil to Throgmorton, May.—CONWAY *MSS*.

ever against the storm cloud—but towards evening a faint blue smoke was seen curling round the ball. Pale tongues of fire flickered out into a coronet of light, and a minute later the cross and the great eagle crashed down upon the floor of the south transept. The lead with which the wood was sheeted ran down in a fiery stream, kindling the surface as it swept along; and very soon the whole spire, from the tower wall to the summit, was a gigantic pyramid of fire.

All London rushed to the Churchyard; bishops, lords, and councillors herded helpless and confused with the crowd of citizens. The cry was to break the communication of the tower with the church. But the dense mass of people surging to and fro choked the avenues by which workmen could be brought up; they were short of tools, and there was no ladder which could reach the battlements. The south transept was kindled by the lead; the nave, east and west, soon followed. The wind was rising, and with beams and blazing rafters falling everywhere, the next fear was for the Bishop's Palace, and for the houses towards the Thames.

Happily the conflagration had been visible far down the river. The Queen had seen it from the windows of Greenwich Palace; Winter's ships were lying in Limehouse Reach, and with his boats' crews and with the pirate Strangways, who was now a valued officer in Elizabeth's service, the young admiral hurried to the scene. The presence of a disciplined body of men brought the crowd to order. The useless hands were ranged in lines to the Thames' banks, passing water-buckets to and fro. As soon as the last remains of the spire had fallen the sailors climbed upon the blazing roof; the Palace was covered with hides and drenched with water, and the communication broken with the cathedral. By ten o'clock the fire had ceased to spread, by midnight it was extinguished.

The wind in the course of the storm had veered round the compass; cinders had fallen in a circle from Fleet Street to Newgate Market; and drops of lead were found far away in gardens in the suburbs; though, strange to say, no life was lost, and no other house was injured. But the Cathedral of Paul's, the world's wonder—which under Edward had been desecrated into a public lounge, a stock exchange, and a stable, which Mary and Pole had purified, and which again was sinking into neglect and profanation—stood a charred and roofless ruin.

The fanatic multitude cried that it was the work of the Papists: the Papists had put gunpowder into the spire, or they had set it on fire by magic. Among the Catholics 'the disaster was terribly discoursed of'; the best did interpret it as Jonah preaching to Nineveh; the malicious did apply it to such signs as chanced to Sodom and Jerusalem.'[1]

For once wisdom was heard from the pulpit. The Bishop of Durham (Pilkington) the following Sunday told the people sharply that it was not for them 'to attribute the calamity to God's displeasure against any special sect or condition of men.' He bade every man look at home, and say *ego sum qui peccavi*. And as to the supposition that it was 'a judgment on the change of religion,' 'he showed out of history that as great or greater calamities had happened when there was no change of religion.' Half London had been burnt in the time of Stephen. The spire which had just fallen was struck in the reign of the saintly Henry the Sixth.

---

[1] Throgmorton to Cecil, June 23.—CONWAY MSS.

If however there was no evidence in the burning of
St. Paul's that God resented the rejection of the nuncio,
the resentment of the Pope might have been looked for
with some certainty. It was only at Philip's intercession that the bolt had been so long withheld. It was
now expected confidently that Pius would reply with
such weapons as were at his command. And Elizabeth
without doubt would have been spared no longer had
not Philip again interposed. Still forcing himself to
hope that de Quadra would succeed in working upon
her, he wrote to Cardinal Pacheco, his minister at
Rome, bidding him request the Pope once more to stay
his hand.

'His Holiness,' he said, 'after the refusal to admit
his nuncio, may desire naturally to pronounce the Queen
of England schismatic and deprive her of her crown.
If he has any such intention, I must request him to
forbear from pronouncing a sentence which cannot be
executed.

'The duty of carrying it into effect will devolve upon
myself, as the most faithful son of the Church. I am at
present in no condition to attempt any such enterprise;
and should I do so the French and Germans will no
doubt take arms against me. The peace of Europe will
be broken, and the Council, the only remedy for the
diseases of the world, will be again postponed.

'Occasion will not be wanting by-and-by when I
am better prepared; and my own person and the arms
of Spain will be then at his Holiness's disposal. He
knows well my zeal in the matter. For this I married
my Queen who is in glory, when her age and constitution gave small promise of children; and the risk to
which I exposed my life in going to that realm is

notorious to the world. When the present Queen destroyed all that we had done, the late Pope proposed to depose her and give England to me. Sensible as I was of his Holiness's kindness, I persuaded him to forbear. You will entreat the present Pope in my name to exercise the same moderation, assuring him at the same time that I aim at nothing but the glory of God.

'You will observe in his reply whether he repeat the offer made to me by Paul the Fourth. I would know his views on that point as soon as possible.'[1]

Thus again Elizabeth was left to de Quadra's skill; and the ambassador to do him justice played his part with meritorious ability. The progress of the love affair will be seen in the two following letters:—

DE QUADRA TO PHILIP.

London, June 30.

'Five or six clergy have been exposed on the pillory as conjurors and necromancers. They were found making a figure of the nativities of the Queen and Lord Robert, with I know not what other strange things—trifles all of them, had they not fallen into the hands of men who were glad to make priests ridiculous.

'The Queen invited me to a party given by Lord Robert on St. John's day. I asked her whether she thought her ministers had done good to their country by making a laughing-stock of Catholics in this way. She assured me the secretary was not to blame. In speaking

---

[1] Philip II. to Cardinal Pacheco, July 11.—MIGNET's *Life of Mary Stuart*. Appendix.

of your Majesty, she said that as long as you were in
England you had been a general benefactor, and had
never injured a creature.

'I professed myself shocked at the doings of the
Council. I told her she should look better to them, and
not allow these headstrong violent men to guide her in
so serious a matter as religion.

'She listened patiently and thanked me for my advice.
In the afternoon we were in a barge, watching the games
on the river. She was alone with the Lord Robert and
myself on the poop, when they began to talk nonsense
and went so far that Lord Robert at last said, as I was
on the spot there was no reason why they should not be
married if the Queen pleased. She said that perhaps
I did not understand sufficient English. I let them
trifle in this way for a time, and then I said gravely to
them both, that if they would be guided by me they
would shake off the tyranny of those men who were
oppressing the realm and them; they would restore
religion and good order; and they could then marry
when they pleased—and gladly would I be the priest
to unite them. Let the heretics complain if they dared.
With your Majesty at her side the Queen might defy
danger. At present it seemed she could marry no one
who displeased Cecil and his companions.

'I enlarged on this point, because I see that unless I
can detach her and Lord Robert from the pestilential
heresy with which they are surrounded, there will be no
change. If I can once create a schism, things will go as
we desire. This therefore appears to me the wisest
course to follow. If I keep aloof from the Queen, I
leave the field open to the heretics. If I keep her in
good humour with your Majesty, there is always hope—
especially if the heretics can be provoked into some act

of extravagance. They are irritated to the last degree to see me so much about the Queen's person.

'Your Majesty need not fear that I shall alienate the Catholics. Not three days ago, those persons whom your Majesty knows of sent to me to say that their party was never so strong as at this moment, nor the Queen and Council so universally abhorred.'

DE QUADRA TO GRANVELLE.

June 30.

'You will see by my letter to the King how we are going on. I keep on terms with the Queen and Lord Robert because the heretics with their quarrels and impertinences may sooner or later drive her out of patience, and nothing is more likely to tempt them to it than her intimacy with me. She on her part knows that it is her interest to keep well with me, because with this love affair of hers she would be a lost woman if the King our master so pleased. As to the rumoured marriages with Sweden or Denmark, she is so infatuated with Dudley that nothing will ever induce her to give him up.

'You will not think me inconsistent if at one time you hear I am quarrelling with her, at another that all is confidence and smooth speeches. You remember the advice of Pontius the Samnite when he had the Romans in the valley—either to feast them and let them go, or to cut all their throats.'[1]

The story returns to Leslie and Lord James, who had left Scotland on their separate errands to Mary Stuart, who was then with the Cardinal of Lorraine at St. Dizier. Leslie was first in the field. He had crossed by

---

[1] *MS. Simancas.*

Brille while Lord James went round by London. As the spokesman of the Gordons, the Athols, the Sutherlands, the Setons, and the Catholic clergy, Leslie invited the Queen to put herself at the head of her natural friends, to arrest at Paris the false brother who aimed at stealing her crown, and with their assistance to crush the heretics and traitors who had sold their country to the Saxon.

Had the armies of France been at her command, had there been no England and no title in question to the English crown, Mary Stuart would doubtless have consented. But she regarded Scotland as the stepping-stone to a higher ambition; the experience of the past year had taught her the danger of violent methods, and she preferred a surer if a longer road. The party who were offering her their services would be her friends at all events; their loyalty was secured by their necessity. Her own policy was to win their opponents the friends of England, to work on their disappointed hopes, and to make their ambition the instrument of her own. Perhaps there was no one in the world whom she more heartily hated than her half-brother; but Leslie returned with a grateful refusal of his proposals, and Lord James who arrived at St. Dizier the day after his departure was affectionately welcomed. In spite of the opposition of Knox, he was empowered by the Estates to offer her the free exercise of her religion. With this condition alone, she professed her readiness to return to Scotland. Lord James tried ineffectually to gain her over to the creed of the Congregation, and his sister in return tempted him with profuse offers of money, benefices, and cardinals' hats, with equal unsuccess. But their differences did not affect the terms on which they parted; for although he was so far true to Elizabeth as to urge her to ratify the treaty of Edinburgh, he was not prepared to insist upon it; and in that one concession she read his own and his party's weakness. The boy-king of France was about to be crowned at Rheims. She proposed to sail immediately after the ceremony; and so heartily she seemed to throw herself on her brother, that she offered to make him Regent of Scotland till her return.

To extort from Mary Stuart the abandonment of her pretensions to the Crown of England, and for this alone, Elizabeth had encountered the cost and peril of the Scottish war; yet even Lord James who of all the Scots was least careless of his obligations, ventured to write to her after leaving his sister, on the point on which she was most sensitive; and to reveal in language of which the hesitation of expression could not obscure the meaning, the part which he and his countrymen were prepared to play.

The Queen of Scots had claimed a present right to Elizabeth's throne; the Commissioners at Leith had resigned those pretensions in her name; and the Scots themselves were of all men in the world the last who should have countenanced her in evading her engagements. But their hungry pride was too strong for their honour.

Lord James Stuart and the English succession.

'You are two young and excellent Queens,' Lord James wrote to Elizabeth, 'whose sex will not permit you to advance your glory by war and bloodshedding. You ought to love each other. Neither of you both is ignorant from what root the contrary affection doth proceed. I wish to God the Queen my sovereign had never taken in hand to pretend interest in, or claim title to, your Majesty's realm. Then you should have been and continued friends. But since on her part something hath been thought of it, I fear that unless that root is removed it shall ever breed unkindness. Your Majesty cannot yield, and she may on the other part think it hard, being so nigh of the blood of England, so to be made a stranger from it. Is there any midway possible? I have thought long of it but never durst speak of it. What if your Majesty's title did remain untouched as well for yourself as for the issue of your body? Inconvenient were it to provide that to the Queen my sovereign her own place was reserved in the succession to the Crown of England—which your Majesty will pardon me if I take to be next by the law of all nations, as she that is next in lawful descent of the right line of King Henry the Seventh; and in the mean time the isle to be united in perpetual friendship?'[1]

'I will acknowledge your present rights,' Mary Stuart virtually said to Elizabeth, 'when you will acknowledge me your successor, and not till then:' and in this language it was plain that all parties in Scotland—treaty or no treaty—were prepared to support her.

If it be asked why Elizabeth should have made a difficulty in consenting, the answer was but too ready. The 'inconvenience' of which Lord James spoke, would in all likelihood have been her immediate assassination.

Already it had been found necessary to surround her with precautions against poison. Not an untasted dish might be brought to her table; not a glove or a hand-

---

[1] Lord James Stuart to Queen Elizabeth, August 6.—*Scotch MSS. Rolls House*. This letter was written before Mary's return to Scotland, though several months after Lord James was at St. Dizier. It may be taken to represent the feelings of the most moderate members of the Scotch Estates.

kerchief might approach her person which had not been scrutinized and she was dosed weekly with supposed antidotes.[1] In spite of precaution, the secret adherents of France, of the Papacy, and of the Queen of Scots, held places in the royal household, and attended in the royal bedchamber. With the prize of the succession once secured, the Catholics would have made haste with their opportunity, lest Elizabeth should marry and destroy their hopes.

More peremptorily than ever therefore Throgmorton was now instructed to demand the ratification of the treaty. On this condition, and this alone, could Elizabeth look forward without misgiving to Mary Stuart's return. As boldly Mary Stuart refused. While the ground was shaking about her she had made pretexts for delay. Secure now of her subjects' support, she was able to answer resolutely that she could not act in such a matter without their consent; and Throgmorton who understood both her and her position to the very letter, implored Elizabeth to lose no time and spare no money in recovering the attachment of the reforming Lords in Scotland. Perilous schemes were on foot for a marriage between the Queen of Scots and Don Carlos of Spain. The English Catholics were longing for it; de Quadra had urged it upon Granvelle as the one true remedy for all evils.[2] 'Your jealousy,' wrote Throgmorton, 'must be cast upon Spain, Austria, and the Queen of Scotland. There lieth the danger and nowhere else. Retain the best party in Scotland, and no prince nor state can do you harm. If Scotland be at your devotion, oh!

---

[1] Minutes for the Queen's person, March, 1561. In Cecil's hand.—BURLEIGH *Papers*, vol. I.

[2] De Quadra to Granvelle, August 2.—*MS. Simancas.*

happy England. It is the most happy state in Christendom.'[1]

Elizabeth unfortunately was still struggling in de Quadra's bird-nets. As late as the 15th of July, Cecil deplored the increasing credit with her of the Spanish ambassador. There were secrets between them which he could not penetrate; only he knew that de Quadra 'seemed to seek by all means overt and covert to further the marriage,' and 'to procure the Lord Robert to have evil thoughts of himself.' Matters were so 'perilous' that he scarcely dared to write about them. 'Happy they,' he exclaimed, 'that live *extra tali jacturam.*'[2]

At this time Europe believed Elizabeth hopelessly abandoned to a passion which was dragging her to disgrace. The Huguenot leaders had ceased to rest their hopes on her; and Mary Stuart anticipated nothing but a splendid and speedy triumph.[3] To the reiterated demands of Throgmorton for the ratification, she replied at last that she would send M. d'Oysel to London with a satisfactory answer. D'Oysel went, but he carried with him instead of satisfaction a request merely that the Queen of Scots on her way to Edinburgh might be allowed to pass through England. Elizabeth was not yet entirely infatuated. To have allowed a Catholic princess, a rival claimant of her crown, who in defiance of promises was obstinately maintaining her preten-

---

[1] Throgmorton to Cecil, May, 1561.—CONWAY MSS.

[2] Cecil to Throgmorton, July 15.—CONWAY MSS.

[3] 'By the Prince of Condé and the Admiral, and by others of reputation for virtue and learning, it hath been told me that the good opinion conceived of her Majesty for her religion, virtue, and wisdom, doth much decay; and that the great good devotion borne her aforetime doth marvellously turn. The causes you can guess.'—Throgmorton to Cecil, June 23.—MS. Ibid.

sions, to pass three hundred miles through a population the most notoriously Romanist in the realm, and with many of whom the Queen of Scots was already in communication, would have been an act of political suicide. D'Oysel professed in Mary Stuart's name the utmost cordiality and good-will; but the single evidence of good-will which Elizabeth could receive was withheld. She replied that when the treaty was ratified she would receive her sister with pleasure; so long as the ratification was refused, smooth words could not be taken in exchange for it, and could scarcely be believed to be sincere.

Elizabeth refuses to allow Mary Stuart to pass through England.

D'Oysel himself was but half faithful to his employer; he allowed the English Council to see how just he considered their suspicions. A letter of the Queen of Scots to Maitland fell into their hands, in which she invited him to undo his work and break the alliance with England which he had been the chief instrument in forming.[1] The position which the Scots were prepared to assume gradually forced itself on Elizabeth's mind; and before the French ambassador left London, she herself, or Cecil in her name, gave the Estates at Edinburgh to understand her opinion of their conduct.

She had dealt openly with them, she said, as all the world knew; she had saved their freedom and defended their religion; while she had asked for nothing for herself and had meddled with nothing. The treaty was a witness of her disinterestedness; and the Queen of Scots had promised that it should be ratified.

'Nevertheless,' she continued, 'how it happeneth we know not, your sovereign—either not knowing in this

---

[1] The Queen of Scots to Maitland, June 29.—*Scotch MSS. Rolls House.*

part her own felicity, or else dangerously seduced by perverse council—being of late at sundry times required by us, according to her bond remaining with us, signed with her own hand, and sealed with the Great Seal of the realm, and allowed by you being the Estates of the same, to ratify the said treaty, maketh such dilatory answers thereto as what we shall judge thereof we perceive that it is meet to require of you. Her answer dependeth, as it should seem by her words, upon your opinion; and we cannot but plainly let you all understand that this manner of answer, without some more fruit, cannot long content us. We have meant well to our sister your Queen; and having promised to keep good peace with her and you her subjects, we have hitherto observed it, and shall be sorry if either she or you shall give us contrary cause. In a matter so profitable to both the realms, we think it strange that your Queen hath no better advice. We therefore require you all, being the Estates of that realm, to consider this deeply and make us answer whereto we may trust; and if you think it meet that your Queen shall leave the peace imperfect by breaking of her solemn promise contrary to the order of all princes, we shall be well content to accept your answer, and shall be as careless to see the peace kept as ye shall give us cause; and we doubt not by the grace of God that whosoever of you shall incline thereto shall soonest repent.'[1]

After this admonition—as natural as it was imprudent—to the Scots, Elizabeth dismissed d'Oysel, bidding him return and tell his mistress to come to England

---

[1] The Queen's Majesty to the Estates of Scotland, July 1.—*Scotch MSS.* (In Cecil's hand.)

when her promise had been fulfilled, and find all hospitality and assistance there. Till that was done, with all regret for the seeming discourtesy, her duty to herself and to the realm compelled her to refuse the Queen of Scots' request.[1]

Mary Stuart was evidently unprepared for the answer; she had anticipated a semi-regal progress through the northern counties. She was mortified to find she was not to see them, save under conditions which would have turned her triumph into a defeat. She wrapped her disappointment in a sentimental mist; she represented herself as a harmless widow, 'impeached of her passage;' and both she and the Queen-mother assailed Throgmorton with all the resources of feminine ingenuity. The ambassador coldly adhered to his commission; to passionate reproaches he had but one answer—'Ratify the treaty;' and at length, when hard pressed, he told Catherine de Medici that 'the insincere dealing of the Queen of Scots was too plain and palpable, and his mistress could not suffer a matter so dangerous to herself and her state to pass unprovided for.'

It was now uncertain whether Mary Stuart might attempt the passage of the Channel. The attitude which she had chosen to assume was an act of war against Elizabeth; and to seize her and carry her prisoner to London would have been consistent with the strictest interpretation of the law of nations. The English Court no doubt hoped that the fear alone might detain the Queen of Scots in France; and Mary herself told Throgmorton that had her arrangements been less advanced, Elizabeth's unkindness might have induced her to post-

---

[1] The Queen's Majesty's answer to d'Oysel, July 15.—*Scotch MSS.*

pone her journey. With the deprecating pathos of which she was so accomplished a mistress, she said that if she was driven by foul weather into an English port, her sister would have her in her hands, to sacrifice her if she was hard-hearted enough to desire it. It might be better for her to die than to live.

Ever graceful, ever charming, never losing an opportunity of winning an Englishman's heart, she embraced the ambassador at her last parting from him at Abbeville, and asked him again if there was no way by which she could gain her sister's confidence.

Once more the hard-hearted Throgmorton, immovable as flint, replied, 'Ratify.'[1]

Thus they parted. Unable to take the English route, the brave woman had resolved to sail direct for Leith, running all risks, and believing that with the escort of three of her uncles and of d'Amville the heir of the Montmorencies, Elizabeth would not dare to meddle with her.

She was going, cost her what it might—going on an errand which cannot now be separated in remembrance from its tremendous end; and Mary Stuart's name will never be spoken of in history, however opinions may vary on the special details of her life, without sad and profound emotion.

She was not yet nineteen years old; but mind and body had matured amidst the scenes in which she had passed her girlhood. Graceful alike in person and in intellect, she possessed that peculiar beauty in which the form is lost in the expression, and which every painter therefore has represented differently.

Rarely perhaps has any woman combined in herself so many noticeable qualities as Mary Stuart; with a

---

[1] Throgmorton to Elizabeth, August.—COTTON MSS., CALIG. E. 5.

feminine insight into men and things and human life, she had cultivated herself to that high perfection in which accomplishments were no longer adventitious ornaments, but were wrought into her organic constitution. Though luxurious in her ordinary habits, she could share in the hard field life of the huntsman or the soldier with graceful cheerfulness; she had vigour, energy, tenacity of purpose, with perfect and never-failing self-possession; and as the one indispensable foundation for the effective use of all other qualities, she had indomitable courage. She wanted none either of the faculties necessary to conceive a great purpose, or of the abilities necessary to execute it, except perhaps only this, that while she made politics the game of her life, it was a game only, though played for a high stake. In the deeper and nobler emotions she had neither share nor sympathy.

Here lay the vital difference of character between the Queen of Scots and her great rival, and here was the secret of the difference of their fortunes. In intellectual gifts Mary Stuart was at least Elizabeth's equal; and Anne Boleyn's daughter, as she said herself, was 'no angel.' But Elizabeth could feel like a man an unselfish interest in a great cause; Mary Stuart was ever her own centre of hope, fear, or interest; she thought of nothing, cared for nothing, except as linked with the gratification of some ambition, some desire, some humour of her own; and thus Elizabeth was able to overcome temptations before which Mary fell.

Yet at the present crisis even the moral balance was in favour of the Scottish Queen. While her sister of England was trifling with an affection for which foolish is too light an epithet, Mary Stuart, when scarcely more than a girl, was about to throw herself alone into the midst of the most turbulent people in Europe, fresh emerged out of revolution, and loitering in the very rear of civilization; she was going among them to use her charms as a spell to win them back to the Catholic Church, to weave the fibres of a conspiracy from the Orkneys to the Land's End, prepared to wait, to control herself, to hide her purpose till the moment came to strike; yet with a purpose fixed as the stars to trample down the Reformation and to seat herself at last on Elizabeth's throne.

'Whatever policy,' said Randolph of her, 'is in all the chief and best-practised heads in France, whatever craft, falsehood, or deceit is in all the subtle brains of Scotland, is either fresh in this woman's memory, or she can fette it with a wet finger.'[1]

Such was Mary Stuart when on the 14th of August she embarked for Scotland. The Cardinals of Guise and Lorraine attended her to Calais. Three other uncles, d'Elbœuf, d'Aumale, and the Grand Prior, embarked with her to see her safe to Edinburgh; and with '*Adieu belle France*,' sentimental verses, and a passionate Châtelar sighing at her feet in melodious music, she sailed away over the summer seas.

The English fleet was on her track, sent out nominally to suppress piracy, yet with dubious orders, like those with which Winter had before sailed for the Forth. There was no command to arrest her, yet there was the thought that 'she might be met withal;' and if the admiral had sent her ship with its freight to the bottom of the North Sea, 'being done unknown,' Elizabeth, and perhaps Catherine de Medici as well, 'would have found it afterwards well done.'

Scotland meanwhile expected her coming with mingled

---

[1] Randolph to Cecil, October 27, 1561.—*Scotch MSS. Rolls House.*

CHAP IV
1561
August

The Scotch Protestants are uncertain of Elizabeth.

alarm, curiosity, and exultation. Maitland it seems, notwithstanding his disappointment about Arran, would still have adhered to the English alliance could he have been sure of Elizabeth. He thoroughly understood Mary Stuart's intentions. He was unprepared to desert the Reformation. 'If the Queen of England will go through with us,' he wrote on the 1st of August to Cecil, 'we will be bold enough.' His hope was that the Queen of Scots would come at once to open war with the Protestants; but he feared 'she would proceed by indirect means, and nothing was so dangerous with the Scots as temporizing.' On the 9th of August Randolph reported that the Congregation, feeling themselves 'without friends abroad,' and with few 'in whom they might assuredly trust at home,' were at a loss what course to take. They did not know what Elizabeth meant to do, or whether to religion as they had established it she was a friend or an enemy. She was known to hate Knox so cordially that it was feared she might assist Mary Stuart to destroy him; and Knox himself wrote to her with some irony to suggest that the Queen of Scots was not believed 'so unfeignedly to favour the tranquillity of her Majesty's reign and realm,' that by ridding Scotland of himself she would be doing her own cause good service.[1]

More distinct graphic and remarkable are two letters from Maitland to Cecil, written on the 10th and 15th of August. 'If,' said Maitland, speaking of the presence of the English fleet in the Channel, 'the Queen's gallies were to be allowed quietly to pass, it would have been better if the passport had been liberally granted.' It

---

[1] Randolph to Cecil, August 9.—COTTON *MSS.* CALIG. B. 10. Knox to Elizabeth, August 6.—*MS. Rolls House.*

was at once useless and unwise to have 'opened their pack and sold none of their wares,' 'or to have declared themselves enemies to those whom they could not or would not offend.' 'If the Queen of Scots was not interfered with she would come among them more irritated against England than ever,' and her appearance 'could not fail to raise wonderful tragedies.' The Protestants might seem to have the upper hand, but there were 'numbers who would be glad to see them overturned, and numbers who would lend their hands to overthrow them.' Mary Stuart would proceed warily: she would first 'undermine the English alliance,' which could be done without difficulty. The Papists hated it without disguise; of the rest, 'some were lukewarm,' some were 'so accustomed to feed on French fare that their stomachs could digest no other,' some would 'be bribed,' some would 'be led by the mere presence of their sovereign to do as she desired,' and many more would care only for their present comfort and convenience.

A few there were undoubtedly 'who would constantly bear out what they had begun,' but their position would be full of difficulty. So long as the Queen was absent they could hold their ground; but Cecil could judge 'what the presence of a princess craftily counselled could bring to pass.' 'She would bide her time.' At first she would quarrel with no one, but she would work her way by degrees. 'Where the accusation of religion would be odious, she would charge the Protestant lords with betraying their country to England.' 'A few thus disgraced and despatched, the rest would be an easy prey, and then might the butchery of Bonner plainly begin.'

Maitland did not wish, he said, that she should be deprived of her kingdom; but he would have 'such things as were necessary to be provided in time,' 'that neither might she by following the advice of God's enemies lose her subjects' hearts, nor those who tended the glory of God and the liberty of their country be made the sons of death.'

The prelude, couched in language which Cecil would most approve, led up to the conclusion which every Scot was most desiring; Maitland was an old chess-player, and knew better than most men how to mask his game.

Maitland desires the recognition of Mary Stuart as heir to the English crown.

There was but one way, he said, to preserve the alliance of the realms, and this he rather indicated than affirmed was the recognition of the Queen of Scots as Elizabeth's successor.¹ This alone would satisfy the vanity of the Scottish nation; this would secure all hearts and smooth all difficulties. Elizabeth might then guide them as she pleased, and the Queen of Scots would be powerless.

Nothing else would answer. Half the Lords were 'Papists unapt for council,' and 'were stirred up privily and comforted by the Queen to disallow the rest.' 'If the Reforming leaders attempted to thwart her, by eschewing Scylla they would fall into Charybdis.'

'I pray you,' the letter concluded, 'let me in this point have your advice; and let me know what the Queen's Majesty will think. Anent the continuance of the amity between the realms, there is no danger of breach so long as the Queen is absent; and if all men were persuaded as I am, and did consider the consequence, little peril would be after her coming; but her presence may alter many things.'²

---

¹ 'On the 25th of October he explained his meaning fully.'—*Vide infra*.
² Maitland to Cecil, August 10, August 15, and October 25.—*Scotch MSS. Rolls House.*

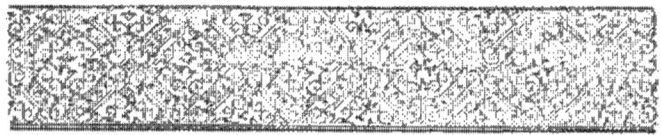

CHAPTER V.

THE galley which bore Mary Stuart and her fortunes reached the Forth without accident, after an uneasy passage of four days. The English vessels saw their prey pass by and dared not stoop upon it. The Queen of Scotland landed on the pier of Leith on the morning of the 19th of August.

Though her coming had been so long talked of, her appearance took her people by surprise. They had made no preparation for her, and Holyrood Palace lay among its meadows with the black precipices of Salisbury Crags frowning over it, like a deserted ruin.

But the Princess who was returning to make her home there was not to be made unhappy by small discomforts. She established herself amidst laughter and kind words in a few hurriedly-arranged rooms. The Puritan citizens serenaded her through her first night with psalm tunes, and she thanked them for their kindness. The dreaded harlot of Babylon seemed only an innocent and graceful girl, throwing herself with confiding trust upon the loyalty and love of her subjects. Her mother's friends expected to be recalled to power. To the surprise of all men, she chose for her chief advisers her brother and Maitland. She issued a proclamation forbidding the Catholics to attempt changes in the established religion. For herself only she pleaded rather than insisted that the promise made to her by the Estates should be observed, and that for the present she might have her own service in the Royal Chapel.

What sour austerity could refuse a request so gracefully urged? The Master of Lindsay and the gentlemen of Fife might croak out texts that 'the idolater should die the death;' Knox might protest that 'one mass was more terrible to him than ten thousand armed men.' The Council were Scots as well as Protestants—they could not 'force the Queen's conscience, and drive her back to France.' Lord James Stuart stood on guard at the chapel door while mass was being sung. Lord John and Lord Robert her other brothers, took charge of the priests. The Puritan noblemen came in from the country full of spirited indignation. A few hours of Mary's presence charmed them into loyal toleration.

'Now, my lord,' said Campbell of Kingsuncleugh to Lord Ochiltree, 'are ye come last of all the rest; and I perceive by your anger that the fire edge is not off you yet; but I fear, after the holy water of the court be sprinkled on you, ye shall become as temperate as the rest. I have been here five days, and at the first I heard every man say let us hang the priest; but after they had been twice or thrice at the abbey, all that fervency was past. I think there is some enchantment whereby men are bewitched.'[1]

Maitland's prophecy was fulfilled more quickly perhaps than he could have himself expected. Even Knox himself Mary Stuart did not despair of subduing. With

---

[1] Knox; *History of the Reformation*, Book iv.

clear collected presence of mind she desired to comprehend her situation exactly, and the resistance for which she had to look; and she took the opportunity of a sermon which he preached at St. Giles's against the mass, the Sunday after her arrival, to measure her strength with her most dangerous enemy.

She sent for him and inquired first about his book 'on the regiment of women.' He said it had been written against the Jezebel of England, and times were changed. His opinion was unaltered, but it was an opinion only on which he had no intention of acting.

She spoke of the rebellion and of the new creed which in spite of princes and governments was thrusting itself by force upon the world.

The power of princes had its limits, the Reformer said. Subjects could not frame their religion according to appetites of sovereigns. The Israelites in Egypt were not of the religion of Pharaoh; Daniel and St. Paul were not of the religion of Nebuchadnezzar and Nero.

She might have resented the comparison, but she contented herself with replying that none of those 'had resisted with the sword.' But Knox answered merely that 'God had not given them the power;' and when she pressed him to say whether he thought subjects might resist their sovereign, he used the comparison which in the next century became the Puritan formula. If a father went mad and offered to kill his children, his children might tie his hands and take his weapon from him: in like manner if princes would murder the children of God, it was no disobedience to restrain them from their evil purpose.

Thus spoke Calvinism the creed of republics in its first hard form. If princes became enemies of God, God's servants owed them no allegiance. The question who was to be the judge was left as usual in such cases for every one to decide for himself.

The Queen sat for some time silent. Fearless as Knox himself, she was measuring with keen precocity the spirit with which she had to deal. She did not mean to quarrel with him, but she could not wholly restrain herself.

'My subjects then,' she said at length, 'are to obey you and not me. I am subject to them not they to me.'

'Nay,' he replied, 'let prince and subject both obey God. Kings should be foster fathers of the Kirk and queens its nursing mothers.'

'You are not the kirk that I will nurse,' she said. 'I will defend the Kirk of Rome for that I think is the Kirk of God.'

'Your will, madam,' Knox answered, 'is no reason, neither does your thought make the Roman harlot the spouse of Jesus Christ.'

So these two parted, each with some insight into the other's nature.

'If there be not in her,' said Knox afterwards, 'a proud mind, a crafty wit, and an indurate heart against God and his truth, my judgment faileth me.'

'He made her weep,' said Randolph, in describing the interview to Cecil; 'as well you know there be of that sex that will do that for anger as well as grief. You exhort us to stoutness. The voice of that one man is able to put more life in us in one hour than five hundred trumpets blustering in our ears.' The same day Korah, Dathan, and Abiram were burnt in effigy in Edinburgh; and but for Lord Huntly's interference, the people were 'minded to have had a priest burnt at the altar at the elevation.'[1]

---

[1] Randolph to Cecil.—COTTON MSS., CALIG. B. 10.

Very swiftly Mary Stuart understood her situation.

In Scotland as throughout Europe the Reformation was the creed of the towns, of the merchants, the tradesmen, and the artisans. It had grown with their growth; it was the expression of their thoughts; and between them and the Catholic Queen there was a chasm which no ingenuity could bridge over. Half a dozen noblemen at most were really Protestants, and even these were still liable to be influenced by many motives external to religion—by patriotism, by national pride, by loyalty, chivalry, and the natural courtesy of gentlemen. The residue of the lords and gentlemen who acted with the Congregation believed only in Protestantism as an excuse for laying hands upon the Church lands; and they dreaded a Catholic reaction only because reaction menaced their chance of filling their lean purses.

The Queen had only therefore to avoid creating alarm by a display of Catholic fanaticism, and her course would be comparatively easy. It was useless to contend against the Reformation so long as England was a Protestant power; but the mass of her own subjects was ready to support her claims on the English succession. The reversion of the crown once secured the English Catholics would rally to her; Philip in all likelihood would give her Don Carlos for a husband, and the rest would speedily follow. Or if Don Carlos was unattainable, there was Lord Darnley the favourite at present among the great English nobility; and the union of the two claims would bring with it double strength. A thousand causes recommended Darnley to the Scots. He was the heir of two great houses, and would command the feudal allegiance of the families of Lennox and Douglas. Before Mary's return, his busy mother Lady

Margaret had sounded Seton, Huntly, Sutherland, and others of the Catholic nobles, on the marriage. Seton had replied 'that he would not only spend his living but give his blood towards setting forth the Lord Darnley;'[1] and a few days only after the Queen's landing, the Earl of Sutherland introduced to her a special messenger, Arthur Lilliard, Darnley's tutor, with a direct proposal from Lady Margaret herself.

Proposed marriage between Mary Stuart and Darnley.

Lord Darnley was but a boy of fifteen, and Mary Stuart's ambition soared to the Spanish throne; but he might be useful as a resource if her other expectations failed her. She received Lilliard characteristically, 'sitting on an old trunk.' She asked innumerable questions of his pupil's 'stature, age, qualities, abilities, and of my Lady Lennox's friends in England and Scotland;' and she dismissed him at last without a definite answer, but with an impression that he had been favourably received.[2]

She kept her counsel so well that no hint of this interview reached the ears of Knox or Randolph. The next step was to send Maitland to Elizabeth with formal messages of courtesy, and to make her understand the conditions on which, and on which alone, the two countries could continue on good terms. Unterrified by Elizabeth's threats the Lords added a message of their own, in which, so far from expressing any willingness to enforce on their sovereign the ratification of the treaty, they showed the most distinct determination to stand by her if Elizabeth insisted on it. Their mistress they said was ready to forgive the ungenerous

---

[1] Articles against Lady Lennox.—*Domestic MSS.*, ELIZ., vol. xxiii. Rolls House.
[2] Ibid.

refusal of the passage through England; but 'if it should chance, as God forbid! that the Queen of England would use any discourtesy towards the Queen their sovereign, or give occasion on her part to violate the good amity and peace between their two Majesties, she might be well assured that they acknowledging themselves to be her subjects, would not forget their duty for the maintenance of the Queen their sovereign's just quarrel.'[1]

It was fortunate for the Queen of Scotland's prospects that the bearer of this communication found Elizabeth in the first tumult of anger and agitation at the discovery of a domestic scandal. According to the will of Henry the Eighth it will be remembered that the next heir to the Crown after Elizabeth and her children was the lady Catherine Grey. The reader has seen this lady coquetting with the Count de Feria and the Spaniards professing Catholic principles, and speculating on an escape to Flanders. Her faith however if she had any, sat lightly on her, for about the time that Mary Stuart sailed for Scotland she was discovered to be enceinte; and on inquiry she declared herself the wife of Lord Hertford, the eldest son of the Protestant Protector. There were reasons for believing that the marriage was no mere act of folly, but that it was connected with secret political combinations. Hertford who was amusing himself in Paris was instantly sent for, Lady Catherine was committed to the Tower, and the Queen wrote to the Lieutenant Sir Edward Warner, that 'there had been great practices and purposes,' that 'many persons of high rank were known to have been privy to the

---

[1] Instructions to the Laird of Liddington by the Queen of Scots. Instructions to the same by the Lords of Scotland, September, 1561.—Keith.

CHAP V.
1561
September

Marriage of
Lady
Catherine
Grey and
Lord Hertford.

marriage,' and that he must make Lady Catherine understand she should have no favour shown her unless she confessed the truth.

Archbishop Parker untied the knot so far as the Church could do it—declaring the ceremony invalid, and the child to be born illegitimate. But the Queen's anger refused to be appeased; and Hertford followed his wife into the Tower to linger there for years. Elizabeth never justified her severity by condescending to explanations; but her unhappy cousin it is likely was expiating the faults of others whom it was less easy to punish.

The affair according to de Quadra took place when Sir Henry Sidney made the first move about the Dudley marriage. The Queen was then believed to be so infatuated that there was no hope of saving her; both Lord Robert and she were known to be making advances to Spain; and Bedford and the Protestants joined themselves with Arundel and Lord Robert's personal enemies to marry the next heir to the son of the Protestant who was the hereditary enemy of the Dudleys. If the Queen married Lord Robert a revolution was expected to follow, and these two were to be the nucleus of a new party.

The secret mover was supposed to have been Cecil, who at that time was in disgrace at Court, and feared that the Queen was about to abandon the Reformation. As soon however as Cecil was assured that the established religion was in no danger he had withdrawn his countenance; the conspiracy, if conspiracy there was, was allowed to drop; and the marriage itself would perhaps never have been heard of except for its unfortunate results.

A single glance below the surface when the explosion

came satisfied Elizabeth that it was dangerous to look further. Lord Robert insulted Arundel; Arundel replied with menacing allusions to Cumnor Hall. The inquiry was sullenly let drop; and the Queen wreaked her anger on the unlucky pair who had offended in being the instruments of the intrigue.[1]

Such is the version of this matter given by the Spanish ambassador, which the English records neither confirm nor discredit. Certain only it is that the discovery of the condition of the heiress presumptive created in Elizabeth a burst of indignation; and the effect of it was to make her for the first time look with less disfavour on the rival pretensions of Mary Stuart. Maitland on being admitted to an interview dared to tell her in his own name and in that of the whole Scottish nobility that claims like those which his mistress possessed on the throne of England could not lightly be signed away. The Estates were unanimously of opinion that the Queen of Scots ought to be declared by Act of Parliament next in succession after Elizabeth and her children; and the ratification of the treaty must be made dependent on her consent.

Elizabeth urged the solemn promises which had been made by the commissioners, and the obligations of the Scots. 'The like,' she said, 'had never been demanded of any prince to declare an heir presumptive in his lifetime.' Maitland answered that by the will of Henry the Eighth 'men had gone about to prevent the Providence of God and shift the one in the place due to the

---

[1] De Quadra to Granvelle, September 6. De Quadra to Philip II., September 13.—*MS. Simancas*. Compare The Queen to Sir Ed. Warner, August 17.—Burleigh *Papers*, vol. I. Cecil to Sussex, August 13.—Wright's *Elizabeth and her Times*, vol. I. Osborne to Chaloner, February 22, 1562.—*Domestic MSS., Eliz.*, vol. xxi. Rolls House.

other;' 'the Queen his mistress was next in blood and would be content to hazard all rather than receive that dishonour to forego her right.'

Elizabeth was strangely tolerant. She said that such language was more like a threat than a request, and if it was made a question of right, she had force at home and friends abroad to defend her. Were she to declare the Queen of Scots her successor she would make a rallying-point for every malcontent in the realm; and with no obscure intimation of her own probable fate, she said 'she was not so foolish as to hang a winding-sheet before her eyes, or make a funeral feast while she was alive.'

Maitland admitted the danger without however appearing to think it of sufficient consequence 'to impede so good a purpose.' He thought too she would secure by consenting the affection of the Scots, and on the whole that she would have the best of the bargain. 'Her gain was assured and in her hand if the treaty was ratified; the gain of the Queen of Scots was only in possibility.'

Even this Elizabeth endured without expression of resentment. She refused positively to name Mary Stuart her successor, knowing that she would be signing her own death-warrant; but she sent Maitland back with a promise that she would do nothing and allow nothing to be done to prejudice the Queen of Scots' title.[1]

With this cautious and forbearing answer, Maitland returned to Edinburgh to find the smooth waters already disturbed. Presuming on her first success the Queen had attempted to open the Chapel Royal for public

---

[1] BUCHANAN; CALDERWOOD.—*Maitland to Cecil, October 7*; BURLEIGH *Papers*, vol. i.

Catholic service. The Protestant mob drove the priest from the altar 'with broken head and bloody ears.' The Earl of Huntly said at the Council that if the Queen would bid him do it 'he would set up the mass in three shires,' and the whole town was buzzing like a nest of angry hornets. The remarkable political sagacity of Knox had looked Mary through and through. In a letter to Cecil he lamented that he had not been resolute from the first, and insisted that she should either leave the mass or leave the country. Maitland and Lord James were blinded; and as for the Queen, 'the Cardinal's lessons were so printed in her heart that substance and quality were likely to perish together.' 'I would be glad to be deceived,' he said; 'but I fear I shall not; in communication with her I espied such craft as I have not found in such age.'[1]

Mary Stuart however made haste to undo her mistake. Instead of supporting Huntly she professed to defer entirely to the wishes of her subjects. The service at Holyrood should for the future be exclusively private; and on Maitland's return she expressed the warmest gratitude for her 'dear sister's' message. She wished she was a man that all differences might be settled by her marrying Elizabeth. She became so attentive to Randolph that she had almost disarmed his suspicions, till she revived them by offering him a pension and one of her ladies for a wife;[2] and Maitland was allowed to hint that even in religion, if her title was recognized, Elizabeth's persuasions might perhaps effect her conversion.[3]

---

[1] Knox to Cecil, October 7.—*Scotch MSS. Rolls House.*
[2] Randolph to Cecil, October 27.—*MS. Ibid.*
[3] Maitland to Cecil, October 25.—*MS. Ibid.*

In vain Knox protested that they were all deceived about her. 'It is astonishing,' Randolph wrote, 'to see how men change. I have to traffic now with other kind of merchants than before. They know the value of their wares, and in all places how the market goeth; and yet it seemeth wonder unto many that the whole state of this realm should be altered by a woman.'[1]

Sir Peter Mewtas followed Maitland to Edinburgh to obtain a distinct understanding about the ratification. Mary told him that she desired nothing more than to be on good terms with her sister. She would ratify, she said, if the treaty was first revised by a Scotch and English commission, and she spoke with such apparent sincerity that the English Council, when Mewtas brought back her answer, were divided—Arundel, Mason, and others of the more moderate party 'thinking it meet for the good of quiet to hearken.'[2]

The Scots unquestionably would have agreed to no revision which did not imply an acknowledgment of the claims of their Queen. They were supporting Mary Stuart in refusing to admit Elizabeth's present right to her own Crown. The single clause in the treaty to which she really objected was that which Cecil had extorted with so much difficulty, and her obstinate resolution bore the worst construction: yet the attitude of the Scots and Catherine Grey's misdemeanours combined to induce Elizabeth to make the best of it, and yield to the utmost which her own safety would permit. She replied in a letter to Mary in which she expressed a sincere desire for the obliteration of unpleasant feelings between them: on her part she would do all which could be in reason

---

[1] Randolph to Cecil, October 27.—*MS. Rolls House*.
[2] Cecil to Throgmorton, November 4.—CONWAY *MSS*.

required of her; and instead of appointing commissioners, she suggested that Mary Stuart should explain her objections to the treaty in a private letter to herself.[1]

Meeting frankness with frankness Mary replied that she would speak as a sister to a sister: she had full confidence in Elizabeth's justice, and would show her the bottom of her heart. She was descended of the blood royal of England; she knew who and what she was, and she would be loath to receive such an injury as to be unjustly debarred from what might in possibility fall to her.[2]

While explaining herself with so much candour to Elizabeth, the Queen of Scots continued her advances to Randolph. She expressed a great wish to see England and to meet her sister; and as of course both Elizabeth's danger from recognizing her, and all objections which the English Council could entertain, would disappear on her conversion to the Reformation, Maitland first, and afterwards Lord James Stuart, assured the English ambassador that her Catholicism was waning, and that she would yield gracefully when Elizabeth would condescend to reason with her.[3] The Catholics themselves took the alarm. 'If the Queens meet,' wrote Randolph, 'the Papists think themselves utterly overthrown; they say plainly she cannot return a true Christian woman.'[4] At all events, converted or unconverted, the Scotch people had set their minds so strongly

---

[1] Elizabeth to Mary Stuart, November 23.—*MS. Rolls House.*
[2] Mary Stuart to Elizabeth, Jan. 5. 1562.—*Ibid.*
[3] 'After this I communed with the Lord James of all these purposes. He liked them well; and he is of that opinion that the Lord of Liddington is, that she will never come to God before the Queen's Majesty draw her.'—*Randolph to Cecil. Ibid.*
[4] Ibid.

on her recognition as heir presumptive to England that Randolph durst not hint so much as a doubt of Elizabeth's compliance;[1] while Maitland told Cecil plainly that if there was further hesitation the Scots would be dangerously alienated, and implored him to further the great object which they had hitherto pursued in common —'the union of the isle.'[2]

Elizabeth, although she would make no promises, seemed to enter warmly into the proposal for an interview; and as it was understood that the meeting of the Queens, unless recognition followed, would do harm rather than good,[3] it appeared as if she meant to give way. Her correspondence with Mary grew more and more cordial. In Maitland she recognized only a loyal servant of his mistress, and herself desired him to correspond closely and confidentially with Cecil.

Mary on her side gave the Protestants no more ground of complaint. She made Lord James Stuart Lieutenant of the Border, and in January she deprived Huntly of the lands of Murray which he held informally under the Crown and bestowed them on her brother.

The Catholic clergy were equally disappointed and dissatisfied. The preachers expected that the authority and the incomes of their predecessors would have been transferred to them unimpaired. Their wishes could not fully be gratified; and two-thirds of the property of the clergy was left in their hands, 'freely given to the devil,' as Knox expressed it. Of the remaining third the devil according to the same authority had his share also, for half of it

---

[1] Randolph to Cecil, January 2.—*Scotch MSS. Rolls House.*
[2] Maitland to Cecil.—*MS. Ibid.*
[3] Ibid.

went to the Crown; but the remaining half was actually given to the ministers;[1] and that an official provision however scanty should be made for them by the Queen was regarded by the Church party as of fatal augury.

Her Council were never weary of praising her sincerity and of insisting on her affection for England and Elizabeth. 'Either,' said Randolph, 'this Queen is truly well disposed to our Queen, or it is the deepest dissembled and the best conveyed that ever was; I refer the judg-

---

[1] The identification of the Catholic ecclesiastics in Scotland with the devil was not wholly a figure of speech. Randolph has left a description of some of their doings, which explains and justifies the passionate anger of the Reformers.

'The bishops,' he wrote, 'are so intolerably licentious of their lives, that it was no longer to be endured; and a better way to plague them there was none than to pluck at their livings, in special by her in whom their whole hope and trust was. I will be bold to trouble your honour with a merry tale. Carlanus, the Italian, took upon him the cure of the Bishop of St. Andrew's in a disease that unto all other men was judged desperate and incurable. He practised upon him divers strange inventions. He hung him certain hours in the day by the heels to cause him to avoid at the mouth that that other ways nature would not expel. He fed him many days with young whelps. He used him sometimes with extreme heats, and as many days with extreme colds. Before his departure he soundeth for the space of six days every day certain unknown words in his ears, and never used other medicine after. It is said that at that time he did put a devil within him, for that since he hath been even the better; and that the devil was given unto him of credit for nine years, so that now the time is near expired that either he must go to hell with his devil or fall again into his old mischief to poison the whole country with his false practices. In token of repentance of his life, beside his old concubine taken from her married husband, he hath this year had (the devil, I trow, was father to the one or both) a couple of children. His bastard brother also, the Bishop of Argyle, hath now two women with child beside his wife. Of the Bishop of Dunblane it is shameful to speak; he spareth not his own daughter. The rest are like to these. The prelates with the rest of the clergy offered as great a sum for one year as that that the Queen hath taken for herself. But that seemeth less than she hath presently need of, her charges being great—all things extreme dear, and her Grace brought up in that licentious court that is without measure in charges. For these causes the wiser sort thought it better to be bold upon the kirkmen than to take of her people, or otherwise burden the realm.'—*Randolph to Cecil, January 15, 1562. Scotch MSS. Rolls House.*

ment to your honour and attend myself the sequel—*nihil simulatum diuturnum.*[1] Knox only remained obstinately incredulous. That Mary Stuart meant well to Elizabeth he as little believed as that she would ever 'embrace the English religion;' and it must be admitted that Knox was right and all the rest were willingly deceiving themselves. While she was holding out hopes of her conversion she was assuring the Pope that she would sooner die than forsake the Catholic faith. While she was expressing her passionate anxiety to please Elizabeth she was scheming for the marriage which Elizabeth most dreaded for her with the Prince of Spain.[2]

Meantime European politics became every day more complicated. Had the Reformers in France made a moderate use of the opportunity which the death of

---

[1] Randolph to Cecil, January 30 and February 12; Maitland to Cecil, January 29; Lord James Stuart to Cecil, January 28.—*Scotch MSS.*

[2] M. de Moret, on his return from Scotland to Paris, said in London that the Protestant Lords were so passionately bent on securing the English succession, that they would countenance for the sake of it even a marriage with the son of Philip the Second. 'Moret tells me,' wrote the Spanish ambassador, 'that she looks to a great marriage for herself and makes no concealment of her desire for the Prince our master. He says that he asked her how her heretics would like it. She told him they would like it very well; and although his religion might annoy them, their anxiety for the establishment of her right in this realm was so earnest that they would make no difficulty about it, provided that it was understood that she would not leave Scotland till she should have a child. Leaving an heir to the crown, she might then go where she would. This, Moret says, is the opinion of Lord James and of the whole or at least the majority of the nobility, among whom there are many Catholics. He tells me moreover that the Queen of Scots assured him she was going on admirably with the Queen of England, who was holding out hopes of the succession to her. She is the more inclined to credit what the Queen of England says, because so many of the principal men in this country have sent to offer her their services. Further he informs me that he is the bearer of letters from the Queen of Scots to the Pope, in which she tells his Holiness that she would sooner die than forsake her religion; and at the same time that she was thinking of opening a correspondence with myself.'—*De Quadra to the Duchess of Parma, January 3, 1562. MS. Simancas.*

Francis created for them they might have won the confidence of the great national party. Catherine de Medici at one time dreaded the House of Guise more than she hated heresy. A strong heterodox element leavened the army; and by playing faction against faction she would have secured to France, in pursuing her own ends, a tempered and progressive liberty. But Calvinism, like all creeds which claim exclusive possession of truth, was violent, intolerant, and propagandist; it regarded Romanism as an enemy to be destroyed—if possible by persuasion—if persuasion failed by the sword. The exiles who had tasted democracy in Switzerland became the missionaries of a faith as much political as religious; and as anarchy became the order of the day Montmorency and the Marshal St. André, the great Gallican leaders, drew more and more towards the Guises. The Cardinal of Lorraine demanded from the Parliament of Paris the revocation of the edicts of January. Confident of his power he even challenged the Protestants to a public discussion before the court. Theodore Beza snatched eagerly at the gage; the Conference of Poissy followed, with three months of argument, recrimination, and at last of mere invective and abuse; and at length it became clear that the new religion was a thing which would either rule all France or must be itself extinguished.

Philip of Spain alarmed for the Netherlands was irritated to the last degree at the folly of Poissy. He was leisurely burning his own homegrown heretics, and his last wish was to refer questions of doctrine to the hazard of argument. He desired Catherine to permit no more such exhibitions. He could not allow the Low Countries to be exposed to the contagion of revolution. He even threatened, if she forgot her duty, to send an army over the frontiers and call to arms all the loyal Catholics in France.¹ Civil war was evidently approaching, and the Calvinists on their side made fresh advances to England for assistance in a Protestant crusade.

The King of Navarre unstable as water had been drifting among the currents uncertain what side to take: 'he changed with the wind;' 'he was afraid of his shadow.' At the end of November however he had been almost brought to promise to disallow the Council of Trent, and to agree to a separate Anglo-Gallican conference.² Even the Queen-mother notwithstanding Philip's menaces was supposed to incline in the same direction. The orthodox preachers at the palace were studiously slighted. During sermon Catherine de Medici went to sleep, the courtiers jested, the King played with his dog.³ 'Here is new fire,' wrote a correspondent of the English ambassadors from the Palace, 'here is new greenwood reeking; new smoke and much contrary wind blowing against Mr. Holy Pope; for in all haste the King of Navarre with his tribe will have another council, and the Cardinal⁴ stamps and takes on like a madman, and goeth up and down here to the Queen, there to the Cardinal of Tournon, with such unquieting in himself as all the house marvels at it.'⁵ All looked well at the Court for the prospects of the Protestants. The Duke of Guise held aloof in Lorraine; d'Elbœuf continued in Scotland with his niece; the halls of the guilds in Paris were appropriated for the Calvinist orations; and the Queen of Navarre, the Prince of Condé, and the Admiral, 'with

---

¹ VARILLAS' *Histoire de Charles IX.*
² Throgmorton to Cecil, November 26.—CONWAY MSS.
³ Shakerly to Throgmorton, December 14.—MS. Ibid.
⁴ The Cardinal of Ferrara came from Rome to Paris in November as legate.
⁵ Shakerly to Throgmorton, December 16.—MS. Ibid.

great routs of ladies and gentlemen,' were daily and ostentatiously present.[1]

The difficulty in the formation of the league lay with Elizabeth, who would join it and would not join it, and changed her mind or her language from day to day. At one time in her affection for the Queen of Scots she made advances to the Guises; she offered her assistance to reconcile them with the King of Navarre, and even volunteered to take their part if Navarre refused.[2] The Dudley love affair was still exhaling about her its fetid vapours. Lord Robert cared not the least with what party he connected himself, and while Elizabeth was corresponding with leaders of the Catholics her lover addressed himself to the Huguenots, offering in his mistress's name and his own the support which they required if they would countenance his marriage;[3] while to the Spanish ambassador again he affected that he was but 'practising;' that his true devotion was to the King of Spain; that both the Queen and he were as anxious as ever to receive one another from Philip's hands.

De Quadra incredulous but amused desired to have his words confirmed by the Queen herself.

'I asked her,' he wrote, in describing the interview to Philip, 'I asked her what your Majesty was to do. She said she could not marry a man whom she had not

---

[1] Sir N. Throgmorton to Chaloner, December 20.—*Spanish MSS. Rolls House.*

[2] 'Esta Reyna procura y solicita la reconciliation de Vendosme con los de Goisa, la qual trata por medio de la Reyna de Escocia, ofreciendoles quanto quieren hasta decir que si Vendosme quisiere agraviarlos ella se pondra de su parte dellos.'—*De Quadra to Philip, January 31, 1562. MS. Simancas.*

[3] 'A Vendosme su hermano y el almirante de Francia M. Roberto ha escrito y enviado secretamente á tratar con ellos amistad y confederacion, prometiendole ellos de ayudar y asistir en lo de su casamiento con la Reyna.'—*De Quadra to Philip, November 27, 1561. MS. Ibid.*

seen; it was likely therefore that she would have to marry a subject, and she knew no one better fitted to be her husband than Lord Robert. She would be grateful therefore if the princes, her allies, and especially your Majesty would recommend him to her that she might be able to say that she was acting with the advice and approval of her friends. Seeing that I did not respond very warmly, she added that it was merely for appearance' sake; whether your Majesty consented or not she would marry Lord Robert when she chose; but if it was done without your Majesty's help, Lord Robert would be little obliged to you.

'I laughed and said she had better make no more delays or excuses. Let her give Lord Robert what he wanted and she might assure herself your Majesty would be well pleased.'[1]

Whatever explanation may be offered of these vagaries, the effect at the time was only to make all parties distrust Elizabeth alike. 'I wish,' exclaimed Cecil in utter despondency, 'I wish she had counsellors of more credit and weight than I; parasites and flatterers do more hurt to princes than any beasts of the field, and I poor soul am forced to bear the blows and stings of these scorpions.'[2]

Elizabeth's vacillation may have occasioned and may excuse a change in France which altered the relations of parties, and the entire circumstances of the approaching

---

[1] De Quadra to Philip. About the time of this conversation Henry Killigrew wrote to Throgmorton—'This afternoon my Lord Robert and my Lord Windsor shooting a match in the park, the Queen's Majesty stole out upon them only accompanied with Kate Carey and two others whom she followed as a maid, and told my Lord Robert openly that he was beholden unto her, for that she had passed the pikes for his sake. It seemeth his favour began but now.'— November 26. CONWAY MSS.

[2] Cecil to Throgmorton, November 27.—CONWAY MSS.

struggle. The King of Navarre suddenly abandoned his party and went over to the Catholics.

The explanation of his apostasy was as simple as it was base: Navarre had no confidence in the success of his cause and he cared little in his heart for anything but women and vanity. If he would separate himself from Condé and the Admiral, Philip offered him the island of Sardinia in compensation for his own lost kingdom, while a further hope was dangled before his eyes that the Pope would divorce him from his Huguenot wife: he might then marry Mary Stuart and be King of England and Scotland.[1] Puzzled by Elizabeth's uncertainty, alarmed and perhaps irritated by the double dealing of the wretched Lord Robert, he yielded to the temptation. As first prince of the blood, lieutenant-general, and quasi-guardian of the King, he carried with him the authority of the Court; and Condé and Chatillon were reduced once more into the position of rebels.

So stood matters in France in the opening of the year 1562; and had Philip listened to the bold advice of Alva, de Quadra, and de Feria, he might have struck in to a purpose which would have changed many things.

'If his Majesty,' wrote de Quadra on the 27th of November to Granvelle, 'intends to interfere in France, he should first secure England, or at least create such divisions in England as shall prevent the Queen from taking part against him. If his Majesty thinks that with smooth words he can persuade the party now in power to alter their policy he deceives himself. They will never be friendly to us, and they will never be neutral. They are and will be the worst enemies that we can have. If

[1] VARILLAS.

they can they will drive the King our sovereign from the Low Countries, and no inducement which the world can offer will move them from their purpose. Interest is nothing, and danger is nothing, in comparison with party spirit and religious passion. It is unsafe to delay longer. If we are to act to any purpose in France we must first act here; England once disposed of his Majesty can restore order elsewhere at his leisure.'[1]

'Too late' might have been the motto of Philip of Spain. Instead of declaring openly for the Catholics acknowledging Mary Stuart and sending an armada into the Channel, his chief fear was that the English Catholics might rise in desperation and thus force him to take a decided part. De Quadra exacted a promise from their leaders that they would not stir without encouragement from the King of Spain; but he was obliged half-reproachfully to tell Philip the truth that not only were the Catholics losing hope, but that they complained of him as the cause of their sufferings. In deference to his wishes they had rejected the proffered hand of France, with the help of which they would have restored the Church, and they were so injured and aggrieved that words could no longer console them.[2]

Philip it is evident had built his hopes on the Dudley marriage; and so anxious was he to bring it about that he would have done all that he was asked to do, and have insisted on no conditions.[3] But de Quadra warned

---

[1] De Quadra to Granvelle, November 27.—*MS. Simancas*.
[2] De Quadra to Philip, January 31.—*MS. Ibid*.
[3] Sir Thomas Chaloner gives a singular account of Philip at this time. 'The king,' he said, 'a good and gentle prince, is a lover of rest and quiet, delighting in hunting and retired militariness with a few of his familiars, to take the more at large the fruition of such pastimes as best delight him.'—*Chaloner to Throgmorton, January 15.* CONWAY *MSS*.

him that in so doing he would be trying the patience of the Catholics too far. Dudley in himself was an object of mere abhorrence to them. Elizabeth could not be relied on; and the marriage once over she would turn round on Philip and be as troublesome to him as ever.[1]

De Quadra in point of fact had found Elizabeth's humour growing dangerous again. Just as she was beginning to believe that she might trust the Queen of Scots, she had discovered Lady Lennox's project of marrying her to Darnley; and there were unpleasant circumstances about Lady Lennox which caused her to be jealously watched. When Elizabeth was arrested as an accomplice in Wyatt's conspiracy, Lady Lennox had insulted her at the palace, and had done her best to persuade Mary to destroy her.[2] The lady's behaviour had been passed over and forgotten; but none the less had she identified herself with the Catholic faction. She had brought up Darnley in the most elaborate practice of Catholic ceremonies.[3] Her husband's castle in Yorkshire was the gathering place of the Catholic noblemen and gentlemen, where at her table Elizabeth was spoken of as a bastard and the family fool was

---

[1] De Quadra to Granvelle, April 3.—MS. Simancas.

[2] 'How that innocent lady cruelly by her was handled is well known. How unfaithfully—the Queen's Highness being sent for sick, caused she pull down her hangings, and above her head being in her wimple caused she keep a kitchen [sic] to her Majesty's displeasure, with casting down of logs, pots, and vessels. What reports made she against her and others, to procure her going to the Tower; what slander at sundry times hath she reported,' &c., &c.—*Notes of the behaviour of Lady Lennox. Domestic MSS.*, ELIZ., vol. xxii.

[3] 'To preserve the hearts of the Papists to regard her untrue title, she hath contemptuously and openly declared her religion. Under colour of her conscience she useth her bedes, auricular confession, pinning of idols and images within and above her bed and the bed of the Lord Darnley, whom she hath grafted in that devilish Papistry.'—*Articles against Lady Lennox. MS. Ibid.* vol. xxiii.

taught 'to rail at the Queen and Lord Robert.' The secrets of the royal household were betrayed there by Francis Yaxlee, a gentleman of the bed-chamber. 'She herself did set forth the Queen of Scots' title, declaring what a good thing it were to have both the realms in one, meaning the conjunction of her son to the Scottish Queen, who should be King both of Scotland and England.'[1]

Some of the worst of these proceedings, together with the proposal which she had made to Mary Stuart, reached Elizabeth's ears. Yaxlee was arrested; the Earls of Cumberland and Westmoreland were sent for to London; Norfolk, Huntingdon, Rutland, and Northampton were ordered into the northern counties to keep the peace; while the Earl of Lennox went to the Tower, and orders were sent out for the instant appearance of his wife.

Resistance was impossible: the Catholics were indignant but helpless; Lady Lennox came to London prepared to face down the accusations against her, but was silently imprisoned; and alarmed at the danger, the Protestants proposed that the Queen should have the same power which had been given to her father of naming her successor by will.[2]

A doubt was raised on Lady Lennox's legitimacy. In the Act of Divorce between her mother Queen Margaret, and her father the Earl of Angus, it was pretended that at the time of their marriage Angus had been already

---

[1] Articles against Lady Lennox.—*Domestic MSS., Eliz.*, vol. xxiii.

[2] 'Tengo por cierto que la cosa pasara en que el Reyno de facultad á la Reyna de testar y elegir heredero á quien quisiese, todo por excluir á la de Escocia y á Miladi Margarita, y porque la succesion cayga en manos de algun herege desta.'

And again—

'El desiño de Cecil que lo gobierna todo no es sino de esclayr á la Reyna de Escocia y á Milady Margarita que son Catolicos y que el Reyno quede en poder de hereges.'—*De Quadra to Philip,* January 31. *De Quadra to Granvelle,* April 3. MS. Simancas.

married to another woman; and Randolph with some
difficulty obtained a copy of the proceedings to be held
as a menace over Lady Lennox's head.

'They may prove what they will,' wrote de Quadra,
'as to legitimacy, but the Lord Darnley will have the
votes of Protestants as well as Catholics. I have been
lately asked whether if he fly to Flanders your Majesty
will receive him. The Catholics rest their whole hopes
on him and his mother. They would rebel if they could,
and forces enough could be raised in the realm if
there was any hope that they would be supported from
abroad.'[1]

Of Philip's interference however or of his allowing
any one else to interfere, there was no hope. Lady
Lennox and her husband were left in the Tower, and
the Queen of Scots made haste to clear herself of a connexion which ran counter to her present interests. Don
Carlos and not Darnley was the real object of her ambition; and she affected and perhaps felt entire indifference to the fate either of him or his mother. The worst
that could happen by their removal from the field was
to leave her the sole representative of the Catholic party.
She was instructed by the Guises to keep on good terms
with England to prevent Elizabeth from meddling in
France. She explained away therefore such circumstances
as seemed suspicious. Autograph letters full of seeming
affection continued to pass between the two Queens; and
the interview was solicited both by Mary and her ministers more ardently than ever. Lord James assured
Randolph, and Maitland insisted to Cecil, that although

---

[1] De Quadra to Philip II., March 13 and 28.—*MS. Simancas.*

earnestly entreated by her uncle, Mary Stuart had refused to 'renew the old league with France;' she would have no friend but Elizabeth and no advisers but themselves; while Maitland threw himself on Cecil's generosity and implored him no longer to oppose a settlement which appeared of so happy promise. The union of the realms was 'the mark at which he had always shot;' Cecil had been 'a father to him,' and he would be proud to be thought 'one of Cecil's creatures,' if Cecil would 'achieve that he had begun and maintain that he had already made.'[1]

To these and similar entreaties, though Elizabeth had seemed to listen favourably, Cecil had remained cold or had answered only 'in parables.' He had his own distrust of Mary which her smooth words had failed to remove; and he regarded Maitland only as illustrating the truth of his own prophecies. Maitland had foretold that the Queen of Scots would gain her subjects over by skilful management; he had been himself the first whom she had conquered.

Meanwhile in France the apostasy of the King of Navarre being once secured, the Duke of Guise with the secret assistance of Philip prepared for a Catholic crusade. The refusal of the Queen of Scots to renew the league with France was probably a concerted measure. The public reception of Mary Stuart in England, after the false game which had been played by Dudley, would do more to injure the hopes of Condé and the Admiral than a Scotch alliance which would insure them Elizabeth's support. The exquisitely futile theological differences between the Lutherans and the Calvinists furnished means to work upon the Germans.

---

[1] Randolph to Cecil, February 22 and February 28. Maitland to Cecil, February 28. Randolph to Cecil, March 31.—*Scotch MSS.*, ELIZ., *Rolls House*.

The Duke of Guise and the Cardinal of Lorraine half
persuaded them that after extirpating the Huguenot
heresy they would reform the French Church on the
Lutheran model. In February the brothers had gone
to the Rhine to see the Duke of Wirtemberg. On their
return through Champagne they separated. Lorraine
went on to Rheims; the Duke with his servants and
train halted on the 1st of March at the village of Vassy,
and Guise as was usual with him entered the church to
hear mass.

The Calvinist meeting-house was close by—set there
probably in deliberate insolence. When the priest began
the Catholic service the Protestant congregation roared
out their psalms. The Duke who for the time had no
thought of using violence sent a message entreating
them to be silent for a quarter of an hour; mass would
then be over and they could sing as they pleased.

The Protestants replying only with louder peals, Guise
repressed his temper bade the priest go on and knelt
quietly down: but his followers were less patient: two
of his pages, German boys, called out at the chapel porch
that the people were dogs and rebels; the congregation
shut the door against them; others of the Duke's train
had gathered round, and still half in sport pushed it open
again; while at the moment hearing the scuffle Guise
himself came out with his sword in his hand.

A stone was flung at him which drew blood, and with
a shout of rage his men dashed at once among the
unfortunate Huguenots—cutting down men, women, and
children. They made no attempt at resistance. A mere
huddled and shrieking crowd were easy victims. The
few who attempted to escape by the roof were shot down
from the outside. The Duke restored order at last; but
not till sixty people had been killed and two hundred

wounded. This 'massacre of Vassy,' infamous as the first of the series of atrocities which culminated in the black day of St. Bartholomew, was the spark which lighted the fire of civil war. Condé demanded justice. The savage populace of Paris muttered in answer that the conqueror of Calais was the best friend of France, and Guise entered the capital in triumph. The Queen-mother was at Fontainebleau, and Condé pressed her to fly with the King. She hesitated, and the prince at first thought of carrying her off by force; but he was overruled by the Admiral: Catherine de Medici with Charles the Ninth were conducted by the King of Navarre into Paris; the Prince withdrew into Orleans with Chatillon and sent out his circulars calling the Calvinists to arms. The Admiral divided with Guise the affections of the army. The old soldiers of Italy gathered about him. The great towns—Lyons, Tours, Poictiers, Bourges, Rouen, Havre, and Dieppe—declared for Condé, shut their gates, and garrisoned themselves. Inferior in numbers, but with the advantage in order, discipline, and resolution, the champions of the Reformation stood prepared like the English Puritans with the Bible in one hand and the sword in the other, to fight out their quarrel. 'Their modesty of demeanour was beyond example. Each company in this army had its minister; and daily prayer was said throughout the camp. Their songs were psalms. When they played they played for sport, and blasphemy was never heard among them. No *filles de joie*, as among the Catholics, loitered among their tents. If a soldier was found with a woman he was forced to marry her.'[1]

So strong Condé became that he was expected daily at

---

[1] This account of Condé's followers rests on the impartial testimony of Varillas.

Paris again; and Guise was forced to temporize. The affair at Vassy was censured in a public edict. Terms were offered for the security of the Protestants, with which their leaders were almost satisfied. There were still hopes that the war might be avoided, when the rage of both parties burst from restraint. At Sens and Blois the Catholic mob flung themselves like wolves on the unhappy Huguenots. Women and children were hacked in pieces. Ministers had their eyes torn out of their sockets and were flung blind and bleeding into the fire. The Calvinists at Tours in revenge plundered St. Martin's tomb, and burnt his bones—an act more agitating to pious minds than a hundred thousand murders. With the passions on all sides at fever heat, the talk of reconciliation died away. The appeal was only to the sword.

The breaking of the storm brought the Lutherans to their senses. The Princes of the Augsburg Confession prepared to arm. Would Elizabeth arm also? or would she leave those to whom again and again she had promised help to their own resources? She hated spending money; she hated the Calvinist theology; she was playing her own game with Mary Stuart. At times she had a constitutional difficulty which increased with the emergency in taking any decided step. But with all her uncertainties she loved liberty. Tales of murder and cruelty never appealed to her in vain: she had her eye on Calais and Normandy and was ready to run some risks for them.

On the 17th of April Throgmorton sent her a detailed account of the position of the two parties. He insisted on the undoubted support which Philip was lending to the Guises; he assured her of the certain existence of a general conspiracy for the extirpation of Protestantism; and himself passionately desirous that she should interfere, he touched the points most likely to influence her decision and indicated what it was desirable that she should do.

Throgmorton urges Elizabeth to support the French Protestants

'Your Majesty,' he said, 'doth see the present state here which is in such terms as it behoveth you greatly well to consider and deeply to weigh what may ensue; and whether it be meet in this dangerous and captious time to have any interview this summer betwixt your Majesty and the Queen of Scotland. Already the ambassador of Spain[1] hath within these three days used such language to the Queen-mother as she may conceive the King his master doth mind to make war to repress the Prince of Condé, if the King her son and she will not—as one that saith he hath such interest in the crown of France by the marriage of his wife, and in respect of the conversation of the Christian religion, as that he will not suffer the same to fall into ruin and danger by heresy and sedition.

'It may chance that in these garboyls some occasion may be offered as that again you may be brought into possession of Calais or of some port of consequence of this side; but howsoever things fall out, it standeth your Majesty upon for your own surety and reputation to be well ware that the Prince of Condé and his followers be not in this realm overthrown. I shall not need to make any long discourse unto your Majesty who is so well advised, but only put you in remembrance what profit, surety, and credit your Majesty hath obtained by maintaining your friends and such as concur with you in religion in the realm of Scotland.

'Assuredly although this papistical complot did begin

---

[1] Perrenot de Chantonnay.

here first to break out, yet the plot thereof was large and intended to be executed and practised as well in your Majesty's realm as Scotland and elsewhere. It may please your Majesty the Papists within these two days at Sens in Normandy have slain and hurt two hundred persons—men and women. Your Majesty may perceive how dangerous it is to suffer Papists that be of great heart and enterprise to lift up their crests so high.'[1]

The arguments which had justified the interference in Scotland were of equal force for the defence of Condé, and Calais was an additional inducement; but Elizabeth's first desire was to mediate. A general religious war through Europe was a terrible possibility; and she was well aware that by supporting subjects against their sovereign she was legitimatizing every conspiracy against herself. By Cecil's advice she sent Sir Henry Sidney to the Queen-mother with an offer to assist her in keeping the peace; while Dudley flinging out his bait as usual on the chance, wrote to Condé of his own and the Queen's interest in him; and to Throgmorton, this precious defender of whatever cause seemed most convenient—'expressed his thanks to God that her Majesty did not so much measure common policy as she did weigh the prosperity of true religion, as well to the world as for conscience' sake.'[2]

It became rapidly clear however that if Elizabeth were to be of use to the French Protestants, she must employ other means than mediation. Catherine de Medici was powerless. The Guises, the Constable, the Marshal St. André, and the King of Navarre, controlled

---

[1] Throgmorton to Cecil, April 17.—CONWAY MSS.
[2] Cecil to Throgmorton, April 24.
Lord Robert Dudley to Throgmorton, May 8. The Queen to Sir H. Sidney, May 10.—CONWAY MSS.

Court and King and threatened only fire and sword. If Elizabeth stood by while they cut the throats of the Huguenots her own turn would come next; and Throgmorton told her she must use her opportunity 'for her surety and perhaps her profit as musicians make melody of discord.' 'At a time,' he said, 'when every state was hovering to make a prey of its neighbour, her Majesty might not be careless; she should prepare with as little display as might be and she should mean more than she showed.'[1]

It was the Scottish question over again only in a more dangerous form. There a collision with Spain had been unlikely if not impossible; here it was certain. Philip did not affect to conceal his own intentions, and knowing the influence which would be brought to bear upon Elizabeth by the Protestants, he wrote to de Quadra to insist that she should remain neutral.

While Elizabeth was uncertain what to do Cecil made the most of the time, directing Chaloner to assure the King of Spain that whatever the world might say the Queen had not assisted the Prince of Condé; the ambassador 'might put it out of all doubt.'[2] A few weeks later he could not have said so without lying; but he made a virtue of the Queen's irresolution while he was able, and at the same time laboured to end it with all his power. He found however when it came to the point of action, a real obstacle of which if his policy was to go forward it was necessary for him to rid himself. Wherever Cecil plotted, he discovered ever the adversary at work with his counterplots. De Quadra had wormed himself into Elizabeth's confidence deeper far than he liked, deeper than he altogether knew. After each interview of the

---

[1] Throgmorton to Lord Robert Dudley, May 8.—CONWAY MSS.
[2] Cecil to Chaloner, June.—Spanish MSS. Rolls House.

subtle Spaniard with the Queen, Cecil found himself compelled to feel 'what roots he had shaken;' and the dangerous course which he was about to enter required absolutely that there should be no secrets between himself and the Queen.

De Quadra had been from the first in close correspondence with the leaders of the English Catholics. He had his correspondents in every English county, in the royal household, and in the families of the Lords. As the representative of the King of Spain, the old English Conservatives the friends of the traditional Burgundian alliance and the advocates of the Austrian marriage, all looked to him. Durham House where he lived was the focus of conspiracy; and by the water-gate leading to the Thames, disaffected Catholics, Irish chiefs, political intriguers, and even ministers of state, sought his presence, sent their messages, and received their instructions from Philip. The latest of these visitors had been Shan O'Neil the great Irish rebel, of whom more will be heard hereafter—who after beating Elizabeth's troops in the field condescended to visit her court, and used the opportunity to offer Ireland to Philip when the battle of the faith was to begin.

Something of these doings was known to Cecil and more was suspected; it was time that they should end, and accident provided the means of ending them. It happened one day that de Quadra had occasion to send his confidential secretary on some matter of business to Cecil. Borghese—so the secretary was called—was the person who ciphered de Quadra's letters, and held the keys of his correspondence. At the instigation of the devil—as his master thought—he went over to the English Government, and offered to betray all that he knew. And he knew but too much. Doctor Turner a priest had been lately despatched to Flanders in the interest of

Lady Lennox, with a detailed account of the names and resources of the disaffected Catholics. Turner had died abroad leaving his papers in the possession of this Borghese who had accompanied him; and Borghese before he restored the originals to his master had taken careful copies of them.

Cecil wished him to return to the ambassador and remain at his post as a spy. Unfortunately the Bishop too had spies of his own in Cecil's household who gave him notice of his servant's treachery. A day or two later the Spanish courier was arrested at Gadshill and stripped of his despatches; two of the young Cobhams were the perpetrators, disguised as highwaymen; and the next news was that Sir George Chamberlain and another of de Quadra's friends were in the Tower. The Bishop's first and natural impulse was to kill Borghese. To take life was against the profession of a priest: nevertheless on occasions these little objections might be waived. On second thoughts he reflected that in England a murder might create a scandal,[1] so he made an excuse to despatch the man to Brussels where the thing could be done more conveniently. Borghese however not trusting the Bishop's scruples escaped while his master was deliberating, took refuge in Cecil's house,[2] and made a complete revelation of every secret that he knew. In vain de Quadra tried to bribe him to go abroad. The mischief was done and could not be remedied. For the first time the Queen learnt the magnitude of the difficulties which surrounded her; and although the delinquents were of

---

[1] 'El castigarle en la vida por vias extraordinarias attende de ser contrario á mi profesion.'

[2] 'The secretary is now departed from the Bishop, and pretendeth to be moved in conscience to utter things against him, because he perceiveth him to labour breach of amity betwixt the princes, and to serve the Pope rather than the King. He requireth that he may avow all these things to the ambassador's face.'— *Cecil to Chaloner, June 8.* Spanish MSS.

too high rank to be immediately arrested, the Bishop could not but fear the worst consequences both for himself and them.[1]

'I have done my best to repair this disaster,' he wrote to Granvelle, 'but I have failed. The devil that has entered into my servant will not be exorcised. I have tried to induce him to leave the realm, I have entreated, bribed, threatened, promised, all to no purpose; and to put him to death as he deserved would have been awkward. I would have consented to it myself, and for the nonce would have broken the rule of my habit; but I should only have irritated them the more and increased their suspicions.'[2]

Finding his position desperate, de Quadra looked his misfortune in the face. He went to Elizabeth, told her (with so worldly wise a person it was unnecessary to mince matters) that he had spared the life of the man to prevent disturbance, and requested her to send him out of the realm. Elizabeth who as yet was imperfectly informed about Borghese's revelations said that she had every desire to gratify the Bishop, but that she could not send a man away merely for revealing secrets of state to her own ministers. Two days after she sent him word that his servant was arrested, and if he had any complaint to bring she was ready to hear it. He replied that he had not asked for the man's arrest, but

---

[1] 'Es grande el mal que sus avisos han hecho y hacen á estos Catolicos, y mas harán cada dia aunque ahora no osa la Reyna meter mano á los mas grandes por no dar ocasion á algun tumulto.'—De Quadra to Antonio de Toledo, June 6. MS. Simancas.

[2] 'Y el acabarle la vida como su maldad merecia, tenia consigo tantos inconvenientes que aunque yo quisiera consentirlo y atravesarme á la regla del habito no fuera sino irritar mas á estos.'—De Quadra to Granvelle, June 8. MS. Simancas.

for his expulsion. He discovered that his secretary was at large in the palace and that Cecil was busy daily taking down his information. He demanded an audience again and it was refused.

'What the man will reveal,' he wrote to Philip, 'will be the names of the persons who come to my house to talk with me, and certain letters of my own which they will be too happy to read. Of actual designs, of actual engagements or promises made by your Majesty, this man can tell nothing for he knows nothing. The worst which he can say is that I have endeavoured to obtain information on the state of the realm by all the means in my power.'[1]

The noblemen chiefly implicated in the exposure were Lord Montague and the Earls of Westmoreland and Northumberland. There was some uncertainty about Lord Derby; and to try his loyalty a letter purporting to be written by Philip and containing large promises of favour was left at his house by an unknown hand. The Earl who believed it authentic sent to de Quadra for an explanation; de Quadra put him on his guard and saved him from committing himself.

To Cecil the most distressing and in every way agitating part of the matter was the account, which till that moment he had never thoroughly understood, of the propositions which Elizabeth and Lord Robert had made to the King of Spain. He saw the delicate ground on which he was treading; while on the other hand the insolence with which the Bishop had written habitually of Elizabeth herself could be made the most and the worst of.

---

[1] De Quadra to Philip, June 6.—*MS. Simancas.*

When the case was complete the Queen again sent for the ambassador, and calmly but coldly said that she had to complain of the language which he had used about her to the King of Spain.

The situation was too desperate for excuse. Looking her straight in the face de Quadra answered that having been pleased to listen to the stories of a servant who had betrayed his trust, she had heard things which there was no occasion for her to have known. He could not but call the precedent a bad one. Whatever he had said or done—good or bad—had risen from occasions which she had herself created. He had acted to the best of his ability, and if the result had been unsatisfactory to her, he had discharged his conscience to God and his master.

'She said,' he continued, in reporting the scene to Philip, 'that I could not deny that I had sent Doctor Turner to Flanders to concert measures to take her crown from her and to give it to Lady Lennox.

'I answered that I had sent Doctor Turner on business of my own, that I had availed myself of the opportunity to inform the Duchess of Parma of the state of England and of the designs of France; Lady Lennox's name might very likely have been mentioned; the French wished to attach her to their party and to marry her son in France, that if the Queen of Scots died they might have another candidate. England and France at that time had appeared to be on the edge of a war; and I had but done my duty in apprising your Majesty of such things. The public peace of Europe was likely to be broken. I was bound to inform myself of the rights of the different pretenders to the throne, of their plans and their connexions, and to prepare your Majesty for all contingencies. This however was all previous to the death of King Francis. Since that time my letters had been occupied entirely with her Majesty's marriage with the Lord Robert, the reception or non-reception of the nuncio, and of the representation of England at the Council of Trent. If her wishes had been defeated in these matters the fault was not mine: she could herself judge between me and others, which had been her truest friends.

'She tried to answer me but she could not. At last I said I should be glad to know what my servant had revealed which had so offended her: I would then tell her the plain truth: I should satisfy her if she wished to be satisfied; if not I must set myself right with your Majesty.'[1]

The Bishop calculated rightly that Elizabeth could not afford to quarrel with him. Both she and Lord Robert had committed themselves with him too deeply. A list of charges was drawn out which he enclosed with his answer to Philip,[2] where the Turner papers on which alone a serious charge could be built were studiously

---

[1] De Quadra to Philip, June.— MS. Simancas.

[2] Articles alleged against the Spanish ambassador by Lord William Howard and Doctor Wotton, with the answers of the said ambassador:—

1. 'That you the ambassador did send to the King of Spain a book of the heretic Doctor Bale, in which the King of Spain and the Spanish nation were evil spoken of; and that you did say that his Majesty might judge from it what was the disposition of the Queen towards him.'

Answer.—'It is true that I did send such a book. I had remonstrated till I was weary of the perpetual books, plays, and songs which were written in the King's dishonour. The Queen had promised many times to stop them, and had not done so.'

2. 'That you the ambassador complained that the Queen had given the Spanish heretics a church, and that they were much favoured both by her and by the Council.'

Answer.—'I wrote that a large house belonging to the Bishop of

omitted. The arrest of the noblemen whom Borghese had named would have been dangerous; and since immediate action was impossible, Cecil did not wish de Quadra to know how much his secretary had betrayed lest he should warn those whom it concerned. To the accusations which were actually brought against the ambassador he replied chiefly by insisting that he had written nothing but the truth; and prudence or necessity compelled Cecil to let the matter drop.

The Bishop insists that he has only told the truth.

The explosion however was not without its good

London had been given to the Spanish heretics, where they preached three times a week. And this is true; and it is true also that they have received favour from the Queen. Money was given to Cassiodorus to enable him to be present at the Conference of Poissy.'

3. 'That you have allowed Shan O'Neil and other persons to attend mass in your house.'

Answer.—' O'Neil attended mass in his own house, and not in mine. My chaplain gave his chaplain, at his desire, twelve consecrated cakes for the Holy Sacrament. It is true that Englishmen and women communicate in my house. I have told the Queen again and again that I cannot refuse to admit them.'[1]

4. 'That you the ambassador wrote to the King of Spain that the Queen was his mortal enemy.'

Answer.—' I do not remember to have used these words of the Queen herself, but of her as directed by Cecil and the rest of the Council. In this connexion the words are too true. Would to God I could say with a good conscience that it was not so.'

5. 'That you the ambassador have told the King of Spain that the Queen intended to foment heresy in the Low Countries with a view of depriving him of those countries and of dividing them among certain heretic Lords there whom she herself would rule: and that you wrote to Cardinal Granvelle bidding him look to what Doctor Haddon was doing there who had gone over on no visible business.'

Answer.—' The Queen has given us serious cause to fear that this is her intention; and the words which she made use of when the Spanish troops were withdrawn implied as much. The heretics who come hither from Flanders are warmly re-

---

[1] Shan O'Neil had attended mass with much else in the Bishop's house, but de Quadra was afraid of getting him into trouble. ' Lo de Shan O'Neil,' he says, ' lo he negado absolutamente diciendo que en mi casa no se ha comulgado por no hacerle daño; pero ya creo que le habrán prendido y que no aprovechará excusarle porque este traydor habrá dicho lo demas que sabe que el dicho O'Neil me habia enviado á decir.'

effects. The Queen probably was ill-pleased that her secret dealings with de Quadra should have reached the Council. There were no more confidential conversations, and the marriage was removed to a greater distance than ever. Lord Robert was mortally offended at the tone in which the Bishop had written of him, and was half irritated into Protestantism. The storm passed away leaving the air purified.

The time was now fast approaching for the proposed interview with Mary Stuart. Elizabeth's views were

ceived. Upwards of 30,000 of them are now settled in London and Sandwich; at which latter place, so convenient for them to come and go, they have a second church. The mischief in the Netherlands is daily increasing, owing to the encouragement of the exiles here. As to Doctor Haddon he is the Queen's Master of Requests and one of the four Commissioners for the prosecution of Catholics in this country. His pretence to have gone over on some insignificant business at Bruges; and inasmuch as this Haddon was one of those who two years ago wrote a scandalous and insolent letter to the officials of one of our towns in favour of certain Flemings who were burnt there, I did but my duty in telling Cardinal Granvelle who he was. Such a man was not likely in the middle of winter to have undertaken a tour through the principal towns of the Low Countries only for his amusement. If the Council here are so suspicious of me that they arrest and examine every one who comes to my house, they need not be surprised if I too have my suspicions in similar cases elsewhere.'

6. 'That you the ambassador told the King of Spain that the Queen had privately married Lord Robert in the Earl of Pembroke's house.'

Answer.—' I wrote what I said to the Queen herself, that it was reported all over London that the marriage had then taken place. She betrayed neither surprise nor displeasure at my words. She told me merely that not only the world outside the palace believed it, but that the same evening the ladies of her own bedchamber, when they saw her enter with Lord Robert, asked whether they were to kiss his hand as well as hers. She had told them that they were not to do so, and that they should not credit such stories. Two or three days after, Lord Robert informed me that the Queen had promised to marry him, but that it could not be this present year. She said herself to me with an oath that if she married an Englishman it should be him. Had I so pleased, I might have written all this to his Majesty; nor do I think I should have done wrong had I told him the world's belief that she was married already. I did not write it however, and sorry I am that I cannot write it with truth.'—*MS. Simancas.*

generous and reasonable. Could she reconcile Condé and the Catholics she would secure toleration in France. She proposed to use the pretensions of the Queen of Scots as a means by which to work upon the House of Guise. Mary Stuart's promises, with the moderation of her proceedings since her return, had gone far to win Elizabeth's confidence. She believed that fenced round with conditions and to secure a great object, the coveted recognition might be ventured.

It was a point on which she stood almost alone in her opinion. Cecil was convinced that Mary Stuart was playing false, and dreaded that the acknowledgment of her claims would bring after it her marriage with Don Carlos. The moderate party in France believed the effect would be only to exaggerate the power of the Duke of Guise; while Catherine de Medici, on the traditionary grounds of French policy, opposed a step which promised to unite Scotland with England,[1] or yet more formidably—should the Carlos marriage succeed—unite both Scotland, England, and Ireland to Spain. All the fears entertained by French statesmen against the marriage of Philip and Mary applied with treble force to this yet larger and more threatening combination.[2]

---

[1] 'Here is great work to impeach the interview betwixt your Majesty and the Queen of Scotland; well I am assured the Queen-mother and the French Councillors do the best they can by all means to set it back.'—*Throgmorton to Elizabeth, July 12.* CONWAY MSS.

[2] Paul de Foix the French ambassador in England, drew out for the Queen-Mother a sketch of the efforts of the House of Valois to prevent the union of England and Scotland. He urged upon Catherine the necessity of persevering in the same course; and he continued—'Il est vraysemblable que la Royne d'Escosse cuyde que l'asseurance de la succession de ce Royaulme d'Angleterre luy aidera au marriage du Prince d'Espaigne; lequel seroit très dangereux et dommageable au Roy tant du vivant de ceste Royne, estant très certain que l'espérance de la succession furoyt que le Prince d'Espaigne auroit les Angloys à sa devotion, que après son décès par

By Lord Robert alone Elizabeth was encouraged in her own views. Lord Robert believed—and Elizabeth may have shared the impression—that the recognition of the Queen of Scots would increase the anxiety of the English Protestants for their own Queen's marriage, that it might induce them in despair of her forming any other connexion to acquiesce in her own wishes.

The Queen of Scots had passed a troubled winter: the Earl of Arran could not part with the hope with which he had been inflated; the Hamilton family with all their dependants pressed her to marry him, and Elizabeth herself would have gladly seen her secured from continental ambitions.[1] Arran however was moody incapable and weak; and the Queen of Scots detested the very thought of him; he would lie in bed a week at a time brooding over his wrongs till he grew distracted, and at length he began to talk wildly of carrying her off from Holyrood by force. In the Earl of Bothwell he had a dangerous companion in discontent. In common with the other Catholic noblemen, Bothwell had found his services to Mary of Guise rewarded with apparent neglect; and being a fierce

---

l'union de cette Isle avec le Bas Pays.' —TRULET, vol. ii. p. 187.

On the 3rd of July, de Quadra wrote to Philip that Catherine de Medici so much dreaded the marriage of the Queen of Scots with the Prince of Spain that she was encouraging the rival marriage with Darnley; and for the same reason, he believed it possible that Elizabeth, though so irritated with Lady Lennox, would consent also. 'Esta Reyna (Elizabeth) no se como vendrá en este casamiento por la poca satisfaccion que de

Miladi Margarita tiene; pero es tanto lo que temo el del Principe N. S. que pienso que podrá ser que por asegurarse de aquel consiente en esta.'— *MS. Simancas.*

[1] 'Randolph told Cecil that he had been asked by the Duke of Chatelherault whether, if the Lords pressed Mary Stuart to marry his son, the Queen of England would oppose it. He replied that he had no doubt she would be much pleased.'—*Randolph to Cecil, February 22. Scotch MSS. Rolls House.*

reckless man, he perhaps worked on Arran's folly to contrive a scheme for the murder of Lord James, of Maitland, and Argyle, and for the transfer of the Queen to their own custody at Dumbarton. To carry off the sovereign was the usual expedient of the Scotch nobles when they desired a change of policy, and the project suited the character of the brave and careless Bothwell.

But Arran already more than half insane was a bad conspirator. Chatelherault having discovered what he intended, confined him in a turret at Hamilton Castle; he let himself down out of a window ninety feet from the ground by a cord, and flying to Knox confessed his guilt; from Knox he went to Lord James Stuart, and from Lord James to the Queen.

What the exact truth was is hard to say, for Arran changed his story from day to day: at one time he said he had been deluded by Lord James's mother, who was a witch; at another he charged his father with having encouraged him; at another he asserted that the plot had originated wholly with the Earl of Bothwell.

Chatelherault, 'the tears trickling from his cheeks as if he had been a child beaten,' protested his own innocence;[1] Bothwell haughtily insisted that the entire story was a fabrication; and Arran was evidently mad. 'Something however there was in it,' so Cecil eventually concluded, 'though not so much as was supposed;' and Mary Stuart realized for the first time the wild risks to which she had exposed herself in her return to Scotland.

Nor did she fare better with Knox and Knox's

---

[1] Randolph to Cecil, April 25.—*Scotch MSS. Rolls House.*

CHAP V
1561

The Scotch
Protestants
and the
Queen.

friends. She was lectured from the pulpit, admonished by the Assembly, requested by petition to leave 'her idol of the mass.' The measure of virtue in the Scotch ministers was the audacity with which they would reproach their Queen; if they were silent, they said that they would make themselves 'criminal of her blood;' they told her 'she was perishing in her iniquity;' they saw through her schemes; 'they would not behold the House of God demolished, which with travail and danger God had created by them;' they 'admonished her plainly of the danger to come;' and, descending to special grievances, they required 'the twa parts' to be taken from 'the dumb dogs'—the bishops and priests—and given, with the manses and glebes, to themselves.

In vain Maitland protested that this was not language for subjects to use to sovereigns; and essentially, after all, Knox was right. He suspected that Mary Stuart meant mischief to the Reformation, and she did mean mischief. Maitland said that if he had a grievance he should complain of it modestly. 'If the sheep,' he answered, 'complain to the wolf that the wolves' whelps have devoured their lambs, the sheep may stand in danger; but the offenders shall have liberty to hunt after their prey.' On the day on which the news arrived of the massacre of Vassy—so frightful a confirmation of Knox's fears—the Queen by accident or design gave a ball at Holyrood. St. Giles's pulpit rung with it, as may be supposed, the succeeding Sunday; and when the preacher was called to answer for his language he told Mary Stuart 'that she was dancing like the Philistines for the pleasure taken in the displeasure of God's people.'

And she endured all this: she even diminished her amusements in deference to the declamation. Could she but secure first the object on which her heart was fixed, she could indemnify herself afterwards at her leisure. The preachers might rail, the fierce Lords might conspire; a little danger gave piquancy to life, and the air-drawn crowns which floated before her imagination would pay for it all.

On the 19th of May, Maitland went to London to make arrangements for the interview. He was directed to ascertain whether if the Queen of Scots came to England she would be compelled to ratify the treaty. If the treaty was to be insisted on without change or qualification, 'then the meeting was nothing profitable, but rather dangerous than otherwise;' and she stipulated for an escort of English noblemen from the Border to Elizabeth's presence, with permission to use, while in England, her own religion.

As bad news came thicker from France, she took warning from Knox's passion. She affected to Randolph the deepest sorrow for her uncles' excesses; she hoped that her sister would not blame her for others' faults. She loved her uncles, she said; she had trusted that they would have been her support in seeking the union of the realms; but, she protested 'with passion, that she would no more think about her uncles;' her only confidence was in her good sister, and to her alone she would cling.[1]

Mary Stuart's anxiety for the meeting, and the terms of it on which she insisted, were not calculated to work favourably on the English Council. 'The matter is liked here by the Queen,' wrote Cecil on the 8th of

---

[1] 'In uttering these words the tears fell from her cheek, which she coloured not so well but some, though they stood far enough off, perceived them.' —*Randolph to Cecil, May 29. Scotch MSS. Rolls House.*

June, 'but, being pondered in Council, it is found to have so many difficulties in it as I doubt what will come thereof. Except the trouble in France shall be ended before the last of this month without our prejudice here, the meeting shall not be this year; the Queen may not by any interview give countenance to the House of Guise; other difficulties are overweighed by the Queen's affection to see her sister.'[1]

'The Queen,' wrote Sir H. Sidney on the same day, 'saith she will to York to meet the Scottish Queen, and yet I believe not to see them meet this year. Our Queen's affection is great to see her, but I think it will not be.'[2]

And yet Elizabeth was determined that it should be, and determined if possible to obtain the sanction of the Council. Maitland brought with him an autograph letter from Mary, which made her personally more anxious than ever. At last, at a formal meeting and in the Queen's presence, the desirableness of the interview was considered and debated at length. Elizabeth answered the unfavourable opinions 'with such fineness of wit and excellency of utterance as for the same with great admiration she was commended;'[3] yet the Council voted without one dissentient voice, on the other side. A speech of Sir Nicholas Bacon made on this occasion survives to explain the reluctance of the English Reformers and the slight confidence which the Queen of Scots had as yet succeeded in obtaining from them.

The Lord Keeper assumed as certain—whatever she might profess to the contrary—that Mary Stuart was

---

[1] Cecil to Chaloner, June 8.—*Spanish MSS. Rolls House.*
[2] Sidney to Throgmorton, June 8.—CONWAY *MSS.*
[3] Sidney to Throgmorton, June 14.—*MS. Ibid.*

under the direction of the House of Guise. The advantage or disadvantage of the interview depended on the real disposition of herself and her uncles towards England.

What that disposition had been there was no occasion for him to repeat. England was Protestant, the House of Guise were fanatically Catholic. They had challenged Elizabeth's crown in the face of the world; and they had proposed to take it from her by force. Was there any proof that this disposition had been changed?

They had been foiled by the expulsion of the French from Scotland: they were unlikely to have forgiven their disappointment. By that means 'the Queen of Scots had not the governance in Scotland which she and they desired—a matter in itself sufficient to continue old displeasures or breed new.' She had not forgotten the refusal to allow her to pass through England, 'nor the sending of ships to sea at the time of her transportation.' These offences alone would have made her an enemy if before she had been a friend, 'specially seeing her affection was joined with ambition to a kingdom.'

As to any change of feeling, was it to be found in the refusal to ratify the treaty? She had promised and promised—but the thing was still undone, though with it every ground for suspicion would have disappeared; and for any other symptom, where was it to be looked for? 'The words were one way, the acts another;' and 'dulce and pleasant speeches' were not materials on which wisdom would rely.

The meetings of princes were so rare that when they occurred they were 'manifestations of great amity.' So open an evidence of an alliance between England and the House of Guise could not but greatly strengthen that house at a moment when the Guises were in arms to support the authority of the Church of Rome, while it would equally weaken and discredit those who had banished that authority; and if the Catholic faction succeeded in France the cause of the Reformation would be shaken through all Christendom.

Danger of commotions in England.

'The governance of France once again obtained by that house,' Bacon continued, 'it is greatly to be feared that Spain and other princes, given as they be, will join in the common cause of Rome; and that being done, then may we assure ourselves that no force or violence shall be left unoffered, no practice unproved, to bring about a change of religion in England; then are we to look for new legates; then will sedition moved by Romish men be many ways attempted—for seeing our maintainers of Rome at the present neither love nor like the state here, nor yet stand in any fear thereof, what will they then do trow you?

'Then are we to look for no aid of any Protestant prince, because we have not only forborne the Protestants in France in this their need and ours and their common cause of religion, but also by this interview strengthened their adversaries and weakened them; and then who doubts but that the House of Guise being by their prevailing brought aloft, will under pretence of religion set abroad all their old titles and quarrels, or at the least violently prosecute the cause of religion here; and what by foreign force and what by devices at home, their enterprises for these titles shall thereby be made more sensible, and shall have for their bringing to pass less danger and difficulty; and what the Scots will then do in furtherance of these quarrels is hard now to know. Yea, although an Englishman can make himself believe otherwise than I can that the House of Guise coming to such governance as they desire, yet considering what tokens of private love and affection have passed between the princes, that therefore neither the old ambition to this kingdom neither the matter of religion could make them do anything that might tend to the trouble of the Queen and state here—if honour can make abode where ambition to a kingdom, and occasion by power of some hope to achieve, comes in place—although I say this might for some respects be believed, yet who can believe that the Queen of Scots would not have the governance of Scotland otherwise than she now hath, or that her uncles will not do their uttermost to bring her to it; or that they, coming to the rule before remembered with the party which the Queen of Scots is able to make in Scotland, shall not be of sufficient power to bring to pass in Scotland what they will, except the Scots be by this realm assisted? And then are the Queen of Scots and her uncles discharged of their bond in honour, and so will become enemies to us, and therefore take occasion to set forth their former titles; and so this realm driven to the defence both of England and Scotland against these their friends and allies, and all the fauterers of Rome both at home and abroad—wherein albeit we have a sea for our defence, and besides thanks be to God be well furnished with ships and munitions of war, yet the foreign enemy being by such conjunction so strong and ourselves at home so divided, it cannot but breed very great peril to the realm.

'Thus in my opinion it is very evident that no hope of good and great fear of ill is to be conceived by this interview, and therefore for my part I cannot allow of it.'[1]

---

[1] Speech of Sir N. Bacon before the Queen, Midsummer, 1562.—HAR-LEIAN *MSS.* 398.

Chap V
1561 June

Elizabeth disregards the opposition, and resolves to meet Mary Stuart.

Elizabeth listened, but she was not convinced; she persisted in her purpose in spite of remonstrance and in defiance of advice. She gave her answer and 'allowed no replication;' 'and although her resolution was groaned at of the best and wisest,'[1] she sent Maitland back to Edinburgh with a promise that she would meet the Queen of Scots at Nottingham on the 3rd of September. The conditions which he had demanded were all acceded to. Mary Stuart while in England would not be pressed to anything which she might conceive to be prejudicial to her interests. Orders were sent to Nottingham to prepare for the reception of the two sovereigns, whose retinues it was calculated would amount to four thousand persons;[2] and so far as de Quadra could learn, Elizabeth and the Scottish minister had arranged between themselves that the Queen of Scots should be recognized at the interview as next in succession; and then and not till then the treaty of Edinburgh should be ratified.[3]

In vain the Council again insisted that in the humour of the northern counties the passage of the Queen of Scots through them would be in a high degree perilous.[4] Lord Robert's entreaties were more effectual than the remonstrances of Bacon and Cecil;[5] the Queen of Scots was to be received at Berwick by the Earls of Northumberland and Westmoreland whose disaffection

---

[1] Sidney to Throgmorton, June 14.—Conway MSS.
[2] Privy Council Register MS.
[3] 'Lo que en estas vistas se ha de tratar es la ratification de la paz que la de Scocia ha de hacer—con tener primero alguna promesa o certification que muriendo esta sin hijos la recibiran aqui á la sucesion deste Reyno.' —De Quadra to the Duchess of Parma, July 3. MS. Simancas.
[4] De Quadra to Granvelle, June 27.—MS. Ibid.
[5] 'Lord Robert is anxious for this interview, because he thinks it will bring the Queen to a resolution to marry.'—Ibid.

to the existing Government was now notorious; and all her expenses while in the realm were to be borne by the English treasury.[1]

Elizabeth's behaviour could be interpreted only as one of those periodic oscillations towards the Catholics to which she was continually liable: and her resolution as soon as it was known produced a burst of excitement among them. 'The Papists have a great voice here— the more it is to be lamented;' wrote an agent of Throgmorton to him from London. 'I have not, since I came last over, come in any company where almost the greater part have not in reasoning defended Papistry, allowed the Guisian proceedings, and seemed to deface the Prince's (Condé's) quarrel and design.'[2] A few days later a singular letter was betrayed into Cecil's hands. It was addressed to Sir Francis Englefield one of Queen Mary's Council, who had refused the oath of allegiance to Elizabeth and was now in exile. The burden of it was that the Catholic bishops—Heath, Bonner, Thirlby, with Abbot Feckenham, and Englefield's other friends in and out of the Tower, 'sent him their commendations,' 'and all trusted to see him in England shortly and to have as great authority as ever he had.'[3] Lady Margaret Lennox with clamour and almost menace demanded her own and her husband's release. The Catholics were showing their hands already in expectation of the results of the interview, and to Mary Stuart herself a Jesuit emissary hastened prematurely across the channel, believing that all was safe. The Queen of Scots elated at the answer brought back by Maitland,

---

[1] Paul de Foix to Catherine de Medici, July 11.—TEULET, vol. II.
[2] William Hawes to Throgmorton, July 15.—CONWAY MSS.
[3] John Payn to Sir F. Englefield, July 24.—*Domestic MSS.*, vol. xxi., Rolls House.

forgot her caution and commissioned Lord Seton to bring the man to her. Lord James Stuart happily heard of it in time. Partially unclosing his eyes he told his sister that 'to see any such man might put her life in peril, and lead to the subversion of the whole state;' 'and somewhat more was said to her grace, that she might know in what case she stood with her subjects at home and her neighbours abroad.'[1]

Simultaneously there came accounts of movements of Spanish troops towards the French frontier. The garrisons of Fontarabia and Pampeluna were increased. De Quadra, by Philip's command, informed Elizabeth officially that his master was about to interfere in France; while Alva at Madrid after some angry words on the affair of de Quadra's secretary, told Sir Thomas Chaloner that religion throughout Europe was made a cloak for anarchy and revolution, and that the Spanish Government would take order in time for its own security.[2] These symptoms and many more confirmed the arguments of Bacon. The Guises from time to time had affected a readiness to treat with the Prince of Condé, but every day made their insincerity more evident. Elizabeth's chief political virtue was the perception of the limits within which she might rely on her own opinion; and pressed on all sides and compelled to look the situation in the face, after driving the Council to desperation she at last gave way and consented to relinquish her project. Sir Henry Sidney was chosen to carry

---

[1] Randolph to Cecil, June 26.— *Scotch MSS. Rolls House.*

[2] Philip II. to De Quadra, June 7. — *MS. Simancas.* Chaloner to Cecil, Mason and Elizabeth, June 3 and July 10. One of Chaloner's expressions deserves recording. Alva had questioned him on the increase of the English fleet. Chaloner answered that it meant nothing; 'but,' he said, 'according to the ancient discipline of England, when the French arm we also arm.'

to Holyrood the intimation of the change. Elizabeth, he was instructed to say, had agreed to the interview in the belief that Condé and the Duke of Guise could have been reconciled. Of this there was no longer any hope. Instead of peace she heard of nothing but murder and ferocity. The Duke of Guise with the assistance of the Spaniards was preparing to exterminate the Protestants; and she therefore felt herself, though with deep regret, compelled for the present summer to abandon a journey to which she had looked forward with so much pleasure.[1]

With this message Sidney reached Edinburgh on the 21st of July. The purport of it was communicated first to Lord James and Maitland, by whom it was privately made known to their mistress; and 'it drove her into such a passion that she did keep her bed all that day.' Her schemings so laboriously constructed had collapsed like a child's card castle.

Yet Mary had schooled herself in patience; she had felt her power over Elizabeth, and delay was not refusal. Forcing herself into self-restraint she admitted Sidney to an audience the day after; and although 'the demonstration of her grief still appeared in words countenance and watery eyes,' she professed herself satisfied with Elizabeth's excuses and willing to believe her assurances of perpetual friendship.[2]

While however Elizabeth still wrote affectionately to 'her good sister,' her ministers found it necessary to come to an understanding with Maitland and Lord James—and to Maitland especially, who had professed himself his especial friend, Cecil wrote out his displeasure in plain terms. So anxious was Maitland to secure the

---

[1] Minute to Sir H. Sidney, July 15.—BURLEIGH *Papers*, vol. I.
[2] Sir Henry Sidney to Cecil, July 25.—*Scotch MSS. Rolls House.*

Queen of Scots' interests that he appeared to have forgotten his earlier opinions and the claims of the English Protestants upon him. Even after such an evidence as Elizabeth had given, in her long resistance to her Council, of her desire to gratify Mary, he had affected to be dissatisfied with her offered concessions, and to consider a mere promise of recognition an inadequate price for the ratification of the treaty. In a tone of affected humility he wrote in answer to Cecil to deprecate his displeasure.[1] But he was no longer dealing uprightly either with his English friends or with his Protestant colleagues in Scotland. 'The Jesuit,' whom Lord James had prevented his sister from seeing, was conveyed secretly by Maitland into her presence, where 'he remained long in purpose.' The man's business was supposed to be connected with the Council of Trent; but Randolph who had shaken himself clear of Mary's fascinations, 'suspected that there was more in it;' and he 'assured' Cecil that the Queen of Scots 'could well enough keep her own counsel when she had no will that any man should be privy of her doings.'[2]

Meanwhile the Protestants in the English Council were improving their victory. Sir Edward Warner was directed to cause 'the late bishops, now prisoners in the Tower,' 'to be more struitly shut up, so as they might not have such common conference as they used to have;' 'much trouble being likely to grow to the Commonwealth if their practices might take effect.'[3] The laws against persons attending mass were set in force more strictly again, and at the beginning of September Grindal and

---

[1] 'It was easy to judge by your letter that your choler was stirred; yet I pray you let it not be extended further than is reasonable,' etc.— *Maitland to Cecil, July 29.—Scotch MSS. Rolls House.*

[2] Randolph to Cecil.—*MS. Ibid.*

[3] *Privy Council Register, July 26.*

Coxe, two of the opposition prelates, suggested the use of torture as a fitting means of obtaining evidence.[1] Cecil himself in a series of brief notes sketched the danger to England if Condé was overthrown. 'Philip and the Guises would become the dictators of Europe; Spain would have Ireland; the Queen of Scots would marry Don Carlos; the Council of Trent would pass a general sentence against all Protestants, and the English Catholics, directed and supported from abroad, would rise in universal rebellion.'[2] He desired Throgmorton to assist him in counteracting the Bishop of Aquila whose influence was still dangerously powerful, by setting the condition of France before Elizabeth in plain colours.

Throgmorton had but to tell the truth; he could say nothing more alarming. One after another the towns which had declared for the Huguenots had fallen. Angers, Tours, Poictiers, Bourges were taken in rapid succession, and in every instance the capture was followed by indiscriminate massacre. The Duc d'Aumale failed at Rouen, and Condé threw in reinforcements; but the siege was only suspended; the Catholics were preparing to return in overwhelming force.

From the south the accounts were even more dreadful; both sides becoming savage there as the famished wolves of the Pyrenees. Later in the summer the Huguenot town of Orange fell into the hands of the Catholics. The

---

[1] 'On a search of Lady Carew's house, neither the priest nor any of his auditors, not even the kitchen maid, would tell anything. Some thought that if the priest were put to some kind of torment, and so driven to confess what he knoweth, he might gain the Queen's Majesty a good mass of money.'—*The Bishops of London and Ely to the Council, September* 13. BURLEIGH *Papers*, vol. i. Intimations of such a kind make Elizabeth's dislike of her episcopal creatures less unintelligible.

[2] 'Perils if the Prince of Condé be overthrown.' In Cecil's hand.—FORBES, vol. II.

inhabitants were hacked in pieces, burnt at slow fires, or were left infamously mutilated to bleed to death. Young wives and maidens, after suffering first what made death welcome to them, were hung out of the windows as targets for the musketeers. Noble ladies first sacrificed to the lust of the soldiers were exposed in the streets to die—either naked or pasted over in devilish mockery with the torn leaves of their Geneva Bibles—the word of a God who for His own purposes left them to endure their agony. Old men and children, women and sick, all perished—perished under cruelties unexampled even in the infernal annals of religious fanaticism. Des Adrets, a Huguenot leader, surprised a detachment of the men who had been concerned in this business at Orange while fresh from the scene. With the cowardice of villains they durst not defend themselves in a fort which was otherwise impregnable—and des Adrets hurled them down over the rocks, dashed them limb from limb; burnt, tore, and tortured them with a rage which tried yet failed to satisfy the cravings of justice. Still parched for blood the Calvinist chief appeared before Montbrisson. It surrendered without a blow; but a plank was run out from the battlements of the castle, and the garrison man by man were driven out upon it and over it—des Adrets sitting below watching the ghastly heap as it rose and shouting to the victims to make haste as they shivered at the hideous leap.

Des Adrets had a life charmed against steel or ball, and a career charmed against defeat; but his successes were on a small scale while his cruelties were paraded in the Catholic camps and shouted from Catholic pulpits. Guise's progress was swift broad and steady. Toulouse fell next amidst horrors of which a Catholic archbishop —so true to his type is the prelate of the Holy Roman Church—but lately invited his flock to celebrate the third centenary. The German help was slow in coming; Condé's troops fell from him, and by the middle of August the Protestant cause appeared to be hopeless.

CHAP. V
1562 August

Desperately pushed the Prince had only England to look to. Normandy was still in his hands; and renewing the proposals which had before been hinted at, and which Elizabeth was once inclined to welcome, he offered to place in her hands the towns of Havre and Dieppe, to be held as securities for Calais, if she on her part would send him men and money. For a French Prince to reintroduce the English into Normandy was a kind of treason. Even among the Calvinists there were men to whom their country was dearer than their creed; and the chivalrous Morvillier, who had defeated the Duc d'Aumale before Rouen, when he heard what Condé proposed resigned his command.[1] Disinterested assistance however was not to be looked for; and without support of some kind the Reformation in France was lost. An Englishman calling himself John Stirrell[2] gave Cecil notice that the proposal would be made[3] on the 3rd of August. Throgmorton wrote to Lord Clinton that Havre would be a cheap bargain 'though it should cost a million of crowns.' The recovery of Calais was the smallest of the advantages which it promised. The Queen would dictate peace on her own terms and have nothing more to fear.[4] In the middle of the month the Vidame of Chartres appeared in London with powers from Condé to conclude the bargain, and the keys of the two towns in his hands.

Condé offers Havre and Dieppe to Elizabeth.

Elizabeth as usual was uncertain and reluctant. On the 17th Cecil 'feared the worst.' He 'doubted much

---

[1] VARILLAS. [2] Probably an assumed name. [3] CONWAY *MSS*
[4] Throgmorton to the Lord Admiral, August 3.—CONWAY *MSS*.

of the Queen's Majesty.' He felt assured she would send no men to Condé; he could scarcely hope that she would lend money.¹ She consented to send a fleet into the Channel under a plea of protecting English commerce, and she sent Henry Knowles to feel the temper of the Germans; but alone and till Knowles's return she refused to move further.

But events were again too strong for her. Gresham reported from Antwerp that her hesitation was ruining her credit. It was said on the Bourse that if she lost the opportunity she might count her crown as lost. He had applied for a loan, but 'the Fuggers had lent their money elsewhere.' 'The moneyed men were afraid to deal further with her.' 'There was none other communication, but that if M. de Guise had the upper hand of the Protestants, the French King, the King of Spain, the Pope, and all those of that religion would set upon the Queen's Majesty for religion's sake.' Therefore 'great doubt was cast upon her estate and credit.' The English nation was at stay; and 'glad was the man that might be quit of an Englishman's bill.'²

Gresham could only recommend Elizabeth to buy saltpetre and set her powder-mills to work without delay.

Alliance between Elizabeth and Condé.

To arguments like these Elizabeth was singularly accessible. On the 25th Cecil was able to tell Throgmorton that he thought she would give way; on the 29th he wrote that the agreement was concluded. An English army would occupy Havre till Calais was restored. The Queen would lend Condé a hundred thousand crowns, and spend forty thousand more on the defence of Rouen.

¹ Cecil to Throgmorton, August 17.—CONWAY MSS.
² Gresham to Cecil, August 8 and August 16.—*Flanders MSS.*

No time was to be lost. As soon as the agreement was known it was supposed that Guise would make some desperate effort, and Throgmorton's life had been already threatened in Paris. Guise himself with Navarre and Montmorency were at Blois. The Queen-mother and the King, not daring 'to commit themselves into the hands of the furious Parisians,' lay with a strong guard at the Bois de Vincennes; while in Paris itself the people 'did daily most cruelly use and kill every person no age or sex excepted that they took to be contrary to their religion.'[1]

Elizabeth's intention was to profess to be at war merely with 'the tyrannical House of Guise,' to deliver from their hands her friend and ally the King of France. Her ambassador therefore would still remain at the Court. But Throgmorton being personally obnoxious to all parties except the Huguenots, and his life being unsafe, it was determined to send Sir Thomas Smith in his place and to recall him to England.

As the news of the English intervention however would precede the arrival of his successor, Throgmorton durst not remain in Paris to face the consequences. He applied for leave to follow the King to the camp of the Duke of Guise; and he attached himself to a convoy of artillery and powder on its way to the Catholic army— the fate of which he perhaps foresaw. It was intercepted by the Admiral and was carried with the ambassador into Orleans.

Neither Elizabeth nor Condé, prepared as they were for some outcry, anticipated the rage with which the conditions of the English alliance were received by the

---

[1] Throgmorton to Elizabeth, August.—CONWAY MSS.

French. Guise first attempted to march on Havre before the English arrived; then finding it impossible to save Havre while Rouen was untaken, and ready to sacrifice every other interest for France, he offered Condé the Edict of January and universal toleration sooner than permit a prince of the blood royal to betray his country. Even Condé himself, staggered by the name of traitor and the desertion of Morvillier, began to hesitate; and Throgmorton had to insist that after allowing Elizabeth to commit herself he could not honourably accept Guise's offer without Elizabeth's consent.[1]

Elizabeth herself too seemed more careful of her own interests than of the interests of religion. Desirous only of securing an equivalent for Calais she declined to send troops to Rouen or to allow them to pass beyond the lines of Havre and Dieppe, while Condé's object was to have an English contingent in the field with him. 'The Prince and the Admiral,' Throgmorton wrote to the Queen, 'say it will be a great note of infamy in them thus to have introduced the English into Normandy only to hold certain towns which they may detain at their pleasure. They would have your Majesty serve their turn as well as your own.' He warned Elizabeth, with a prescience of the inevitable future, that if she thought only of herself, and if the two parties were eventually reunited, she 'would have the whole force of France combined against her.'[2]

Unfortunately the warning was thrown away. Elizabeth wished well on the whole to freedom, and was ready at the last emergency to fight for it; but truth and

---

[1] Throgmorton to Cecil, September 9.—CONWAY MSS.
[2] Throgmorton to Elizabeth, September 24.—FORBES, vol. ii.

right in her mind were never wholly separated from advantage. She drove hard bargains and occasionally overreached herself by excess of shrewdness. Condé when he understood her resolution sent to Havre to charge the governor not to allow the English to enter. Either the Vidame however or some one else was not so scrupulous. 'It stood upon us,' said Cecil, 'not to neglect the matter, and by other means we obtained a probability to receive us if we would enter.'[1]

On the 2nd of October the first detachment of the English army sailed from Portsmouth, and on the 4th Sir Adrian Poynings with three thousand men was in possession of the town. The command in chief was given to the Earl of Warwick, Lord Robert Dudley's elder brother, who was to follow at leisure with the remainder of the troops.

Simultaneously the Catholics had re-formed the siege of Rouen. On the 28th of September Guise sat down before it in force, accompanied by Navarre, St. André, the Constable, the Queen-mother, and the boy King. The garrison was too small by far for the works which they had to defend; and the first step taken by Poynings was to risk Elizabeth's anger and to allow five hundred volunteers to ascend the river and attempt to make their way through Guise's lines. Killigrew of Pendennis, 'Strangways the rover,' young Leighton of Shropshire, friends of Peter Carew and Wyatt, were the leaders of the expedition. The men were chiefly the west country privateers who on Mary's death had emerged from their pirate nests into Elizabeth's service. The boats were fired on at the shallows of Caudebècque; Killigrew was hurt and Strangways was mortally wounded. A barge

---

[1] Cecil to ——, October 11.—Wright's *Elizabeth*, vol. I.

ran on the sands; the crew were taken prisoners and carried into Guise's camp, where they were hanged on trees with a scroll above their heads—'pour avoir venus contra la volunté de la Royne d'Angleterre au service des Huguenotz.'[1] The rest cut their way into Rouen, to play the part of brave men there before they joined their lost companions; while the troops left at Havre worked day and night entrenching and fortifying, and endeavouring by strictness of demeanour and discipline to conciliate the inhabitants.[2]

---

[1] Sir T. Smith to Sir N. Throgmorton, October 17.—FORBES, vol. I.

[2] Order to be observed by the English soldiers now serving in New Havre, set forth by Sir Adrian Poynings, lieutenant to the Queen, in the absence of the Earl of Warwick:—

1. That every captain and soldier, immediately after their arrival in the church or market-place, shall devoutly together yield thanks to God by singing of some psalm or other prayer that shall be appointed for their good passage and safe arrival.

2. That every soldier behave himself towards the French in all loving, courteous and gentle manner; and that no man, of what degree soever he be of, presume to lodge himself other than shall be appointed by such officers as have authority for the same, pain of imprisonment.

3. That no soldier presume to take any victual or any other thing by violence or otherwise from the French without agreeing and paying for the same, upon pain of death.

4. No soldier make quarrel or broil with the French upon pain of death.

5. No Englishman to draw weapon in the town on pain of death.

6. No Englishman upon any quarrel outside the town to draw weapon upon pain of loss of his right hand and banishment from the town.

7. No blow to be struck without weapons, either day or night, pain of loss of right hand.

8. No soldier to pass the gates without license.

9. No soldier to steal or embezzle weapon or armour, pain of death.

10. That soldier that is taken swearing any detestable or horrible oath, or shall be found drunk, shall receive six days' imprisonment for the first time, and pay a day's wages to him that shall present him, so the same be presented within three hours after; and for the second default shall receive ten days' imprisonment and be banished the town as a disordered person.

11. That no soldier use any unlawful game, as dice, cards, tables 'making or marring,' pain of six days' imprisonment.

12. Soldier taken outside his lodgings without his sword and dagger, one day's imprisonment.

13. No soldier shall lend any money upon any weapon or armour,

Elizabeth herself meanwhile was endeavouring to justify her interference to her brother-in-law of Spain. A Spanish army was already in Guienne; a Spanish contingent was on its way to join Guise; and Philip in a solemn letter had adjured Elizabeth, if she valued her throne to give no countenance to rebels and traitors, and to allow herself to be guided by de Quadra.[1]

Elizabeth in reply insisted that the Duke of Guise was and ever had been an enemy of England. He had conspired against her own title in favour of his niece; he had 'evicted Calais from the English Crown;' which, although bound to restore by treaty, he made no secret of his intention to keep. The disturbance in France gave her an opportunity of recovering it which she refused to neglect; Calais alone she protested was her object; and in pursuit of it she expected rather countenance and help from her allies than menace and opposition. When Calais was restored she promised to recall her troops from French soil.[2]

In England the irritation of the Catholics bubbled over in an abortive movement on the part of a nephew of Reginald Pole. The grandchildren of the Countess of Salisbury retained the appellation and something of

---

ten days' imprisonment and loss of the money lent.

14. Sentinels leaving their post on the walls, death.

15. That no soldier keep any woman other than his wedded wife.—*Rolls House MS.*

[1] Philip II. to Elizabeth, September 11.—*Spanish MSS. Rolls House.*

[2] 'To the recovery whereof we do heartily require you to use such a mean as may stand with the indifferency of your friendship, and with the opinion that the world had conceived how ready you ought to be to procure the restitution of the town of Calais to this our crown; and in so doing we assure you we shall be found most ready to revoke our forces, and to live as we did before these troubles in full and perfect rest.'—*Elizabeth to Philip II., September 30. MS. Ibid.*

the interest of 'the White Rose.'[1] The Earl of Huntingdon, the child of Lady Salisbury's daughter, was the Protestant candidate for the succession. Geoffrey Pole, Reginald's brother, who had turned Queen's evidence against his mother and Lord Montague, had left two sons behind him, Arthur and Edward. Arthur the eldest, an extravagant and profligate youth, had married a daughter of the Earl of Northumberland; though ready to be guided by his friends, he held his title to be as good as or better than his cousin's; and growing discontented with England he proposed to de Quadra to enter the service of Philip, with a dozen other gentlemen.

De Quadra, to whose caution young Pole did not recommend himself, declining his advances, he went next to the French ambassador and professed an anxiety to join the Duke of Guise.

Paul de Foix, to whom he appeared but a wild harebrained boy, advised him to keep out of mischief, and added that the Duke of Guise would not regard with much favour a rival pretender who might interfere with Mary Stuart. De Foix however afterwards consulted de Quadra. Pole pretended that he could carry with him the good wishes of half the peerage. He agreed to make over such claims as he possessed to the Queen of Scots, if on coming to the throne she would revive in his favour the dukedom of Clarence; and as he professed himself able to raise Wales in insurrection, Guise considered that he might possibly be useful, and offered to receive him. With his brother, his brother-in-law Antony Fortescue, and a number of other

---

[1] Viniendo la corona á los de aquella casa del Duque de Clarencio que llaman de la Rosa Blanca.—*De Quadra to Philip. MS. Simancas.*

youths, he attempted to escape from the Thames; but he was betrayed, taken, and thrown into the Tower. His intention he did not attempt to conceal. He was tried for treason and condemned to die; but Elizabeth wisely spared him.[1]

A far graver danger threatened the country a few days after the arrest of Arthur Pole.

The Queen, spending October at Hampton Court, felt herself one day faint and unwell. Never suspecting that her sensations were the first symptoms of small-pox, she went into the air, caught cold, and in a few hours was in high fever. The eruption was checked. She grew rapidly and alarmingly worse. On the night of the 15th Cecil was sent for in haste, and the physicians told him that unless there was a change for the better she had but a few days to live. The following morning there was no improvement. The Council were called down from London; and such of the peers as were within reach hastened to join them. The solitary cord which held England together was threatening to snap; and all the passions, doubts, fears, jealousies, distrusts, and superstitions which distracted the country were soon represented within the palace. Should the Queen die no ray of light or hope could have been seen through the black mass of impending cloud. In the evening she sunk into a stupor, 'without speech;' and with blank faces, in the ante-chamber of the room where she was believed to be dying, the Council sat into the night to consider the fatal question of the succession.

So far as de Quadra could learn there were three opinions. One group of statesmen (he does not mention their names) took their stand on the will of Henry the

---

[1] De Quadra to Philip, September and December, 1562.—*MS. Simancas.*

Eighth, and declared for Lady Catherine Grey. Bedford, Norfolk, and Pembroke, disliking their experience of female sovereigns, were in favour of Huntingdon, and so was Lord Robert Dudley, who was now on good terms with him. The Queen of Scots was barely named. 'The wisest and most dispassionate protested against deciding anything with haste and dividing the realm.' The aged Winchester recommended that the conflicting titles should be examined by the Crown lawyers and judges; and that they should all bind themselves to maintain that person, whoever it might be, who should be found to have the soundest claim. In this last opinion the rest were said to have concurred.[1]

In a matter of European importance the Spanish ambassador was likely to have been well informed. His account may be accepted as substantially correct: and it speaks well for the good sense of Elizabeth's advisers: but their moderation was not exposed to further trial; at midnight the fever cooled, the skin grew moist, the spots began to appear, and after four hours of unconsciousness Elizabeth returned to herself. The Council crowded round the bed. She believed that she was dying: her first words before she had collected her senses were of Lord Robert, and she begged that he might be made Protector of the Realm. As she grew more composed, her mind still running on the same subject, she said she loved Lord Robert dearly, and had long loved him; but she called God to witness that 'nothing unseemly' had ever passed between them.[2] She com-

---

[1] De Quadra to the Duchess of Parma, October 16 and 17. De Quadra to Philip, October 25.—*MS. Simancas.*

'Protestó la Reyna en aquel punto que aunque amaba á Milord Roberto ya le habia siempre amado mucho, era Dios testigo que no habia pasado entre ellos cosa desconveniente.'

mended her cousin Lord Hunsdon to the care of the Council, and still in expectation of immediate death mentioned others of her household for whom she wished provision to be made. She was then left to rest.

By the morning the eruption had come out—and the danger was over. The Queen rallied as rapidly as she had sunk, and England breathed again; only the succession question, having been brought so close with its tremendous issues, demanded solution with louder peremptoriness; the cry rose that Parliament must meet, and in some way or other put an end to the uncertainty; the country would endure no longer a protraction of its present peril.[1]

For many days the Queen remained confined to her room, unable to attend to business. Meanwhile a letter arrived from Spain, and de Quadra demanded an audience of the Council to communicate its contents.

He was received with unusual form, the Bishop of Rochester as Grand Almoner leading him in, which he interpreted into an intended insult. The letter was a command from Philip more positive than before that

---

[1] Rumours—true, false, or a mixture of both—informed de Quadra six weeks later that a meeting was held at the house of Lord Arundel to reconsider the question. Norfolk was present, and Lord William Howard; and the object was to further the claims of Lady Catherine Grey, to whose son Norfolk's infant daughter was to be betrothed. The discussion lasted till two in the morning, and ended without result. When the Queen heard of it she cried for anger. She sent for Arundel to reproach him; and Arundel, de Quadra was told, replied that if she intended to govern England with her caprices and fancies, the nobility would be forced to interfere.—*De Quadra to Philip, November 30. MS. Simancas.* Whether these and similar stories were fictions or realities, it is to be remembered that they were related by an ambassador who was in close and daily intercourse with Elizabeth, that they were addressed to Philip, who was intimately acquainted with her; and the laws of human imagination forbid men to invent under such circumstances what is wholly inconsistent with probability.

England should take no part in the French war, and that the troops—if troops had already been despatched—should be recalled on the instant.

Cecil replied that Elizabeth could not allow the House of Guise to become dominant again. The Queen-mother and the King were prisoners in their hands; and going bravely to the point he said that England would not sit still and see the Protestants murdered.

De Quadra answered that he knew nothing of the Guises; but this he knew, that to call in question the existing Government in France was alike frivolous in itself and an insult to his own master, who considered it so good that he would support it if necessary with the whole strength of Spain. To encourage subjects in rebellion for a heretical creed was a scandal which could lead only to a general war in Christendom; and those he said were ill friends to their sovereign who encouraged her in forsaking the duties of a Christian prince.

Cecil who knew that on this point half the Council agreed with the Bishop, turned the discussion upon Calais, where he was more sure of sympathy. Calais he said had been lost in the King of Spain's quarrel. The Guises had taken it, and meant to keep it; and come what would it should be wrested out of their hands.

Both sides were losing temper. The Bishop said that Calais was lost through no fault of the King of Spain; it was lost by the folly and incapacity of those who had charge of the town, and those who said otherwise to make his master odious lied.

There was not a man in England Cecil fiercely retorted who did not know that the war had been undertaken solely to please Philip.

Pembroke, Arundel, and Clinton, who had been on

Mary's Council, declared that Cecil was right. They had done their best to prevent the war; but the King and Queen had insisted upon it. De Quadra again contradicted them, and the meeting broke up in a storm of reproach and menace.[1]

Yet there was a party, and a large party, who disapproved on principle of the expedition to Havre as cordially as they had disapproved of the wars of Philip and Mary. The occupation of Boulogne had promised fairly and had ended in disaster.[2] Poinings for the present held Havre firmly, and a thousand men were in Dieppe; but at Dieppe the English had been received with outcry and opposition, and if Rouen fell might look to be immediately attacked there.

Whether Rouen could be relieved appeared every day more doubtful. Rochefoucault who was to have joined Condé from the south, had been intercepted and cut up by the Spaniards. A promised German contingent could not march for want of money; and the Prince wrote pressingly to Elizabeth for an additional 5000 men. Elizabeth however, afraid of committing herself with Spain, would not or durst not venture deeper than she had already entered. Condé seeing her centring her strength exclusively in the coast towns, believed justly that she was thinking more of Calais than of him; while Guise and Navarre again promised the Protestants a 'peaceable assurance of their religion' if they would join

---

[1] De Quadra to Philip, October 25. —*MS. Simancas.*

[2] 'What account I may make of these doings I must require time to teach me. Sir John Raynsford, when Boulogne was gotten, seeing every man to rejoice and laugh thereat, said he would keep his laughing till two years were past. If those two years expired, he saw the thing liked as well as then it was, he would laugh too. What the end thereof was, a great many be alive that can remember.' — *Mason to Chaloner*, October 12. *Spanish MSS.*

in 'expelling the English from the realm as the antient enemies of the crown.'[1]

The Prince notwithstanding his suspicions sent an honourable refusal; and before he despatched his letter let the English ambassador read it. Yet a correspondence continued with Guise's camp. 'There is great fear,' reported Throgmorton, 'great dissimulation, or much inconsistency.' 'I do well perceive,' he said, 'that the divorce among these folks is not so desperate but that the same may be soon enough accorded, and the same little to serve our purpose.' He advised Elizabeth to reinforce her garrisons at Havre and Dieppe, that if the Protestant leaders proved to be 'other men than they ought to be,' 'she might be in case to have reason at their hands.'[2]

Meanwhile the work at Rouen grew hourly hotter. A German army under d'Andelot was at last on its way to Condé; and Guise was determined to take the place before they could come up. The numbers engaged were no longer so unequal; the garrison after the entry of the English volunteers were almost 6000 men, and the besiegers were 10,000 at the most. But Guise had contrived to surprise St. Catherine's Hill, the most commanding of all the defences, and covered by the batteries erected there thinned the numbers of the defenders by a succession of desperate assaults. One fortunate accident occurred to cheer the Protestant party. On the 15th of October Navarre, whom they hated as an apostate, was shot in the trenches through his shoulder. The ball could not be extracted, for he could not endure the pain. When he thought himself better he had his mistress

---

[1] Throgmorton to Elizabeth, October 23.—CONWAY MSS.
[2] Ibid.

with him in his tent; he was an inveterate sensualist, and the wound inflamed and mortified. He received the last sacraments from a priest, but his physician, a Calvinist in disguise, avenged the cause which he had deserted by working on his terrors; and the wretched man died in the anguish of darkness.[1]

The loss of Navarre was a heavy blow to Guise, for Condé succeeded his brother as first prince of the blood. But it came too late to save Rouen: on the 21st the besieged made a successful sally, destroying batteries and carrying off guns; on the 25th a general assault all along the lines was led by Guise in person, which though not immediately successful left few of the defenders in a condition for further resistance, except the English and a handful of Scots. Again with daylight the storming columns came on. Alone and uncommanded—for their leaders were wounded or dead—these few gallant men held their ground till noon, when they were cut down almost to the last man, and the Duke of Guise entered Rouen over their bodies. Killigrew was taken half dead, and eventually recovered; about forty escaped down the river and made their way to Havre; the rest were killed.[2]

The expected atrocities of course followed. A few of the principal citizens were kept alive to be hanged in cold blood as traitors. The town was given up to the indiscriminating ferocity of the Catholic soldiers, who massacred till they were weary.

The Protestants in France were consoled by the death of Navarre. The loss of so many English soldiers, present as they were against her orders, it was feared would exasperate Elizabeth beyond comfort or endurance.

---
[1] VARILLAS.
[2] VARILLAS.—*John Young to Cecil, Nov. 2. Domestic MSS. Rolls House.*

430   *History of England.*

<small>Chap V
1562
November</small>

Elizabeth however showed invariably to advantage in serious trials. So much afraid were the Council of the effect upon her that Lord Robert was set to prepare the way. He told her that there had been a terrible assault, and that it was doubted whether the town could hold out. He supposed that the Queen would have blamed the English commander for having allowed his men to go on the service;' but she said only that if Poinings had broken his orders he had better have sent a larger force; 'his blame would have as much for five hundred as for a thousand;' and 'she showed a marvellous remorse that she had not dealt more frankly' herself.[1]

<small>The English at Havre.</small>

The truth when she knew the worst confirmed her resolution. She hurried off Warwick to his command, and determined to 'stuff Newhaven with men.' Dieppe being exposed and the inhabitants dangerous, it was relinquished, and the force of the expedition was concentrated. Seven ships and a fast galley were kept at sea to command the Channel, and at the beginning of December 7000 men were within the lines at Havre. As usual with English expeditions the troops were sent but half-provided, and when they arrived they were ill-clothed and ill-lodged. The winter was cold and wood and coal were largely wanting. Sickness set in and Warwick wrote for 'two thousand mattresses with speed, or a third of the men would be unfit for service.'[2] Still the Government, eager and confident, clung tenaciously to what they had undertaken.

By this time Condé had received his long-looked-for reinforcements. The plague had broken out in Orleans and forced him to the field; and on the 8th December

---

[1] Lord R. Dudley to Cecil, October 30.—*Domestic MSS. Rolls House.*
[2] Warwick to Cecil, December 3.—Forbes, vol. ii.

he marched out, accompanied by the Admiral and Throgmorton at the head of 8000 men—a small force after all in numbers, but composed of the best troops in France. Before leaving the city he hanged an abbot and a member of the Parliament of Paris, in return for the massacre at Rouen. He then moved on Pluvieres, which he took in two days, 'putting the captains, soldiers, and all such as bare arms, to the sword.' There d'Andelot joined him with the Germans; and he advanced towards Paris, closely watched at a distance by Guise. Both sides were unwilling to risk a battle. Condé paused at the suburbs not venturing to enter the city; and Catherine de Medici supported by Montmorency made a last effort for peace. Commissioners met on the 1st of December. The terms which the Prince demanded were an 'interim' till the close of the Council of Trent; Catholics and Protestants 'to live according to their consciences;' a general amnesty; and his own recognition as the prince next to the crown.

CHAP V
1562
November

Proposals for peace.

All this the Queen-mother was ready to grant. The difficulty was the English alliance and the promise of Calais to Elizabeth. The blood of the volunteers at Rouen gave his allies claims upon him which the generous Condé would not repudiate; but he showed Throgmorton his evident desire that the Queen of England would content herself with having earned the gratitude of the Huguenots, and not 'seek to mix particular causes in quarrel for religion.' A courier was instantly despatched to London. Elizabeth answered that 'the Prince had bound himself by a solemn act under his hand;' if he broke faith with her he should never count upon her help again; and she trusted he would give the world no cause to accuse him of ingratitude. If he would be constant to his engagements she would assist him farther; but she

CHAP V.
1561
December

Elizabeth insists on the restoration of Calais.

said pointedly that she had sent orders to Warwick to keep Havre against all comers Protestant or Catholic.[1]

In the same despatch—as a fatal weapon to punish Condé if he flinched—the secret articles which he had signed in his extremity, binding himself to the restoration of Calais, were enclosed to Throgmorton to be used as occasion might require.[2]

The Conference broke up. The Catholics fiercely withdrew their promises of toleration. Condé true to his faith and false to France fell back from Paris, closely followed by Guise, the Constable, and St. André, intending to retire to the coast of Normandy, where the English army would take the field with him.

Far wiser as well as nobler it would have been could Elizabeth have forgotten those 'particular causes.' Her true policy which the Spaniards dreaded that she might pursue, was to leave Calais to its fate, throw her influence into the scale of moderation, and establish a peace which would paralyse the power of the Guises. She could have done it had she pleased; and then de Quadra said she would have placed herself beyond reach of danger. A government at Paris composed of Catherine de Medici, Montmorency, and Condé, would have joined with Elizabeth in holding down the ambition of the Queen of Scots. The English Catholics would cease to conspire from a sense of the hopelessness of their cause, and the Reformation could establish itself in Europe.[3]

It is remarkable that the first serious blunder of

---

[1] Elizabeth to Throgmorton, December 14.—CONWAY MSS.
[2] Ibid.
[3] 'Soy de opinion que se hará algun concierto pernicioso del qual resulte que la religion in Francia no quede remediado y aqui se pierda del todo; porque como estos Catolicos ven flaqueza en lo de Francia, descaecerán totalmente de la esperanza que tenian de ser favorecidos, y se rindirán á la fuerça; o si tal concierto no se hiciese á lo menos se asegurará esta Reyna de los de

Elizabeth's Government was the one measure on which both the great parties in the country were agreed. The blind anxiety of national pride refused to rest till England recovered a town which it would hold only to its own injury, which would and must be a never-ceasing irritation to France, and an open wound. Elizabeth, though not incapable of a more generous policy, preferred an object which seemed practicable, direct and tangible; and her shrewdness for once overreached itself. The Spanish Government with adroit insight changed their tone as they saw her strike into the false road. They knew what she refused to see that neither Condé nor Châtillon would surrender permanently to England an acre of French soil; and as they saw Elizabeth commit herself they withdrew their menaces, and encouraged her warmly 'to secure a pawn for the recovery of Calais.' 'I have to do with curious men,' wrote Chaloner from Madrid; 'so as we make not religion the cause of our stir they seem well contented.'[1] The Duke of Alva complimented Elizabeth's ambassador on the skill with which the English had chosen their opportunity; and assuring him that Philip was sincerely anxious for the success of the enterprise at Havre, expressed a fear only that it might fail for want of strength to carry it out.[2]

To prevent Condé from joining Warwick, Guise de-

Guyes y de la Reyna de Escocia, de manera que se pierda la esperanza que los dichos Catolicos de aqui tienen de ser remediados por aquel medio; lo qual podria ser facilmente que hiciese ligandose y juntandose el Rey de Francia con esta Reyna contra la de Escocia, caso que aquella se causse con algun principe que les de amparha é entrambos; porque como otras veces tengo dicho en este articulo, sou muy concordes y conformes la Reyna de Francia y esta, y ahora anda esta sospecha mas que nunca.' — *De Quadra to Philip, November. MS. Simancas.*

[1] Chaloner to Cecil, November 21. —*Scotch MSS.*

[2] Alva's conversation with Chaloner throws some light on the strength of England in the sixteenth century—'If the French quarrel was

termined to force a battle, and clung to his rear, watching for some opportunity when the magnificent cavalry of the Admiral would have least room to act. On the 18th of December the armies were but a few miles apart, near Dreux. The Eure divided them, and the rough woody country on the banks of the river was almost what the Catholics desired. A narrow strip of open ground lay in front of Condé's position, but closed in as it was all round with scrub and brushwood, Guise supposed that he had found what he wanted; and to prevent the Protestants from renewing their retreat he crossed the river on the night of the 18th, occupied a small village in the line by which Condé would have to pass, and prepared to attack him at daybreak. Two hours before dawn he heard mass and took the sacrament; with the first streaks of light he had his men strongly posted among copsewood and hedges, with the river in his rear.

Had it been possible Condé would have declined the engagement. He was outnumbered; three-fourths of his infantry were Germans, and he did not trust them; but except through Guise's lines there was no escape. The action opened with artillery. The Germans as the Prince had foreseen were instantly thrown into confusion; and Montmorency, who commanded the Catholic

---

made up,' the Duke said, 'England might perhaps feel what the power of France did import; I confess your men are hardy and want not courage, but in discipline and furniture of war they are far to seek.'

'Which objection of the Duke,' says Chaloner, 'I thought not meet at that present to leave wholly unreplied to; I told him that the state of things was lately so redubbed, as he should have cause to be of another opinion. In number of apt bodies to make soldiers, I think you will confess, I said, that we be on as fair footing as France, or rather before them, accounting but their own race. As for the power of France, I wist not what more account we should now make of their force, divided and ruled by a child, that proof showeth we made of them aforetime.'—*Chaloner to Cecil, December. Spanish MSS.*

centre, believing that a single charge would end the battle, dashed forward into the open ground where neither Guise nor St. André on the right and left wing could support him. Drawn up in reserve, with four thousand horse from the old army of Italy, Châtillon saw his enemy throw himself into the single spot where a horse could gallop. Down came the Protestant cavalry with levelled lances; the Catholics out of breath with running could not form to receive them, and through and through their broken ranks Châtillon rode. The Constable fell shot through the cheek, and was borne off a prisoner; the Duc d'Aumale was mortally wounded; eight cannon were carried off in triumph, and the whole centre was dashed into ruins.

If the rest of the army had behaved tolerably a victory was within Condé's grasp which would have ruined Guise's fame and ended the war. The Duke however with St. André drew together upon the ground which Montmorency had left vacant. The Germans advancing in disorder and finding themselves opposed by an unbroken force turned back without a shot or a blow. In vain d'Andelot laboured to rally them. They threw away their arms and allowed themselves to be chased from the field.

The fight was renewed by the reserve; but the Calvinist infantry were far overmatched. Condé fighting desperately was borne to the ground; his horse was killed under him and he was taken; while the Catholic horse, composed chiefly of the French nobles and their retinues, took courage and engaged Châtillon. With these however, wanting as they did all qualities of soldiers except courage, the Admiral's trained troopers made rapid work; and then turned on Guise in time to rescue the few companies of foot who were struggling against overwhelming numbers. Thrice Châtillon charged upon the solid squares. The third time St. André was made prisoner and killed by accident as he was borne away over a horseman's saddle-bow. The squadrons were forming for a final effort to rescue Condé when their pikes were found bent and twisted, their swords broken, their pistols clogged and useless, from the hard service of that desperate day. The short winter's afternoon was closing; and sullenly and slowly the Admiral gave the order to withdraw.

The loss on both sides was about equal. Out of thirty thousand who had been engaged eight thousand lay dead upon the field. Of the Catholic Triumvirate Guise only remained. The Constable was a prisoner and St. André dead; the young counts and gentlemen who had formed the Catholic cavalry were killed or taken. On the other hand the Prince of Condé was a prisoner also. The Germans had been broken into a rabble; and of the whole Calvinist army the horse only held together in effective force—capable perhaps if they had hurled themselves once more on Guise's thinned and wearied masses of crushing them in pieces; but unable any longer to keep the field as an army. The Admiral pursued his way unmolested towards Havre; d'Andelot conducted Montmorency into Orleans; the Duke of Guise was left in possession of the field of battle; and Throgmorton, who was parted from his friends during the action, was two days later brought into the Catholic camp.

So ended the battle of Dreux, remarkable for the carnage which considering the numbers engaged was beyond example; and for the capture on either side of the chief leaders of the opposing factions. After a drawn battle, in the already lukewarm humour of Condé, the war was likely to assume a new phase unfavourable to the hopes of England.

It is time to return to the Queen of Scots. After the failure of the interview, her uncles by whose advice she had been labouring hitherto to disarm suspicion, recommended her to throw off the mask and fall back upon the Catholics. She had gained little by conciliation: their own successes at the end of the summer promised again to give them the disposal of the force of France; and while Maitland still affected to be blind and kept his eye fixed on the English succession, Lord James, a less able but a truer and far nobler man, saw that his confidence in his sister perhaps had been mistaken, and that Knox had been more right than himself.

Of all the reactionary noblemen in Scotland the most powerful and dangerous was notoriously the Earl of Huntly. It was Huntly who had proposed the landing at Aberdeen; it was Huntly who had sworn that if the Queen would but speak the word the mass should be 'set up again.' In his own house the chief of the house of Gordon had never so much as affected to comply with the change of religion; and to him and his policy the Duke of Guise now advised Mary to incline.

A number of causes combined at this moment to draw attention to Huntly. He had refused to part with the lands of Murray which had been given to Lord James. One of his sons Lord John Gordon commonly called Laird of Finlatter, who had been imprisoned for murder, had escaped to the north, and was supported by his father in setting the law at defiance;[1] and uneasy about

---

[1] Lord John Gordon's history throws singular light on the inner life of the Scotch nobility. Randolph writes to Cecil—'Touching the Laird of Finlatter, there is here a strange story. If your honour call it to remembrance, there was one Finlatter, Master of the Household to the

CHAP V
1562.
August

The Earl of Murray determines to punish the Earl of Huntly.

Mary's intentions, and fearing what Huntly might do next if he was left unpunished, Lord James—or to call him henceforth by the name under which he is so well known, the Earl of Murray[1]—resolved to anticipate attack, to carry the Queen with him to visit the recusant lord in his own stronghold, and either to drive him into a premature rebellion or force him to submit to the existing government.

Murray's reasons for such a step are intelligible. It is less easy to understand why Mary Stuart consented to it. 'Whether,' says Knox, 'there was an agreement between the Papists of the north and the Papists of the south, or to speak more plainly between Huntly and the Queen, was not known; but suspicion was wondrous vehement

---

Queen-mother, that had commission many times to confer with your honour and the rest of the Commissioners at your being at Edinburgh. This Finlatter was disinherited by his father, and his land given to John Gordon second son to the Earl of Huntly. Two principal causes there were that moved Finlatter's father thus to do: the one that he solicited his father's wife being his mother-in-law to dishonesty, not only with himself but with another man; the other which is marvellous strange that he took purpose with certain as well-conditioned as himself, to take his father and put him into a dark house, and there to keep him waking until such time as he became stark mad; and that being done, thought to enter himself in possession of the house and lands. This being revealed, and care taken given unto his father that this was true, he having no other issue by persuasion of his wife who was a Gordon gave the whole land unto John Gordon, who after the death of the said Finlatter married her and so had right unto the whole living. To see how God hath plagued the iniquity of this same woman—in one month after his marriage John Gordon casteth his fantasy unto another, and because that he would not depart from the land which was hers for her lifetime, he locketh her up in a close chamber where she yet remaineth; and for the deliverance of her and for the unjust dealing of John Gordon towards her much controversy is risen in this country, and are of the chief causes why he enterprised such things as he hath done, thinking he shall be forced to put her to liberty and forego the land as long as she liveth.'—*Sept.* 30, 1562. *Scotch MSS. Rolls House.*

[1] The Earldom was his, although he had not yet assumed the title. At this time he was styled Earl of Mar, but his repeated change of name creates confusion.

that no good will was borne to the Earl of Murray.' Huntly's family in explanation of the events which followed, affirmed that 'the trouble which happened to the Gordons' was 'for the sincere and loyal affection which they had to the Queen's preservation;' and that throughout there was a secret understanding between the Queen and the Earl. It may be that Mary Stuart was prepared for either contingency. She was going with but a moderate escort to that Aberdeen to which she had been before invited. If the Catholic noblemen were as powerful as they pretended they could destroy her brother and set her at liberty from the thraldom in which she had been held. If Huntly had overrated his strength, she would gain a step in the confidence of Elizabeth, and allay the rising suspicions of Murray and his friends. Divided between her zeal for orthodoxy and her hope of the English succession, she might account either conclusion as an advantage gained, and it was essential for her to test the relative powers of the different parties among her subjects.

The expedition itself she thoroughly enjoyed. The northern autumn was wet and cold; but Mary Stuart was as much at her ease galloping a half-broken stallion over the heather as when languishing in her boudoir over a love-sonnet; to Randolph who accompanied the party she said she wished she was a man, 'to know what life it was to lie all night in the field or to walk on the cawsey with a Glasgow buckler and a broadsword;' and the glittering cavalcade swept gaily through the country, knight and yeoman, lord and dame, in all three thousand horse.

On the 31st of August they reached Aberdeen, where an invitation met them from Huntly to visit his house at Strathbogie. 'It was the fairest and best in all the

CHAP V
1562
August

country;' and the Earl had made large provision for the Queen's reception; but the reply was a demand only for the surrender of his fugitive son; and when Lord John Gordon did not appear, the Queen willingly or unwillingly passed on through the heart of the Huntly clan to Inverness. The Earl of Sutherland—another Gordon—who was in the royal train, was secretly in league with his kinsman; and Lord John hung on the skirts of the march watching an opportunity to carry Mary off; but the chance did not present itself.

Having the disposition of the authority of the sovereign Murray's object was to make his power felt. On reaching Inverness he required the castle gates to be opened. The Gordon in command more loyal to Huntly than to the Queen refused to admit her, and though the Earl made haste to apologize and sent orders the next day to place the castle and all in it at her disposal the captain was hanged over the battlements.

Having strangled a wolf cub thus in the heart of the den, Murray had accomplished one part of his purpose; and not caring to remain longer where the horses and perhaps their riders also would soon have starved, he turned back upon his steps. The Earl of Huntly finding that if he meant to do anything he must do it promptly and by force made an effort to intercept him. A thousand Gordons lay in a wood on the banks of the Spey the night before the Queen passed. But their hearts failed them, and they scattered before she appeared. On the 24th of September she was again at Aberdeen. The time of reckoning was now come for the Earl himself. Murray was resolved not to leave the country till he had brought him on his knees, and though Huntly still affected loyalty and 'laid the fault on his son,' yet as his son was known to be with him either in Strathbogie or the neighbourhood he was informed that the Court would remain at all risks in Aberdeen till Lord John was taken or had surrendered.

In the quadrangle of Huntly's house stood a single cannon—an awful emblem of power and sovereignty. It had been dismounted and concealed in a cellar. Murray sent for it; and the Earl, 'with very humble words and tears and sobs,' promised that it should be given up. Lady Huntly—reported by the Protestants to be a witch—'led the messenger into the chapel of the house,' furnished with crucifix, candle and altar. 'Good friend,' she said to him, 'you see here the envy that is borne unto my husband: would he have forsaken God and his religion as those that are now about the Queen, my husband would never have been put at as he now is. God and he that is upon this altar will preserve us and let our true hearts be known. Tell your mistress my husband was ever obedient to her and will die her faithful subject.'[1]

A fortnight passed. The house where the Court lodged was one night almost burnt over their heads by the Gordons. Young Kirkaldy of Grange on the 9th of October made a dash on Strathbogie, and would have made the Earl prisoner had he not 'scrambled over a low wall without boot or sword,' and escaped by the speed of his horse. Lord John in revenge destroyed an outlying party of the Queen's guard; Huntly himself was reported to have retired to Badenoch, 'where neither men nor guns could be taken in the winter;' while from the south came news that Bothwell had

[1] Randolph to Cecil, September 30.—*Scotch MSS. Rolls House.*

escaped out of Edinburgh Castle; not it was supposed without the Queen's knowledge. Lord Gordon, Huntly's eldest son and Chatelherault's son-in-law, was reported to be working on the irritation of the Hamiltons at Arran's imprisonment; and the Duke and his whole house were expected to rise in insurrection.

There was matter in this news for grave anxiety; and had Huntly remained in the Highlands Murray might have found the work which he had taken in hand too hard for him. But fortune stood his friend. Misled by a false report that the Queen's escort had been tampered with, the Earl came down again from the mountains. Information was brought into Aberdeen that he was but a few miles off with not more than seven hundred men about him. Swift as lightning Murray Morton and Grange were on his track. He was surrounded in a bog called Corrichie Burn, from which there was no escape; and after a sharp skirmish in which two hundred of his followers were killed he was taken with his two sons Lord John and Lord Adam.

His own fate was a strange one. 'The Earl without blow or stroke being set on horseback before him that was his taker suddenly fell from his horse stark dead without word that ever he spoke.'[1] Adam Gordon being then but a boy of seventeen was dismissed to be the scourge in manhood of the northern Protestants. Lord John after a full confession was beheaded in the market-place at Aberdeen. 'The Queen took no pleasure in the victory and gloomed at the messenger who told of it.' Her brother read her a cruel lesson by compelling her to be present at the execution; while Maitland for once

---

[1] Randolph to Cecil, October 28 and November 2.—*Scotch MSS. Rolls House.*

'remembered that there was a God in Heaven,' and made a speech on the ways of Providence.[1]

Mary Stuart might have preferred a different result. She made haste to turn to her advantage Murray's triumph. Elizabeth the day before she was taken ill, had written to her a remarkable letter—not, like so many others, prepared by Cecil and signed by herself, but an original composition altogether peculiar and characteristic. Though the style was confused the tone was noble. The object was to explain the interference in France and to deprecate Mary's resentment.[2] One

---

[1] Knox.

[2] 'MY OWN DEAR SISTER,—Were it not a thing impossible for us to forget our own hearts, I should fear you might think that I had drunk the waters of Lethe; but there is I assure you no such river in England; and of the fault if fault there be you are yourself the chief cause; for if your messenger who you told me long ago was coming had not delayed so long, I should have written to you as usual; but when I heard that you were going so long a pilgrimage and so far from the English border, I thought that this had perhaps hindered you; while on my part I was kept silent by another motive—I feared to distress you with the tale of the tragedies with which each week my own ears were grieved. Would to God they had been as unknown to others as they were passed over in silence by me; and I promise you on my honour that till the ravens cried out upon me I would have stopped my ears with oblivion. But when I saw that all my advisers and my subjects considered me too blind—too dull— too improvident—I roused myself from that slumber. I thought I was unworthy to rule such a realm as this which I possess, did I not make Prometheus as familiar with my councils as I had long made Epimetheus. And when I remembered that it touched your interests also —my God, how did it gnaw my heart! not for myself, you know it well, but for her to whom I wish all the good that can be devised, fearing lest you should think that the old sparks are kindled into new flame.

'Notwithstanding when I saw that necessity has no law and that we must guard our own homes when those of our neighbours are on fire, I had no such suspicion of you as that you would refuse to take off the veil of nature and regard the naked cause of reason.

'Far sooner would I pass over those murders on land; far rather would I leave unwritten those noyades in the rivers—those men and women hacked in pieces; but the shrieks of the strangled wives, great with child —the cries of the infants at their

defect however there was in this letter: it contained no word upon the subject nearest to the heart of the Queen of Scots, while rumours reached her of the discussions of the Council on the succession when Elizabeth was supposed to be dying, in which her name and claim had been passed by almost in silence.

Maitland therefore was at once set to work. He wrote to Cecil to say that although Huntly's rebellion

mothers' breasts—pierce me through. What drug of rhubarb can purge the bile which these tyrannies engender? My own subjects in many places have lost goods, ships, and life, and have been baptized with another name than their sponsors gave them at their baptism—a name till late unknown to me, now too familiar—too often heard—the name of Huguenots. The blame of this treatment has been cast on the poor soldiers, but the fault rests with the wicked leaders of the quarrel, who when complaint is made to them, instead of correcting one ill deed commit twenty.

'I received letters from the King and Queen—letters which they cannot deny—from which I learn clearly that the King is but King in name, and that others have the power. And seeing this I have set myself to prevent the evils which might follow if the quarry of this realm was in their talons. But I shall so rule my actions that the King shall hold me a good neighbour, who rather protects than destroys. Your kinsmen shall have no cause to deem me vindictive. I shall do them no hurt unless they commence with me. You shall have no ground to charge me with deceit. I have even accomplished more than I have promised wherever it has been possible; and I promise you it shall not stand with me, but there shall be soon a sound peace between all who will be ruled by reason. I send my fleet, and I send my army, but with no thought except to do good to the King, and to all, unless they will first injure me; and that the world may know the desire I have for peace, and remove all suspicions which may be engendered of me, I make this declaration without any reserve whatever. I trust therefore you will think as honourably of me as my good will towards you deserves; and though I am not ignorant what arts will be or have been used with you in this respect to induce you to withdraw from the affection which I am assured you bear me; I nevertheless have such trust in this heart which I hold so precious,[1] that I think the rivers will sooner run upwards to the mountains than it shall change towards me. The fever under which I am suffering forbids me to write further.'—*Queen Elizabeth to the Queen of Scots*, October 15. *Scotch MSS. Rolls House. Translated from the French Original.*

[1] The Queen of Scots had sent to Elizabeth a heart set with diamonds.

had been crushed, his mistress was in 'perplexed case.' With reason or without reason England was at war with France; and France, which at all times had befriended Scottish liberty—France, whose alliance Scotland could not afford to lose—was calling on her for assistance. The Queen of Scots herself had an interest in her dowry which she would forfeit by refusal, while from England it appeared that she was to receive nothing but Elizabeth's regard, which did not go 'beyond her person.' Had Elizabeth died in her last illness the Queen of Scots would have sacrificed the friendship of France and have gained nothing in exchange. Could she but have confidence that 'quarrels should never rise between herself and any person in that realm,' she would value the English alliance 'more than all the uncles in the world:' but the only security which could give her that confidence was the recognition of her title; and 'it was whispered in the late storm' that the English Council intended to prefer another candidate. Maitland for his part said he could ill believe it, 'seeing none was so worthy or had so good a title.' The union of the realms was of priceless moment: and 'if religion moved anything,' the late appearance of his mistress in arms against the leader of the Papists ought to disarm suspicion.[1]

A fortnight later Randolph said that Scotland was full of rumours traced to the authority of the Clerk of the English Council, that 'during the late discussion one voice only had been raised for the Queen of Scots, and that in the Parliament about to be held she would be debarred from the succession.'[2] Unable to endure the suspense longer, Mary Stuart at last despatched Maitland

---

[1] Maitland to Cecil, November 14.—COTTON MSS. CALIG. B. 10.
[2] Randolph to Cecil, November 28.—MS. Ibid.

to press her claims openly on Elizabeth; 'to demand access to the Parliament House' and declare her title before the Estates of the Realm; and if the Lords and Commons refused to entertain it, to 'tell them plainly that she would seek her remedy elsewhere.'[1]

So wrote Mary grasping fiercely at the prize which she trusted to have purchased by Huntly's blood; while Randolph informed Cecil that the distrust of Knox was still as fixed as ever. 'He had no hope that she would ever come to God, or do good in the Commonwealth; he was so full of mistrust in all her doings, words, and sayings, as though he were either of God's privy council, that knew how he had determined of her from the beginning, or knew the secrets of her heart so well that he was assured she neither did or would have for ever one good thought of God or of his true religion.'[2]

---

[1] 'You shall in our name and in our behalf publicly and solemnly protest that we are thereby injured and offended, and [must seek] such remedy as the law and consuetude has provided for them that are enormously and excessively hurt.'—*Instructions given by the Queen of Scots to Maitland.* KEITH, vol. ii.

[2] Randolph to Cecil, December 16.—*Scotch MSS. Rolls House.*

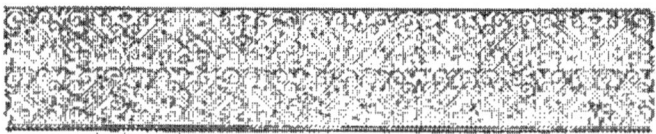

CHAPTER VI.

IN the face of enormous difficulties Elizabeth and her ministers had restored England to its rank in Europe. They had baffled Spain, wrested Scotland from the Guises, and played with accomplished dexterity on the rivalries and jealousies of the Romanist powers. By skill and good fortune they had brought the Catholics at home to an almost desperate submission; and now, with the country armed to the teeth, they were subsidizing a Protestant rebellion in France, and fastening themselves once more upon the French soil.

The expenses of so aggressive and dangerous a policy had been great, yet Elizabeth's talent for economy had saved her from deep involvements; and while courtiers whined over her parsimony, the burden of public debt bequeathed by Mary had received no increase, and was even somewhat diminished. The wounds were still green which twenty years of religious and social confusion had inflicted on the commonwealth; but here too there were visible symptoms of amendment: above all, the poisonous gangrene of the currency the shame and scandal of the late reigns had been completely healed.

No measure in Elizabeth's reign has received more deserved praise than the reformation of the coinage. The applause indeed has at times overpassed her merit;

for some historians have represented it as accomplished at the cost of the crown; whereas the expense, even to the calling in and recoining the base money, was borne to the last penny by the country. Elizabeth and her advisers deserve the credit only of having looked in the face, and of having found the means of dealing with a complicated and most difficult problem.

When the ministers of Edward the Sixth arrived at last at the conviction that the value of a shilling depended on the amount of pure silver contained in it, and that the base money therefore with which the country had been flooded must be called down to its natural level, the people it was roughly calculated had lost something over a million pounds. An accurate computation however was impossible, for the issues of the Government large as they were had been exceeded by those of private coining establishments in England and abroad, where the pure coin left in circulation was melted down and debased.

The evil had been rather increased than diminished by the first efforts at reformation. The current money was called down to an approach to its value in bullion, and it was then left in circulation under the impression that it would no longer be pernicious; but the pure shillings of Edward's last years could not live beside the bad, and still continued either to leave the country or to be made away with by the coiners. The good resolutions of further reform with which Mary commenced her reign disappeared as she became straitened for money; the doctrinal virtues superseded the moral; and relapsing upon her father's and her brother's evil precedents, she poured out a fresh shower of money containing but three ounces of silver with nine of alloy, and attempted to force it once more on the people at its nominal value.

The coining system acquired at once fresh impetus; and Elizabeth on coming to the throne found prices everywhere in confusion. Amidst the variety of standards and the multitude of coins recognized by the law, the common business of life was almost at a stand-still. Of current silver there was such as remained of Edward's pure shillings, containing eleven ounces and two pennyweights of silver in the pound; the shillings of the first year of Mary containing ten ounces; and the old shillings of Henry the Eighth containing eleven ounces.

Of testers or sixpences the coin in common use, there were four sorts: the tester of eight ounces of silver in the pound, the tester of six, the tester of four, and the tester of three; with groats, rose pence, and other small coins, of which the purity varied in the same proportion. The testers of eight, six, and four ounces had been issued originally as shillings, and had been called down to sixpences. These three kinds were all of equal value, 'for that which lacked in fineness exceeded in weight,'[1] and they were really worth fourpence halfpenny. The fourth kind the tester of three ounces was worth only twopence halfpenny; but 'the worst passed current with the best' in the payment of the statute wages of the artisan or labourer. The working man was robbed without knowing how or why, while the tradesman and farmers aware that a sixpence was not a sixpence, defied the feeble laws which attempted to regulate the prices of produce, charged for their goods on a random scale, and secured themselves against loss by the breadth of margin which they claimed against the consumer.

The earliest extant paper on the subject in the reign

---

[1] Paper on Coinage: endorsed in Cecil's hand, Mr. Stanley's opinion.— *Domestic MSS.*, ELIZ. vol. xiii.

of Elizabeth is the composition of the Queen herself. With the rise in prices the landowners generally had doubled their rents, while the rents of the Crown lands had remained unchanged. The ounce of silver in the currency of the Plantagenets, instead of being coined into the five shillings of later usage, had been divided only into a quarter of a mark, or three shillings and four pence. Elizabeth proposed to return to the earlier scale, and retaining the same nominal rent of which she found herself in receipt, to allow 'the tenants of improved rents to answer their lords after the rate of the abatement of value for every pound a mark;'[1] while all outstanding debts or contracts might be graduated in the same proportion.

The objections to this project it is easy to see would have been infinite. It fell through—was heard of no more. But in their first moments of serious leisure, immediately after the Scotch war, in September 1560, the Council determined at all hazards to call in the entire currency, and supply its place with new coin of a pure and uniform standard. Prices of all kinds could then adjust themselves without further confusion.

The first necessity was to ascertain the proportions of good and bad money which was in circulation. A public inquiry could not be ventured for fear of creating a panic, and the following rudely ingenious method was suggested as likely to give an approximation to the truth. 'Some witty person was to go among the butchers of London, and to them rather than to any other, because they retailed of their flesh to all manner

---

[1] 'Wherein', she said, 'the lord shall not be much hindered, being able to perform almost every way as much with the mark as he was with the pound.'—(Opinion of her Majesty for reducing the state of the coin, 1559.) Domestic MSS. Eliz.

of persons in effect—so that thereby of great likelihood came to their hands of all sorts of money of base coin: and to go to a good many of them—thirty-six at least— and after this manner, because they should not understand the meaning thereof, nor have no suspicion in that behalf—requiring all of them to put all the money that they should receive the next forenoon by itself, and likewise that in the afternoon by itself, and they should have other money for the same; promising every one of them a quart of wine for their labours, because that there was a good wager laid whether they received more money in the afternoon—whereof nine score pounds being received of the butchers, after the manner aforesaid, being all put together, then all the shillings of three ounces fine and under, but not above, should be tried and called out—as well counterfeits after the same stamp and standard as others; and after the rest of the money might be perused and compared one with another.'[1]

Either by this or some other plan, the worst coin in circulation was found to be about a fourth of the whole, while the entire mass of base money of all standards was guessed roughly at 1,200,000*l.* How to deal with it was the next question. Sir Thomas Stanley offered several schemes to the choice of the Government.

1. The testers, worse and better together, might be called down from sixpence to fourpence; a period might be fixed within which they must be brought to the Mint, and paid for at that price. The 1,200,000*l.* would be bought in for 800,000*l.*; the bullion which it contained, being recoined and reissued at eleven ounces fine, would be worth 837,500*l.*; and the balance of 37,500*l.* in

---

[1] 'A manner to make a proof how many sorts of standards are current commonly within this realm.'—LANSDOWNE MSS. 4.

favour of the Government, together with the value of the alloy, would more than cover the expenses of the process. If the Queen wished to make a better thing of it, the worst money might be sent to Ireland, as the general dirt heap for the outcasting of England's vileness.

2. The bad coin might be called in simply and paid for at the Mint according to its bullion value, a percentage being allowed for the refining.

3. If the Queen would run the risk she might relieve her subjects more completely by giving the full value of fourpence halfpenny for the sixpence, three halfpence for the half groat, and so on through the whole coinage, allowing three-quarters of the nominal value, and taking her chance—still with the help of Ireland—of escaping unharmed.[1]

Swiftness of action, resolution, and a sufficient number of men of probity to receive and pay for the monies all over the country were the great requisites.[2] The people were expected to submit to the further loss without complaint if they could purchase with it a certain return to security and order. Neither of Stanley's alternatives were accepted literally. The standard for Ireland had always been something under that of England. But the Queen would not consent to inflict more suffering on that country than she could conveniently help. The Irish coin should share in the common restoration, and be brought back to its normal proportions.

On 27th of September the evils of an uneven and vitiated currency were explained by proclamation. The people were told that the Queen would bear the cost of

---

[1] Mr. Stanley's opinion.—*Domestic MSS.*, Eliz. vol. xiii. Rolls House.
[2] Bacon to Cecil, October 14, 1560.—*MS. Ibid.* vol. xiv.

The Reign of Elizabeth.

refining and recoining the public moneys if they on their side would bear cheerfully their share of the loss; and they were invited to bring in and pay over to persons appointed to receive it in every market town the impure silver in their hands. For the three better sorts of tester the Crown would pay the full value of fourpence halfpenny, and for the half groats and pence in proportion. For the fourth and most debased kind, which was easily distinguishable, it would pay twopence farthing.

To stimulate the collection a bounty of threepence was promised on every pound's worth of silver brought in. Refiners were sent for from Germany; the Mint at the Tower was set to work under Stanley and Sir Thomas Fleetwood; and in nine months the impure stream was washed clean, and a silver coinage of the present standard was circulating once more throughout the realm.

Either a large fraction of the base money was not brought in, or the estimate of the quantity in circulation had been exaggerated. The entire weight collected was 631,950 lbs.; 638,000*l.* (in money) was paid for it by the receivers of the Mint, and it yielded when melted down 244,416 lbs. of silver, worth in the new coinage of eleven ounces fine 733,248*l.* So far therefore there was a balance in favour of the Crown of 95,135*l.*; but the cost of collection, the premiums, and other collateral losses reduced the margin to 49,776*l.* 9*s.* 3*d.* Thirty-five thousand six hundred and eighty-six pounds, fifteen shillings and sixpence (35,686*l.* 15*s.* 6*d.*) was paid for the refining and re-minting; and when the whole transaction was completed Elizabeth was left with a balance in her favour of fourteen thousand and seventy-nine pounds, thirteen shillings, and ninepence (14,079*l.* 13*s.* 9*d.*)[1]

The cost of the process.

Thus was this great matter ended, not as it has been represented by means of two hundred thousand crowns raised by Gresham in Flanders. The two hundred thousand crowns indisputably were raised there, but it was to buy saltpetre, and corselets, and harquebusses; and the reform of the coin cost nothing beyond the thought expended on it.

Social condition of England.

But the country was sick of other disorders less easy to heal. The silent change in the relations of rich and poor, the eviction of small tenants, the creation of a new race of men on the ruins of the abbeys, whose eyes were more on earth than heaven, the universal restlessness of mind, and the uprooting of old thought on all subjects divine or human, had confused the ancient social constitution of the English nation. Customs and opinions had vanished, and laws based upon them had become useless or mischievous. The underroll of the peasant insurrection was still perceptible in the weakness of the Government and the anarchy of the country population.

The petty copyholders dispossessed of their tenures had contracted vagrant habits; the roads were patrolled by highwaymen who took purses in broad daylight in the streets of London itself; and against these symptoms was contending the reactionary old English spirit which had gathered strength under Mary, the single good result

---

[1] 'Charges of refining the base money received into the Mint since Michaelmas 1560 until Michaelmas 1561, and of the charges of the workmanship on coining to fine money thereof made; with a note of the provisions and other charges incident to the same, the waste of melting and blemishing being borne.'—LANSDOWNE *MSS.* 4.

of her reign. Grass lands were again browning under tillage, farm-houses were rebuilt, and the small yeomen fostered into life again; but a vague unrest prevailed everywhere. Elizabeth's prospects during her first years were so precarious that no one felt confident for the future; and the energy of the country hung distracted, with no clear perception what to do or in what direction to turn.

The problem for statesmen was to discern among the new tendencies of the nation how much was sound and healthy, how much must be taken up into the constitution of the state before the disturbed elements settled into form again.

A revolution had passed over England of which the religious change was only a single feature. New avenues of thought were opening on all sides with the growth of knowledge; and as the discoveries of Columbus and Copernicus made their way into men's minds, they found themselves not in any metaphor but in plain and literal prose, in a new heaven and a new earth. How to send the fresh blood permeating healthily through the veins, how to prevent it from wasting itself in anarchy and revolution—these were the large questions which Elizabeth's ministers had to solve.

In this as in all else Cecil was the presiding spirit. Everywhere among the State papers of these years Cecil's pen is ever visible, Cecil's mind predominant. In the records of the daily meetings of the Council Cecil's is the single name which is never missed. In the Queen's cabinet or in his own, sketching Acts of Parliament, drawing instructions for ambassadors, or weighing on paper the opposing arguments at every crisis of political action; corresponding with archbishops on liturgies and articles, with secret agents in every corner of Europe or with foreign ministers in every court, Cecil is to be found ever restlessly busy; and sheets of paper densely covered with brief memoranda remain among his manuscripts to show the vastness of his daily labour and the surface over which he extended his control. From the great duel with Rome to the terraces and orange groves at Burleigh nothing was too large for his intellect to grasp, nothing too small for his attention to condescend to consider.

In July 1561, under Cecil's direction letters went round the southern and western counties desiring the magistrates to send in reports on the working of the laws which affected the daily life of the people, on the wages statutes, the acts of apparel, the poor laws, the tillage and pasture laws, the act for 'the maintenance of archery,' and generally on the condition of the population. A certain Mr. Tyldsley was commissioned privately to follow the circulars and observe how far the magistrates either reported the truth or were doing their duty; and though the reports are lost Tyldsley's letters remain, with his opinion on the character of the English gentry.

If that opinion was correct the change of creed had not improved them. The people were no longer trained in the use of arms because the gentlemen refused to set the example. 'For tillage it were plain sacrilege to interfere with it, the offenders being all gentlemen of the richer sort;' while 'the alehouses'—'the very stock and stay of false thieves and vagabonds,' were supported by them for the worst of motives. The peers had the privilege of importing wine free of duty for the consumption of their households. By their patents they

were able to extend the right to others under shelter of
their name; and the tavern-keepers ' were my lord's servants, or my master's servants; yea, and had such kind
of licences, and licence out of licence to them and their
deputies and assignees, that it was some danger to
meddle with them.'[1] The very threat of interference
either with that or any other misdemeanour in high
places caused Cecil to be generally detested.[2] Go where
he would, Tyldsley said, ' he could find no man earnestly
bent to put laws in execution;' ' every man let slip and
pass forth:' so that ' for his part he did look for nothing
less than the subversion of the realm to which end all
things were working.'

---

[1] The intention of the exemption had been the encouragement of 'hospitality' in the great country houses. Times were changing, and the old-fashioned 'open house' was no longer the rule. Without abolishing the privilege the council restricted the quantity which each nobleman was allowed to import. Dukes and archbishops were allowed ten pipes annually; marquises nine pipes; earls, viscounts, barons, and bishops, six, seven, and eight.—*Domestic MSS., Eliz.* vol. xx.

[2] 'This be you most sure of that as much evil as can be invented by the devillish wit of them that be nought is spoken against you.

'It is not yet four days past since one of my men said unto me, "Sir, would to God ye would not meddle so much as ye do, nor be so earnest;" for, said he, "if ye heard so much as I do hear, ye would marvel. For even they that do speak you most fairest to your face do name you behind your back to be an extreme and cruel man, with a great deal more than shall need to rehearse; and they say," said he, "that all these doings is long of Mr. Secretary Cecil. I do know," said he, "all this to be truth, for I do hear it amongst their servants, and belike they have heard it of their masters at one time or another. And further," said he, "when I was last in London, there was a business in hand as touching what wages watermen should take going from one place to another, which thing was much cried out upon; and they say that Mr. Cecil was all the doer of that matter too. Surely," said he, "he is not beloved; and therefore for God's sake sir be you ware. I have not spoken any of this to the intent that I would have you either to leave off or to slack any part of all your godly doings, but rather if I could to sharp you further against the devil and all his wicked instruments."'—*Mr. Tyldsley's Report, September* 3, 1561. *Domestic MSS.,* Eliz. vol. xix.

CHAP VI
1561
Religion, morality, and the English clergy.

Equally unsatisfactory were the reports of the state of religion. The constitution of the Church offended the Puritans; the Catholics were as yet unreconciled to the forms which had been maintained to conciliate them; and to the seeming cordiality with which the Liturgy was at first received, a dead inertia soon succeeded in which nothing lived but self-interest. The bishops and the higher clergy were the first to set an example of evil. The friends of the Church of England must acknowledge with sorrow that within two years of its establishment the prelates were alienating the estates in which they possessed but a life interest—granting long leases and taking fines for their own advantage. The Council had to inflict upon them the disgrace of a rebuke for neglecting the duties of common probity.[1]

The marriage of the clergy was a point on which the people were peculiarly sensitive.[2] Though tolerated it was generally disapproved, and disapproved especially in members of cathedrals and collegiate bodies who occupied the houses and retained the form of the religious orders. While therefore canons and prebends were entitled to take wives if they could not do without them, they would have done better had they taken chary advantage of their liberty. To the Anglo-Catholic as well as the Romanist a married priest was a scandal, and a married cathedral dignitary an abomination.

'For the avoiding of such offences as were daily conceived by the presence of families, of wives and children

---

[1] Articles for the Bishops' obligations, 1560.—*Domestic MSS.*, ELIZABETH.

[2] The frequent surnames of Clark, Parsons, Deacon, Archdeacon, Dean, Prior, Abbot, Bishop, Frere, and Monk, are memorials of the stigma affixed by English prejudice on the children of the first married representatives of the sacred orders.

within colleges, contrary to the ancient and comely order of the same,' Elizabeth in 1560 forbade deans and canons to have their wives residing with them within the cathedral closes under pain of forfeiting 'their promotions.' Cathedrals and colleges, she said, had been founded 'to keep societies of learned men professing study and prayer;' and the rooms intended for students were not to be sacrificed to women and children.[1]

The Church dignitaries treated the Queen's injunction as the country gentlemen treated the statutes. Deans and canons, by the rules of their foundations, were directed to dine and keep hospitality in their common hall. Those among them who had married broke up into their separate houses, where in spite of Elizabeth they maintained their families. The unmarried 'tabled abroad at the ale-houses.' The singing-men of the choirs became the prebends' private servants, 'having the Church stipend for their wages.' The cathedral plate adorned the prebendal side-boards and dinner-tables. The organ-pipes were melted into dishes for their kitchens; the organ-frames were carved into bedsteads, where the wives reposed beside their reverend lords; while the copes and vestments were coveted for their gilded embroidery, and were slit into gowns and boddices. Having children to provide for, and only a life-interest in their revenues, the chapters like the bishops cut down their woods, and worked their fines, their leases, their escheats and wardships, for the benefit of their own generation. Sharing their annual plunder, they ate and drunk and enjoyed themselves while their oppor-

---

[1] Proclamation by the Queen for the eviction of wives out of colleges. (In Cecil's hand.)—*Domestic MSS.*, ELIZ., vol. xix.

tunity remained; for the times were dangerous, 'and none could tell what should be after them.'

'They decked their wives so finely for the stuff and fashion of their garments as none were so fine and trim.' By her dress and 'her gait' in the street 'the priest's wife was known from a hundred other women;' while in the congregations and in the cathedrals they were distinguished 'by placing themselves above all other the most ancient and honourable in their cities;' 'being the Church—as the priests' wives termed it—their own Church; and the said wives did call and take all things belonging to their church and corporation as their own;' as 'their houses,' 'their gates,' 'their porters,' 'their servants,' 'their tenants,' 'their manors,' 'their lordships,' 'their woods,' 'their corn.'[1]

Celibacy had been found an unwholesome restriction; married clergymen might have been expected to do their duties the better rather than the worse for the companionship; and such complaints as these might be regarded as the inevitable but worthless strictures of malice and superstition. But it was not wholly so. While the shepherds were thus dividing the fleeces the sheep were perishing. In many dioceses in England a third of the parishes were left without a clergyman, resident or non-resident. In 1561 there were in the Archdeaconry of Norwich eighty parishes where there was no resident incumbent; in the Archdeaconry of Norfolk a hundred and eighty parishes; in the Archdeaconry of Suffolk a hundred and thirty parishes were almost or entirely in the same condition.[2] In some of these churches a curate at-

---

[1] Complaints against the Dean and Chapter of Worcester.—*Domestic MSS.*, Eliz., vol. xxviii.
[2] Strype's *Annals of the Reformation*, vol. I.

tended on Sundays. In most of them the voices of the priests were silent in the desolate aisles. The children grew up unbaptized; the dead buried their dead. At St. Helen's in the Isle of Wight the parish church had been built upon the shore for the convenience of vessels lying at the anchorage. The Provost and Fellows of Eton were the patrons, and the benefice was among the wealthiest in their gift; but the church was a ruin through which the wind and the rain made free passage. The parishioners 'were fain to bury their corpses themselves.' And 'joining as it did hard to one of the chief roads of England, where all sorts of nations were compelled to take succour and touch, the shameful using of the same church caused the Queen's Council and the whole realm to run in slander.'[1]

'It breedeth,' said Elizabeth in a remonstrance which she addressed to Archbishop Parker, 'no small offence and scandal to see and consider upon the one part the curiosity and cost bestowed by all sorts of men upon their private houses; and on the other part the unclean and negligent order and spare keeping of the houses of prayer, by permitting open decays and ruins of coverings of walls and windows, and by appointing unmeet and unseemly tables with foul cloths, for the communion of the sacrament; and generally leaving the place of prayer desolate of all cleanliness and of meet ornament for such a place, whereby it might be known a place provided for divine service.'[2]

Nor again were the Protestant foreigners who had

---

[1] Presentation of George Oglander.—*Domestic MSS.*, ELIZ., *Rolls House*.
[2] The Queen to the Archbishop of Canterbury, 1560. (Cecil's hand.)—*Domestic MSS.*, vol. xv.

taken refuge in England any special credit to the Reformation. These exiled saints were described by the Bishop of London as 'a marvellous colluvies of evil persons, for the most part *facinorosi ebriosi et sectarii.*' Between prelates reprimanded by the Council for fraudulent administration of their estates, chapters bent on justifying Cranmer's opinion of such bodies—that 'they were good vianders, and good for nothing else'—and a clergy among whom the only men who had any fear of God were the unmanageable and dangerous Puritans, the Church of England was doing little to make the Queen or the country enamoured of it. Torn up as it had been by the very roots and but lately replanted, its hanging boughs and drooping foliage showed that as yet it had taken no root in the soil, and there seemed too strong a likelihood that notwithstanding its ingenious framework and comprehensive formulas, it would wither utterly away.

'Our religion is so abused,' wrote Lord Sussex to Cecil in 1562, 'that the Papists rejoice; the neuters do not mislike change, and the few zealous professors lament the lack of purity. The people without discipline, utterly devoid of religion, come to divine service as to a Maygame; the ministers for disability and greediness be had in contempt; and the wise fear more the impiety of the licentious professors than the superstition of the erroneous Papists. God hold his hand over us, that our lack of religious hearts do not breed in the mean time his wrath and revenge upon us.'[1]

Covetousness and impiety moreover were not the

---

[1] Sussex to Cecil, July 22, 1562; from Chester.—*Irish MSS. Rolls House.*

only dangers. The submission of the clergy to the changes was no proof of their cordial acceptance of them. The majority were interested only in their benefices, which they retained and neglected. A great many continued Catholics in disguise: they remained at their post scarcely concealing if concealing at all, their true creed, and were supported in open contumacy by the neighbouring noblemen and gentlemen.

In a general visitation in July 1561 the clergy were required to take the oath of allegiance. The Bishop of Carlisle reported that thirteen or fourteen of his rectors and vicars refused to appear, while in many churches in his diocese mass continued to be said under the countenance and open protection of Lord Dacres: and the clergy of the diocese generally he described as wicked 'imps of Antichrist;' 'ignorant, stubborn, and past measure false and subtle.' Fear only he said would make them obedient, and Lord Cumberland and Lord Dacres would not allow him to meddle with them.[1]

The Border of Wales was as critical as the Border of Scotland. In August of the same year 'the Popish justices' of Hereford commanded the observance of St. Lawrence's day as a holyday. On the eve no butcher in the town ventured to sell meat; on the day itself 'no gospeller' durst work in his occupation or open his shop. A party of recusant priests from Devonshire were received in state by the magistrates, carried through the streets in procession, and so 'feasted and magnified as Christ himself could not have been more reverentially entertained.'[2]

In September, Bishop Jewel going to Oxford reported

---

[1] The Bishop of Carlisle to Cecil.—*Domestic MSS.*, vol. xviii.
[2] The Bishop of Hereford to Cecil.—*Domestic MSS.*, vol. xix.

the fellows of the college so malignant that 'if he had proceeded peremptorily as he might,' he would not have left two in any one of them; and here it was not a peer or a magistrate that Jewel feared, but one higher than both, for the Colleges appealed to the Queen against him; and Jewel could but entreat Cecil with many anxious misgivings to stand by him. He could but protest humbly that he was only acting for God's glory.[1]

The Bishop of Winchester found his people 'obstinately grovelled in superstition and Popery, lacking not priests to inculcate the same daily in their heads;' and himself so unable to provide ministers to teach them, that he petitioned for permission to unite his parishes and throw two or three into one.[2]

The Bishop of Durham called a clergyman before him to take the oath. The clergyman said out before a crowd, 'who much rejoiced at his doings,' 'that neither temporal man nor woman could have power in spiritual matters but only the Pope of Rome;' and the lay authorities would not allow the Bishop to punish a man who had but expressed their own feelings; more than one member of the Council of York had refused the oath and yet had remained in office; the rest took courage when they saw those that refused their allegiance 'not only unpunished but had in authority and estimation:' and distracted 'with the poisonful and malicious minds about him,' the Bishop said that 'where he had but little wit at his coming he had now almost none left him, and wished himself a sizar at St. John's again.'[3]

---

[1] Jewel to Cecil, *Domestic MSS.*, vol. xix.
[2] *MS. Ibid.*, vol. xxi.
[3] *MS. Ibid.*, vol. xix.

Finally in 1562 the Bishop of Carlisle once more complained that between Lord Dacres and the Earls of Cumberland and Westmoreland, 'God's glorious gospel could not take place in the counties under their rule.' The few Protestants 'durst not be known for fear of a shrewd turn;' and the lords and magistrates looked through their fingers—while the law was openly defied. The country was full of 'wishings and wagers for the alteration of religion;' 'rumours and tales of the Spaniards and Frenchmen to come in for the reformation of the same:' while the articles of the secret league between the Guises and Spain for the extirpation of heresy circulated in manuscript in the houses of the northern gentlemen.[1]

The Queen's own conduct had been so uncertain, she had persisted so long in her determination to invite the Queen of Scots into England, with a view in some form or other of acknowledging her as her successor, she had given so marked an evidence of her retrogressive tendencies in appointing these very Earls of Westmoreland and Cumberland to receive Mary Stuart on the Border, that no one ventured to support a spiritual authority which in a year or two might vanish like a mist. And it was not till Elizabeth had been driven at last into the French quarrel, had given up the interview, and had sent her troops to Havre to co-operate with the Huguenots, that the reforming party recovered heart again; and the Romanists discovered that unless they were prepared for immediate rebellion they must move more cautiously.

The first effect of their disappointment was a curious one. On the 7th of August de Quadra wrote to the

---

[1] *Domestic MSS.*, vol. xxi.

Spanish minister at Rome begging him to ask the Pope in the name of the English Catholics whether they might be present without sin at 'the common prayers.' 'The case,' de Quadra said, 'was a new and not an easy one, for the Prayer-book contained neither impiety nor false doctrine. The prayers themselves were those of the Catholic church altered only so far as to omit the merits and the intercession of the saints; so that except for the concealment, and the injury which might arise from the example, there would be nothing in the compliance itself positively unlawful. The communion could be evaded: on that point they did not ask for a dispensation. They desired simply to be informed whether they might attend the ordinary services.' The Bishop's own opinion was that no general rule could be laid down. The compulsion to which the Catholics were exposed varied at different times and places; the harm which might arise to others varied; nor had all been equally zealous in attempting to prevent the law from passing or in afterwards obstructing the execution of it. While therefore he had not extenuated the fault of those who had given way to the persecution, he had in some cases given them a hope that they had not sinned mortally. At the same time he had been cautious of weakening the resolution of those who had been hitherto constant. If the Pope had more decided instructions to give, he said he would gladly receive them. There was another class of cases also which there was a difficulty in dealing with. Many of the English who had fallen into heresy had repented and desired to be absolved. But the priests who could receive them back were scanty and scattered; and there was extreme danger in resorting to them. In some instances they had been arrested, and under threat of torture had revealed their penitents' names.

The Bishop said he had explained to the Catholics generally that allowance was made for violence, but they wished for a general indulgence in place of detailed and special absolution; and although he said that he did not himself consider that this would meet the difficulty, he thought it right to mention their request.[1]

The question of attendance on the English service was referred to the Inquisition, where the dry truth was expressed more formally and hardly than do Quadra's leniency would have preferred.

'Given a commonwealth in which Catholics were forbidden under pain of death to exercise their religion; where the law required the subject to attend conventicles; where the Psalms were sung and the lessons taken from the Bible were read in the vulgar tongue, and where sermons were preached in defence of heretical opinions, might Catholics comply with that law without peril of damnation to their souls?'

Jesuitism was as yet but half developed. The Inquisition answered immediately with a distinct negative.

Although the Catholics were not required to communicate with heretics, yet by their presence at their services they would assume and affect to believe with them. Their object in wishing to be present could only be to pass for heretics, to escape the penalties of disobedience; and God had said, 'Whosoever is ashamed of me and of my words, of him will I be ashamed.' Catholics, and especially Catholics of rank, could not appear in Protestant assemblies without causing scandal to the weaker brethren.

In giving this answer Pope Pius desired to force the

---

[1] De Quadra to Vargas, August 7.—MS. Simancas.

Catholics to declare themselves, and precipitate the collision which Philip's timidity had prevented.

On the other point he was more lenient. He empowered de Quadra, as a person not amenable to the English Government, to accept himself the abjuration of heretics willing to forsake their errors, and to empower others at his discretion to do the same whenever and wherever he might think good.[1]

Before the order of Pius had reached England, the impatience of the Catholics had run over in the abortive conspiracy of the Poles. In itself most trivial, it served as a convenient instrument in the hands of Cecil to irritate the Protestants. The enterprise in France appealed to the loyalty of the people who flattered themselves with hopes of Calais, and the elections for the Parliament which was to meet at the spring of the new year were carried on under the stimulus of the excitement. The result was the return of a House of Commons violently Puritan; and those who were most anxious to prevent the recognition of the Queen of Scots found themselves opportunely strengthened by the premature eagerness with which her claims had been pressed.

Maitland's intended mission to London had been postponed till the meeting; but meanwhile Sir William Cecil had ominously allowed all correspondence between them to cease;[2] and Randolph on the 5th of January wrote from Edinburgh of the general fear and uneasiness that 'things would be wrought in the approaching Parliament which would give little pleasure in Scotland.'[3] Diplomacy however still continued its efforts. Notwithstanding the rupture with the Guises, the admission

---

[1] Pius IV. to de Quadra.—*MS. Simancas.*
[2] Maitland to Cecil, January 3.—*Scotch MSS. Rolls House.*
[3] Randolph to Cecil.—*MS. Ibid.*

The Reign of Elizabeth. 475

of Mary Stuart's right was still played off before Elizabeth as a condition on which France might be pacified and Calais restored: and there was always a fear that Elizabeth might turn back upon her steps and listen. To end the crisis, Sir Thomas Smith advised her to throw six thousand men some moonlight night on the Calais sands. The garrison had been withdrawn after the battle of Dreux to reinforce the Catholic army, and not two hundred men were left to defend the still incomplete fortifications.[1] But Elizabeth was as incapable as Philip of a sudden movement, and she had no desire to exchange her quarrel with the Guises—which after all might be peaceably composed—for a declared war with a united France. She knew that she had not deserved the confidence of the Huguenots, and she had already reason to fear that they might turn against her.

The day after the battle of Dreux, Throgmorton unable to rejoin the Admiral, was brought in as a prisoner into the Catholic camp. The Duke of Guise sent for him, and after a long and conciliatory conversation on the state of France, spoke deprecatingly of the injustice of Elizabeth's suspicions of himself and his family, and indicated with some distinctness that if she would withdraw from Havre Calais should be given up to her.[2]

---

[1] Sir T. Smith to Elizabeth, January 2.—FORBES, vol. ii. The beneficial effects of the French conquest had already been felt in the Pale. Before the expulsion of the English it was almost a desert. Sir Thomas Smith held out as an inducement for its recovery, that it had become 'the plentifullest country in all France.'

[2] 'If they cannot accord among themselves, then I perceive they mind to treat with you favourably, and I believe to satisfy your Majesty about Calais, provided that from henceforth you do no more aid the Prince and the rebels.'—Throgmorton to Elizabeth, January 3. CONWAY MSS.

'These men have two strings to their bow—to accord with the Prince and to accord with her Majesty also; but not with both at once to both's satisfactions.'—Throgmorton to Cecil, January 3. FORBES, vol. ii.

Elizabeth catching at an intimation which fell in with her private wishes, replied with a promise 'that nothing should be done in Parliament to the displeasure of the Queen of Scots.' Mary Stuart had recovered credit by her expedition to the north; and her confidence in Elizabeth's weakness again revived: not indeed that Elizabeth was really either weak or blind, but in constitutional irresolution she was for ever casting her eye over her shoulder, with the singular and happy effect of keeping the Catholics perpetually deluded with false expectations, and of amusing them with hopes of a change which never came.

Her resolution about the Scottish succession promised a stormy and uneasy session; and Cecil before its commencement still uncertain how far he could depend upon her, made another effort to rid the court of de Quadra. The Spanish ambassador was suspected without reason of having encouraged the Poles. He was known to have urged Philip to violence, and to be the secret support and stay of the disaffected in England and Ireland. Confident in the expected insurrection of the Low Countries, Cecil was not unwilling to risk an open rupture with Spain, which would force Elizabeth once for all on the Protestant side.

A few days before Parliament was to meet, an Italian Calvinist in the train of the Vidame of Chartres was passing Durham Place when a stranger who was lounging at the gate drew a pistol and fired at him. The ball passed through the Italian's cap and wounded an Englishman behind him. The assassin darted into the house with a crowd at his heels; and the Bishop knowing nothing of him, but knowing the Italian to be a heretic, bade his servants open the water gate. The fugitive sprung down the steps, leapt into a boat, and was gone. Being taken afterwards at Gravesend, he confessed under torture that he had been bribed to commit the murder by the Provost of Paris. De Quadra, who had made himself an accomplice after the fact, was required to surrender the keys of his house; and his steward refusing to comply, the mayor sent workmen who changed the locks.

De Quadra went to the palace to complain; but the Queen without permitting herself to be seen, referred him to the Council; and Cecil at last told him that he could not be allowed to remain at Durham Place. All the Papists in London attended mass there; every malcontent, every traitor and enemy of the Government, came there at night to consult him. The disturbance which had broken out in Ireland was due to the advice given by de Quadra when O'Neil was in London; and but for the care which the Queen had taken of him he would probably have long before been murdered by the mob.[1]

De Quadra was not a man to be discomposed by high words. He replied that whatever he had done he had done by his master's orders; and complaints against himself were complaints against the King of Spain. If he had seemed to act in an unfriendly manner, the times were to blame; if he did not profess the English religion, he professed the religion of Christendom; and those noble and honourable men who came to his house to mass came where they had a right to come and did not deserve Cecil's imputations.

---

[1] De Quadra to Philip, January 10.—*MS. Simancas*. The account of the matter sent by the English Council to Sir Thomas Chaloner, agrees closely with that of de Quadra, dwelling only in fuller detail on the midnight conferences of conspirators and traitors held at Durham Place.—*Spanish MSS., January* 7. *Rolls House.*

Hot words passed to and fro. Cecil charged the Bishop with maintaining traitors and rebels. De Quadra said it was not he or his master who were most guilty of using religion as a stalking-horse to disturb their neighbours' peace.

Cecil said the Bishop had encouraged Pole and Fortescue. The Bishop answered truly enough that he had had nothing to do with them or their follies.

'The meaning of it all,' de Quadra wrote to Philip, 'is this: they wish to dishearten the Catholics whom the Parliament will bring together from all parts of the realm. I am not to remain in this house because it has secret doors and entrances which we may use for mischief. They are afraid, and they have cause to be afraid. The heretics are furious at seeing me maintain the Catholics here with some kind of authority, and they cannot endure it; but a few days ago the Lord Keeper said that neither the crown nor religion were safe so long as I was in the realm. It is true enough, as Cecil says, that I may any day be torn in pieces by the populace. Ever since this war in France, and the demonstrations in Paris against the heretics, the Protestant preachers have clamoured from the pulpit for the execution of "Papists." Even Cecil himself is bent on cruelty; and did they but dare they would not leave a Catholic alive in the land.

'But the faithful are too large a number, and if it comes to that they will sell their lives dear. London indeed is bad enough: it is the worst place in the realm: and it is likely—I do not say it in any fear, but only because it is a thing which your Majesty should know—that if they force me to reside within the walls of the city something may happen to me. The Council themselves tell me that if I am detected in any conspiracy my privilege as ambassador shall not save me. They wish to goad me on to violence that they may have matter to lay before the Queen against me.'¹

Believing or pretending to believe that de Quadra notwithstanding his denial was really implicated in the affair of the Poles, Cecil overshot his mark. Chaloner was instructed to demand the Bishop's recall; and meanwhile he was allowed still to reside in Durham Place, but with restrictions upon his liberty. The water gate was closed, sentinels were posted at the lodge, the house was watched day and night, and every person who went in or out was examined and registered.²

While this fracas was at its heat, on the 12th of January Parliament opened, and with it the first convocation of the English Church. The sermon at St. Paul's was preached by Day, the Provost of Eton; that at Westminster by Dr. Nowell. The subject of both was the same: the propriety of 'killing the caged wolves'— that is to say the Catholic bishops in the Tower—with the least possible delay.³

The session then began. The Lord Keeper in the usual speech from the throne dwelt on the internal disorders of the country, the irreligion of the laity, the disorder and idleness of the clergy. He touched briefly on the events of the three last years; and in speaking by name of the House of Guise, he said that if they had

---

¹ De Quadra to Philip, January 10. —MS. Simancas.

² De Quadra to Philip, January 27. —MS. Ibid.

³ 'El Martes se abrió el Parlamento, y lo que se predicó tanto en Westminster en presencia de la Reyna como en San Pablo en el sinodo eclesiastico fué principalmente persuadir que se matassen los lobos encerrados; entendiendo por los obispos presos.'—De Quadra to ——, January 14. MS. Ibid. It is mournful to remember that Nowell was the author of the English Church Catechism in its present form. See note at the end of this volume.

not been encountered in Scotland they must have been fought with under the walls of York.

Then passing to France, he said that the Queen by the same cause had been compelled to a second similar interference there. He alluded pointedly to a disloyal faction in England, by whom the foreign enemies were encouraged. He spoke shortly of the late devilish conspiracy, and then concluded with saying that reluctant as they knew the Queen to be to ask her subjects for money, they would be called upon to meet the expenses which she had incurred in the service of the Commonwealth.

Speech of Sir Thomas Williams.

Sir Thomas Williams the Speaker of the Lower House followed next in the very noblest spirit of English Puritanism. With quaint allegoric and classical allusions interlaced with illustrations from the Bible, he conveyed to the Queen the gratitude of the people for a restored religion and her own moderate and gentle Government. He described the country however as still suffering from ignorance, error, covetousness, and a thousand meaner vices. Schools were in decay, universities deserted, benefices unsupplied. As he passed through the streets, he heard almost as many oaths as words. Then turning to the Queen herself he went on thus—

'We now assembled, as diligent in our calling, have thought good to move your Majesty to build a fort for the surety of the realm, to the repulsing of your enemies abroad: which must be set upon firm ground and steadfast, having two gates—one commonly open, the other as a postern, with two watchmen at either of them—one governor, one lieutenant, and no good thing there wanting; the same to be named the Fear of God, the governor thereof to be God, your Majesty the lieutenant, the stones the hearts of your faithful people, the two watchmen at the open gate to be called Knowledge and Virtue, the two at the postern gate to be called Mercy and Truth.

'This fort is invincible if every man will fear God; for all governors reign and govern by the two watchmen Knowledge and Virtue; and if you, being the lieutenant, see Justice and Prudence, her sisters, executed, then shall you rightly use your office; and for such as depart out of this fort let them be let out at the postern by the two watchmen Mercy and Truth, and then shall you be well at home and abroad.'[1]

All that was most excellent in English heart and feeling — the spirit which carried England safe at last through its trials—spoke in these words. Those in whom that spirit lived were few in number: there was never an age in this world's history when they were other than few; but few or many they are at all times the world's true sovereign leaders; and Elizabeth among her many faults knew these men when she saw them, and gave them their place, and so prospered she and her country. The clergy cried out for the blood of the disaffected; the lay Speaker would let them go by the postern of Mercy and Truth.

These introductions over the House proceeded to business. The special subject of which all minds were full had been passed over both by Bacon and Williams; but the Commons fastened upon it without a moment's delay. There were no signs of the Queen's marrying, notwithstanding her half promise to her first Parliament. She had been near death, and the frightful uncertainty as to

---

[1] Speech of Sir Thomas Williams.—D'EWES' *Journals*, pp. 64, 65.

what would follow should she die indeed was no longer tolerable.

On the 18th the question was talked over: the different claimants and their pretensions were briefly considered, and as had been anticipated the tone of feeling was as adverse as possible to the Queen of Scots. The Scottish nobles had not been forgiven for having supported her in refusing to ratify the treaty. To secure their sovereign the reversion of the English crown they were held to have repaid the assistance which had saved them from ruin with the basest ingratitude. Sir Ralph Sadler broke out with a fierce invective upon the 'false, beggarly, and perjured' nation, whom 'the very stones' in the English streets would rise against.[1] Another speaker challenged Mary Stuart's pretensions on the ground of English law. It was admitted on all sides, this person said, that the Queen of Scots' succession had been 'barred' by the will of Henry the Eighth; but some people pretended that the will had not been signed with his hand, some that he had never made a will at all; there was no mention of it on the Patent Rolls;[2] and if the original had existed why was it not produced? This last question could not be answered;[3] but there was proof enough of the reality of the will; there were abundant entries of this and that detail of it which had been acted upon; and of the executors there were still many who survived. The dispute however was not narrowed to that single issue. The Queen of Scots was an

---

[1] SADLER *Papers*, vol. iii. p. 303.
[2] This is true. Neither is there any record of the will on the Roll, nor any sign of erasure where the entry ought to have been.
[3] This mysterious concealment can only be explained as the deliberate act of Elizabeth, who was determined to maintain Mary Stuart's rights, and who felt that it would be impossible if the will was produced.

alien, and no person could inherit in England who was not born of English parents on English soil. Lady Lennox was an alien also; for though she was born at York it was but in a passing visit; her father Angus was a Scot, and when he married her mother he had another wife living. The only legal heir was the heir appointed by Henry the Eighth—Lady Catherine Grey, the injured and imprisoned wife of Hertford.[1]

The result of the first discussion was the resolution to prepare an address to the crown. But de Quadra was able to learn that the question would not be settled; the Queen was determined to keep her promise to Mary Stuart; and Cecil on the 14th wrote to Sir Thomas Smith that however Parliament might press her 'the unwillingness of her Majesty to have a successor known' would prevent a conclusion.[2] The strength of Elizabeth's resolution would soon be tried. Meanwhile on the 20th Cecil explained to the Commons the cause of the interference in France.[3] On the 25th he was heard at the bar of the House of Lords on the same subject; and his speech was chiefly directed against Philip, whom he accused of having entangled England in war while its titular king, and then of having betrayed it at Cambray; of having taken part with the Queen's enemies in

---

[1] Oration spoken in Parliament.—*Domestic MSS.*, Eliz., vol. xxvii. Lady Catherine Grey's popularity had been increased by an accident which had redoubled Elizabeth's displeasure. Sir Edmund Warner, taking pity on his young prisoner, had allowed her husband to have access to her room; the result was a second infant; and fecundity was a virtue especially valued in an English princess. 'Este negocio de Catalina,' wrote de Quadra on the 27th of January, 've cobrando fuerças entre estos de la nueva religion, y el parir la hace bien quieta del pueblo.'—*De Quadra to Philip. MS. Simancas.*

[2] Cecil to Sir T. Smith, January 14.—Wright's *Elizabeth and her Times*, vol. i.

[3] Dewes' *Journals*.

CHAP VI.
1563
January

A penal law against the Catholics.

Speech of Lord Montague.

every difficulty in which she had been involved; and of having lent his strength to make the Duke of Guise sovereign of France and Mary Stuart Queen of England —'Queen of England,' 'as she was already styled by her household at Holyrood.'[1]

A penal Bill against the Catholics was next laid before the Upper House. It was described as 'a law against those who would not receive the new religion,' bloody in its provisions as the preachers desired, and contrived rather as a test of opinion than of loyalty.

At once and without reserve or fear the Catholic Lords spoke out: Northumberland said the heretics might be satisfied with holding other men's bishoprics and benefices without seeking their lives; when they had killed the clergy they would kill the temporal lords next; and the Earl swore that he would speak as his conscience bade him; he would protest against the law; and he believed that most of the lords who heard him were of the same opinion with himself.[2]

Montague followed on the same side and at greater length:—

'A law was proposed,' he said, 'to compel Papists under pain of death to confess the Protestant doctrine to be true. Such a law was neither necessary nor was it just. The Catholics were living peaceably, neither disputing nor preaching nor troubling the commonwealth in any way. The doctrine of the Protestants if they had a doctrine had been established against the consent

---

[1] De Quadra to Philip, January 27.—MS. Simancas.

[2] De Quadra to Philip.—MS. Simancas. The Supremacy Bill, which ultimately passed, was brought into the House of Lords on the 25th of February. De Quadra's letter describing Northumberland's speech was written on the 27th of January, and must therefore refer to some other Bill—unnoticed in the meagre journals—which was thrown out. The ambassador distinctly says that there was a vote—'viniendo á votare los Señores.'

of the ecclesiastical estate; and it was absurd so long as
the world was full of disputes and the opinions of those
best able to judge were divided, for one set of men to
compel another to accept their views as true or to pretend that there was no longer room for doubt. The
Protestants might be content with what they had got
without forcing other men to profess what they did not
believe and to make God a witness of the lie. To take
an oath against their consciences or else to be put to
death was no alternative to be offered to reasonable men;
and if it came to that extremity the Catholics would
defend themselves. A majority might be found to vote
for the law if the bishops were included; but the bishops
were a party to the quarrel and had no right to be
judges in it. The bishops had no business with pains
and penalties; they should keep to their pulpits and
their excommunications and leave questions of public
policy to the lay lords.'[1]

Had Montague been despotic in England the Protestants would have had as short a shrift as the Huguenots
were finding in France; but even a Catholic of the sixteenth century when in opposition could be more temperate than a Protestant in power. The Bill was lost
or withdrawn to reappear in a new form: and the peers
who had checked the zeal of Bonner and Gardiner had
the credit of staying in time the less pardonable revenge
of their antagonists.

On the French question there were analogous differences of opinion. When the temper of Parliament had
been felt it was found that notwithstanding the Puritan
constitution of the Lower House the feeling was in

---

[1] *Annals of the Reformation.* STRYPE, vol. i.

favour only of the recovery of Calais. The Lords and Commons 'resolved to yield their whole power in goods and bodies to recover Calais, to maintain Newhaven and any war which might arise thereof;' but they were not so ready to contribute to the charge 'of supporting the army of the Protestants.'[1] The disposition of the people was the same as the disposition of the Queen; and Elizabeth warned on many sides that she could not trust Condé, and only half trusting Chatillon, wrote to Sir Thomas Smith that in a doubtful quarrel she could not press her subjects too far. He need not hint to the Admiral that there was 'any slackness' on her part; but 'she would be glad if some indirect means could be devised' to compose the religious difficulties—though 'toleration was not stablished so universally as the Admiral desired'—provided England could have 'its right in Calais and the members thereof,' and the money which she had lent Condé partially if not wholly repaid.[2]

Both Queen and country were falling back on the 'hollow dealing' which she had regretted so bitterly on the fall of Rouen; and then as ever it was found dangerous to follow private objects behind an affected zeal for a noble cause. Six thousand Englishmen paid with their lives for this trifling with Chatillon, while the coveted Calais was forfeited for ever; the Huguenots obtained the half toleration which Elizabeth desired for them; and they found the value of it on the day of St. Bartholomew.

But to return to the succession.

In the interval of these discussions the address of the

---

[1] Elizabeth to Sir T. Smith, January 25.—FORBES, vol. ii.
[2] Ibid.

Commons was drawn; and on the 28th the Speaker with the whole House attended to present it in the gallery of the palace. Commencing with an elaborate compliment on the Queen's services to the country Sir Thomas Williams proceeded to say that the nation required for their perfect security some assurance for the future. Her Majesty had been dangerously ill, and the Commons had supposed that in calling them together so soon after her recovery she had intended to use their assistance to come to some conclusion. He reminded her of Alexander's generals; he reminded her—more to the purpose—of York and Lancaster; and the realm he said was beset with enemies within and without. There were 'a faction of heretics in her realm—contentious and malicious Papists—who most unnaturally against their country, most madly against their own safety, and most treacherously against her Highness, not only hoped for the woful day of her death but also lay in wait to advance some title under which they might revive their late unspeakable cruelties. The Commons saw nothing to withstand their desires but her only life; they feared much to what attempt the hope of such opportunity—nothing withstanding them but her life—might move the Catholics; and they found how necessary it was that there should be more set and known between her Majesty's life and the unkindness and cruelty they intended to revive.' Ignorant as they were to whom the crown ought to descend, and being unable to judge of the limitation of the succession in King Henry's will, their first desire was that her Majesty would marry, their second that she would use the opportunity of the session to allow some successor in default of heirs of her body 'to be determined by Act of Parliament;' while they on their part 'for the preservation and surety of her

Majesty and her issue' would devise 'the most penal, sharp, and terrible statutes to all who should practise against her safety.'

By the nomination of a Protestant successor Elizabeth had everything to gain; while if Mary Stuart were acknowledged her life would not be safe for a day. Her policy in every way was to acquiesce in the prayer of the Commons; and yet she listened with ill-concealed impatience. She said briefly that on a matter of such moment she could give no answer without further consideration, and she then abruptly turned her back on the deputation and withdrew.[1]

If de Quadra was rightly informed she had been half prevailed on to name the Earl of Huntingdon, with the condition that she herself should have Lord Robert. But Dudley had made no advances in the favour of the Peers, and Huntingdon was a Puritan and Dudley's brother-in-law; Lord Arundel with the Howards still inclined to Lady Catherine Grey, of whom the Queen could not endure to hear; and thus all parties were at issue.

The Upper House followed the Lower with an address to the same purpose. Elizabeth said bitterly that 'the lines which they saw in her face were not wrinkles but small-pox marks; God had given children to St. Elizabeth, and old as she was he might give children to her; if she appointed a successor it would deluge England in blood.'[2]

Both Houses were profoundly angry. The Protestants supposed that the Queen was sacrificing the Reformation and the country to her secret passion for Lord Robert; that she was studiously allowing the Scottish Queen's

---

[1] 'Con tanto les volvió las espaldas y se entró en su aposento.'—*De Quadra to Philip, February 6. MS. Simancas.*

[2] Ibid.

pretensions to drift into tacit recognition. Day after day throughout the session the subject continued to be harped upon. A Bill was proposed by Cecil by which if the Queen died the Privy Council were to continue in office with imperial authority till Parliament could decide on the future sovereign. But this too came to nothing,[1] and the Queen continued to give evasive answers till the prorogation of Parliament should leave her free again.

And yet the Protestant party were determined to carry something which should answer their purpose; and at once—though the first penal law had been lost—enable them to hold down the Catholics, and in case of Elizabeth's death, to prevent Mary Stuart's succession.[2] To check the exultation of Montague and his friends at their first success in Parliament, Cecil contrived another demonstration against de Quadra. On the day of the Purification the foreign Catholics in London came as usual in large numbers to hear mass at Durham Place. The guard at the gate took their names as they passed in; and before the service was over an officer of the palace guard entered from the river, arrested every Spaniard, Fleming, and Italian present, and carried them off to the Fleet. They were informed on their release that thenceforward no stranger, not even a casual visitor to the realm, should attend a service unsanctioned by the laws.[3]

On the 20th of February a Bill was introduced, by which, without mention of doctrine, Protestant or Catholic, all persons who maintained the Pope's authority or refused the oath of allegiance to the Queen, for the first

---

[1] Draft of an Act of Parliament, in Cecil's hand. — *Domestic MSS.* vol. xxviii.

[2] 'Esta ley contra los Católicos no se ha hecho con otra fin mas principal que de excluir la de Escocia desta succesion por via indirecta.'— *De Quadra to Philip*, February 20.

[3] De Quadra to Philip, February 6 and February 20.

offence should incur a premunire, for the second the pains of treason. Should the Bill pass it was believed to be the death-warrant of the imprisoned bishops; and even in the Lower House voices were raised in opposition. Cecil in a passionate speech declared that the House was bound in gratitude not to reject what was necessary for the Queen's security. Her life was in danger because she was the defender of English liberty; the King of Spain desired her to send representatives to Trent; she had refused, and he was threatening her with war; and the Pope was offering millions of gold to pay the cost of an invasion of England. The Queen herself would die before she would yield, but her subjects must stand by her with laws and lives and goods. There was no help elsewhere. The Germans used fine words, but they failed at the pinch. The Emperor had been gained over by the Pope. Their reliance must be on themselves and their own arms, and nowhere else.

After Cecil rose Sir Francis Knowles, who said that there had been enough of words: it was time to draw the sword. The Commons were generally Puritan. The opposition of the Lords had been neutralized by a special provision in their favour, and the Bill was carried. The obligation to take the oath was extended to the holder of every office, lay or spiritual, in the realm. The clergy were required to swear whenever their ordinary might be pleased to tender them the oath; the members of the House of Commons were required to swear when they took their seats; members of the Upper House were alone exempt, the Act declaring with perhaps designed irony that the Queen was otherwise assured of the loyalty of the peers.[1] Without this proviso de Quadra was

---

[1] 5 ELIZ. cap. I.

assured that they would have refused to consent; and even with it he clung to the hope that the Catholic noblemen would be true to themselves. But he was too sanguine, and Cecil carried his point.

Heath, Bonner, Thirlby, Feckenham, and the other prisoners at once prepared to die. The Protestant ecclesiastics would as little spare them as they had spared the Protestants. They would have shown no mercy themselves, and they looked for none.

Nor is there any doubt what their fate would have been had it rested with the English bishops. Immediately after the Bill had received the royal assent, the hated Bonner was sent for to be the first victim. Horne Bishop of Winchester offered him the oath, which it was thought certain that he would refuse, and he would then be at the mercy of his enemies. Had it been so the English Church would have disgraced itself; but Bonner's fate would have called for little pity. The law however stepped in between the prelates and their prey—as Portia between Shylock and Antonio—and saved them both. By the Act archbishops and bishops might alone tender the oath; and Bonner evaded the dilemma by challenging his questioner's title to the name. When Horne was appointed to the see of Winchester his predecessor was alive; the English bishops generally had been so irregularly consecrated that their authority until confirmed by Act of Parliament was of doubtful legality; and the judges of the Court of Queen's Bench caught at the plea to prevent a needless cruelty. Bonner was again returned to the Marshalsea, and Horne gained nothing by his eagerness but a stigma upon himself and his brethren.[1]

The remaining business of the session passed over

---

[1] *Annals of the Reformation.* STRYPE, vol. i. part 2, pp. 2 to 8.

without difficulty: the grant of money was profusely liberal;[1] an Act was passed for the maintenance of the navy, which will be mentioned more particularly in a future chapter; a tillage Act revived the statutes of Henry the Seventh and Henry the Eighth for the rebuilding of farm-houses and breaking up the large pastures.[2] The restoration of the currency made a wages Act again possible, but the altered prices of meat and corn required a revision of the scale. The magistrates in the different counties were empowered to fix the rate according to the local prices, their awards being liable to revision by the Court of Chancery, to which returns were to be periodically made.[3] Other remarkable provisions were added to restore the shaken texture of English life. During the late confused time the labourer had wandered from place to place doing a day's work where he pleased. Masters were now required to hire their servants by the year, neither master to part with servant nor servant with master till the contract was expired, unless the separation was sanctioned by two magistrates.

These acts all indicated a recovered or recovering tone. The solid English life, after twenty years of convulsion, was regaining consistency.

---

[1] Two fifteenths and tenths on personal property, and an income-tax of ten per cent. for two years.

[2] 5 Eliz. cap. 2.

[3] 5 Eliz. cap. 4. Wages varied with the time of year, and the rates were read out every month in the parish churches. The average in 1563 may be gathered with tolerable accuracy from the scale which was ruled for the county of Bucks before the passing of the Act. The price of food after the restoration of the currency was found to have risen a third. The penny, which in terms of bread, meat, and beer, had been worth under Henry the Eighth twelve pence of our money, was now worth eight pence. The table of wages in Bucks in 1561 was for the common labourer sixpence a day from Easter to All Hallows; five pence a day from All Hallows to Easter; and eight pence a day in the hay and corn harvest.—TYLDSLEY'S Report. Domestic MSS., vol. xix.

The well-being of the people however turned on the success of Elizabeth's policy, and hung on the thread of her single life; while neither Lords nor Commons had as yet received an answer to their addresses. On the 16th of February she sent a message by Cecil that she had not forgotten them, and entreating their patience: but ten days passed and nothing was done; and by that time Maitland had arrived from Scotland with an offer from his mistress—of course as a condition of recognition—to make herself 'a moyenneur of a peace' with France, which would give back Calais to England. There was a hope that by such an offer even the unwillingness of Parliament might be overcome; and Maitland was prudently feeling his way when one of those strange adventures occurred which so often crossed the path of the Queen of Scots, and gave her history the interest— not perhaps of tragedy, for she was selfish in her politics and sensual in her passions—but of some high-wrought melodrama.

In the galley in which she returned to Scotland there was present a young poet and musician named Châtelar. Gifted, well-born, and passionate, the handsome youth had for some months sighed at her feet in Holyrood. He went back to France, but he could not remain there. The moth was recalled to the flame whose warmth was life and death to it. He was received on his return with the warmest welcome. Mary Stuart admitted him to her labours in the Cabinet, and he shared her pleasures in the festival or the dance. 'So familiar was he with the Queen early and late that scarcely could any of the nobility have access to her.'[1] She leant upon his

---

[1] KNOX.

shoulder in public, she bewitched him in private with her fascinating confidence;[1] and interpreting her behaviour and perhaps her words too favourably, he one night concealed himself in her bedroom. He was discovered by the ladies of the bedchamber before the Queen retired; and the next morning she commanded him with a sharp reprimand to leave the court. But Mary Stuart pardoned easily the faults of those whom she liked. Châtelar was forgiven, and again misconstruing her kindness, four nights later the poor youth repeated his rash adventure. He came out upon the Queen while she was undressing, and 'set upon her with such force and in such impudent sort that she was fain to cry out for help.'

Hearing her shrieks Murray rushed into the room. Châtelar was of course seized and carried off and tortured. Confessing the worst intentions with wild bravado, he was executed a week after in the Market Place at St. Andrew's, chanting a love-song as he died; and the Queen after some natural distress recovered her spirits.

She had probably nothing worse to accuse herself of than thoughtlessness; and the truth might have been told without danger of compromising her. It is strange

---

[1] Randolph, who was describing what he had himself seen, said in a letter to Cecil, 'Your honour beareth the beginning of a lamentable story, whereof such infamy will arise as I fear, howsoever well the wound be healed, the scar will for ever remain. Thus your honour seeth what mischief cometh of the over-great familiarity that any such personage showeth unto so unworthy a creature and abject a varlet, as her Grace used with him. Whatsoever colour can be laid upon it, that it was done for his master's sake (Châtelar had been in the train of M. d'Amville), I cannot but say it had been too much to have been used to his master's aid by any princess alive.'—Scotch MSS. Rolls House.

that Maitland, in a fear that it might affect the success of his mission, thought it worth his while to cover the story with an incredible lie. Maitland had two objects in London—one to secure the succession for his mistress by assuring Elizabeth that she had nothing to fear from so true a friend; the other to consult the Spanish ambassador on the marriage with the Prince of Spain which of all things on earth Elizabeth most dreaded for her. It was this last object chiefly which he thought the Châtelar affair might hinder; he therefore told de Quadra that Châtelar before his death had declared that he had been employed by the Huguenots to compromise Mary Stuart's reputation; he had concealed himself in her room, intending to be seen in leaving it, and then to escape.[1]

Two days after Châtelar was executed Mary Stuart lost a far nobler friend. A pistol-ball fired from behind a hedge closed the career of the Duke of Guise under the walls of Orleans. The assassin Poltrot was a boy of nineteen. Suspicion pointed to the Admiral and Theodore Beza as the instigators of the crime; and Chatillon never wholly convinced the world of his innocence, for Poltrot himself accused him while the horses were tearing him in pieces. However it was, that single shot shattered the Catholic confederacy and changed the politics of Europe. The Guise family fell with

---

[1] 'Las personas,' de Quadra adds, 'que le enviáron á esta tan gran traycion, dice Ledington que han sido mas de una; pero la que principalmente le dió la instruccion y recaudo fué Madame de Curosot.'—*De Quadra to Philip, March 28.* Madame de Curosot was probably Charlotte de Laval, the wife of the Admiral. This preposterous story passed current with the Spaniards, and reappears in a despatch of de Chantonnay to Philip. — TEULET, vol. v. pp. 2, 3.

their head into sudden ruin. The Duc d'Aumale, badly wounded at Dreux, lived but to hear of his brother's murder, and followed him in a few hours. The Grand Prior died of a cold caught in the same battle.[1] Of the six brothers who but a few months before held in their hands the fortunes of France three were dead; of the three remaining the Marquis d'Elbœuf was shut up in Caen Castle, closely besieged by Chatillon; the Cardinal of Lorraine was absent at Trent; and the Cardinal of Guise was the single member of the family who had no capacity. The other great leaders of France had disappeared with equal suddenness: Montmorency was a prisoner in Orleans, Condé a prisoner in Paris; St. André was dead, Navarro was dead; Catherine found herself relieved of rivalry and able to govern as she pleased. The Queen of Scots had no longer a friend in France who cared to stand by her; and well indeed after this blow might she lament to Randolph the misery of life, and say with tears 'she perceived now the world was not that which men would make it, nor they the happiest that lived the longest in it.'[2]

Mary Stuart's prospects in England had been on the eve of arrangement, when Elizabeth, relieved of the dread of the Duke of Guise, believed herself again at leisure to trifle, or to insist on new conditions on which the recognition should be made.

The following letters and abstracts of letters for a moment lift the veil of diplomacy, and reveal the inward ambitions, aims, and workings of the different parties:—

---

[1] VARILLAS.
[2] Randolph to Cecil, April 1.—*Scotch MSS. Rolls House.*

SUMMARY OF A LETTER FROM THE BISHOP OF AQUILA TO THE KING OF SPAIN.[1]

March 18.

The Bishop of Aquila understanding that Maitland the Secretary of the Queen of Scots desired to speak with him, invited the said Secretary to dinner. The conversation turned chiefly on two points—the succession of his mistress to the English crown and her marriage.

On the first Maitland said that with the Queen of England's permission he had discussed with Cecil the terms on which the Queen of Scots would relinquish her present claim on the English crown, provided the succession was secured to her in the event of the Queen of England's death without children.

The conditions he said had been arranged; and the two Queens were to have met to conclude the agreement; when the death of the Duke of Guise changed all, and he could no longer hope that his mistress's right would ever be admitted.

The Bishop seeing that Maitland was perplexed, and wishing to learn whether he had anything more on his mind, said that if his mistress would marry where the Queen of England wished she might then no doubt have all that she desired.

Maitland replied that to this there were two objections: in the first place the Queen of Scots would never marry a Protestant; in the second place she would marry neither Catholic nor Protestant at the will of or in connection with the Queen of England, not though the succession could be absolutely made sure to her.

---

[1] The original letter of de Quadra is not preserved. The translation is from a contemporary abstract.

CHAP VI.
1563
March

The husband whom Elizabeth would give her would be but some English vassal; and if she married below her rank her difficulties would remain as great as ever. To be nominated as successor would be of no use to her unless she had power to enforce her rights;[1] while she would forfeit the good will of the Catholics by seeming to give way. The Earl of Arran she abhorred; the Duke of Ferrara whom the Queen-mother of France proposed to her she despised. She would sooner die than marry any one lower in rank than the husband whom she had lost.

The Bishop asked what she would think of the Archduke Carlos of Austria.

Maitland replied that the Archduke would satisfy neither his mistress nor her subjects. He was a mere dependent on the King of Spain, and could not be thought of unless the King of Spain—as was not likely —would interfere in England on a large scale, emphatically and effectually.

The Scots desire a marriage between Mary Stuart and the Prince of Spain.

The Secretary then spoke at length of the fears of the Queen of England lest the Prince of Spain should marry his mistress. The Queen-mother too, he said, feared it equally and with good reason, for if the King of Spain would consent he might add England, Ireland, and Scotland to his dominions. Nothing could be more easy, so great was the anxiety of the English Catholics for that marriage and for the union of the crowns. When the Bishop objected that the Scots might oppose it on the ground of religion, the Secretary admitted that the nobility of Scotland were generally Protestant; but they were devoted to the Queen, and would be content that she should marry a Catholic if it was for the interests of

---

[1] 'Porque sin fuerças proprias nunca podria executar la declaration que se hiciese.'

the realm. Means could be found to work upon them. The Catholics at first might be allowed mass in their private houses—by and by they would have churches. Lord James was most favourable to the marriage, and if the Bishop wished he would come to London and speak with him.

As to the feeling in England, the Bishop confirms Maitland's account from his own knowledge. One nobleman offers if it can be brought about to serve the King of Spain with a thousand horse; others are almost as forward; and the state of the realm is such that the union of the island under a single powerful and Christian prince is the sole means by which religion can be reformed. The whole body of the English Catholics desire the Bishop to represent this in their names to the King of Spain as spoken from their very heart and soul; they assure him that it is their universal wish, and that no obstacle can prevent it from being carried into effect if his Majesty will only consent.

DE QUADRA TO PHILIP II.

London, March 28.

'Maitland tells me that four or five days ago, speaking of the affairs of France and of the Queen of Scots' marriage, the Queen of England said that if his mistress would be guided by her she would give her a husband that should be all which she could desire; the Queen of Scots should have Lord Robert, on whom God had bestowed so many charms that were she herself to marry she would prefer him to all the princes in the world.

'Maitland by his own account replied that her Majesty was giving a wonderful proof of her affection for the Queen his mistress in offering to bestow upon her an object so dear to herself. If his mistress came to love

CHAP VI
1563
March

Elizabeth proposes Lord Robert for the Queen of Scots.

Lord Robert as much as her Majesty loved him, he feared even so she might not marry him for fear of depriving her Majesty of what she so much valued.

'After more of these courtesies the Queen said, "Would to God' the Earl of Warwick was as charming as his brother—we might then each have had our own." Maitland would not understand the hint; but she kept to the subject and went on, "Not that my Lord Warwick is ill-looking or ungraceful, but he is rough, and lacks the sweet delicacy of Robert; he is brave enough and noble enough to deserve the hand of a princess."

'Maitland did not like the ground on which he found himself, so to end the conversation he said that the Queen his mistress was still young; her Majesty had better first marry Lord Robert herself; if she had children it would be all which the realm required of her; should no such event happen, and should God call her to his mercy, his mistress might inherit both crown and husband; and with one or the other of them there could be no doubt of a family. The Queen laughed, and the subject dropped.

'There has been a proposal in the Upper House to limit the succession to the heads of four or five English families, leaving the Queen to choose among them. The plan was Cecil's, and the object was of course to secure the crown to some one of his own party; while the pride of the great houses named would be flattered with the distinction, whether her choice rested on them or not. The Queen herself wishes to be allowed to bequeath the crown by will. They will perhaps pass a resolution excluding women to make sure of keeping out the Queen of Scots.'

SUMMARY OF A LETTER FROM DE QUADRA TO THE
KING OF SPAIN.[1]

April 3.

'The Queen is really anxious for this marriage between the Queen of Scots and Lord Robert; but she is not likely to succeed. Maitland demands the recognition, and threatens great things if it is not conceded. With the succession secured to her, he tells the Queen that she will be content to remain on good terms. If she is left in uncertainty, he says that she must seek other friends abroad.

'Cecil answers that if means can be found to provide for his mistress's safety during her lifetime, and to prevent a religious revolution from following afterwards, the claims of the Queen of Scots shall be admitted forthwith. Maitland rejoins that this is nothing but words. He has now gone to France. At parting he told me that if his mistress could not have our Prince she would do what she could to obtain the King of France. The Archduke Carlos she will not hear of. Her own subjects and the English Catholics alike object to the Archduke, and would prefer Lady Margaret's son Lord Darnley.

'Rawlet the Secretary of the Queen of Scots assures de Quadra that the Lord James and the whole Scotch nobility, Protestant as well as Catholic, wish for the Prince of Spain. Ten or twelve English peers and knights also have memorialized the Bishop about it, and some of them are willing to swear fealty to the Prince and the Queen of Scots together.'[2]

Unaware of the pit which threatened to open under her feet, and warming herself with the project of the

---

[1] Contemporary abstract.   [2] *MS. Simancas.*

Lord Robert marriage, which would elevate her favourite and as she supposed would be a shelter to herself, Elizabeth meanwhile felt herself able to dismiss the Parliament and to answer the addresses of the Houses before they separated.

On Saturday the 10th of April she went down to the Lords to give her assent to the acts of the session. Sir Thomas Williams paid her the usual compliments, comparing her to the great queens of fable or history—to 'Palestina,' who reigned before the deluge, to Ceres who followed her, and other benefactresses of mankind real or imaginary; without entering again upon painful subjects, he contented himself with expressing a wish at the close of his speech to see her happily married.

A formal answer of a corresponding kind was read by Bacon—and then Elizabeth rose and in her own style spoke as follows:

'Since there can be no duer debt than prince's word, to keep that unspotted, for my part, as one that would be loth that the self thing that keeps the merchant's credit from cruze, should be the cause that prince's speech should merit blame, and so their honour quail: an answer therefore I will make, and this it is:

'The two petitions that you presented me, in many words expressed, contained these two things in sum as of your cares the greatest—my marriage and my successor—of which two, the last I think is best to be touched; and of the other a silent thought may serve; for I had thought it had been so desired as none other tree's blossoms should have been minded ere hope of my fruit had been denied you. But to the last, think not that you had needed this desire, if I had seen a time so fit, and it so ripe to be denounced. The greatness of the cause therefore and need of your returns doth make me say that which I think the wise may easily guess—that as a short time for so long a continuance ought not to pass by rote, as many telleth tales, even so as cause by conference with the learned shall show me matter worthy utterance for your behoof, so shall I more gladly pursue your good after my days, than with my prayers be a means to linger my living thread.

'And this much more will I add for your comfort. I have good record in this place that other means[1] have been thought of than you mentioned, perchance for your good as much, and for my surety no less, which if presently could have been executed had not been deferred. But I hope I shall die in quiet with *Nunc Dimittis*, which cannot be without I see some glimpses of your following after my graved bones. And by the way if any doubt that I am as it were by vow or determination bent never to trade that life (of marriage), put out that heresy; your belief is awry—for as I think it best for a private woman, so do I strive with myself to think it not most meet for a prince—and if I can bend my will to your need, I will not resist such a mind.'[2]

With this oration Parliament was prorogued; and Elizabeth had kept her word to the Queen of Scots.

With the Parliament ended also the first convocation of the English Church—of the doings of which some-

---

[1] *i. e.*—The Lord Robert marriage as the condition of the recognition.

[2] A manuscript version of this speech, at Hatfield, leaves little doubt that the text as given by D'Ewes is substantially correct. The few varieties of reading do not affect the more complicated passages, and we are obliged to conclude that Elizabeth really spoke with these intricate and strange involutions. A date upon the MS., April 10, 1563, fixes the occasion on which the speech was delivered.

thing should be said—although what convocation might decide affected little either the stability or the teaching of the institution which it represented.

The Church of England had been reproached with teaching no definite doctrine. It was proposed that 'Nowell's Catechism,' 'Edward's Articles,' and 'Jewel's Apology,' lately written at Cecil's instigation, should be bound together and receive authoritative sanction—'whosoever should speak against the same to be ordered as in cases of heresy.' An effort was made to get rid of vestments and surplices, organs and bells—'the table to stand no more altarwise;' the sign of the cross to be abolished in baptism; and kneeling at the Communion to be left indifferent, or discountenanced as leading to superstition.

The more advanced Calvinists demanded the reinvigoration of that aged iniquity, the Ecclesiastical Courts, with a new code of canon law; the clergy meanwhile to have power to examine into the spiritual condition of their parishioners; to admonish them if their state was unsatisfactory; to excommunicate them if admonition failed; and excommunication to mean the loss of civil rights, imprisonment, fine, and the secular arm. Adulterers and fornicators were to be put to open shame, flogged at the cart's tail, banished or imprisoned for life; and moral offences generally were to be dealt with by similar means.

It was no doubt well that English people should understand the faith which they professed; it was well that they should be prevented so far as possible from committing sin; but it would not perhaps have contributed in the long run to the end desired, if the clergy had been again empowered to deal with these things in their own peculiar manner.

This last ambition was quenched and did not reappear.

Six formulas committing the Church to ultra-Protestantism were lost by the near majority of fifty-nine to fifty-eight, while the discussion generally resulted in the restoration of thirty-nine of the original forty-two articles of Edward as a rule of faith for the clergy. The Bishop of Worcester introduced a measure to prevent his order from making away with the Church property. Petitions were presented for a more strict observance of Sunday, which came to nothing. This in the main was the work aimed at or accomplished by convocation: more moderate than might have been expected from the spirit in which the session had opened. The clergy were learning their position, and as a body were willing to work heartily on the narrow platform to which their pretensions had been limited. They too disappeared with the Parliament, and the Queen was left to extricate herself as she could from the embroglio in France.

Although she knew nothing of the overtures of the Scots to Spain, there was much in Philip's attitude which was seriously menacing. His ambassador in Paris was advising the Government to refuse the restoration of Calais, while he himself professed to Chaloner his hope that England would recover it. Many thousand Spaniards were serving in the French army, while more were preparing to join them; and it seemed as if his chief anxiety was to stimulate the war.

The King of Spain had deeply resented the treatment of his ambassador. The Bishop of Aquila, he told Elizabeth, had been placed in England to preserve the alliance between his subjects and hers; and in what he had done had but obeyed the orders which he had received with his appointment.[1] Gresham reported from

---

[1] Philip II. to Elizabeth, April 2, 1563.—*Spanish MSS. Rolls House.*

Flanders, as the belief on the Bourse, that 'there would be much ado with the summer for religion, when King Philip would disturb all he could to maintain Papistry;' and Gresham's own uniform advice to Elizabeth was to buy saltpetre, cast cannon, and build ships.[1]

More important and far more alarming was the likelihood of a peace in France in which England as the phrase went, 'was to be left out at the cart's tail.' To the extent to which Elizabeth had been seeking objects of her own behind her affectation of a desire to help the Huguenots, the Huguenot leaders felt themselves entitled to desert her could they obtain the toleration which was of moment to themselves. Elizabeth had been ready to sacrifice them could she recover Calais by it. The Prince of Condé must have felt his conscience easy in repaying her in her own coin.

On the 7th of March Sir Thomas Smith believed that he had obtained what Elizabeth wanted; and that he would have peace and Calais in a month.[2] The Queen-mother had been ingeniously deluding him, that she might have evidence of treachery to lay before Condé, whom on the 8th of the same month she met with the Constable on an island in the Loire.

The eclipse of the Guises enabled the interest of France once more to be preferred to the interest of Rome. Catherine offered Condé his brother's place as Lieutenant-General, with a moderate toleration—something perhaps in advance of that of which Elizabeth had advised the acceptance—for the Calvinists. The Calvinists should pray to God as they pleased if they would cease to molest the Catholics. The 'strangers' on both sides

---

[1] Gresham to Cecil, March 21.—*Flanders MSS.*
[2] Smith to Cecil, March 7.—*Forbes*, vol. ii.

should be sent home; the Spaniards should retire from
the south, the English should evacuate Normandy. The
Prince had promised Elizabeth that he would agree to no
terms without giving her notice—and he kept his word.
He wrote both to her and to Sir Thomas Smith, saying
that he had taken arms for the freedom of conscience,
which was now conceded; he assumed, without mentioning Calais, that Elizabeth had assisted him for the same
object; and the object being secured there was no longer
occasion for continuing the war.[1]

In vain Elizabeth required him to remember his
honour and promise; in vain she bade him beware 'how
he set an example of perfidy to the world.' She was but
receiving the measure which she had prepared for her
allies. Peace was signed in France on the 25th of
March, and notice was sent to Warwick that the purpose
of the war being happily accomplished, he was expected
to withdraw from Havre.[2]

The Prince however was unwilling to press matters to
extremity. On the 8th of April he protested in a second
and more gracious message, that neither by him nor by
the Admiral had the town been placed in English hands;
but he offered in the name of himself, the Queen-Regent,
and the entire nobility of France, to renew solemnly and
formally the clause in the Treaty of Cambray for the
restoration of Calais in 1567; to repay Elizabeth the
money which she had lent him, and to admit the English
to free trade and intercourse with all parts of France.

Could Elizabeth have temperately considered the value
of these proposals she would have hesitated before she

---

[1] Condé to Elizabeth, March 8. Condé to Sir T. Smith, March 11.—Forbes, vol. ii.
[2] Warwick to the Council, March 31.—Forbes, vol. ii.

refused them; but she was irritated at having been outwitted in a transaction in which her own conduct had not been pure. The people, with the national blindness to everything but their own injuries, were as furious as the Queen. The garrison at Havre was only anxious for an opportunity of making 'the French cock cry cuck.'[1] They promised Elizabeth that 'the least molehill about her town should not be lost without many bloody blows;' and when a few days later there came the certainty that they would really be besieged, they prayed 'that the Queen would bend her brows and wax angry at the shameful treason;' 'the Lord Warwick and all his people would spend the last drop of their blood before the French should fasten a foot in the town.'[2]

The French inhabitants of Havre had almost settled the difficulty for themselves. Feeling no pleasure, whatever they might affect, in having 'their antient enemies' among them, they opened a correspondence with the Rhingrave. A peasant passing the gates with a basket of chickens was observed to have something under his clothes. A few sheets of white paper was all which the guard could discover; but these when held to the fire revealed a conspiracy to murder Warwick and admit the French army.[3] The townspeople, men, women, and children, were of course instantly expelled; and the English garrison in solitary possession worked night and day to prepare for the impending struggle.

It was with no pleasure that Condé felt himself obliged to turn against Elizabeth the army which her own money had assisted him to raise. She had answered

---

[1] Pelham to Throgmorton, April 5.—CONWAY MSS.
[2] Pelham to Throgmorton, April 15.—MS. Ibid.
[3] Henry King to Chaloner.—Spanish MSS.

his proposals by sending to Paris a copy of the articles which both the Prince and the Admiral had subscribed. 'No one thing,' she said, 'so much offended her as their unkind dealing after her friendship in their extremity;' while Sir Thomas Smith, on the other side, described Condé as a second King of Navarre going the way of Baal Peor, and led astray by 'Midianitish women.' Yet had Elizabeth's own dealings been free from reproach, it was impossible for Condé, had he been ever so desirous of it, to make the immediate restoration of Calais a condition of the peace. Had the war been fought out with the support of England in the field till the Catholics had been crushed, even then his own Huguenots would scarcely have permitted the surrender. Had he held out upon it when the two factions were left standing so evenly balanced, he would have enlisted the pride of France against himself and his cause, and identified religious freedom with national degradation. Before moving on Havre he made another effort. He sent M. de Briequemaut to explain his position and to renew his offers enlarged to the utmost which he could venture. The young King wrote himself also accepting Elizabeth's declaration that her interference had been in no spirit of hostility to France, entreating that she would continue her generosity, and peace being made, recall her forces.[1] The ratification of the treaty of Cambray was promised again, with 'hostages at her choice' for the fulfilment of it, from the noblest families in France.

But it was all in vain. Elizabeth at first would not see Briequemaut. She swore she would have no dealings with 'the false Prince of Condé,' and desired, if the French King had any message for her, that it should be

---

[1] Charles IX. to Elizabeth, April 30.—FORBES, vol. II.

presented by the ambassador Paul de Foix. When de Foix waited on her with Charles's letter she again railed at the Prince as 'a treacherous inconstant perjured villain.'[1] De Foix, evidently instructed to make an arrangement if possible, desired her if she did not like the Prince's terms to name her own conditions, and promised that they should be carefully considered. At first she would say nothing. Then she said she would send her answer through Sir Thomas Smith; then suddenly she sent for Bricquemaut, and told him that 'her rights to Calais being so notorious, she required neither hostages nor satisfaction; she would have Calais delivered over; she would have her money paid down; and she would keep Havre till both were in her hands.'

Bricquemaut withdrew, replying briefly that if this was her resolution she must prepare for war. Once more de Foix was ordered to make a final effort. The Council gave him the same answer which Elizabeth had given to Bricquemaut. He replied that the English had no right to demand Calais before the eight years agreed on in the treaty of Cambray were expired. The Council rejoined that the treaty of Cambray had been broken by the French themselves in their attempt to enforce the claims of Mary Stuart, that the treaty of Edinburgh remained unratified, and that the fortifications at Calais and the long leases by which the lands in the Pale had been let proved that there was and could be no real intention of restoring it; 'so that it was lawful for the Queen to do any manner of thing for the recovery of Calais; and being come to the quiet possession of Havre without force or any other unlawful means, she had good reason to keep it.'[2]

---

[1] De Quadra to Philip, May 9.—*MS. Simancas.*
[2] 'A conference between the French King's ambassador and certain of her Majesty's Council, June 2.'—CONWAY *MSS.*, Cecil's hand.

On Bricquemaut's return, Catherine de Medici lost not a moment. The troops of the Rhingrave, which had watched Havre through the spring were reinforced. The armies of the Prince and of the Guises lately in the field against each other were united under the Constable, and marched for Normandy.

In England ships were hurried to sea; the western counties were allowed to send out privateers to pillage French commerce; and depôts of provisions were established at Portsmouth, with a daily service of vessels between Spithead and the mouth of the Seine. Recruits for the garrison were raised wherever volunteers could be found. The prisoners in Newgate and the Fleet—highwaymen, cutpurses, shoplifters, burglars, horse-stealers, 'tall fellows' fit for service—were drafted into the army in exchange for the gallows;[1] and the Council determined to maintain in Havre a constant force of six thousand men and a thousand pioneers, sufficient it was hoped, with the help of the fleet and the command of the sea, to defy the utmost which France could do.

Every day there was now fighting under the walls of the town, and the first successes were with the English. Fifty of the prisoners taken at Caudebeque, who had since worked in the galleys, killed their captain and carried their vessel into Havre. A sharp action followed with the Rhingrave, in which the French lost fourteen hundred men, and the English comparatively few.

Unfortunately young Tremayne was among the killed, a special favourite of Elizabeth, who had distinguished himself at Leith, the most gallant of the splendid band of youths who had been driven into exile in her sister's time, and had roved the seas as privateers. The Queen was prepared for war, but not for the cost of war. She

---

[1] *Domestic MSS., Eliz.*, vol. xxviii.

had resented the expulsion of the French inhabitants of Havre: she had 'doubted' if they were driven from their homes 'whether God would be contented with the rest that would follow;'[1] she was more deeply affected with the death of Tremayne; and Warwick was obliged to tell her that war was a rough game; she must not discourage her troops by finding fault with measures indispensable to success; for Tremayne, he said, 'men came there to venture their lives for her Majesty and their country, and must stand to that which God had appointed either to live or die.'[2]

The English had a right to expect that they could hold the town against any force which could be brought against them; while the privateers like a troop of wolves were scouring the Channel and chasing French traders from the seas. One uneasy symptom alone betrayed itself: on the 7th of June Lord Warwick reported that a strange disease had appeared in the garrison, of which nine men had suddenly died.[3]

But the intimation created little alarm. For three more weeks the English court remained sanguine, and talked not only of keeping Havre, but of carrying the war deeper into Normandy. 'I was yesterday with the Queen,' wrote de Quadra on the 2nd of July. 'She said she was about to send six thousand additional troops across the Channel, and the French should perhaps find the war brought to their own doors. Cecil and the Admiral said the same to me. They have fourteen ships well armed and manned besides their transports, and every day they grow more eager and exasperated.'[4]

---
[1] The Queen to Warwick, May 22.—FORBES, vol. ii.
[2] Warwick to Cecil, June 9.—*Domestic MS.*
[3] Warwick to Cecil, June 7.—*MS. Ibid.*
[4] De Quadra to the Duchess of Parma, July 2.—*MS. Simancas.*

But on that day news was on the way which abridged these large expectations. 'The strange disease' was the plague; and in the close and narrow streets where seven thousand men were packed together amidst foul air and filth and summer heat, it settled down to its feast of death. On the 7th of June it was first noticed; on the 27th the men were dying at the rate of sixty a day; 'those who fell ill rarely recovered; the fresh water was cut off, and the tanks had failed from drought. There was nothing to drink but wine and cider; there was no fresh meat, and there were no fresh vegetables. The windmills were outside the walls and in the hands of the enemy; and though there was corn in plenty the garrison could not grind it. By the 29th of June the deaths had been five hundred. The corpses lay unburied or floated rotting in the harbour. The officers had chiefly escaped; the common men, worse fed and worse lodged, fell in swathes like grass under the scythe, and the physicians died at their side.'

The Prince of Condé notwithstanding the last answer to de Foix had written on the 26th of June a very noble letter to Elizabeth. 'To prevent war,' he said, 'the King and Queen, the Princes of the blood, the Lords of the Council, the whole Parliament of Paris would renew the obligation to restore Calais at the eight years' end. It was an offer which the Queen of England could accept without stain upon her honour, and by agreeing to it she would prove that she had engaged in the quarrel with a chief eye to the glory of God and the maintenance of the truth.'[1]

Elizabeth had fiercely refused; and when this terrible news came from Havre she could not—would not—realize its meaning. She would send another army, she

---

[1] Condé to Elizabeth, June 26.—FORBES, vol. ii.

CHAP VI
1563
June

would call out the musters, and feed the garrison from them faster than the plague could kill. Cost what it would Havre should be held. It was but a question of men, money, and food; and the tarnished fame of England should be regained.[1]

And worse and worse came the news across the water. When June ended, out of his seven thousand men Warwick found but three thousand fit for duty, and the enemy were pressing him closer, and Montmorency had joined the Rhingrave. Thousands of workmen were throwing up trenches under the walls, and thousands of women were carrying and wheeling earth for them. Of the English pioneers but sixty remained alive, and the French cannon were already searching and sweeping the streets. Reinforcements were hurried over by hundreds and then by thousands. Hale vigorous English countrymen they were landed on that fatal quay: the deadly breath of the destroyer passed upon them, and in a few days or hours they fell down and there were none to bury them, and the commander could but clamour for more and more and more.

The work of the plague.

On the 11th of July but fifteen hundred men were left. In ten days more at the present death rate Warwick said he would have but three hundred alive.[2] All failed except English hearts. 'Notwithstanding the deaths,' Sir Adrian Poynings reported, 'their courage is so good as if they be supplied with men and victual they trust by God's help yet to withstand the force of the enemy and to render the Queen a good account thereof.'[3]

---

[1] The Council to Warwick, June 29. Elizabeth to Warwick, July 4.—FORBES.

[2] Warwick to the Council, July 11.—FORBES, vol. ii. Endorsed 'Haste post haste for thy life! Haste, haste, haste!'

[3] Sir Adrian Poynings to Cecil, July 6.—*Domestic MSS.*, ELIZ.

Those who went across from England, though going as they knew to all but certain death, 'kept their high courage and heart for the service.'[1]

Ship after ship arrived at Havre with its doomed freight of living men, yet Warwick wrote that still his numbers waned, that the new comers were not enough to repair the waste. The ovens were broken with the enemy's shot, the bakers were dead of the plague. The besiegers by the middle of the month were closing in upon the harbour mouth. A galley sent out to keep them back was shot through and sunk with its crew under the eye of the garrison. On the 19th their hearts were cheered by large arrivals, but they were raw boys from Gloucestershire, new alike to suffering and to arms. Cannon had been sent for from the Tower, and cannon came, but they were old and rusted and worthless. 'The worst of all sorts,' wrote Warwick, 'is thought good enough for this place.' It was the one complaint which at last was wrung from him.

To add to his difficulties the weather broke up in storms. Clinton had twenty sail with him, and three thousand men ready to throw in. If the fleet could have lain outside the harbour the ships' guns could have kept the approaches open. But a south-west gale chained Clinton in the Downs; the transports which sailed from St. Helen's could not show behind the island, and there was a fear that the garrison cut off from relief might have been overpowered in their weakness and destroyed.

Too late for the emergency and still with sullen unwillingness to yield, the Queen on the 20th sent over Throgmorton to accept Condé's terms. But the French court was with the besieging army, and knew the con-

---

[1] Sir Adrian Poynings to Cecil, July 9.—*Domestic MSS., Eliz.*

dition of Warwick's troops too well to listen. The harbour was by that time closed; the provisions were exhausted; the French understood their power and meant to use it. Warwick, ordered as he had been to hold the place under all conditions, 'was prepared to die sword in hand' rather than surrender without the Queen's permission; but in a few days at latest those whom the sword and pestilence had spared famine would make an end of. Fortunately Sir Francis Knowles, who was in command at Portsmouth, had sent to the court to say that they must wait for no answer from France; they must send powers instantly to Warwick to make terms for himself. A general attack had been arranged for the morning of the 27th. Lord Warwick knew that he would be unable to resist, and with the remnant of his men was preparing the evening before to meet a soldier's death, when a boat stole in with letters, and he received Elizabeth's permission to surrender at the last extremity.

Surrender of Havre.

War, plague, and storm had done their work and had done it with fatal efficacy. Clinton was chafing helplessly at his anchorage 'while the French were lying exposed on the beach at Havre.' He could not reach them, and they could but too effectually reach Warwick. Knowing that to delay longer was to expose the handful of noble men who survived with him to inevitable death, and himself wounded and ill, the English general sent at once to the Constable to make terms. The Constable would not abuse his advantage, and on the 29th of July Havre was restored to France, the few English troops remaining being allowed to depart with their arms and goods unmolested and at their leisure.

The day after the weather changed, and Clinton arrived to find that all was over, and that Warwick himself was on board a transport ready to sail. The Queen-mother sent M. de Lignerolles on board Clinton's ship to ask him to dine with her. He excused himself under the plea that he could not leave his men; but he said to de Lignerolles 'that the plague of deadly infection had done for them that which all the force of France could never have done.'[1]

Thus ended this unhappy enterprise in a disaster which terrible as it seemed was more desirable for England than success. Elizabeth's favouring star had prevented a conquest from being consummated which would have involved her in interminable war. Had it not been for the plague she might have held Havre; but she could have held it only at a cost which before many years were over would have thrown her an exhausted and easy prey at the feet of Philip.

The first thought of Warwick, ill as he was, on reaching Portsmouth was for his brave companions. They had returned in miserable plight, and he wrote to the Council to beg that they might be cared for. But there was no occasion to remind Elizabeth of such a duty as this: had she been allowed she would have gone at once at the risk of infection to thank them for their gallantry.[2] In a proclamation under her own hand she commended the soldiers who had faced that terrible siege to the care of the country; she entreated every gentleman, she commanded every official, ecclesiastical or civil, in the realm to see to their necessities 'lest God punish them for their unmercifulness;' she insisted with generous forethought 'that no person should have any grudge at those poor captains and soldiers because the town was rendered on

---

[1] Clinton to Cecil, July 31.—*Domestic MSS.*, Eliz.
[2] Lord Robert Dudley to the Queen, August 7.—*Domestic MSS.* vol. xxix.

CHAP VI
1563
August

The garrison of Havre spreads the plague in England.

conditions:' 'she would have it known and understood that there wanted no truth, courage, nor manhood in any of them from the highest to the lowest;' 'they would have withstood the French to the utmost of their lives; but it was thought the part of Christian wisdom not to tempt the Almighty to contend with the inevitable mortal enemy of the plague.'[1]

Happy would it have been had the loss of Havre ended the calamities of the summer. But the garrison scattering to their homes carried the infection through England. London was tainted already, and with the heat and drought of August the pestilence in town and village held on its deadly way.

The eruption on the skin which was usual with the plague does not seem to have attended this visitation of it. The first symptom was violent fever, burning heat alternating with fits of shivering; the mouth then became dry, the tongue parched, with a pricking sensation in the breast and loins; headache followed and languor, with a desire to sleep, and after sleep came generally death, 'for the heart did draw the poison, and the poison by its own malice did pierce the heart.' When a man felt himself infected 'he did first commend himself to the highest Physician and craved mercy of him.' Where he felt pain he was bled, and he then drank the 'aqua contra pestem'—the plague water—buried himself in his bed and if possible perspired. To allay his thirst he was allowed sorrel-water and verjuice, with slices of oranges and lemons. Light food—rabbit, chicken or other bird—was taken often and in small quantities. To prevent the spread of the contagion the houses and streets and staircases were studiously cleaned; the windows

---

[1] Proclamation by the Queen, August 1.—*Domestic MSS.*

were set wide open and hung with fresh green boughs of oak or willow; the floors were strewed with sorrel, lettuce, roses, and oak leaves, and freely and frequently sprinkled with spring water or else with vinegar and rosewater. From cellar to garret six hours a day the houses were fumigated with sandalwood and musk, aloes, amber, and cinnamon. In the poorest cottages there were fires of rosemary and bay. Yet no remedy availed to prevent the mortality, and no precaution to check the progress of the infection. In July the deaths in London had been two hundred a week; through the following month they rose swiftly to seven hundred, eight hundred, a thousand, in the last week of the month to two thousand; and at that rate with scarcely a diminution the people continued to die till the November rains washed the sewers and kennels clean, and the fury of the disorder was spent.

The Bishops attributing the calamity to supernatural causes, and seeing the cause for the provocation of the Almighty in the objects which excited their own displeasure, laid the blame upon the theatres, and petitioned the Government to inhibit plays and amusements.[1] Sir William Cecil not charging Providence till man had done his part found the occasion rather in the dense crowding of the lodging-houses, 'by reason that the owners and tenants for greediness and lucre did take unto them other inhabitants and families to dwell in their chambers;' he therefore ordered that 'every house or shop should have but one master and one family,' and that aliens and strangers should remove.[2]

The danger alarmed the Council into leniency towards

---

[1] Grindal to Cecil, February 22, 1564.—LANSDOWNE *MSS.* 7.
[2] Sir Wm. Cecil's Injunction.—*MS. Ibid.*

the state prisoners. The Tower was emptied. The Catholic prelates were distributed among the houses of their rivals and successors; Lady Catherine Grey was committed to the charge of her father's brother, broken in health, heart, and spirit, praying but praying in vain, that 'her lord and husband might be restored to her,' and pining slowly towards the grave into which a few years later she sank.[1]

The victims who died of the plague were chiefly obscure; one person however perished in it whose disappearance the reader will perhaps regret.

The story must go back for a few pages.

The King of Spain after receiving de Quadra's letter which contained the proposals of the Queen of Scots for the Prince of Spain took time to consider his answer, and at length on the 15th of June replied as follows:—

PHILIP II. TO THE BISHOP OF AQUILA.

June 15.

'I have pondered over the conversation which has passed between you and Maitland on the marriage between his mistress and the Prince my son, and I am much pleased with the discretion which you showed in your replies.

'Perceiving as I do that if this marriage can be brought about it may be the beginning of a better state of things in England, I am willing to admit the consideration of it; and if you believe that those who have spoken with you on the subject are persons whom you can trust, you will use their assistance to bring the thing about.

'You will learn from Maitland and from the Queen of

---

[1] Letters of Lord John and Lady Catherine Grey. — LANSDOWNE MSS.

Scots what friends they most rely upon in England. You will judge whether the names which they mention are of sufficient weight, and you will at once communicate with me. Above all you will be secret, for the good to be looked for depends on the marriage being completed before anything is heard of it. If the French know that I have given my consent there is no step to which their fears will not drive them to prevent the consummation of it, or if we persist in spite of them, to hinder the good fruit which may be otherwise looked for. As to the Queen of England and the heretics, you can imagine for yourself what they are likely to do. You must therefore be most cautious with whom you speak on the subject, and in your choice of agents through whom to communicate with the Queen of Scotland.

'The Emperor also you will observe, after what has passed between the Cardinal of Lorraine and himself,[1] can know nothing of the wishes of the Queen of Scots herself or of her subjects; he looks on his son's affair as already settled; and I may say for myself that were there any likelihood of that marriage taking effect I should prefer it to the other.[2] I should not move in the matter at all till the Emperor was undeceived were it not for what you tell me of the unwillingness of that Queen and her advisers to accept the Archduke, and of the small advantage which they anticipate from the Austrian connexion.

---

[1] The Cardinal of Lorraine, in a personal interview with Ferdinand, had proposed a marriage between his niece and the Archduke Carlos.

[2] A note in the margin of the letter, in Philip's autograph, shows his extreme slowness and caution:—'De punto en punto me vieis avisando de lo que en esto pasará, sin venir á convencion ninguna; mas de entender lo que arriba se dice, hasta que yo os avise de lo que en ello se me ofriciese y se hubiese de hacer; aunque podreis asegurarles que mi intencion es la que aqui se dice.'

'I am alarmed especially at the possibility of her marrying a French King again, for I cannot but remember the trouble which her last alliance in that quarter occasioned me. Should she marry in that quarter, I know but too well that at no distant time I shall be forced into war to protect the Queen of England from an invasion such as was intended before; and you can judge yourself whether that is an event to which I can look with pleasure.

'You will ascertain what support the Scots can count upon in England, and you will not prevent them from increasing their party; but you will not involve yourself with any particular person further than you have already done. Let them do the work by themselves, let them gain what friends they can among the Catholics and others whom they trust. If anything is discovered it must be their affair and not mine.

'As for what you say of the dependence of the English Catholics upon me, I am anxious to do the very utmost which I can for them. You will animate and console them as usual; only of all things in the world you must be careful not to let your own hand be seen. You know what would follow.

'I am very sorry for the Act which the Queen has obtained from Parliament against those who will not accept her as Head of the Anglican Church. The bishops and other Catholics are now in danger of death. They have begun already you tell me with the Bishop of London.

'I am glad to hear that the Emperor has remonstrated, though I fear it will do little good. I have myself also written to the Queen; and you will yourself do and say whatever promises to be most effective to make them change their purpose. I know that I can depend on you in this, feeling as you do so acutely about it.'[1]

To Philip's letter a few lines were added by the Duke of Alva:

ALVA TO THE BISHOP OF AQUILA.

June 16.

'Although his Majesty in his own letter has told you how important it is to be secret in the affair of the marriage of the Queen of Scots, I cannot but myself reiterate the same caution. The world must know nothing till all is actually over, or no good will come of it.

'You will therefore charge those with whom you have to deal to allow no hint of our purpose to transpire. You will let us know step by step how the negotiation proceeds, and his Majesty will take measures accordingly.'

No answer could have promised better for Mary Stuart's hopes; but it had been long in coming, and the diplomacy of conspiracy was restless and feverish. Maitland after his visit to France returned to London in July to learn what de Quadra had heard. He had as yet heard

---

[1] Ferdinand, immediately on the passing of the Act, wrote to beg that no violence might be used towards the Catholic bishops. The ingenuity of the lawyers might have been less successful had not Elizabeth been able to shield herself behind Ferdinand's and Philip's letters. Archbishop Parker also lent his assistance. In a circular to his brother bishops he desired them, with the Queen's and Cecil's connivance, not to offer the oath to any one a second time without referring to himself; 'not,' he said, ' that he had warrant to stay the execution of impartial laws,' but being ready ' to jeopard his private estimation if the purpose which the Queen would have done, might be performed.'—STRYPE'S *Life of Parker*, vol. I. pp. 249, 250.

CHAP VI
1563
July

Possibility of other marriages for the Queen of Scots.

nothing, and Maitland's views meanwhile had been qualified by a conversation with Catherine de Medici. The Queen-mother as Philip had foreseen dreaded nothing so much as this Spanish marriage; and to prevent it she had promised that if the Queen of Scots would remain unmarried for two years, Charles the Ninth and the Crown of France would again be at her service. Construing Philip's silence unfavourably, Maitland allowed de Quadra to see that he thought well of the French connexion. In vain de Quadra spoke of the Archduke Carlos. Maitland would not hear of him unless with a distinct understanding that Philip would make his mistress Queen of England. It was yet possible too for the Queen of Scots to extort favourable terms from Elizabeth.

Before Maitland returned to Scotland, Elizabeth in her parting interview bade him tell Mary Stuart that if she married into the houses of Austria, France, or Spain, she would take it as an act of war.[1] She would prefer a marriage at home for her. But there were the Protestant Princes; there was the King of Denmark; there was the Duke of Ferrara: any one of these she might choose, or any French nobleman not of royal rank, and she should be named successor at once.

Maitland entered too far into these views for de Quadra's peace. He feared that Mary Stuart herself in her passionate desire for recognition might consent after all to some marriage detrimental to the interests of Catholicism,[2] and in dread of such a catastrophe, and not

---

[1] 'No podria de dejarla de tener por enemiga.'—*De Quadra to Philip, June 26. MS. Simancas.*

[2] 'Es de temer que la golosina de ser declarada sucesora deste Reyno no

haga aquella Reyna condescender en algun casamiento menos conveniente á las cosas de la religion.'—*De Quadra to Philip, June 26.—MS. Simancas.*

trusting Maitland, the Spanish ambassador on his own
responsibility sent an English friend to lay before her
the wishes of the Catholics, and to assure her that
whether she obtained the Prince of Spain, or accepted
the Archduke Carlos, Philip in either case would support
her claims in England by arms.'[1]

At this crisis the letters of Philip and Alva reached
London. De Quadra regretted that his commission was
so cautiously worded; but he lost not a moment in de-
spatching his own secretary Luis de Paz, to Holyrood.
As a blind to the English Government he sent him first
to Chester under pretence of inquiring into the seizure
of a Spanish ship by pirates. At Chester de Paz found
that the pirates in question were Scots—and went on as
if to seek redress at Edinburgh. There he saw Mary
Stuart, Maitland, and Murray. His message was received with delight by all of them. The Queen of Scots
wrote to the Duchess of Parma, relinquishing with eager
gratitude every other prospect for herself. The Bishop
of Ross hurried off to London to de Quadra to agree to
all conditions which Philip might ask.[2] The long and
dangerous labours of the indefatigable ambassador were
at last it seemed about to prosper and bear fruit—when
in the moment of success he was taken away. Luis de
Paz returned to London on the 26th of August to find
him dying. 'He knew me,' Luis wrote, 'and answered
bravely when I spoke to him. He was grieved to end
his services at a moment when he hoped to be of use.
His last words were, "I can do no more."'[3]

So died a good servant of a falling cause—faithful even

---

[1] 'Que tenga fuerzas para conseguir su derecho á este Reyno.'—*MS. Simancas.*
[2] Note of the mission of Luis de Paz to Scotland, by Diego Perez.—Mignet's *Life of Mary Stuart.* Appendix C.
[3] 'No puedo mas.'—*Memoir of Luis de Paz. MS. Simancas.*

Chap VI
1563
August

Death and character of the Bishop of Aquila.

unto death. The Bishop of Aquila had the character of his race and his profession. In the arts of diplomatic treachery he was an accomplished master. Untiring and unscrupulous, skilled in the subtle windings of the heart, he could stimulate the conscience into heroism, or play with its weakness till he had tempted it to perdition— as suited best with the ends which he pursued with the steadiness of a sleuthhound. He would converse in seeming frankness from day to day with those whom with his whole soul he was labouring to blast into ruin. Yet he was brave as a Spaniard should be—brave with the double courage of an Ignatius and a Cortez. He was perfectly free from selfish and ignoble desires, and he was loyal with an absolute fealty to his creed and his King. It was his misfortune that he served in a cause which the world now knows to have been a wrong cause; but qualifications in themselves neither better nor worse than those of Alvarez de Quadra won for Walsingham a place in the brightest circle of English statesmen.

How it might have fared with Mary Stuart and Don Carlos had de Quadra lived to complete the work for which he was so anxious, the curious in such things may speculate. The Prince of Spain had the intellect and the ferocity of a wolf; the Queen of Scots had a capacity for relieving herself of disagreeable or inconvenient companions. Yet they would scarcely perhaps have made their lots more wretched than they actually were: we wonder at the caprices of fortune; we complain of the unequal fates which are distributed among mankind—but Providence is more even-handed than it seems; Mary Stuart might have been innocent and happy as a fishwife at Leith; the Prince of Spain might have arrived at some half-brutal usefulness breaking clods on the brown plains of Castile.

Philip's orders had been so well observed that no hints had transpired of what was intended. The Archduke Carlos was the supposed candidate in the Spanish and Imperial interest. The Cardinal of Lorraine had arranged the marriage with Ferdinand. It had been talked of in the Council of Trent. It had been argued upon in a Parliament which met at Edinburgh in the preceding June. The name of the Prince of Spain was mentioned from time to time, but rather as a vague surmise; and the last thought which entered the mind of any one was that Philip would seriously substitute his son for his cousin. The Austrian match was the object of Elizabeth's fears; and what she had said to Maitland she directed Randolph to submit formally to the Queen of Scots herself.

CHAP VI
1563
August

To settle the succession in some way, and if possible to settle it in Mary Stuart's favour, she said, was her most ardent desire. She had combated hitherto the wish of Parliament to disinherit Mary. On public grounds she was anxious for the union of the realms—and privately she considered the Queen of Scots' claim to be the best. But the Queen of Scots if she was to succeed to the English crown must make up her mind to accept the Reformation, if not as her own conviction yet as the public law of the realm. If she chose to marry a Catholic prince, if she chose to make herself the representative of a Catholic party and policy, Parliament would unquestionably renew the attempt to bar her title; the country would not submit again to the Pope and the Inquisition, and Elizabeth would herself be unable to take her part further.[1]

Elizabeth informs Mary Stuart of the conditions on which she may be recognised.

---

[1] 'To consider her own particular which in the way of friendship towards her we do most weigh, we do assure her by some present proof that we have in our realm, upon some small report made thereof (of

'She did not believe,' Elizabeth continued—and the clause is in her own handwriting; 'she did not believe that the Queen of Scots meant anything against herself;' and 'she might perhaps be borne in hand that some number in England might be brought to allow' her general schemes. But she warned her sister not to be 'abused' by foolishness. 'If she tried that way she would come to no good.' For both their own sakes and for the sake of both the countries she implored the Queen of Scots to avoid a course which might 'become a perpetual reproof to both of them through all posterity.' If she married the Archduke, England must and would accept that act as a declaration of hostility. If she would take advice which she might assure herself was well meant towards her, she would marry some one to whom no suspicion could be attached. Her title should then be examined, and should receive the fullest support which she herself could give it—'her own natural inclination being most given to further her sister's interest and to impeach what should seem to the contrary.'

As to the person—an English nobleman would best please the English nation; and measuring the attractiveness of the offer by her self-sacrifice in making it, Elizabeth said that 'she could be content to give her one

---

the Austrian marriage), we well perceive that if we do not meddle and interpose her authority, it will not be long before it shall appear that as much as wit can imagine will be used to impeach her intention for the furtherance of her title. And considering the humours of such as mind—except our authority, or the fear of us shall stay them—their own particular, what can our sister think more hurtful to her than by this manner of proceeding by her friends that be not of her natural nation nor of her kingdom—first, to endanger the amity betwixt us; secondly, to dissolve the concord between the two nations; thirdly, to disappoint her of more than ever they shall recover.'— *Elizabeth to Randolph, August 30.* COTTON MSS., CALIG. B. 10.

whom perchance it could be hardly thought she could agree unto.' But she would not bind the Queen of Scots to this choice or to that; England required only that she should not marry any one 'of such greatness as suspicion might be gathered that he might intend trouble to the realm;' she might take a husband where she pleased 'so as he was not sought to change the policy' of the English nation, which it was certain 'that they would in no wise bear.'[1]

What right, it has been asked impatiently, had Elizabeth to interfere with Mary Stuart's marriage? As much right, it may be answered, as Mary Stuart had to pretend to the succession of the English crown. Those who aspire to sovereignty must accept the conditions under which sovereignty can be held. The necessities of State which at the present day bar the succession of a Roman Catholic, were stronger a thousandfold when a Catholic sovereign might bring back with her the fires of Smithfield: and the fault of Elizabeth was rather in forbearing to insist upon a change of creed than in being willing to accept a successor with a less effective security for her harmlessness.

Nor was it Elizabeth only who had a right to be alarmed. Murray, Argyle, and Maitland had been led astray by vanity and idle ambition. In their eagerness to give a sovereign to England they had half lost their interest in the Reformation, or had closed their eyes to the dangers to which they exposed it. But there were those in Scotland to whom the truth of God was more than crowns and kingdoms—to whom the re-

---

[1] Instructions to Randolph, August 20.—COTTON MSS., CALIG. B. 10. Matter committed to Thomas Randolph, August, 1563.—*Scotch MSS. Rolls House.*

volution which had passed over their country was too precious to be fooled away by courtiers' weakness or a woman's cunning. Knox knew as well as Mary knew the fruit which would follow if she married a Catholic prince. He had laboured to save Murray from the spell which his sister had flung over him; but Murray had only been angry at his interference, and 'they spake not together familiarly for more than a year and a half.'[1]

The falling off of his friends threw the weight of the battle upon Knox. In 'the Parliament time,' when the Lords thinking then only of the Austrian Carlos had been congratulating one another on the great match intended for their Queen, Knox rose in the pulpit at St. Giles's and told them all 'that whenever they professing the Lord Jesus consented that a Papist should be head of their sovereign they did as far as in them lay to banish Christ from the realm; they would bring God's vengeance on their country, a plague on themselves, and perchance small comfort to their sovereign.'

It was language which should not have been needed, for it was language which they should themselves have used. It was language which with the necessary change of diction any English statesman would have used from the Revolution till the present day. It contained but a plain political truth of which Knox happened to be the exponent.

Mary recognized her enemy. Him alone she had failed to work upon, and believing herself sure of the Lords she gave her anger its course.

In imagination Queen of Scotland, England, Ireland, Spain, Flanders, Naples, and the Indies—in the full tide of hope and with the prize almost in her hands, she was

---

[1] Knox's *History of the Reformation*.

in no humour to let a heretic preacher step between her
and the soaring flights of her ambition. She sent for
Knox, and her voice shaking between tears and passion,
she said that never had prince been handled as she;
she had borne his bitterness, she had admitted him to
her presence, she had endured to be reprimanded, and
yet she could not be quit of him; 'she vowed to God
she would be avenged.'

Quiet, collected—seeing through and through her,
yet with a sound northern courtesy, the Reformer answered that when it pleased God to open her eyes she
would see that he had done nothing to offend her; in
private he had been silent; 'in the preaching place' he
must obey God Almighty.

'But what,' she asked, 'have you to do with my
marriage?'

He said his duty was to preach the Evangel: the
nobility were so much addicted to her affections that
they had forgotten their duty, and he was therefore
bound to remind them of it.

'But what,' she repeated, 'have you to do with my
marriage? what are you within this commonwealth?'

'A subject born within the same, madam,' he replied;
'and one whose vocation and conscience demands plainness of speech; and therefore, madam,' he went on, 'I
say to yourself what I spake in yonder public place—
whenever the nobility shall consent that you be subject
to an unfaithful husband, they renounce Christ and betray the realm.'

The Queen again sobbed violently.

Knox stood silent till she had collected herself. He
then continued—'Madam, in God's presence I speak; I
never delighted in the weeping of any of God's creatures;
yea I can scarcely abide the tears of my own boys whom

my own hand corrects; but seeing I have but spoken the truth as my vocation craves of me, I must sustain your Majesty's tears rather than hurt my conscience.'

Soon after this conversation Randolph brought Elizabeth's message. In his account of the interview he gives a noticeable sketch of Mary Stuart's personal habits.

Active and energetic when occasion required, this all-accomplished woman abandoned herself to intervals of graceful self-indulgence. Without illness or imagination of it she would lounge for days in bed, rising only at night for dancing or music; and there she reclined with some light delicate French robe carelessly draped about her, surrounded by her ladies, her council, and her courtiers, receiving ambassadors and transacting business of state. It was in this condition that Randolph found her. She affected the utmost cordiality; she listened graciously to his communication; she professed herself grateful for Elizabeth's interest in her; she desired him to be cautious to whom he spoke, and referred him for her answer to Maitland and Murray. But with all her address she could not conceal from him that more was intended than she allowed to appear. Her want of interest in the Austrian marriage was evident, and Randolph himself feared 'she might be more Spanish than Imperial.'[1] A month later John Knox had discovered the secret and made haste to tell Cecil what was impending. It was no Austrian prince on whom Mary's eyes were fixed. The King of Spain had consented to give her his son. The Queen of France offered her the hand of Charles the Ninth. She would take Don Carlos if Philip kept his word. If Don Carlos

---

[1] Randolph to Cecil, September 4.—*Scotch MSS. Rolls House.*

failed her she would take the French King. The
majority of her Council had consented to what would
be their own destruction, and 'the greater part would
before long draw the better after them.' The Queen of
England would be amused with smooth answers; but
the mask would soon be laid aside. There was still
hope of the constancy of the Earl of Murray. But if
Murray followed the rest 'the rage of the storm would
overthrow the force of the strongest'—'all through the
inordinate affection of her that was born to be a plague
to the realm.'

'Thus,' Knox concluded, 'you have the plainness of
my troubled heart; use it as ye will answer to God and
as ye tender the commonwealth; the Eternal assist you
with His Spirit.'[1]

In the midst of these encompassing perils Elizabeth
bore herself bravely. The death-rate in London at the
end of December was still two hundred a week; the
country was smarting under the disaster at Havre; the
French difficulty was likely to lead to a general war[2] in
which Spain would take part; and Mary Stuart married
to a Catholic prince formed the ominous centre round
which the clouds were forming. Yet Elizabeth to the
world appeared to be given up to amusement, caring for
nothing but pleasure, and wasting her fondness upon
idle and tawdry favourites. 'The Queen,' wrote Francis
Chaloner to his brother, 'thinks of nothing but her love

---

[1] Knox to Cecil, October 5.—*Scotch MSS.* A postscript adds—'The loch between Leith and Kinghorn is left void. What strange fowl shall first alight there God knoweth.'

[2] 'By many intelligences here, I see none other but war to ensue between us and the French King ere it be long. God send grace that King Philip's subjects be not also our enemies, for we suspect as much.' —*Francis Chaloner to Sir Thomas Chaloner,* December 18. *Spanish MSS. Rolls House.*

affairs; she spends her days with her hawks and hounds and her nights in dances and plays. Though all things go ill with England she is incapable of serious thought. The court is as merry as if the world were at our feet; and the ingenious fool who can devise the best means of trifling away time is the man most admired and prized.'[1]

Yet Elizabeth was but concealing her real nature behind a mask of levity. Her spirits rose with trouble, and her high qualities were never more thoroughly awake.

Notwithstanding the struggle in Normandy, peace still existed in name between England and France; but Catherine demanded as an indemnity for the aggression on French territory a formal surrender of the English claim on Calais. Elizabeth answered that she would brave all consequences before she would submit 'to that dishonour;'[2] and a declaration of war was daily expected. Philip had offered to mediate, but with the key to Philip's policy in her hand she left him unanswered till his ministers complained to her ambassador of her scanty courtesy;[3] and then for reply she bade Chaloner tell Philip that in her past difficulties, though he had many opportunities of helping her, she had received nothing from him but 'good words;' he desired to have her at his feet, acting under his orders, and humbly petitioning for his support; but never in that position

---

[1] 'Regina tota amoribus dedita est, venationibusque aucupiis choreis et rebus ludicris insumens dies noctesque; nihil serio tractatur, quanquam omnia adversae cedant; tamen jocamur hic, perinde ac si orbem universum debellati fuerimus. Et qui plures pugnandi modos ridiculo studio excogitaverit, quasi vir summo pretio dignus suspicitur.'—*Spanish MSS.*

[2] Elizabeth to Chaloner, December, 1563.—*MS. Ibid.*

[3] Chaloner to Elizabeth, December 19.—*MS. Ibid.*

should Philip see her; she doubted whether a protracted residence of an ambassador at the Court of Spain was any longer expedient; she had half resolved to continue her diplomatic intercourse with him only through the Regent in Flanders; better an open enemy than a treacherous friend; if the worst came she could encounter it.[1]

In her bearing towards Mary Stuart she showed at the same time large forbearance and a clear foreseeing statesmanship. She knew the Queen of Scots' intentions beyond all uncertainty, but she still hoped to win her over to a safer course with the prospect of the succession;[2] while Mary Stuart on her part would not risk a quarrel till the Spanish affair had gone further. De Quadra's death had broken the link of her communication with Philip, and since the visit of Luis de Paz she had heard no more from him.

After a delay of some weeks she had replied to Randolph's message, thanking Elizabeth for her advice; to gain time and to avoid committing herself to a refusal, she desired to be told explicitly which of the many candidates for her hand would be 'allowed' in England and which would not; and again with more distinctness what would be done for her if she married as Elizabeth wished.

It is quite certain that the Queen of Scots had no real

---

[1] Elizabeth to Chaloner.—*Spanish MSS. Rolls House.*

[2] Luis Romano, who was left in charge at the Spanish embassy after de Quadra's death, wrote to Philip on the 3rd of December that Elizabeth had been speaking of the marriage between the Queen of Scots and the Prince of Spain, and had said positively it should never be. 'No, no!' 'que no se hará.' It was thought, he said, that she would tempt the Queen of Scots to give it up by the largeness of her offers on the other side.—*MS. Simancas.*

Chap. VI
1563 November

intention of being guided by Elizabeth. Maitland had told de Quadra that she would not marry a Protestant even if her recognition was an accomplished fact. The inquiry therefore could only have been finesse. Elizabeth with less temptation to insincerity, replied 'that the principal marriage which would make all other marriages fortunate, happy, and fruitful was the conjunction of the two countries and the two Queens;'

Elizabeth again addresses Mary Stuart.

but she warned the Queen of Scots that 'whatever mountains of felicity or worldly pomp' she might promise herself by going her own way, she would find her hopes in the end deceive her; the fittest husband for her would be some English or Scottish nobleman; but if she preferred to look elsewhere all Christendom was open, excepting only—as the Queen of Scots desired her to be explicit—the royal Houses of Spain, France, or Austria. A marriage into either of these could be construed only into a renewal of the schemes which she had entertained 'in her late marriage with the French King; but no other restriction should be placed upon her choice and no other difficulty raised.' Elizabeth trusted only that her selection 'might be such as should tend to the perpetual weal of the two kingdoms—the conjunction whereof she counted the only marriage of continuance and blessedness—to endure after their own lives to posterity to the pleasure of Almighty God and the eternal renown of themselves as queens and good mothers of their countries.'

To the last question of the Queen of Scots—what should be done for her if she complied—Elizabeth answered that she would 'proceed forthwith to the inquisition of her right by all good means in her favour; and finding it fall to her advantage, upon plain understanding had what manner of marriage she should make, she would proceed to the denunciation of her title as she would do for her own natural daughter.'[1]

It was long before Randolph was allowed an audience to give this second message. The Queen of Scots had quarrelled again with Knox, whom she attempted to provide with lodgings in Edinburgh Castle; the lords had interfered, and anger and disappointment had made her ill.

Moreover she was still waiting for letters from Spain which would not arrive. She was waiting and would have long to wait; for the fire of resolution no longer fanned by de Quadra's letters had grown faint again, and other schemes and other anxieties were distracting Philip's mind from Scotland. The death of Guise and the compromise between Condé and Catherine had destroyed the party which he had raised in France. Ferdinand of Austria was on the edge of the grave. There was a project for marrying the daughter of Maximilian, who would succeed to the empire, to Charles the Ninth; and this alliance might serve to renew the broken league among the Catholic powers, or at all events might relieve him of his fear that the prize might be secured by Mary Stuart. A grave difficulty lay in the character of Don Carlos himself. 'The cruel and sullen disposition of the Prince of Spain' was becoming more dangerous as he grew towards manhood. His brain had been hurt by a fall. His appetite was so furious that no gluttony could satisfy it. His passions were so violent that the King himself durst not thwart him lest he should die in the suffocation of his rage.'[2] Such a youth was no promising subject of a matrimonial

---

[1] Elizabeth to Randolph, November 17.—COTTON MSS. CALIG. B. 10. Scotch MSS. Rolls House.
[2] Minutes of Sir Thomas Chaloner, December 19.—Spanish MSS.

intrigue—no safe foundation on which to build a policy.

Towards England Chaloner described Philip as 'uncertain whether the ancient league or present personal respects should most prevail with him.' The best-informed Spaniards held a war to be eventually inevitable; but they did not expect it immediately. The Pope was labouring to bring about a cordial action between the Catholic sovereigns, and it was thought he would eventually succeed; but the critical condition of Flanders—fermenting on the edge of rebellion—would probably postpone for the present the rupture with Elizabeth. Philip, Chaloner said, was 'a prince of good disposition, soft nature, and given to tranquillity,' who if left to himself would leave England in peace; but Alva, Ruy Gomez, de Feria, and others by whom he was surrounded were men of another temperament; and Elizabeth's wellwishers in Spain advised her to make peace with France in time, and reserve her strength for the future struggle.[1]

The condition of Don Carlos however forbade the further mooting of the Scotch or any other marriage for him, and Mary Stuart's hope of sharing the Crown of Spain, whatever else she might expect from Philip, faded away. It was necessary for her to turn her thoughts elsewhere; and uncertain what to do she at length admitted Randolph to her cabinet once more.

She was again in bed. It was after dinner. Murray, Maitland, Argyle, and a number of other noblemen were present.

'Now Mr. Randolph,' she said, kissing as she spoke a diamond heart—a present from Elizabeth—which hung

---

[1] Minutes of Sir Thomas Chaloner, December 19.—*Spanish MSS.*

about her neck: 'Now Mr. Randolph I long to hear what answer you have brought me from my good sister. I am sure it cannot be but good.'

Randolph delivered his message.

She listened without interest till he spoke of her recognition, when she became at once attentive. She expected however to hear some person named as the husband desired for her.

'You have more to tell me,' she said, 'let me hear all.'

Randolph answered that his commission extended no further.

Lord Argyle approached the bed. 'My Lord,' she said to him, 'Randolph here would have me marry in England. What say you?'

'Is the Queen of England become a man?' said Argyle.

'Who is there, my Lord,' said she, 'that you would wish me to marry?'

'Whoever your Majesty can like well enough,' the Earl answered. 'I would there was so noble a man in England as you could like.'

'That would not please the Hamiltons,' said the Queen.

'If it please God and be good for your Majesty's country,' Argyle rejoined, 'what matter it who is displeased?'

She passed the subject off.[1]

She dismissed Randolph without an answer, and weeks passed before she sent for him again. He spoke to Murray and Maitland, to all those lords who were

---

[1] Randolph to Cecil, December 13, December 21, and December 30.— Scotch MSS. Rolls House.

under the deepest obligations to England, but they were cold and reserved.

'The Lord everlasting bring it to pass,' he wrote to Elizabeth, 'that we may rather rejoice in the birth of your Majesty's body before any other without the same, whom God may put in your heart to yield your right unto after your Majesty's days.'[1]

---

[1] Randolph to Elizabeth, January 21, 1564.—*Scotch MSS. Rolls House.*

NOTE TO VOL. VII., p. 479.

EXTRACT from the Sermon of Dr. Nowell made at the opening of Parliament, January, 12, 1562-3, from a manuscript in the library of Caius College, Cambridge:—

'Furthermore, where the Queen's Majesty of her own nature is wholly given to clemency and mercy, as full well appeareth hitherto; for in this realm was never seen a change so quiet and so long since reigning without blood (God be thanked for it); howbeit those which hitherto will not be reformed, but obstinate and can skill by no clemency or courtesy ought otherwise to be used. But now will some say, "Oh, bloody man that calleth this the house of right, and now would have it made a house of blood." But the Scripture teacheth us that divers faults ought to be punished by death, and therefore following God's precepts it cannot be accounted cruel; and it is not against this house, but the part thereof to see justice ministered to them who will abuse clemency. Therefore the goodness of Her Majesty's clemency may well and ought now therefore to be changed to justice, seeing it will not help. But now to explicate myself, I say, if any man keeping his opinion, will, and mind, close within himself, and so not open the same, then he ought not to be punished, but when he openeth it abroad then it hurteth and ought to be cut off: And especially, if in anything it touch the Queen's Majesty; for such errors or heresy, ought not, as well for God's quarrel as the realm's to be unlooked unto, for clemency ought not to be given to the wolves to kill and devour as they do the lambs, for which cause it ought to be foreseen; for that the Prince shall answer for all that so perish, it lying in her power to redress it, for by the Scriptures murderers, breakers of the holy day and maintainers of false religion ought to die by the sword.

. . . .

'Also some other sharpe laws for adultery, and also for murder, more stricter than for felony—which in France is well used, as the wheel for the one, the halter for the other, which if we had here I doubt not within few years would save many a man's life.'

www.ingramcontent.com/pod-product-compliance
Lightning Source LLC
Chambersburg PA
CBHW031940290426
44108CB00011B/622